THE AUTHOR

Kate Lock was born in Oxford, where she grew up and began
her career as a journalist on the *Oxford Star*. She moved to
London, where she worked for *Radio Times* for six years and
she continues to write for the magazine on a freelance basis.
She has written two other novelisations: Jimmy McGovern's
The Lakes (as K.M. Lock) for BBC/Penguin and *Where the
Heart Is: Home* (Headline). Kate lives in York with her husband,
Stephen and daughter, Isis.

This book is published to accompany the television series *EastEnders*.
Executive Producer: Matthew Robinson

Published by BBC Worldwide Ltd, Woodlands, 80 Wood Lane,
London W12 0TT

First published 1998
Copyright © Novelisation: Kate Lock 1998
The moral right of the author has been asserted.

ISBN 0 563 38483 2

Editorial Consultant: Jake Lushington

Commissioning Editor: Viv Bowler
Project Editor: Lara Speicher
Copy Editor: Julian Flanders
Book Design: Lisa Pettibone
Cover Design: Town Group Creative
Picture Researcher: Susannah Parker

Typeset by Keystroke, Wolverhampton

Printed and bound in Great Britain by MacKays of Chatham
Colour separations by Radstock Reproductions Ltd, Midsomer Norton
Colour section printed by Lawrence Allen Ltd, Weston-super-Mare
Cover printed by Belmont Press Ltd, Northampton

EastEnders

BLOOD TIES
The Life and Loves of Grant Mitchell

Kate Lock

PROLOGUE

THE FALKLANDS, 1982

'See you in Stanley.' Private 'Tiny' Johnson paused as he lit a cigarette, the orange flame flaring in the dark. His face was briefly illuminated as he bent his head towards the flame. He glanced up and met Grant's eyes for a second. 'Or in Hell.'

'Nah mate, this is hell. Tabbin' in wet socks all day through bloody bogs, then freezing your arse off at night on a mountainside.' Private Grant Mitchell sounded nonchalant, but it was pure bravado. He was nineteen years old and more frightened than he'd ever been in his life. They were preparing to charge the Argentinians, who were dug in above them on Mount Longdon. It was nothing like manning army check-points in Belfast, his only other experience of action. It was nothing like anything he had ever known before. He was going to have to run straight into enemy fire without even being able to see the bastards, like going 'over the top' in old war films. Except this wasn't a film, it was real. And he might really die.

His life in London's East End seemed light years away. He thought of his brother, Phil, his mother, Peggy and his young sister, Sam, who had all come to wave him off at Southampton. He had sailed on the *Canberra*, along with almost two and a half thousand other troops. They made cracks about being on a luxury cruise to the South Atlantic, but none of them had known what they were letting themselves in for. Sitting in the dark, waiting for the signal to move, a child's voice at the back of his head whimpered, I want to go home.

'I need to kill a few Argies just to get me circulation goin' again,' he blustered, hoping his shaking fingers weren't noticeable. Tiny, who had been in the paras for ten years, gave a hollow laugh.

'You're shit-scared, Grant, ain'tcha? Go on, admit it. Want

me to hold your hand?'

'Leave it out,' he said defensively. 'I can hack it. Piece of cake.'

'Yeah? You're still wet behind the ears, what do you know?'

'Enough.'

'Is that right? You ever killed anyone before?' Grant was silent. 'Thought not,' Tiny said. 'Well, take a tip from me. It ain't no joking matter.'

'Alright, lads?' The corporal went past doing last-minute checks along the start line. 'Ready for the off?'

'Sir.' The men began to get themselves together, adjusting kit, stubbing out fags, picking up weapons. The low murmuring and morale-boosting jokes of the past ten minutes petered out as the company tensed itself for the attack. Grant heard a metallic scraping and caught the glint of a blade next to him. He turned to see Dougie Briggs fixing his bayonet, then noticed others were doing the same. So this was it. It was going to be real fighting, man to man, not firing at bobbing specks in the distance like some funfair shooting gallery. That was all they'd done so far; for all he knew they'd been slaughtering sheep. Hardman Dougie had been going mental, thinking they weren't going to see action. The only reason Dougie had joined up, as he frequently boasted, was to kill legally. Grant didn't share Dougie's bloodlust. It was simply that there had never really been any career alternatives. Fighting was all he knew.

Grant fixed his bayonet, heart beating fast. Suddenly, the fear evaporated and he felt elated, powered by the adrenalin pumping through his veins. The misery of wet clothes and blistered feet, the exhaustion of trekking over the gruelling Falklands terrain was all forgotten. He was alive to the sensations of every nerve-ending, his rigorously trained body ready to respond in an instant to whatever demands he made of it. He was in control: the perfect human fighting machine.

It was a steepish climb over hillocky ground, the men fanning out as they picked their way around outcropping boulders towards the Argentinians holed up ahead. They advanced stealthily, without drawing enemy fire, until the corporal who was leading them stepped on a mine. It exploded, throwing his body several feet into the air, seeming to Grant to hang there as if suspended before the man's screams punctured the silence. Then all hell broke loose. Small arms and mortar fire rained down on them and instinctively Grant ducked behind the nearest boulder. Something rattled past him and he assumed it was a loose rock, until it went off further down the slope and he realized they were lobbing grenades. He saw Tiny's hulking form crouched behind an inadequate low outcrop ahead and yelled at him to keep his head down. He was too exposed; a sitting duck for the snipers with their infra-red night sights above them.

A bullet ricocheted off the side of Grant's boulder and he realised he wasn't much better protected. More grenades thudded past. He heard another, blood-curdling scream and his guts churned liquid. They had to get out of their position, fast. Dougie indicated more substantial cover some thirty yards ahead and made a dash for it. Grant shouted to Tiny to follow and pepper-potted across the open ground, making quick bounds and dropping down on his belly, until he caught up with Dougie. Tiny, breathing heavily, brought up the rear.

'That was a bit bloody close,' Tiny growled. Dougie put his finger to his lips and pointed. There was an Argentinian position within striking distance, several dark figures clearly visible moving behind a stone wall. They were concentrating their fire on another company which had got pinned down in a narrow gulley to their right and obviously hadn't spotted the three paras sneaking up on the left flank.

'Let's give 'em their balls back,' Dougie said, pulling out a grenade.

The bunker blew up quite spectacularly.

'That one's from Maggie!' Dougie crowed. He cocked his rifle and turned a manic grin on Grant and Tiny. 'And now one from us.' They kept low, scuttling forwards like spiders and scrambling over the remnants of the wall, dropping down into a deep trench. Two Argentinian soldiers lay dead. Another was still, somehow, alive, his features so mangled that when Dougie stood over him with his gun it was impossible to read the man's expression. Dougie pumped a round into him. Next to him, Tiny was making sure the corpses were good and dead, too.

Grant picked his way along the trench, which was littered with stuff: packets of cigarettes, tinned food, clothing. They had obviously been dug in for some time. He spotted a bulky-looking sleeping bag at the far end and prodded it with the butt of his rifle. There was a whimper. 'Come out, you bastard,' he yelled, kicking the body inside hard. He heard another, terrified squeal.

'Found a live one?' Dougie and Tiny pricked up their ears.

'Sounds like it.' Grant grabbed the zip and yanked it open, rifle at the ready. Inside there was a young Argentinian soldier. He was curled up in the foetal position but appeared to be un-hurt by the shelling. He looked desperately thin, bony ankles sticking out of his absurdly baggy uniform. Grant caught him by the collar and hauled him to his knees. The boy – he was obviously no more than sixteen – stared at him with wild eyes.

'What's that you're supposed to say? "Arriba" something?' Grant called over his shoulder to Tiny. They'd all been told the Spanish for 'put your hands up' but his head was whirling, all sorts of junk flying round in it, and he couldn't think straight.

'Not goin' to bottle out now, are you Grant?' Dougie leered. 'You ain't been blooded, yet, have you, mate? Gotta do it sometime.'

Grant hesitated. He knew he should take him prisoner, but his head was pounding, bursting, the pulse beating a deafening tattoo in his ears. Dougie's words echoed in his brain, repeating a long-ago taunt from his childhood, 'Bottlin' out, Grant? Call yerself a Mitchell?' He remembered – felt again – the blow coming out of nowhere, smashing against the side of his head and sending him sprawling on the floor. He remembered the huge fist held over him and the mighty shadow it cast on the wall, like a giant's arm waiting to crush him. He knew, with a sickening certainty, that it was going to knock him down again and again, until he couldn't get up. Suddenly, fleetingly, he was a small, helpless boy sobbing on the ground, doubled up in agony and terror.

'What's the matter? You yellow?' Dougie's voice egged him on with more jeers from the past. Grant stared at the snivelling young soldier with the streaked and dirty face cowering in front of him and saw himself. The thought nauseated him. He despised the kid for being so weak, so pathetic. He wanted to obliterate the image, wipe it clean out of his mind, along with the humiliation, the beatings, the persecution. A mist seemed to be coming down over his eyes, and in the fog he saw the soldier reach into his pocket with a sudden, quick movement. Thinking he must have a revolver hidden, Grant fired.

Everything happened in slow motion after that, like a grisly dance of death in a Peckinpah movie. The Argentinian's mouth dropped open in surprise as he staggered backwards and half-fell against the trench wall. The gun in Grant's hands kept pumping bullets, ejaculating rounds into the jerking body. Even so, the soldier did not die instantly, but scrabbled and clawed in the mud making appalling gurgling noises in his throat.

Grant, revolted, kept shooting, screaming, 'Die, will yer? Die, you bastard,' until he had used up a whole magazine. He stood over the slumped form, bayonet raised, waiting, daring it to twitch one more time. His lungs rasped like bellows and his ears were ringing from the shots. Nothing. His enemy was slain. His past was dead.

Dougie slapped him on the back. 'You got him alright, Grant,' but Tiny said nothing. Grant followed his eyeline. Protruding from the dead soldier's pocket was a white handkerchief. Tentatively, he checked for a gun – but there was none. Suddenly, Grant felt the massive injection of frenzied energy draining from his limbs and the next thing he was aware of was his legs crumpling under him. He sank on the ground, tipping over sideways, and found himself lying almost on top of the corpse. The smoothness of his skin was what struck him the most. He noticed it with the utmost clarity. The kid was too young even to shave. It was like meeting his own ghost. Grant screamed.

CHAPTER ONE

The scream sliced into Sharon's sleep, ripping open her dream. She had been having an odd — though pleasantly erotic — dream about Grant, in which they were swimming naked in a huge tank, diving and playing and tumbling like a couple of otters. They seemed to be on display; she could make out faces gawping at them through the glass. She had swum over to the side, revelling in the sleek feel of the water on her skin, and saw Pauline Fowler looking at her disapprovingly. Her sour face made Sharon laugh. She noticed Arthur Fowler standing next to her, and beside him, her friend Michelle and little Vicki, 'Chelle's daughter. Indeed, most of the residents of Albert Square seemed to be there, watching them, pointing and gossiping. It was then that she realized they were in Albert Square and the tank was on a platform in the garden in the centre of it. She barely had a chance to register the fact that half of Walford was viewing them so shamelessly exposed when she heard the scream.

At first, she thought it was part of the dream, this dreadful, primitive howl. She trod water, looking about her, blonde hair streaming in her eyes. It was followed by another, and another, the noise tugging her to the surface. She burst out of sleep gasping, as if she'd been holding her breath, and sat bolt upright in bed. Through the thin partition wall of the guest-house she heard Grant scream again.

'Grant! Grant! Are you alright?' Sharon pounded on the wall. There was no reply. She leapt out of bed and ran next door, rattling his door handle frantically. 'Grant! Speak to me! Grant!' She paused, listening hard. No voices. The screaming had stopped but she thought she could hear sobbing. 'Grant. It's me, Sharon. What's going on? You okay?'

'Hang on.' Grant's voice sounded husky. Sharon heard a bed creak but it seemed a long time before he opened the door. 'What do you want?' His tone was defensive. It was impossible to make out his face properly in the darkened room but she thought his eyes looked shiny.

'To see if you were alright. You were shouting out. I thought you were being murdered in your bed.'

'I – I had a nightmare, that's all.'

A light came on in the hallway and the guesthouse proprietor, Mrs McDonald, appeared in a candlewick dressing-gown, her hair awry. 'Wha's goin' on? Is someone hurt? I heard a scream as made ma blood run cold.'

'Bad dream.' Sharon smiled sweetly at her, making as if to return to her room. 'Nothing to worry about. Sorry to have disturbed you. Goodnight.'

They watched her trail back down the corridor, muttering something to herself. 'Nosy old bag,' Grant hissed. He ran a hand over his close-cropped hair. 'I don't think I'll be going back to sleep in a hurry. Do you fancy a scotch?'

Sharon was about to comment, 'At this time of the morning?' – it was four o'clock – but thought better of it. 'Go on then, why not?' she said. Grant retrieved a bottle they'd bought on a tour of the nearby whisky distillery the previous day and poured a large shot into a toothmug, downing it in one. He closed his eyes for a second, shook his head, opened them again and gave Sharon a tight smile.

'Better?' she asked.

'Much.' He poured himself another and handed her one in the engraved tumbler they'd purchased as a souvenir for Grant's brother, Phil.

'Cheers.' She took a swallow and felt it burn a fiery trail down her throat. Grant knocked his back more slowly this time, observing her over the top of the mug. 'Brrr.' Sharon, who was clad only in a thin nightie, shivered violently. 'They don't believe in central heating up here, do they?'

'Supposed to be good for you. Toughens you up.' Grant

seemed to be relaxing. He drew back the curtain and stared out at the night. 'Get into bed if you like,' he said casually, without looking round.

'Your bed?' Sharon hesitated. 'With you?'

'Why not?'

'Well, we haven't ... I mean, we said we'd get to know a bit about each other first, take it slowly ...'

Grant turned round. 'I'm only talking about keeping your feet warm.' He grinned. 'And mine, too, if you don't mind. I won't try it on, I promise.'

Sharon took another swig of the malt and felt braver. 'Okay.' She got in. Grant surveyed the space left in the single bed.

'Budge up.' She moved over close to the wall, suddenly a little overwhelmed by his masculinity, the hardness of his muscles, the faint smell of sweat, the impression of pent-up energy he gave off as his body came into close contact with hers. She drained the rest of her whisky.

'Thanks. I – I'd better go now.'

He put a hand on her arm. 'No.'

'What?' Sharon began to feel alarmed.

'I'm sorry.' He hit the side of his head with the flat of his hand. 'I didn't mean it to sound like an order. It's just that . . .'

He paused, glancing out at the darkness. They sat listening to the silence. Eventually he said, 'This quiet. It gives me the creeps. There's always some noise in Albert Square, whatever time it is.'

'Yeah, don't I know it. Drunks I sling out of the Vic who don't seem to have homes to go to.'

Grant turned to her. 'Will you stay with me? Please, Sharon. Keep me company. I'll sit in the chair if you like.' His eyes were wide. Sharon was touched. She sensed that it was rare for him to lower his guard like this; Grant and his brother Phil had earned their reputation as tough blokes.

'Okay,' she whispered. He went to get out but this time she stopped him. 'Stay.' She snuggled down under the duvet. 'Come here. I'll hold you.'

He put his face close. 'You sure?'

'For goodness sake.' She held out her arm. 'Will you hurry up? It's freezing under here.'

'Are ye no stopping for Hogmanay?' Mrs McDonald quizzed as Grant went to pay the bill.

'We'll have enough pissed up Scotsmen to deal with back home,' he replied curtly. Her pencilled-in eyebrows shot up.

Sharon, trying hard to suppress giggles, explained smoothly, 'I work in a pub in the East End of London. It's the busiest night of the year for us.' Mrs McDonald pursed her lips. 'I always say the Scots know how to have a good time,' Sharon continued desperately. Grant hoisted their luggage, tucking two fishing rods under his arm.

'Did ye catch anythin'?' the landlady enquired, slightly mollified.

'Cold,' he replied, shoving the front door open with his shoulder and going out. Sharon, defeated, fled after him.

'She's got a point,' she said, as they drove alongside the loch, a wintry sun glittering weakly on the water. 'This was supposed to have been a fishing trip. We can't really go back empty-handed, can we? They'll all think ...' Sharon glanced at Grant quickly. 'Well, you know what people are like.'

'Hmmm.' He drummed his fingers on the wheel. 'Phil and I usually bring home a few for the freezer.'

'But we haven't got time now ...'

Grant winked. 'No problem. We'll just find a fishmonger.'

New Year's Eve festivities were in full swing when they arrived back at the Vic. Eddie Royle, the Vic's landlord, had arranged a karaoke competition which had brought out more wannabe Sinatras, Presleys and Whitney Houstons than he had bargained for. Grant and Sharon, having made their entrance during a noisy rendition of 'It's Got to be Perfect', were greeted with cheers, whistles and a barrage of sarky comments about the condition of Grant's tackle, which they did their best to ignore.

Michelle, though, was not put off the scent so easily and the following day she approached Sharon, urging her to spill the beans. Sharon, who still didn't know what to make of Grant's behaviour, was uncharacteristically offhand with her best mate.

'There's nothing to tell, so just drop it, okay?' she snapped, moving down the bar to serve another punter.

Meanwhile, in the Bridge Street café, across the road from the Vic, Grant was getting the third degree from a persistent Phil. 'You must be losing your touch, my old son,' he laughed, when Grant denied having done the deed with Sharon. 'What is it between you two, then? "Just good friends"?'

'Yeah. And what's it got to do with you?' Grant flared.

'Keep your hair on. We don't want to fall out over no woman, do we?' Phil replied, amused. He swilled down the last of his coffee and ambled out of the café. 'Just good friends.' The phrase resounded in his head. He wanted it to be more than that, much more. Sharon was a revelation: warm, kind, sexy, funny; altogether drop-dead gorgeous. At twenty-one, she had a worldliness beyond her years and her poise and self-confidence took his breath away. He had never wanted a woman as much as he wanted her. And he had never been so afraid of rejection in his life.

Fortunately, Sharon made the first move, turning up on Grant's doorstep bearing the salmon that they'd brought back from Scotland. 'Do you want your half?'

He laughed. 'I wouldn't know what to do with it.'

'Well, in that case, come over to the Vic for your tea,' she said brightly. 'I'll cook. It'll be lovely with a sauce.' Grant found himself agreeing eagerly

Later, when he met her for a drink in the bar before tea – Sharon lived in the flat above – she said she wanted to ask him a serious question. Suddenly, Grant felt his mouth go dry.

'It's been on my mind ever since Scotland, but it didn't seem the right time,' Sharon began haltingly, unsure of how to put it. Grant's night terror had really shaken her but the next morning he had acted as if nothing had happened, which was almost as disturbing. She took a deep breath. 'Something bothered you up there, didn't it?' Grant looked blank. 'Like the trip brought back bad memories,' she probed gingerly.

'No, I don't think so. Except perhaps previous fishing trips when the company wasn't so pleasant.'

She saw that he wasn't going to open up and decided not to press it. 'Well, anytime you want to talk about it.'

Grant stood up abruptly. 'Let's go upstairs and eat that fish, shall we? We don't want it spoiling after all our hard work.'

Sharon grinned. 'Not to mention all our hard cash.'

Two weeks later, Grant was still holding Sharon at arm's length. Rather than face any more questions, he had retreated into his shell, avoiding her and being surly with Phil and the customers who bought their cars into the brothers' auto repair shop.

The Mitchells had set up the gaff in the arches beneath the railway bridge in 1990, the same year they moved to Albert Square. Phil had had a substantial gambling win, after which they had been warned off a patch further up the river, and he had used the money to set up the business. Grant, who had done a mechanics course in the army, helped out, so did Ricky Butcher, a young apprentice mechanic. But Phil was the mainstay. He had learned the trade running their father's garage. Like their father, the brothers tended to operate in the grey area just outside the law and had an eye for the main chance. Unlike their father, who couldn't control his gambling and went bust, they generally came out on top.

When they had first arrived in Walford, the brothers had rapidly earned the nicknames 'Tweedledum' and 'Tweedledee' because they looked so alike. Stockily built with broad shoulders, both were balding early, although twenty-eight-year-old Grant, the younger by a year and a half, was better looking. He had intense blue eyes which could freeze to flint when angry and gave off an air of danger that women found irresistible.

Phil, with his beard and rounder, ruddy face, was almost cuddly by comparison. His mild appearance was deceptive; Phil was an equally hard nut who had frequently lent his bulk to jobs that required both belligerence and muscle, from bouncer to debt-collector, not to mention some of a more criminal nature. Only last year he had got involved in a scam dealing in forged MOT certificates, which had been a winner until it backfired rather badly. They had a bent brief, Marcus Christie, working on it; Phil's case had yet to go to the magistrate but he was not looking forward to it much.

But, for now, Phil was intent on keeping his head down and his nose clean and getting on with some graft, which was why his moping brother was beginning to get to him. 'If you're gonna frighten off the punters with that face, you might as well make yourself useful doing something else.'

'Like what?'

'That red Escort needs a complete respray.'

'It's a crock.'

Phil laughed grimly. 'Payment for services rendered. Don't look a gift horse in the mouth.'

'Who's it a gift for?'

'You. If you fix it.'

After that, Grant became completely absorbed in his work.

Sharon was getting fed up. Grant seemed to be giving her the cold shoulder and she couldn't understand why. When Wicksy, her boyfriend, had dumped her last summer, she had vowed to give herself time before getting involved again. The emotional wounds had cut deep; she and Wicksy had run the Vic together and had planned to take over the tenancy, but his commitment had dwindled and their application was turned down. He left Walford soon after, breaking Sharon's heart and destroying her dream of managing the pub that she'd grown up in.

The lunchtime rush was over, but Michelle was still sitting on a barstool, toying with an orange juice. 'You gonna be all day with that?' Sharon asked tersely.

'Just waiting.'

'Waiting for what?'

'For you to tell me why you've been so flamin' miserable lately.' 'Chelle cocked an eyebrow. 'It's Grant, isn't it?'

Sharon sighed heavily. 'Yeah.'

'Thought you two had got on well on holiday.'

'So did I. Now he don't seem to want to know.'

'Has he been using you?' 'Chelle looked angry. ''Cos if he has …'

'Hold your horses. I told you. We didn't do anything.'

'Really?'

'Cross my heart. Well, we did sleep together. But we didn't sleep together, if you get my drift.' Sharon fiddled with her teatowel.

'Sounds pretty intimate to me.'

'It was. I saw a different side to him. He was gentle, sweet. Vulnerable.'

Michelle snorted. 'Grant?'

Sharon grinned. 'I know how he can be. But he was a pussy cat after his …' she glanced about and lowered her voice. 'He had this nightmare. He was screaming in his sleep. It was awful, 'Chelle. I've never heard a grown man cry out like that before. I stayed with him after that and I thought we'd got closer, but now it's like it never happened.'

'But you still like him?'

'Yes.'

'Does he know that?'

'He don't give us the chance. He's avoiding me.'

'You gotta tell him. Sort it out, one way or the other.'

'Enter the lion's den, you mean?'

Michelle grinned. 'Shouldn't be a problem. You said he was a pussy cat.'

Having mustered her courage and applied a fresh coat of lipstick, Sharon went over to the Arches. She met Phil on his way out to pick up two teas from the café. 'He's all yours,' he said, jerking his thumb at the workshop. 'Though why you want to bother with him, I can't think.' It did not bode well. Sharon walked hesitantly into the garage. She did not see Grant until it was too late.

'Ow! Who the ...?' Grant pulled himself out from underneath a car, his face creased with anger. The first thing he saw was Sharon's legs. From his vantage point, they went up a long way before her skirt started. He sat up, smiling apologetically. 'Sorry. Didn't see you.'

'Neither did I. Are you okay?'

'No harm done. A lot of men have to pay to be walked over by women in high heels.'

She giggled, relieved the ice had been broken. 'Look, I came over because I wanted to talk – not to question you again,' she added hurriedly, as he immediately began to put on a shuttered look.

He brushed his oily hands on his overalls self-consciously. 'What about?

'Us.' He looked at her intently. She cleared her throat. 'I – I really like you, Grant. But you've gone all distant. I've gotta know where we stand.'

Caught off-guard, he shuffled his feet awkwardly. 'Is that "like" as in "good friends"? Or "like" as in "more than good friends"?'

'As in more than ...' Sharon breathed softly.

He met her eyes. 'I'm glad. Because I feel the same way. I just wasn't sure if you did.' They smiled at each other, and it might have turned into something more had Phil not returned with the teas. 'I got you something,' Grant said hurriedly. He pulled back the cover from the car behind him to reveal a gleaming red Escort. Digging in his pocket, he produced a bunch of keys. Sharon's jaw dropped.

'It's fantastic. But I can't drive. I thought you knew that.'

'Free driving lessons thrown in,' he grinned. 'Ten o'clock Thursday do you?'

'You're on.'

★

'You got it running, then?' Phil commented, as Grant reversed the Escort out for Sharon's first lesson.

'Sweet as a nut.'

'Did the trick?'

'Let's hope so.' Grant waved. 'See you later.' He drove round the corner full of confidence, planning to take Sharon out to a country pub somewhere. When he saw her loading a stack of suitcases into a taxi outside the Vic he was so surprised he stalled it.

'Sharon!'

She looked up. 'Hi, Grant.' He got out and went over. 'Look, I'm sorry, I was going to tell you but I've hardly had a second to think straight.' She gestured towards the luggage. 'My mum – Angie – rang me from the States yesterday. She's taken it into her head to get married and wants me over there. The wedding's in Florida. The ticket arrived this morning. All paid for. I didn't have much option.'

Grant's face fell. 'So it's goodbye.'

'Only for a little while.'

The cabbie stuck his head out of the window. 'Better get going if you're going to make that flight, love. Traffic's murder this morning.'

Grant put a hand on Sharon's shoulder. 'I think you should say goodbye to me properly.'

'Properly?'

'Like this.' He kissed her full on the mouth and, when she didn't resist, pulled her close against him. Sharon responded enthusiastically.

'Ahem.' Dot Cotton, who was passing with her shopping bag, made a disapproving noise. Sharon and Grant drew apart, giggling.

'See you soon,' he said, helping her into the cab. He watched her drive off, his heart lighter than he had ever known it before.

CHAPTER TWO

Sunbathing by the pool at Angie's kitsch pink mansion (her new husband had made a fortune in packaging), Sharon savoured the memory of Grant's kiss. She closed her eyes, reliving the ripples of pleasure she had felt when he took her in his arms. After they had said goodbye she had sat in the taxi grinning like an idiot, watching Grant wave until he disappeared from view. 'Looks like your boyfriend's going to miss you,' the cabbie observed.

'He's not my ... I mean, we're not ... well, not yet ...' She looked out of the window, trying to hide the secret smile that kept springing involuntarily to her lips. The cabbie eyed her in the mirror. 'How long are you going away for?' When she told him she was going to America for six weeks, he winked at her and said, 'Long time to wait, eh, love?', making her blush.

But now it was almost over, Sharon reflected, coming out of her reverie and gazing up at the cloudless blue sky. It had been great catching up with Angie again, but she had a life of her own to get back to. Florida was lovely, but right now, Walford was where she wanted to be.

Grant had missed Sharon, but he wasn't one to moon about. During her absence, he took the opportunity to date a sultry brunette called Miranda who worked as a secretary at Luxford and Copley, the Vic's brewery. Grant claimed it was part of an elaborate scam to gain a sneak preview of the questions for the forthcoming quiz night against the Vic's rivals from the Rose and Crown. Michelle, who saw the two of them in the pub together, was sceptical when he told her it was purely business and even more so when he asked her not to mention it to Sharon.

Having no qualms about combining business and pleasure, Grant had also lent Miranda the Escort as part of the bribe, an arrangement that rebounded on him when Sharon came back from the States a day early. She rushed straight round to the Arches, eager to pick up where they'd left off, and was regaling him with holiday anecdotes when Miranda sashayed in.

'You were right about its performance,' she said huskily, dropping the car keys into his hand. 'Most men can't live up to that kind of promise.' She kissed him on the cheek and stroked his jaw with a lingering finger. 'Any time you want to prove me wrong, of course …' Grant winced as the door slammed shut behind Sharon.

Later Grant went round to the Vic to protest his innocence, but Sharon was in no mood for explanations. 'Save it, Grant. I know what I saw. I'm just thankful I found out early what a rat you are.' She gave him a poisonous look and moved down to the other end of the bar to serve Big Ron, one of the market traders.

'She'll calm down later,' Phil advised as his brother sulked over a pint. He downed his own drink and got up. 'Come on. We've got a mystery motor to see to.' Grant followed him, equally curious to investigate the crashed car that had been left at the garage. The driver had scooted off in a hurry, saying he'd be back later to move some stuff out of the boot. The police arrived not long afterwards, sniffing around and asking questions, which had sent Phil into a flat spin. His case about the forged MOT certificates had been referred up to a higher court and he couldn't afford to be associated with anything dodgy. Whatever was in the boot, they both agreed, it was unlikely to be a picnic hamper.

Ricky was as keen to find out what was in the boot as the Mitchells, and eagerly helped them force the lock. Just as he was about to open the lid there was a loud knocking on the workshop door, making all three of them jump.

'Ssh.' Phil held a finger to his lips. Grant cast around for a cosh and picked up a wrench.

The hammering was repeated. Grant weighed the wrench in his hand, ready. He couldn't believe it when he heard Sharon's voice.

'Grant. Let me in. Grant!' The three of them looked at each other. Phil shook his head.

'I know you're in there. Kathy saw you. I'm sorry about earlier, but what was I to think?' She banged on the door again and, getting no reply, eventually gave up, shouting a final, 'Well, if *that's* how you feel …'

'This'd better be worth it,' Grant said grimly.

It was a bizarre haul: a doll, a broken briefcase, envelopes, a street map, train timetables and some stamps. 'That can't be it,' Ricky said, disappointed.

'Bingo.' Phil prised open the briefcase. It was stuffed with forged fivers, plus the original forgery plates that they'd been run off.

'Wow. This is so alright innit? Like finding treasure or summat,' Ricky enthused. Phil gave Grant a look. They both knew what a hopeless blabbermouth Ricky was.

'Here.' Phil opened his wallet. 'Why don't you take a holiday for a few days – go somewhere hot, have fun. You've earned it. We'll keep things ticking over here.'

'Thanks.' Ricky pocketed the cash. 'I will.'

'They're not too bad,' Grant remarked, after a happy Ricky had departed. He held up one of the fivers to the bare light bulb dangling from the ceiling. 'You've gotta look quite hard to spot it.' He waited until Phil's back was turned and slipped a wad into his jacket pocket. He had a lot of making up to do.

It took Grant considerable flannelling before Sharon was satisfied with his explanation about the brewery secretary and the bribe, and even more for her to believe his story about wearing a personal stereo in the workshop, accounting for his apparent deafness when she knocked. Relieved that they had made it up, he ordered drinks all round – Michelle was at the bar, too, celebrating her new job selling timeshares – paying with a couple of the forged fivers.

Immediately, he regretted the decision. Eddie, who was serving him, held the notes in the air and studied them closely. Eddie was a former copper – a bent copper at that – and was well known to the Mitchells. There was no love lost between them: last year Eddie had got hold of some forged driving licences Grant had been intending to flog for a small fortune and had flushed them down the loo. However, he seemed not to notice the missing watermark on the fivers and put them in the till. Grant relaxed and gave Sharon his undivided attention, well chuffed at having put one over on him.

Sharon was cleaning the bar the next day when Eddie came up to her, granite-faced. 'Know what this is?' He thrust a note under her nose. Sharon squinted at it.

'It's a fiver.'

'It's a forgery. And if I find out where it came from there'll be hell to pay.' He glared at her. 'From now on, you check every single one, okay? And if you find one, you call the nick. Got it?'

She shrugged. 'Okay, okay. Why am I getting it in the neck?'

He narrowed his eyes. 'I think you're protecting someone.'

'And what evidence do you have for that?' she retorted furiously.

'I don't like the company you keep.' Sharon, fuming, went on with her work, angry with her boss for implying that Grant might have been responsible. But the more she thought about it, the more the thought wouldn't go away. What if he was? It was just the sort of stunt the Mitchell brothers would try. It ate away at her until, finally, she could bear it no longer and went to the Arches to have it out with them. She found only Phil, who denied all knowledge, but his look of panic when she told him that Eddie had called the old bill spoke volumes.

The next day she tried again to talk to Grant, calling on him at home. Grant lived in the flat downstairs from Phil at 43 Albert Square. Den had originally bought it for Sharon to share with Michelle and Vicki, but 'Chelle had moved back next door to Pauline and Arthur's and Sharon had let it until the end of last year, when Grant made her an offer for it.

Once again, she found herself shut out: Grant refused to open the door, shouting some pathetic excuse about it being in a mess. Increasingly humiliated by his behaviour towards her, she stalked off, vowing to end the relationship once and for all. 'He doesn't want a girlfriend,' she told Michelle. 'He wants a lady in waiting. I'm fed up with chasing round after him. I've had enough.'

She tracked him down at the Arches later on that evening, catching him red-handed counting out forged fivers. 'Oh, so you do take an interest in something, then?' she said sarcastically, walking straight in unannounced.

Grant spun round. 'Sharon!'

'Don't worry, it's none of my business. I've just come to bring you these.' She held out the keys to the Escort.

'Is there something wrong with it?' he asked.

'You could say that. You gave it to me, remember?'

'Sorry?'

'The car was one part of the package, you were the other part. I'm chucking 'em both back.' She slung the keys on the desk and turned on her heel.

'Please Sharon,' Grant pleaded. 'Look, I'll tell you anything you want to know.'

'I don't want any more lies, Grant. I want the truth.'

Grant took a deep breath. 'Alright ...' He told her about the crashed car, the strange driver and the forged notes. He conveniently omitted to mention the two heavies who had turned up the previous evening, pretending to want to do a deal over the forgery plates for the fivers. That had been a set-up while his flat was done over and they lifted the plates, which he and Phil had stashed away there. At least he hadn't lied to Sharon when he said the place was a mess.

'And that's the truth?' Sharon insisted.

'On my father's life.'

'I thought he died years ago.'

Grant reconsidered. 'On Phil's life.' He saw she believed him and seized the moment. 'Look, Sharon, I don't want to lose you. I know I've been behaving like a bit of a prat recently, but it doesn't mean I don't care for you ...' It was all Sharon wanted to hear. Her face softened and she moved towards him. Grant leaned forward to kiss her but before their lips could meet they were interrupted by the garage door slamming shut.

'Very touching,' said a voice. 'But you've got something that belongs to me and I've come to collect.'

The man gave Sharon the creeps, but Grant seemed to know who he was. 'Go on home, I'll deal with this.' He gave her a little shove.

'But . . .'

'No buts.' He propelled her towards the door. 'I'll see you later.' She was left standing outside in the cold and the dark once again, thinking, 'This is getting to be a habit'. Shivering – and not only from the chill wind – she walked back past the children's playground and round the corner to the Vic, wondering what on earth she was getting herself mixed up with. More to the point, who.

'What's wrong?' asked Eddie, as they cleared up after lunch a few days later. They had called a truce over the fivers business after no more appeared in the till. These days Eddie was being positively nice. It made a change from Grant's unpredictable moods. He had been like a bear with a sore head all morning.

Sharon, feeling a twinge of disloyalty, nonetheless needed to confide in someone. 'My love-life. Feels like it's one step forward and two steps back all the time.' She laughed lightly, but Eddie wasn't fooled.

'Well, if you will date a Mitchell ...' He patted a bench. 'Sit down and tell me about it.'

'I know you don't think much of Grant, but there's more to him than people think,' Sharon said, taking a gulp of the large gin and tonic he poured her. 'I know he'll never win a game of Trivial Pursuit but he's a sweet bloke – it's like going out with a big, grinning kid, a cheeky kid. Trouble is, he's like a kid in other respects, an' all. He's thoughtless. Not in a nasty way – in a childish way.'

'You'll make up, won't you?'

Sharon swilled the ice in her glass. 'We're not really together, so we've not really broken up. I just don't know if I want to be disappointed again – seems to come as part of the deal.'

'There's always an alternative,' Eddie said softly, moving closer to her. 'I'm everything Grant's not. He's a wheeler-dealer; I'm straight. He's a big kid; I'm mature. He's rough-hewn; I'm class. And I'm reliable. I'd never let you down.'

'Sounds the perfect package,' Sharon replied, grinning.

'So how about it?'

'What?'

'Me. You could do worse.'

It was then that she realized he was serious. 'Never say yes on the rebound. Me mum taught me that,' she said, leaping up to clear away more glasses.

Grant's day started off badly and it had been getting worse ever since. He and Phil had done a deal with the car-owner that had turned out to be an arch con. The forgery plates were a red herring: it was the stamps that were valuable. It was only after Phil and Grant had posted them off, as arranged, that they discovered the stamps were rare misprints worth £5000 each.

Grant had pinned his hopes on making money from the stuff in the car. The bloke had promised them a large sum for going through with the operation and Grant already had plans for the money. He told Sharon they could get out of Walford and buy a place in Spain, and she had seemed keen. But he and Phil had come out of it all empty-handed and now he was having to pretend to her that he hadn't meant what he said. Sharon was accusing him of blowing hot and cold, when nothing could have been further from the truth. He'd had dreams of them running a bar together by a beach, with no more hassles, no more interference. A chance to wipe the slate clean. And maybe, just maybe, with his golden girl by his side and the sun on his back, the nightmares would have gone away, too.

To cap it all, when Sharon came round to see him at the Arches that afternoon, she had dropped a hint about him having competition. Grant immediately suspected Eddie of making a pass and his anger had been brewing like a gathering storm ever since. Sharon swore it was nothing, but Grant's blood was up. 'Typical! Cocky sod! That's the old bill for you, they think they can do what they like!' She told him to forget it and returned to work, but he couldn't let it drop.

Back home, he paced up and down like a caged tiger. All he could see was Eddie's white grin, taunting him. It became a disembodied image, a mocking Cheshire-cat leer, mouthing 'sucker' at him through tombstone teeth, daring him to do something about it. At last, Grant could bear it no longer. Driven by a frustration he could scarcely contain, he went outside. He was not aware of his feet touching the ground or even opening the door to the Vic.

Eddie was about to lock up – the towels were on the taps, bar stools on tables – but welcomed him genially.

'Come in, Grant. We've just got a few glasses to rinse, then I'll let you have Sharon.'

'You'd have had her yourself earlier if you'd had the chance.' He grabbed Eddie by the collar. 'She told me.'

Sharon tried to intervene. 'You've got it all wrong, Grant! I explained earlier.'

'No, it's Royle that's got the wrong idea.' Grant shoved him against the bar, sending empties crashing. Eddie was a big man, taller than Grant, and no stranger to aggro, but Grant had powerful muscles. He had also been trained to kill. 'Come on!' he shouted, challenging him. And that was the last thing he remembered before the red mist came down.

'Grant!' Sharon's voice penetrated the storm in his brain. 'Grant! Stop it! For God's sake, stop it, Grant, you're killing him!' Grant looked at her, unsure of who she was. She shook him by the shoulders. 'Grant. It's me, Sharon. Let it go, Grant. Let it go.' He hung his head, his breath was coming in great rasping sobs. Eddie was lying on the floor beneath him, a pool of blood around his head. He raised his eyes, wanting – but not daring – to ask what had happened. Sharon swallowed. 'Leave him, Grant. Go home.' Slowly, Grant got to his feet and left without saying a word.

'Is this a private party, or can anyone join in?' Phil asked. He had been awakened by the opera music belting out full volume on Grant's stereo, as had the Fowlers next door, judging by the rapping on the wall. Grant did not reply. He swayed slightly in the doorway to his darkened flat, apparently unaffected by the noise. Phil came in and closed the door. 'If you've really got to play something, I've got a Motorhead CD upstairs.' He switched the light on. '*That* I could sleep to. But please, Grant, not fat Italians coughing up their tonsils.' Phil reached out to turn down the stereo but Grant's hand clamped his wrist.

'Leave it,' Grant said warningly. Phil noted his white knuckles and sensed trouble. Grant looked like a zombie. He heard a siren wailing and drew the curtain back. An ambulance had pulled up outside the Vic, blue light flashing. Phil gave Grant, who seemed not to have noticed, a worried glance, and went to join the crowd of curious onlookers who had emerged from their houses. He caught Sharon's dead-eyed stare as Eddie Royle was stretchered into the ambulance and read it in an instant. From across the Square, the volume of the aria became louder and louder.

★

Grant was in hyper mode by the time Phil returned, saying he couldn't sleep and that he was going to the snooker hall. He denied knowing anything about any bother at the Vic and seemed uninterested in Eddie Royle's fate. Deeply concerned, Phil had no choice but to accompany him. Grant challenged a couple of regulars to a doubles match, then upped the odds when he and Phil won. It wasn't until Grant's cueing started to fall apart that Phil noticed his swollen hand. Grant said he'd shut it in a car door but refused to stop the game, continuing to play mechanically and uselessly as if he was entirely unaware of anything or anyone else around him. They lost that game, and the next, and the stake of three hundred pounds, but Grant remained oblivious.

'Eh, Phil, your brother's a nutter,' one of the players remarked. 'He must be on something, or he's finally flipped ...'

'Come on,' Phil guided Grant towards the door, refusing to rise to the bait. 'Let's go and get that hand seen to.'

Sharon sat chewing her nails in the hospital waiting area, feeling completely stunned. Eddie was being operated on but he had a ruptured artery in the skull that had formed a blood clot – not to mention four broken ribs and numerous cuts and bruises – and the nurse had been reticent about his chances. She had quizzed Sharon about Eddie's relatives, and when Sharon mentioned that his father was Irish, she asked if Eddie was a practising Roman Catholic. The next thing Sharon saw was a priest hurrying down the corridor.

She told the policeman who turned up to question her that Eddie had fallen down the stairs. He made it clear he didn't believe her.

'Look, I've told you everything I know,' she maintained, rattled.

He sighed. 'This wasn't a lucky punch you know. In my book, a man who can inflict damage like that really shouldn't be walking round.'

At that moment, Phil and Grant came in, Grant nursing a bruised and swollen hand. Phil spotted the copper and quickly lead Grant over to the Admissions desk. He waited until the policeman had gone and came over to Sharon.

'What have you told the old bill?'

Sharon looked at him coldly. 'You don't even care about Eddie, do you?'

'That's not the point ...'

'I ain't told them nothing – yet. But if Eddie don't pull through, you aren't going to keep the lid on this. Besides ...' she paused, remembering the sight of Grant pulverising Eddie, 'maybe I should talk. Maybe that brother of yours really is better off behind bars.'

Phil stiffened. 'Sharon, there's things you don't understand.'

Michelle had been waiting up for Sharon, keeping an ear open for a cab, but it was half-past two before she heard her return. 'Sharon? What happened?' she asked, running outside. Sharon turned a mascara-streaked face towards her. 'Oh, no, no,' Michelle breathed.

Sharon sniffed. 'It's alright. He's had an operation and he's going to be okay, but it was touch and go for a while.' She unlocked the door of the Vic and surveyed the wrecked bar, stools overturned, broken glasses, upturned ashtrays. Blood. ''Chelle,' she whispered, 'would you stay with me a few nights till Eddie gets back?'

'Yeah, sure. I'll just get some clothes.' Michelle paused. 'Not like you to be frightened of staying on your own.'

Sharon glanced out at the street. Phil and Grant were getting out of a taxi. Michelle followed her gaze. 'It's Grant, isn't it?' she said, the full horror of Eddie's 'accident' slowly dawning. 'It's Grant you're frightened of.'

'I already told you,' Grant said. 'I caught my hand in the car door.'

'Yeah, yeah,' Phil retorted, disbelieving. He let them into

Grant's flat and poured out two large measures of scotch. 'Look, we've gotta get our story straight, bruv. Sharon might say something.' Grant stared into his whisky, glassy-eyed. 'But first,' Phil continued, 'you've gotta tell me what really happened.'

Grant took a deep breath. 'Me and Eddie had a fight.'

'What about?'

'I don't know.'

'Oh, come off it Grant!'

'It's the truth ... I don't know,' Grant yelled. 'I can't remember anything.'

'Alright, alright, calm down.' Phil's brow furrowed.

'Phil.' Grant's voice shook slightly. 'It's happened again, hasn't it?'

CHAPTER THREE

Eddie turned his heavily bandaged head towards Phil. It was clearly an effort. 'You're offering me money to keep my mouth shut?' His expression — what Phil could see of it under the wrappings — was one of incredulity.

'If you like. Look, he's my brother, what do you expect?' Phil had the grace to look ashamed. He had blagged his way past the ward sister, desperate to find out what Eddie was going to do. He was relieved to hear he didn't intend to press charges — Eddie was determined to sort Grant out himself — and had offered him 'compensation'. Eddie was obviously not impressed.

'Stuff your money,' he croaked, leaning his head back on the pillow.

Phil sighed. 'I'm only trying to do what's right.'

'Right for who?'

Phil got up to leave, sickened by the whole mess. This wasn't his quarrel but he had no choice in the matter. Grant was his responsibility. Their mother, Peggy, had laid down the law about that the last time Grant went crazy. That was when he came out of the army, nine years ago. Now, the warning bells were ringing again.

'You know he's disappeared?' he remarked casually, regarding Eddie from the foot of the bed.

Eddie opened an eye — the other was swollen shut — and gave Phil a baleful look. 'Well, let's hope for his sake it's permanent.'

Sharon was equally unwelcoming and apparently as unconcerned as Eddie to hear that Grant had gone walkabout. 'If you find him, tell him to stay away,' she spat. Michelle glanced at her, concerned, as Phil shambled out of the Vic. Sharon was white as a sheet, with huge dark circles under her eyes. Michelle knew she hadn't slept — she had heard her padding about all night — and was deeply concerned.

'Don't waste your energy thinking about him,' she said, coming over and putting an arm round her shoulders. 'He's not worth it.'

Sharon turned haunted eyes to her. 'I keep seeing his face. It was like I didn't know him ... how can someone change just like that?'

Michelle shrugged. 'You're better off out of it.' She gave her shoulders a squeeze. 'You look wiped out. Go upstairs and lie down. Clyde and I can manage here.' Sharon smiled gratefully. 'Thanks. I might just do that.'

She dozed fitfully, her dreams once again invaded by Grant. This time they were terrifying dreams; dreams in which he stared at her with bulging eyes, his face a rigid mask of anger. She awoke, perspiring, and glanced at the clock: nine-thirty. I've got to pull myself together. They must be frantic downstairs, she thought, getting up. Throwing open the window to get a breath of fresh air, she caught sight of Grant passing in front of the Vic. He turned into the gateway to number 43. Without pausing to think, she slipped out of the Vic and waited by the railings opposite his flat. It wasn't long before he came out again, carrying a large holdall.

'Going without saying goodbye?' she said, stepping out of the shadows.

Grant started. 'Sharon.'

'Is that it, then?' she said sarcastically.

He flinched. 'Look, I don't want to argue with you.'

'Well, that's a relief. I've seen one of your arguments, remember?'

'I don't want to talk about it.' He strode away down Bridge Street, walking purposefully.

'Grant,' Sharon sobbed, her resolve crumbling. She ran after him. 'I just want you to explain what this is all about.'

Grant stopped under the railway viaduct and turned to face her. 'What's the point? There's nothing here for me anymore. Tell me one person who won't be glad to see the back of me.' His eyes challenged her briefly, then he turned on his heel again.

'Me,' Sharon whispered softly, too softly for him to hear, her face wet with tears.

Phil was working at the Arches, his mind only half on the job, when Grant reappeared the next day. He looked weary and dishevelled, as if he'd slept rough, but otherwise he appeared to have returned to normal.

'Where the hell have you been?' Phil exploded to hide his relief. He had been imagining all sorts of scenarios, one of which involved dragging the canal.

'To sort myself out.' Grant sat down, lowering his pack.

Phil nodded at Ricky. 'Go to the café and get us some teas. Take your time.' He handed him some change.

'And a bacon sarnie,' Grant shouted after him.

'So you ain't eaten, either?'

'Not much.'

'Where did you go?'

Grant looked up. 'Army Recruitment Centre. I'm gonna re-enlist.'

'Why, Grant? I mean, army life and you ... well, you ain't exactly cut out for it, are you? Not after ...'

Grant stood up abruptly. 'It's the only life that makes any sense to me.' He went out, bumping into Ricky and slopping hot tea on him.

'Ow!' Ricky complained. 'D'you want your sandwich? Grant? Grant! Oh, be like that, then.' Ricky unwrapped the sandwich and took a large bite.

When a fragile Eddie returned to the Vic, Sharon tried to stay out of his way, letting John, his father, settle him in. John, who had come back from Ireland as soon as he heard about his son, was as much in the dark as everyone else about Eddie's 'accident'. Only Sharon and Grant and Eddie knew the truth, and Sharon, who had avoided visiting Eddie in hospital, was nervous about what he would say. She was summoned by him later — Eddie was recuperating upstairs — and told that Grant was barred.

'And if you find that difficult to cope with and want to leave, I won't stop you,' he said, adding, with heavy irony, 'I'll even write you a good reference.' Sharon got the message. Eddie was asking her to choose her loyalties: Grant or the Vic.

Being put on the spot by Eddie rankled. After all, thought Sharon, the Vic was hers by rights. Den and Angie, Sharon's adopted parents, had run it for years. She had grown up there, under the severe gaze of Queen Victoria, whose bust still surveyed the bar. She knew every inch of crumbling plaster, every knot of wood. Who the hell was Eddie to evict her? Some Johnny-come-lately who wasn't even born in the East End? His nerve made her blood boil. The more she thought about it, the less she wanted to stay under the same roof as Eddie. Until the Vic was hers officially, that was. It was a day she frequently fantasized about. Then, Sharon decided, she'd bar him.

As far as Grant was concerned, he was out of her life already, whether she liked it or not. She was still trying to come to terms with Phil's news about Grant re-enlisting, but his departure from Albert Square seemed inevitable: Phil had not been able to dissuade him and, privately, Sharon was glad. It saved her from making a decision to end their relationship; a decision she was not sure she would have been strong enough to keep. She tried to convince herself that it was the best thing for both of them. If she'd got in any deeper ... Sharon gave herself a little shake. It was no use thinking like that. Better to say a civilized 'goodbye' and get on with her life. She glanced at her watch. There was no time like the present.

Grant had his belongings packed and piled in the hallway.

'I won't come in,' Sharon said formally. 'I've just come to wish you good luck.'

He gave her a tight smile. 'Is that all?'

'What else is there to say?'

Grant shook his head. 'Nothing.' He looked at her searchingly. 'It's been …'

'Don't. Don't say that.' She turned to go.

'Sharon, wait.' Grant stepped out of the door. 'I'd do anything to make it up to you.'

'Won't you be too busy parachuting out of a mess tin to do that?'

He put a hand on her arm. 'Really.' For a moment, they connected and she dropped her guard.

'There is something, actually,' she confessed, an idea gleaming.

'Name it.'

'Do you want a housesitter while you're away? I've gone right off living with Eddie.'

Grant dug in his pocket and handed her a key. 'The place is all yours.'

It wasn't until the domineering figure of Peggy Mitchell turned up on the doorstep, demanding to know her son's whereabouts, that Sharon realized living in Grant's flat might have its drawbacks.

'You knew he was off to re-enlist and you didn't try to stop him?' Peggy, a diminutive but formidable blonde, interrogated her within seconds of being introduced.

'I didn't really see any reason why I should; I thought is was his decision,' Sharon replied, taken aback at her ferocity.

'Oh, God!' Peggy threw up her hands in disgust. Phil, who had got wind of Peggy's arrival, tried to smooth things over, telling her it was nothing to do with Sharon. 'Well, in that case I want to speak to my son in private,' Peggy returned coldly, glaring at Sharon.

'Nice to meet you too, Mrs Mitchell,' Sharon replied,

equally cool. She arose with dignity and left for work, but not before hearing Peggy ask, rather too loudly, 'Is she the reason Grant's gone off?'

Sharon suppressed a snort. If that was what having a close family was all about, she was almost thankful that Angie had been too sozzled most of the time to interfere. At least, now that she was teetotal, now they were mates, equals if you like, she thought. Phil seemed to have shrunk to an obedient little boy the minute Peggy stalked into the room.

Just walking into the Recruitment Centre had given Grant the old, familiar buzz. Army life, being part of a group, not an individual, suited him. He revelled in the camaraderie, the mutual dependency. It was intimate, yet impersonal; thrilling, yet secure; demanded total commitment but no emotional entanglement.

He had passed the medical without a problem but for some reason the doctor wanted him to see a psychiatrist. Normally, nothing would have induced him to see a shrink, but he guessed it must be routine these days. The last time he'd been through an army medical was at sixteen. Things were bound to have changed since then.

'Relax, Mr Mitchell, you're not in the army yet,' the psychiatrist said as Grant stood to attention in front of him.

'Sir.'

'Been in the wars a bit?' He indicated Grant's hand.

'Just a couple of busted bones, Sir. Nothing permanent.'

He pored over Grant's medical notes. 'So I gather. Otherwise, you're in pretty good shape. It says here you have a fresh tattoo on your upper arm.' He looked up at Grant questioningly.

'It's the emblem of the parachute regiment, Sir.' Grant had had it done the previous day.

'Hmm.' He consulted his notes again, taking his time reading. 'Five years in the paras. See much action?'

'A tour of duty in Northern Ireland, Sir, and the Falklands campaign.'

'Ah, yes, the Falklands.' The psychiatrist, a bookish man wearing a bow tie, adjusted his glasses. 'I have here a letter from your old commanding officer. Perhaps we should start there.'

Grant gave him the version he had come to think of as the truth. It didn't tally with the version that terrorized him at night. The psychiatrist made no comment.

'Alright,' he said, when Grant had finished. 'Let's return to your hand. I believe you got it injured in a fight?' Grant sighed. He'd been over all this with the quack. As far as he was concerned it was a waste of time. He just wanted to get back in. 'Were you provoked?' the psychiatrist asked, leaning back in his chair and observing him.

'Yeah.' Grant momentarily forgot the 'Sir'. 'Alright, so I lost my temper,' he admitted hotly. 'Who doesn't? A bloke winds you up, you lose your rag. Big deal.'

'You must have hit him fairly hard.'

'Well of course I hit him hard. What was I supposed to say? "Look, mate, I'm gonna kill you, but I'm not going to hit you hard"?' He found himself breathing rapidly and made an effort to calm down.

'You wanted to kill him?' The psychiatrist raised an eyebrow.

'Figure of speech, Sir.'

'Do you have a girlfriend, Mr Mitchell?'

Grant was puzzled. 'Of course, Sir.'

'How does she feel about your re-enlisting?'

'She wants what I want, Sir,' he replied, after a moment's hesitation. 'No offence, Sir, but what has this got to do with me being in the army?'

'Mr Mitchell, I am trying to understand what civilian life means to you. Is anything troubling you? Are you sleeping alright?'

'Can't complain,' Grant said stiffly, wary now.

'Is that a yes or a no?' The psychiatrist waited. Grant did not respond. 'When you had this fight, were you having trouble sleeping?'

'I can't remember.'

'Try. It's not unusual for men involved in combat to develop sleeping problems, nightmares and such. Has this happened to you?' He leaned forward, forearms on the desk, eyeing Grant intently.

'You think my fight had something to do with what happened over there, don't you? With all due respect, Sir, a brawl in a pub in Walford is hardly the Falklands ... though Eddie Royle and the Argies have got a bit in common.'

The psychiatrist sat back again. 'I see,' he said slowly. 'Well, I think that about covers it.'

Grant didn't feel like facing anyone. The psychiatrist had said he'd receive a letter and Grant had a sinking feeling in the pit of his stomach about it. He couldn't put his finger on what he'd said that might have blown it – enough of his mates in the paras used to get into rucks when they were in civvies, after all – but there was something about the look on the bloke's face when he'd talked about Eddie that made him uneasy.

He took refuge in the Arches, creeping in after dark with a bag of fish and chips for his tea. One of the cars was unlocked and he slid into the driver's seat, leaving the door open so he could see by the interior light. He sensed, rather than heard a movement behind him and swung round sharply. A young girl with long, blonde, tousled hair got up from the back seat, looking scared.

'God, you didn't half give me a fright.' She smiled sheepishly.

'Sam!' Grant was stunned. The last person he expected to find himself camping out with in the chilly garage was his baby sister. 'What the hell are you doing here?'

She shrugged. 'Not a lot. Give us a chip.'

'Does mum know you're here?'

'Hope not, or we're both in trouble,' Sam said conspiratorially. 'She's already on the warpath lookin' for you.'

He sighed. 'Why can't she just let things alone? She's always interfering.'

'S'actly what I mean,' Sam agreed, munching. 'I'm right fed up with bein' at home, havin' to watch her and that boyfriend of hers carryin' on. They don't take no notice of me anyways, 'cept to have a go. D'you know what she did today, just 'cos I went to see Ricky?' Normally Grant would have pricked up his ears at the mention of his apprentice's name. Ricky and Sam had the hots for each other ever since she'd first visited the Arches, a relationship he and Phil disapproved of almost as much as Peggy did. Sam paused, having run out of breath. 'Carted me back 'ome, telling me it weren't up to me to say what was a big deal an' what weren't.' She looked up at Grant from under her fringe. 'That's why I'm here.'

'Sam, you're only fifteen,' Grant, who was only half-listening, reminded her absent-mindedly.

'Well, what about you? You're twenty-eight and even you can't make your own decisions.'

'What are you on about?' Grant was paying attention now.

'Mum moving heaven and earth to stop you re-enlisting. She even sent Phil out to look for you.'

'Wonderful.'

'So what's happened? Why ain'tcha in Aldershot?'

Grant crumpled up the chip wrapper and hurled the ball out of the car window with unnecessary force. 'Haven't you got any homework to keep you quiet?'

Peggy Mitchell was used to having things done her way. She had always ruled the roost, even when the boys' father, Eric, was alive. Eric had disciplined them – that, in her view, was a father's role – but Peggy was the one that taught them what was what. And top of her list came the family. In her book, families stuck together. She herself came from a large East-End family near Stepney and the same values had been imbued in her from an early age. 'Blood is thicker than water.' How many times had she heard her old dad say that, Peggy reflected, as she trotted briskly towards the Bridge Street Café in Albert Square, where Phil had told her he would meet her with the runaway Sam.

At forty-nine, she was still an attractive woman, although she had a hard set to her face. After Eric had died following a long, drawn-out battle against cancer she'd had hopes of doing something with her life. Eric, who was all set to become a champion boxer when she married him, had been a bitter disappointment. He never made the big time, turning instead to boozing, gambling and dodgy dealing. She had even considered leaving him, but Sam had come along – a late baby and a genuine accident – putting the mockers on any chance of escape. She had always slightly resented her pretty daughter because of that, and now that Eric was gone and she had resumed a long-standing affair with Kevin, who owned a mini-cab firm, Sam was in the way. It was with torn loyalties that Peggy approached the café to remonstrate with her.

'Grant! What are you doing here?' Sharon gasped, taken by surprise. She switched the hoover off and pushed a strand of hair out of her eyes, realizing she looked a mess.

Grant put down his rucksack. 'I've come back.'

'But the army …?'

He shook his head. 'No joy. Not the right temperament, apparently.' He said it lightly, but the news had been like a punch in the guts. The letter had arrived that morning and he was still reeling from it.

'Oh.' Sharon didn't know what to say. There was obviously more to this than Grant was letting on, but it didn't seem the right time to ask. She looked around at her stuff, which had overtaken his living-room – photos of herself with Den and Angie, favourite pictures, ornaments, books. 'I'm sorry, I've completely invaded you. I suppose you want your flat back, don't you?'

'No, you're alright.' Grant flexed his hand, which was still garish with bruises. 'I can move in upstairs.'

'Sure Phil won't mind?'

'He'll be glad of the company.'

They were interrupted by a sharp knock at the door. Grant opened it to find his mother standing there. She had Sam by the scruff and was trailing a defeated-looking Phil. 'Oh, so you're back,' she said tartly. 'I take it this is a flying visit?'

'No, mum. I'm not going.'

Peggy stomped past him, dragging Sam. 'Well, I'm glad you've come to your senses. It's a pity you had to put us through all this rigmarole to start with. I've been worried sick.' She caught sight of Sharon and stopped. 'You still 'ere?'

'Mum, I've said Sharon can stay. So just leave it, okay?'

'So where are you going to sleep?' Peggy eyed Sharon beadily.

'I'll move in with Phil.' Grant glanced questioningly at his brother. Phil shrugged.

'Well, you're all going to be cosy.' Peggy sat down in a high-backed armchair and surveyed them regally. ''Cos we've agreed Sam's going to move in as well.' She snapped open her handbag and took out a compact. 'I suppose there's one good thing,' she continued, reapplying lipstick. 'Phil can look after both of you.'

CHAPTER FOUR

'Oh, no, not again,' Phil groaned, jolted out of sleep by Grant's screams. He rubbed his eyes and peered at the clock: midnight. He went into the living-room where Grant was sleeping on a camp bed. Grant was still in the throes of his nightmare, tossing and scrabbling under the blanket, shouting, 'No! No!'

'Hey, hey, you're alright.' Phil knelt down and put a hand on his shoulder, shaking him gently to wake him. A light went on in the hall and Sam appeared in the doorway.

'What's going on?'

'It's okay, Sam, he's just having a bad dream. Go back to bed. Well, go on,' Phil insisted, as she hesitated. 'He'll be alright. I'm used to it.'

Grant stirred and opened his eyes wide. He sat up, his sweat-drenched T-shirt clinging to him. 'I don't think I wanna go back to sleep,' he said, shuddering.

'Fine by me,' Phil replied. 'Let's go out for a walk.' They slipped on tracksuits and trainers and went out into the Square. Phil breathed in deeply. 'Take a breath of that fresh air.' He glanced at Grant, who was still looking stunned, and started jogging on the spot. 'Let's have a little trot round, eh? Tire you out like they used to do in the army. Bit of tabbing. Come on.' It was many laps of the Square before Grant felt tired enough to sleep, by which time Phil, who was less fit than his brother, was utterly exhausted.

Sharon, in the flat below, had also been awoken by Grant's screams. She had been deeply perturbed and brought it up with Phil later, when she went round to the Arches to arrange her first driving lesson with Grant. 'Is that the Mitchell Brothers School of Motoring?' she enquired lightly.

'Since you're getting your lessons for free, the Muggs

Brothers School of Motoring'd be more like it,' Phil snapped, appearing from underneath a bonnet. He was knackered and feeling the strain after dealing with Grant – who had bounced into the kitchen that morning as fresh as a daisy – and was in no mood for niceties.

'I didn't ask. He offered them,' Sharon retorted, stung.

'Yeah, well, he's always had a generous nature. Trouble is, there's always bin someone round to exploit it.'

'I dunno why you're taking it out on me, unless it's something to do with last night.'

Phil immediately clammed up, turning his back on her and rifling through a toolbox. He liked Sharon but she wasn't the girl for Grant. Ever since she'd started messing with his head, he reflected, Grant had regressed. The blackouts, his losing control, the nightmares; Phil had hoped it was all buried and forgotten but now his brother was being tortured by demons and it was all Sharon's fault.

'I heard him shouting,' Sharon persisted. 'He was like that in Scotland. What happened?'

Phil wiped his hands and came over to her, his colour high. 'What always happens. I looked after him. So why don't you just do us a favour and mind your own business?'

Sharon stood her ground. 'I do happen to care about him, Phil.'

'Care about him? You don't know the meaning of the word. Do you know what that involves?' He glared at her. 'That "noise" you heard last night. That was caring about him. Tell me, do you really want him? As he is? Damaged goods?' Sharon flinched. 'No. You don't,' Phil continued softly. 'Well, I'll tell you something else you don't know. If you're waiting for him to ask you, you'll wait for ever, 'cos deep down inside he just ain't got the confidence.'

Now Sharon was really cross. 'You've spent years looking after him and you still ain't got it sorted out. So why should I know all the answers?'

'You don't even know what the questions are,' he spat.

'So, help me.'

'I'll give you one piece of advice.' Phil put his face threateningly close. 'With Grant, it's all or nothing. So if you ain't man enough to take him on as he really is, do us all a favour and get out of his life. For good.'

However committed he was to Grant, even Phil had to admit that babysitting his brother and sister wasn't his idea of a fun Saturday night. From the living-room, the sound of a military band on the television blasted out – Grant, compensating for having his offer of a date turned down by Sharon – making it hard for Phil to think, let alone hold a conversation.

He sighed heavily and banged on Sam's door. 'Sam! Please! Just one minute!' There was no reply. He tried again. 'Look, mum's gone out now, can't we just talk about it?' Sam had locked herself in her bedroom in a major strop following a disastrous tea party at the Butchers', during which Ricky had breezily announced that they were engaged. Pat and Frank had taken it surprisingly well, considering, but Peggy had come down on Sam like a ton of bricks and frogmarched her out of the house. Phil, too, had received an almighty rollicking, after which Kevin had been dispatched to make it crystal clear to Ricky that if he came within fifty feet of Sam again he would not live to tell the tale.

Phil gave up and returned to the living-room. 'Can't you knock that thing on the head?' he said irritably, slumping down on the sofa.

'I like it,' Grant replied, keeping his eyes glued to the parade of marching regiments. Suddenly he sat bolt upright. 'There's Tiny!'

'What?'

'Never heard of him.'

'Yes you have. He's still in, lucky sod.'

Phil cursed inwardly. Grant didn't need any more reminders of his past in the paras. 'Leave it out, will yer? Can't you switch over?'

'You must remember him.'

'You've never mentioned him before.'

'Yes, I did. We called him Tiny because he was so big.'

'Doesn't ring a bell,' Phil returned grumpily.

Grant's face was lit up. 'I've told you all about him. We played together in the platoon five-a-side football team.'

'You told me you never got picked.'

His face grew darker. 'Of course I did. I played midfield.'

'Alright, alright, fine, don't get carried away.' Phil got up. 'Look, can't we go somewhere for a drink?'

Grant stood up too, his excitement turning to anger. 'You don't believe me, do you? You think this is some loony tune made up by your deranged brother.'

'Jesus, it's been a hard enough day as it is, Grant. Don't start again.'

'Say you believe me,' Grant insisted.

'I do.'

'No you don't! Say it!'

Phil noticed the cords standing out in Grant's neck and wondered what they were in for now. He didn't have the strength for another all-nighter.

'I believe you, I believe you! I believe you just saw your best mate, Tiny what's-his-name, on the telly! Your best mate ever in the whole army and that you won the platoon cup! Is that enough?' Phil pulled on his jacket. 'I'm off for a drink.'

'I've got a photograph somewhere, and a winner's medal,' Grant yelled after his brother's retreating back. The door slammed.

Agitated, he paced up and down the room, trying to remember where they both were. Sideboard drawer? He yanked it out and emptied the contents on the floor, scrabbling through them frantically. There was no sign of the photograph or the medal. Grant racked his brains. Finally, he realized: they must be in Sharon's flat. But Sharon was on a girls' night out with Michelle. He started hunting for his spare key, turning out pockets and rifling through bags. He had to find that photo.

★

As it happened, Sharon's plans for the evening had been cancelled after Michelle cried off at the last minute in order to cook a meal to impress her new housemate. Michelle had been desperate to move out from under Pauline's stifling influence and had just succeeded in renting rooms for herself and Vicki in a house in Victoria Road owned by Rachel, a college lecturer. Sharon, nose out of joint, retired to her flat with a bottle of red wine and drank it, falling asleep on the sofa.

The next thing she was aware of was a tremendous crash and the sensation of being showered with something. She woke up choking on a pall of thick, white, gritty dust. Thinking there had been an explosion, she curled into a ball and put her arms over her head. Her hair was full of bits of plaster. There was a second, thunderous blow and another cloud of plaster and dust rained down on her, shooting out from the wall opposite as if someone was attacking it from the other side with a heavy implement.

'God almighty!' she screamed, terrified. Suddenly, she felt as if she was in a horror movie. Only this was real.

There was a moment of silence.

'Sharon?' called Grant's voice from the stairwell linking the two flats. A million questions were speeding through Sharon's mind, but she was too petrified to articulate any of them. 'Sharon?' Grant's voice shouted again, more urgently this time. 'Sharon?' He gave the wall a third blow and the head of a sledge-hammer burst through the thin plaster wall, making her shrink back in fright. As the dust settled, she could make out his eyes staring at her through the hole.

'What the hell do you think you're doing?' she gasped, trying to sound brave.

'I needed to get something and the door was locked.'

She couldn't believe she was hearing him correctly.

'Look, I didn't think you were in there,' Grant continued. He made it sound entirely reasonable. He examined the hole and for a second she thought he was going to keep pounding it until he could climb through. 'I'll come round,' he said. She heard his footsteps retreating and strained her ears. He was trying the back door, rattling it hard. 'Sharon, it's locked.' She held her breath, not daring to move or speak. 'Sharon, don't be so silly,' he shouted, sounding angry. 'I just want to talk to you.' Still she stood frozen to the spot. Suddenly there was a tinkling of breaking glass and she heard the key being turned in the lock. Without thinking twice, Sharon grabbed the empty wine bottle and cracked it against the coffee table, breaking it in half. Armed with the jagged bottle neck, she waited.

Having sunk three pints and two whisky chasers, Phil's mood had improved considerably. He won a game of darts against Pete Beale and was up against Arthur Fowler next.

'How's that brother of yours?' Arthur asked matily. 'Not in tonight?' Phil smiled to himself. It wasn't many weeks ago that Pete, Arthur and Frank Butcher had tried to orchestrate a showdown in the Vic with Grant as payback for Eddie. It had come to nothing because Grant, for once, hadn't risen to the bait. If he had, Arthur definitely wouldn't have as many teeth left as he was showing at the moment.

'He's fine,' Phil replied, throwing an arrow and scoring treble twenty. 'Having a quiet night in front of the box.' He felt a faint pang of guilt and wondered, wearily, if he should go back and check. Grant had, after all, been in a funny mood, getting all worked up over that army bloke. Phil decided against it. He was on a winning streak and didn't want to break his concentration. Besides, he told himself, Grant didn't want mollycoddling. Too much fussing around would only wind him up more. The trick was to be there for him in a crisis. Like he'd always been, ever since they were little. Ever since... Arthur raised his arm to throw and Phil flinched involuntarily. The movement, combined with a sudden evocative whiff of something familiar, took him back to his childhood, to the gym where his father used to train. Phil remembered the smell of leather and sweat and the overpowering odour of embrocation as if it were yesterday. He remembered the other stuff, too.

'Ooh, me shoulder,' Arthur Fowler complained, flexing his arm. 'Pauline's rubbed it with Tiger Balm but it's no better. It's put me throwing action right out.'

'It's me,' Grant said, laughing nervously. 'What are you doing?'

Sharon tightened her grip on the bottle.

'Get out, Grant.' He took a step towards her and she lifted it threateningly.

Grant stopped. 'I was looking for something. I couldn't get in so I thought I might as well start on the new door. You did know I was planning to knock one through there.' He crossed to the sideboard and started rummaging through drawers, tipping their contents onto the floor. 'Who do you think I am?' he asked aggressively, glancing back at her. 'Jack the Ripper?'

Sharon stared at him in disbelief. He had smashed through the wall, punched through the glass in the door and now he was turning the furniture upside-down and pretending this was normal behaviour? 'What are you doing?' she whispered hoarsely.

'I'm looking for this photograph to prove to my know-all big brother that he doesn't know everything,' he ground out, still hunting.

'You're crazy,' Sharon said, backing away. 'You must be. You're out of your mind.'

'It's my wall. I can do what I like with it.'

Sharon's mouth fell open. 'You ... you stupid bastard, you screwed-up ...' The bubble of fear inside her burst, dissolving into anger instead. She picked up an ornament and would have thrown it at him had he not held up a warning hand.

'If you throw that, Sharon ...'

'Yeah? You'll what?' Her blood was up now and she was spoiling for a fight.

'Just don't throw it, alright?'

'Or what? You'll beat the living daylights out of me like you did Eddie?'

'Put it down, Sharon,' he said, getting up off the floor.

'I saw you, Grant! I saw what you were like. I saw you hitting him!' Grant was silent, his eyes unreadable. 'I'm gonna move out,' Sharon said, determined. 'Now.' She started to walk towards the bedroom but he barred her way. 'Look,' she sighed, trying to keep the quiver out of her voice, 'whatever's the matter with you I don't think I want to know about it. You just plain bloody frighten me and that's all there is to it.'

Grant's eyes blazed. 'I have never laid a finger on a woman in my life.'

'You'll get round to it,' she hissed, 'but it's damn well not going to be me!'

He held her by the shoulders, making her face him, his fingers digging deep into her skin.

'What, you really think I'd hurt you?'

'I don't think I'm going to stay around to find out.' She tried to wrench free from his grasp but he had hold of her hard. 'Let – me – go,' she said fiercely. He looked at his hands as if he had only just realized what he was doing, and relaxed his grip.

'Look, what happened with Eddie ...' he stumbled. 'I was out of order, bang out of order. I know that.' He tried to embrace her but she refused to respond. 'I could never hurt you,' he continued, his voice husky. 'If anyone laid a finger on you, I'd ... I don't know what I'd do. You're the most important thing in the world to me.'

Sharon looked at his face. He had tears in his eyes. 'Please don't leave me, not over something stupid like tonight,' he begged. She tried not to feel moved at his wretchedness, reminding herself of Eddie's battered body.

'What did happen between you and Eddie?' she asked, more gently this time. He tried to change the subject but she wouldn't let him, threatening to leave if he didn't tell her the truth.

Eventually, he said, 'There aren't words for some of the things I've seen.'

'In the Falklands?'

'Yes.'

'Tell me.' He opened his mouth, but what came out was not words but a great, juddering, heartrending sob. Sharon's last atom of resistance crumbled. 'I'll make some tea,' she said gently. 'And we're going to sort this out. We're going to get through this. Yes?'

'I don't think I can,' he whispered.

Sharon squared her shoulders. 'So, let's find out.'

By the time he got home, Phil was too drunk to notice the hole in the wall. And by the time he got up – late – the following morning, he was too enraged about the damage (it was glaringly obvious in broad daylight) to think about anything else, least of all mementoes of Grant's army chums. It wasn't until a couple of days later that he remembered the conversation that had led to the wall being bashed down, but wisely kept his mouth shut. Grant had not produced any proof, nor had he mentioned the paras since. Phil took it to be a good sign. Grant also seemed to be more relaxed, which was a novelty. He put it down to the punishment Grant was giving the wall – they had decided to make a proper job of the connecting door – which was obviously doing wonders for working off his frustrations.

'How long do you reckon it'll take to finish?' Sharon asked, passing Grant a can of beer. She had come home after an evening out with a mate to find Grant labouring on the door.

'I should have it cracked by tomorrow. Then I'll be able to drop in in the middle of the night.' Sharon stopped smiling.

'Only joking,' Grant said.

They had proceeded to have quite a drinking session and the next thing Grant was aware of was waking up in the chair with a stiff neck, surrounded by a sea of crumpled beer cans. He went to the kitchen and made tea, taking a cup to Sharon. There was no response when he knocked on her door, so he went in. He hadn't seen her in bed since that night in Scotland, getting on for six months ago. She was even more beautiful without make-up, he thought, gazing down at her sleeping: younger, softer, vulnerable. Without the carefully applied mask of cosmetics she normally wore, she had lost the brittleness of her public image – the face she painted on for the Vic's customers – and looked like a little girl.

'Tea,' he whispered, bending over her. Sharon stirred and passed a hand over her face.

'Oh God. Don't look at me like this. Go away.'

'Alright, alright, I'll turn my back.' He put down the breakfast tray and went to draw the curtains.

'No!' Sharon groaned, 'Too bright. My hair's a mess.' She dived under the duvet. 'What are you still doing here, anyway?' she asked indistinctly.

'I fell asleep. Not long after you crashed out. You had nothing to worry about,' he added. 'I'm far too much of a gentleman to take advantage of a lady when she's not exactly sober.'

Sharon made a muffled response that sounded like, 'How have you managed so far, then?' Grant grinned and left the room. He could tell she was warming to him.

Later that morning, Sharon, still feeling groggy, made her way to the launderette, hoping fervently that it wasn't Dot Cotton's shift on the service washes. If it was, she'd get no peace, and she wanted time to herself to think. As she went in, she noticed Michelle deep in discussion with her Uncle Pete on his fruit and veg stall. Sharon waved but Michelle didn't see and went hurrying off across the Square.

Sharon sat down, disappointed. She had been feeling rather left out of Michelle's life of late. Lulled by her washing churning in the suds, she reflected that Michelle seemed to be totally taken up with Rachel. She was even running around organizing a housewarming party with her. To Sharon's mind, it was a waste of time. Rachel was an outsider: different class, different roots, different job, different accent. Sharon and Michelle, on the other hand, had grown up in Albert Square. They had played together, gone to school together, even dated together, and confided in each other about everything. Well, almost everything, she corrected herself. It had been a long time before Michelle had had the guts to tell her that little Vicki's father was none other than Sharon's adoptive dad.

The revelation, a year ago, had come just as Sharon was trying to come to terms with Den's mysterious death. One minute she was trying to cope with the news that police divers had discovered his body in the canal; the next, she was trying to get her head round the fact that her dad had slept with her best friend and that Vicki was her half-sister. The incident had marked a loss of innocence for both Sharon and Michelle, ruling off their old, easy-going relationship and starting them on the road to a more volatile, if more worldly knowledge of each other. Things had been strained for a while, but that was all in the past. Sharon had guarded Michelle's secret, but it made her sad to think that Vicki didn't know they were family. With Den and Angie gone she didn't have anyone else.

Her thoughts turned to Grant. She still didn't know how she felt about him. She'd been appalled when he attacked Eddie and terrified when he bludgeoned down the wall, but now it was like he was a different person. This Grant was attentive, sweet, respectful, caring. It was disarming. The problem was knowing which was the real Grant: the violent madman or the gentle giant …

Michelle, who popped into the Vic that evening, had no doubts on that score. 'You be careful,' she warned, downing a quick half. 'I wouldn't like to be locked in a room with him.' To her surprise, Sharon found herself defending Grant.

'You've got him completely wrong. He's the perfect gentleman.' Michelle's eyebrows almost disappeared into her fringe.

'Which is why you're holding him at arm's length, then, is it?' she commented pithily, emptying her glass and leaving.

Sharon was still chewing this over when she got back to the flat. With Grant it was all or nothing. That was what Phil had said and she knew he was right. When Grant had begged her not to go, she had been touched by his need for her, flattered, even. It gave her power; a thrilling power over a powerful man. A power you abused at your peril. The danger sharpened her desire. Suddenly, she wondered why she had waited so long.

To her surprise, Grant was still working on the door, even though it was late.

'Nearly there,' he said, fiddling with the lock. 'There we go.' He closed the door. 'A perfect fit. Da da!' He grinned, pleased with himself, then tried to open it again. The door stuck fast. 'Oh no.' He rattled the handle. 'It's locked itself.'

'Haven't you got the keys?'

'They're upstairs at Phil's.' He passed his arm over his forehead wearily. 'And before you ask, he's out. Sam's got my set but mum's dragged her back into custody because she found out she was seeing Ricky again.'

Sharon laughed. 'Well, they can hardly keep their hands off each other, those two.' She met his eyes for an instant and they both glanced away, embarrassed.

'I suppose I could always smash another hole in the wall,' Grant joked.

'You could always stay here,' Sharon said, serious.

'What, a couple more cans of lager and fall asleep on the sofa?'

'No,' she smiled, her mind made up. 'I think we should forget the beer. I seem to remember you saying you'd never take advantage of a girl if she'd had a drink. Well, I'm stone-cold sober.'

This time Grant held her gaze, his eyes boring into her. His hands clasped her waist and drew her close. 'Are you sure?' he murmured, his lips brushing her hair. Sharon kissed him.

'Let's find out, shall we?' she whispered, leading him towards the bedroom.

CHAPTER FIVE

Sharon stretched luxuriously, flexing her toes. Still drowsy, she turned to embrace Grant. But he wasn't there. Rubbing her eyes, she struggled up onto one elbow and peered about the darkened room. Grant, fully dressed, was tying his trainers. He looked up guiltily. 'Morning.'

'Morning.' She glanced at his feet. 'Getting your running shoes on, I see.'

He shifted uncomfortably. 'It's nothing personal. It's just — well, I've got some business to see to. At the Arches.' He got up. 'Catch you later, alright?'

'Alright,' she replied, disappointed. There was a knock on the door, making both of them jump.

'You'd better get it,' he said, disappearing into the kitchen. Sharon sighed and pulled on a dressing-gown. What was it with blokes the morning after? It was as if they had to pretend it never happened. She put on her slippers and shuffled to the door.

'Blimey, you look like you've been pulled through a hedge backwards,' Michelle said breezily, stepping in uninvited.

'Thanks. Remind me to return the compliment the next time I get you out of bed.'

'Oh. Sorry. Having a lie-in were you?'

Sharon grimaced. 'Not any more.'

From the kitchen came the sound of the kettle boiling. Michelle waited for Sharon to offer her a cup of coffee, but she didn't. 'I won't stop,' she said, taking the hint. 'I just dropped by to invite you to the housewarming party. Any time from one o'clock. Bring a bottle.' Grant's head appeared around the kitchen door. Michelle gawped. Grant stared back, his expression belligerent. 'And a friend,' she added reluctantly.

★

'You're not seriously telling me you really want to go to this thing?' Grant demanded after Michelle had gone.

Sharon huffed, exasperated. 'I thought you wanted to go?'

'I was just windin' her up. D'you think I'd go after what that uptight cow said last time?' Rachel's previous attempt at socializing with Grant and Sharon – a dinner party to which Michelle had invited them along for moral support – had deteriorated into a slanging match after Rachel had decried boxing as 'entertainment for Neanderthals' and the army as 'a dumping ground for psychopaths'.

'So what do you want to do?' Sharon asked.

Grant considered. 'Game of snooker and a curry?' Sharon felt a brief pang. A few frames down the snooker hall was hardly romantic; she would have preferred to have been wined and dined somewhere intimate with candles and soft music. They had, after all, just spent their first night of passion together. 'Well?' Grant said impatiently. Sharon put on a bright smile. Grant wasn't the type to wear his heart on his sleeve. She would just have to get used to that.

'Sounds great.'

Phil was on his way to the Arches when he spotted a vagrant making a nuisance of himself outside the launderette. Normally, he would have walked on by – it wasn't unusual to see beggars, especially outside the Tube station – but there was something familiar about this one. He was tall and stringy with lank black hair and a beard and wore a ripped and torn parka.

'Hey, you, hop it,' Phil shouted, as the tramp accosted a woman laden with groceries, snarling abuse at her when she hurried on past. He swivelled round and Phil found himself looking into the ravaged face of Nick Cotton.

At first, he wasn't even sure that it was Nick. The guy was trembling and sweating and stank to high heaven and his face was so dirty it was hard to tell. His bloodshot eyes darted about nervously, as if unable to bear Phil's scrutiny. One look at his unfocused gaze and huge pupils was enough to tell Phil he was on drugs. And judging by the state of his arms, he was obviously an addict.

'Well, if it ain't me old mate Phil Mitchell.' Nick Cotton reached out a grimy hand. 'Spare us some change, mate, will yer?' Phil regarded it with distaste.

'You gotta nerve, coming back here again after what you did,' he spat.

'Tha's all in the past now, int it?' Nick gave a wheedling smile. 'All buried and forgotten.'

'Yeah, just like Dot would've been if you'd had your way.' Two years ago, Nick had almost succeeded in poisoning his mother in an attempt to get his hands on the fortune she had won playing bingo. Dot had eventually called his bluff and Nick had been forced to do a runner. No one had been sorry to see the back of him; he was regarded as a bad lot whose appearance inevitably spelt trouble whenever he turned up in the Square.

'I never went through wiv it,' Nick protested. 'When it came down to it, I just couldn't hurt me old ma. Anyways, I'm a changed man now.'

'You look it.' Phil grabbed hold of him by the arm. 'So changed I can't see you fitting in here no more. Not that you ever did. Now get out of here before they take you away with the rest of the rubbish.' He gave him a shove, sending Nick stumbling towards an alleyway stacked with reeking dustbin bags.

'You ain't getting rid of me,' Nick shouted wildly, picking himself up. 'I've come 'ome. For good.'

Grant had already opened up and was doing a respray job by the time Phil got to the lock-up. 'When did that one come in?' Phil shouted, pointing at the car.

Grant stopped and removed his mask. 'First thing. You weren't here so I said we'd take it. Rush job.'

'Is it kosher?'

'What do you think?' Grant looked at him scornfully. 'The bloke's paying way over the odds, cash. Said we were recommended. I could hardly turn him down, could I? Ruin our reputation. This is easy money.'

'Easy come, easy go,' muttered Phil, thinking of Nick Cotton.

'What?'

'Nothing. Just be careful who you deal with.'

Phil's jitters were increased ten-fold later that morning when his solicitor, Marcus Christie, turned up unannounced at the garage.

'I have good news,' Christie said, picking his way carefully around oily pieces of engine in his expensive brogues. 'It appears the police are going to have to drop the case against you. They don't have enough evidence to make it stick and without more concrete proof the CPS won't look at it.' He cast a look about the workshop, eyebrows arched. 'All *you* have to do, Mr Mitchell, is keep a low profile, so to speak.' Brushing away a fleck from his immaculate navy suit, he continued, 'Of course, if the police were to discover anything else at all incriminating … well, I don't need to tell you that would alter things greatly to your disadvantage.' He held out his hand then, noticing Phil's streaked palms, withdrew it. 'Good-day to you.'

'Smug git,' Grant muttered as Christie left. 'Who does he think he is?'

'A rich bastard we pay to keep us out of schtook,' Phil reminded him grimly. 'And he was doing us a favour. So for Christ's sake, get rid of that flamin' motor.'

Despite Sharon's initial misgivings, her evening out with Grant went well. He seemed to have got over his earlier moodiness and she found herself relaxing and enjoying his company. They ended up tumbling into bed again and this time, to her relief, Grant was warmer towards her in the morning, holding her in his arms and stroking her hair gently. Sharon, suspecting he thought she was still asleep, kept her eyes closed, though it was hard to stop the smile tugging at the corners of her mouth.

Only one thing spoiled Sharon's new-found happiness and that was the feeling Grant was still holding out on her. Whenever she showed an interest in his business he was either frustratingly noncommittal or changed the subject.

'It's like I only know a fraction of what's going on with him,' she complained to Michelle later when she bumped into her in the market. 'When I ask, he just makes some excuse and fobs me off. Look.' She opened the carrier bag she was holding and produced a new dress. 'He just gave me the money, told me to get something nice. Den used to do the same. Give me money to buy sweeties and tell me to run along.'

'Well, I wouldn't knock it,' Michelle remarked, fingering the dress. 'Play your cards right and you could do rather well.'

Sharon sighed. 'You know what I mean, 'Chelle. If this is gonna be a serious relationship, I don't want there to be secrets between us.'

'Big "if".'

'Yeah, well, I still want to know the truth.'

'And what if you don't like it?'

'That's my look-out. I'm a big girl. I can handle it.'

'Okay,' Michelle said slowly. 'You could start by finding out where he gets his money from, since he's so free with it. *Then* see if you still want to have a serious relationship.'

Their conversation was interrupted by a commotion around Pete Beale's stall. 'Stand back, give the poor sod some air,' Pete shouted as traders and shoppers crowded round. 'Somebody call an ambulance, for crying out loud!' Kathy, Pete's ex, came hurrying past on her way to the café, where there was a payphone.

'What's happened?' Sharon asked nervously.

'It's Nick Cotton,' she replied. 'Pete was just setting up and he found him. Looks like an overdose.'

Nick Cotton's sorry condition was the talk of the Square for the rest of the day, but Sharon was unable to get Michelle's challenge out of her head. What if Grant was involved in something dodgy? Would she be able to turn a blind eye? The Mitchell brothers had a reputation. There was the business with the stamps and the forged fivers and that mess with the MOT certificates. Either she let sleeping dogs lie, Sharon decided, or she found out now what she was letting herself in for. It was no contest.

Back home, she dug out Den's old address book and looked up a contact of his, Johnny, who had been in the motor trade for years.

'Funny you should ring,' he wheezed. 'The old bill have already been sniffing round here asking a load of questions. Word is they're onto summat.'

'Did they mention the name Mitchell?'

Johnny paused. 'As in Phil and Grant Mitchell?'

'Yes.'

'You're not involved with them, love, are you?' Johnny spluttered 'Your dad'll be turning in 'is grave.'

'Depends what you mean by "involved",' Sharon replied cagily. 'What exactly do they do?'

When Johnny told her that the Mitchells did up stolen cars, Sharon found she wasn't as shocked as she once might have been. Being with Grant was obviously beginning to rub off, she concluded. The revelation confirmed what she'd half-suspected, but hadn't wanted to admit to herself: she was sleeping with a crook. The thought was quite a turn-on. Grant made all the men she'd ever dated look like wimps in comparison. He couldn't have been further from safe, boring Duncan, the priest; Ian Beale had been just a kid when they went out, and he showed up Wicksy, whom she used to idolize, as little more than a poncy playboy.

'Thanks, Johnny, you're a gent,' she said, her decision made. 'How much do you think the police know?'

'I'll keep you posted, love,' he said.

*

Johnny came into the Vic two days later wearing a cap pulled well down over his eyes. Sharon hardly recognized him; he seemed to have shrunk and withered since she'd last seen him, his skin leathery and kippered by the cigarette smoke he was constantly wreathed in.

'What are you doing here?' she hissed under her breath as he ordered a half of bitter.

'Careful.' Johnny cast a sidelong look at Eddie. 'Once a copper ...' Sharon registered the hint. 'Just passing through,' Johnny continued in a louder voice. 'I was going to stop off on business, as usual, but someone else is keeping an eye on things instead.'

'Oh, yes?' Sharon inquired innocently as Eddie passed behind her. 'Here's your change.'

'Ta love.' Johnny took a draught and smacked his lips. 'That's good. It's getting really hot out there.'

'Really?' She swabbed the bar with a towel nonchalantly.

'Yeah. And the filth. All over the place. Know what I mean? You need to watch your step.' He drained the rest of his glass and put it down in front of her.

'Thanks for the warning,' Sharon said, feeling panic rise inside her. She had to tell Grant.

'Alright if I pop out for a minute?' she said casually to Eddie.

'As a matter of fact, it's not, Sharon,' he replied tersely. 'There's a whole pub of customers waiting to be served.'

'I won't be long.'

'Listen,' Eddie growled, 'I don't think you're understanding me, Sharon. Whatever it is can wait.' Sharon was taken aback. Eddie was usually pretty relaxed about his staff taking breaks, but he had been on her case all morning. Now she came to think of it, he seemed distinctly edgy.

'Looks like Grant's not the only one being watched,' Johnny muttered, confirming her suspicions. Eddie must have set Grant up. She'd seen him deep in conversation with another man, a stranger in a mac, who had been in the pub several times recently. How stupid I was not to realize, she cursed herself, wondering desperately how to create a diversion.

Fate intervened in the form of Nick Cotton, who had been discharged from hospital and headed straight back to Albert Square.

'Oi, you! What's your game? C'mon, out!' Eddie shouted, as Nick began hassling customers for money. Sharon, seeing Eddie distracted, seized her chance and ran out to the back to phone Grant. He did not take the news well, but she didn't give him time to argue.

'Do as I say. Just get in a clean car and drive away fast.'

'But there's a VW we've still got in the lock-up. And some number plates in the red tool box. If they find those …'

'I'll sort it,' she insisted. 'Now just go!'

She returned to the bar to find Eddie looking for her.

'Women's problems,' she said brightly.

Grant had never taken orders from a woman in his life before – apart from his mum – and he was riled at being put on the spot by Sharon. What did she know about it anyway? He and Phil had both kept schtum about the stolen motors. Still, the urgency in her voice told him this was no wind-up and his instinct was to trust her. With Phil lying low at a mate's, there was no one else he could turn to. He *had* to trust her. He grabbed the keys to Sharon's Escort, which was on the forecourt outside, slammed the garage doors shut and drove off at speed through the market, scattering a pile of cardboard boxes. Glancing in the rear-view mirror he spotted an unmarked police car, which had obviously been parked in Turpin Road, do a three-point turn and follow him. He gritted his teeth and put his foot down. The further he could get them from the lock-up, the better. Sharon would need as much time as he could buy to get rid of the car and the plates. It was only as he was pulled over on Mile End Road that he remembered. Sharon couldn't drive yet.

★

With Johnny's help, Sharon had managed to give Eddie the slip a second time. She ran round to the Arches, retrieved the number plates and threw them onto the passenger seat of the nifty Golf Gti. Turning the ignition key with trembling fingers, she reversed out in a cloud of exhaust, revving madly. The car stalled. I must be mad, she thought. What on earth am I doing? Grant had only given her two driving lessons, both of which had been a disaster. All the things he'd told her about clutch control had gone clean out of her head. But it was too late to stop now; she was committed. Sharon took a deep breath, restarted the car and crunched it noisily into first gear. Cursing, she kangaroo-hopped down the road. As Bonnie to Grant's Clyde, it wasn't an inconspicuous getaway, but Johnny was waiting for her on the corner of Turpin Road and George Street and took her place at the wheel.

'I'll keep it safe for yer – least I can do for Den's little princess when she's in trouble,' he said, winking. 'But you can tell Grant it'll cost him. I ain't *that* generous.' He departed with a wave, leaving Sharon to face Eddie.

'So the wanderer returns,' he said sarcastically as she entered the bar. 'Very nice of you to drop in, Sharon.' One glance at his face told her they both knew what was going on.

'Sorry. I had to pop out for some air.' Sharon returned, deadpan. 'I suddenly felt very sick.' Looking him in the eye, she added, 'Well, I'd better get on clearing up the glasses. Best to get everything straight, isn't it?'

'Anything?' The copper in the squad car, which had been called in for backup, strolled over to Grant's Escort, which the plain-clothes detective was going over with a fine tooth-comb.

The detective shook his head. 'Nothing.' Grant, who was leaning against the bonnet, arms folded in an air of studied resignation, was trying to make out the chatter on the police radio. It sounded hopeful.

'Their lock-up's clean as well,' the first copper said.

Grant suppressed a smirk. 'I told you so,' he jeered.

'You can keep your mouth shut,' the detective snarled. 'We've got your number. Next time you won't be so lucky. In the meantime …' He signalled the first officer. 'Sergeant. Book him for speeding.'

Strangely, Grant didn't mind about the ticket. He didn't even feel angry when he saw the state of the workshop. He turned a deaf ear to Phil chuntering on about walking back right into a hornet's nest and barely rose to the bait when Peggy and Kevin accosted him. All he knew was that Sharon had come through for him, and that meant everything.

Peggy was on the warpath because Sam – who she had personally shepherded to school with Kevin – had somehow given them the slip and disappeared. Ricky was missing, too, and when Phil discovered an RAC route map to Gretna Green at the lock-up (in the only envelope the police hadn't torn open), there was only one conclusion to be drawn. Grant, Phil and Kevin were immediately despatched up the M6 to stop the pair of them eloping. As far as Peggy was concerned, it was a race against time with her daughter's virtue on the line. Phil and Grant, who had realized Ricky must have nicked one of the stolen number plates to disguise his camper van, had a less noble motive.

The drive up to Scotland made Grant wistful for Sharon. He hadn't had the chance to tell her how he felt before he left and, when he rang her from a motorway service station, he found himself suddenly struck dumb. Yet he couldn't stop thinking about her, wanting her. It was as if she had bewitched him. They were the other side of Carlisle before the penny dropped: he was in love. By the time they got to Gretna he had formulated a plan. Ricky's and Sam's names were not on the register – it turned out there was a three-month waiting list – but Grant's and Sharon's soon were.

CHAPTER SIX

Eddie hadn't said anything. He didn't have to. His relationship with Sharon, which had been on shaky ground ever since Grant landed him in hospital, had reached an all-time low since the foiled police raid. His old colleagues in the Met had been giving him grief, particularly Inspector Manning, who had been keen to nail Phil Mitchell for the forged MOT certificates a year ago and was desperate for a result. Without anything new to convict him on, Phil Mitchell was going to walk free. Not only that but the personal score Eddie had planned to settle with Grant had come to nothing. It was all Sharon's fault. She had to go, he decided, good barmaid or not.

He hit on a foolproof way to do it. When Sharon came in for her lunchtime shift he gave her an ultimatum: Grant or the job.

'You can't do that!' she said angrily.

'Call it "irreconcilable differences" if you like,' Eddie replied, 'but this time I mean it, Sharon. He's a bad influence, he's got a bad reputation and I won't have my staff associating with him. It's your choice.'

They were interrupted by a nervous young policeman who wanted to know the whereabouts of Dot Cotton.

'What's that Nick of hers done this time?' Eddie asked wearily. 'I've had to throw him out of here once already.'

'Nick?' The rookie looked confused. 'It's Charlie Cotton I need to see her about, her husband.'

The news came out when Dot's elderly friend, Ethel Skinner, returned to the Vic later, all of a-twitter. 'Oh dear, oh dear, oh dear,' she wailed, chin wobbling. 'Have I gone quite white?'

'No,' Eddie said, wiping a glass. 'Should you have done?'

'Yes with what I've been through this afternoon,' she replied indignantly, her rouged cheeks even pinker than usual. 'I want a brandy please. A large one.'

Pauline Fowler, who was at the bar with Kathy Beale, overheard and soon Ethel had a sizeable audience.

'What's happened?' Kathy asked. 'Are you ill?'

'No, it's not me. It's Dot ... well, not exactly Dot, more Charlie.'

'Charlie?' Pete Beale put a supportive hand on her shoulder. 'What's he been up to?'

Ethel took a gulp of her brandy. 'He's been found deceased. On the M25. Dot's terribly upset.'

'I can't think why,' Pauline declared. 'He was only a waste of space when he was here.' Charlie, a long-distance lorry driver who only ever dropped into Dot's life when he needed something, was about as universally unloved as his son.

'Funny that, you know, Sharon,' Eddie remarked. 'How some women always find dodgy characters irresistible.' He enjoyed having a dig at Sharon. The fact that she'd turned him down still rankled. He had been humiliated at the time, coming out with his feelings like that and being so laughingly rejected, but underneath nothing had changed. He still fancied her, fantasized about her even, and her voluptuous presence behind the bar was a constant reminder of what Grant had got and he hadn't. And he couldn't stand it any more.

Grant returned from Scotland later that day with Ricky and Sam in tow. Sam was wearing a ring and looking pleased with herself; Ricky was bullish.

'Couldn't you stop them?' Peggy was beside herself when she heard that her daughter was now going under the name of 'Mrs Butcher'.

'No, Mum, we couldn't. They got married at a different registry office,' Grant explained wearily. 'We checked out as many as we could but by the time we found them it was too late.' Peggy opened her mouth to give him another ear-bashing but he held up his hand and walked away. 'Not now, Mum, please. I'm knackered.'

He went straight round to the flat, hoping that Sharon was in. She was.

'Successful mission?' she asked, smiling.

Grant rubbed his jaw. 'Well I didn't manage to stop Romeo and Juliet getting themselves hitched. But ...' He took a deep breath. '... I did manage to do something else.'

'Are you going to give me a clue?'

'Nope.'

'Is it a present?' She ran her hands teasingly over his body. 'Come on, where have you hidden it?'

'Naughty.' Grant caught hold of her wrists and held them up. 'Got you.' He pulled her to him and kissed her hard, feeling her melt into him. He knew then that his impulse had been right. 'I brought you this,' he said softly, pulling a piece of paper out of his back pocket. Sharon unfolded it and her mouth dropped open. It was a provisional marriage booking for the wedding of Mr Grant Mitchell and Miss Sharon Watts at Gretna Green on 15 October.

'Grant, I – I don't know what to say,' she stammered.

'Say "yes",' Grant whispered, putting his arms round her waist. Sharon struggled free.

'Can I think about it?'

Sharon was being very secretive about something, thought Michelle, making her way across the Square to Grant's flat. She had promised her some juicy gossip, but had refused to say any more in the Vic. Michelle was intrigued.

'Come on, then, tell,' she insisted, settling herself on Sharon's sofa.

'It's where to start that's the problem.'

'Well, just get on with it, then.'

Sharon poured her a glass of wine. 'Eddie's told me I've got to give up Grant or lose my job.'

'What? He can't do that. It's unfair dismissal. He's completely out of order.' Michelle was steaming.

'There's more.'

'More? What else does he want you to do?'

'Not Eddie, Grant. He's asked me to marry him.'

Michelle stared at her friend, gobsmacked. 'You're not actually, seriously considering it, are you?' Sharon studied her glass without answering. 'You are, aren't you? Oh, Sharon.'

'I know you've never liked him but you don't know him like I do,' Sharon said defensively.

'Alright, so he's kind to animals and helps little old ladies cross the street.' Michelle paused. 'For heaven's sake, Sharon, wake up! The man's a crook!'

'I know.' Sharon looked wretched. 'But he's here and he loves me. Alright, he doesn't show it. He's not that sort. But he does care.'

'So what do you want me to say?' Michelle demanded. 'You've already made up your mind.'

'No, I haven't.' Sharon finished her glass and poured them both more wine. 'When I'm with him, everything feels right and it's complete. But then when I'm on me own, I think about all the other stuff. The life that Den handed Angie.'

'Well, exactly. You don't want that for yourself, do you?'

'No. I grew up in the middle of it and it stinks,' she said slowly. 'But deep down I can't see me in a semi-detached in Walthamstow with two point five kids and a nice little hatchback either.'

'You don't have to go to extremes.' Michelle took Sharon's hand. 'Look, you're the sister I never had. I wouldn't want anything bad to happen to you ...'

'Bit late for that now, isn't it?' Sharon said, trying to laugh it off.

'You might think what happened in the past is bad but believe me it can get a lot worse. Tell Eddie to stuff his job if that's what you want. As for Grant, string him along, live with him, sleep with him, but please, Sharon, don't marry him.'

★

Sharon tried to tell herself that Michelle was just being a prophet of doom, but she was troubled by the pleading expression on her friend's face. She spent a sleepless night chewing over Michelle's words and the following morning decided to tackle Grant about his motives.

'Thought it was about time we made it legal,' he replied lightly, patting the space in the bed next to him.

Sharon almost exploded. 'Legal? Don't make me laugh. That's a four-letter word to you.' She sat stiffly upright on the edge of the mattress. 'Now come on, what's your game. You got some scam going I can't figure out?'

'Me?' Grant was a picture of wounded innocence.

'I mean it, Grant! I've got to know.'

Seeing her agitation, he tried to put his feelings into words. 'Alright … but it's not easy …' he swallowed. Sharon's eyes were fixed on his face.

'See, I could always pull the birds, but that was just indoor Olympics. I was just as happy out with the lads or with me head stuck under an engine.'

'So what's changed?'

'Dunno. I met you and we became friends. Somehow that seemed more important than how quick I could get you into bed.' He paused. The words sounded so clumsy. It was as if they were clogging his throat so that what was real, underneath, couldn't get out. 'And now …' he paused, fingering the duvet cover. 'Yes?' Sharon coaxed.

'Now … I can't imagine what it would be like if you weren't around.'

Sharon, her face relaxing into a broad smile, kissed him.

'Grant. What you're trying to say is that you love me. Is that it?'

'Yeah. I s'pose it must be,' he said.

Sharon still hadn't given Grant an answer. She still wasn't sure what it was going to be. The voice in the back of her head reminded her to think about what Grant did to Eddie; to remember his anger, the violence that could spark from his eyes, the storm that seemed to rage in his mind. But it was only a small, quiet voice and she did not want to listen to it anyway. Grant had calmed down a lot, she told herself. And, like he'd said, he would never lay a finger on her. She was sure it was only because he had been so restless and rootless in the past that he'd been so volatile. She could change all of that. She understood him. Plus, he could do something for her. Together, they would be a force to be reckoned with.

It was finding the ring that finally persuaded her. Sharon — musing that she was already acting like a wife — discovered it in Grant's sock drawer when she was putting away his laundry (it had not taken him long to move back downstairs). Curiosity overcame her and she opened the small, black box to find a diamond ring. Its beauty took her breath away. Surreptitiously, she tried it on her third finger. It fitted perfectly.

She was admiring it on her hand when there was the sound of a key in the lock and Grant called her name. 'I'm in here,' she shouted, hurriedly removing the ring and replacing the box. When he came into the bedroom she was diligently folding his T-shirts.

'I want to talk to you,' Grant said, as if he'd prepared a speech.

'Me first.' Sharon's insistence took him by surprise.

'Okay.' He sounded relieved. She turned to face him, folding her arms.

'Everybody in the world thinks I must be out of my tree to have anything to do with you. Everywhere I go someone's doing a number on your character.'

Grant was stunned. 'Don't spare my feelings, Sharon.'

'They all tell me you're dangerous to know.' She eyed his crestfallen face. Grant, sensing a big disappointment in the offing, said nothing. 'But,' Sharon continued brightly, 'I've decided I like living dangerously. So, Grant, I'm gonna do you the biggest favour of your life.' She paused, building up the suspense. 'I'll marry you.'

'Sharon, I ...' After thinking the worst, Grant was so amazed he was rendered practically speechless.

She held up her hand, 'Wait. There's two conditions.'

'What?' He was coasting now, ready to agree to almost anything.

'No secrets. No lies. I don't care what you do as long as you don't bring it home and you don't lie about it.'

'I'd never lie to you.'

'And the other thing's the Vic,' Sharon said, warming to her theme. 'I want that pub. It belongs to me and I'm gonna have it. I don't care what you do or how you go about it, but I want you to get me that pub.'

Sharon threw down the gauntlet to Eddie by wearing her ring to work that evening. She made a point of showing it off, causing Pete Beale to splutter, 'Didn't know you was left-handed', when she gave him his pint with an ostentatious flourish.

Kathy, who was at the bar with Pete, exclaimed 'Blimey, Sharon. Not Grant Mitchell?'

Sharon smiled. 'I know what I'm doing.'

'Well, I hope you do,' she replied, looking dubious.

Eddie, watching it all with a face like thunder, beckoned her out back. 'You know what aggravates me, Sharon, is not that you didn't take my advice, it's that you've got the gall to waltz into my pub flashing that rock like Liz Taylor on heat and you didn't even have the common decency to come and speak to me first.' He was breathing hard.

'And what would have been the point?' Sharon asked sweetly. 'You see, I've been thinking about our little chat, and I've made up my mind.'

Eddie flushed livid. 'Obviously. Well, let me tell you something. I spent half my life banging up cheap crooks like Grant Mitchell and I know exactly what you're in for and quite honestly, I don't envy you one little bit, because one day you're going to regret it.'

'No,' Sharon said, harder now. 'You're gonna regret it. I don't have to choose. I'm gonna marry Grant Mitchell and I'm gonna stay at the Vic and if you don't like it Eddie, you know what you can do.'

'Fine,' Eddie turned on his heel and walked away. 'You're fired,' he threw over his shoulder.

When Sharon broke the news to Grant, she thought for a moment that he was going to rush off and beat up Eddie again. She hadn't told him about Eddie tipping off the police for precisely that reason, and kicked herself as soon as she realized Grant was in the mood to do some damage. He had been out celebrating their engagement with Phil and had come home pretty tanked up. Sharon watched anxiously as he shrugged on his bomber jacket and pulled on a pair of leather gloves.

'Where are you going? It's past midnight.'

'I'm going to make that bastard pay for what he's put you through.' He yanked a black woollen hat down over his ears.

'Grant! You mustn't!' Sharon tried to stand in his way but he simply lifted her up and put her to one side.

'Don't worry,' he said with a wicked grin. 'I won't resort to violence. Nothing drastic like that. Just a little hostage-taking.' Ten minutes later, having broken into the pub, he returned bearing the wooden bust of Queen Victoria, which had stood on the bar for as long as anybody in Walford could remember. She looked very disapproving. Sharon, relieved it was nothing worse, couldn't help laughing. But the joke backfired when the following day Eddie announced that the bust was no loss as he was thinking of changing the name of the pub. Sharon, hit where it hurt, was doubly determined to win the Vic back and pushed Grant to start sounding out his contacts.

'I'm not sure my contacts are that good,' he admitted. 'Pubs ain't exactly been my field – until now.'

'Then you'll just have to make new ones, won't you?' Sharon replied, pert.

'Okay, you want the Vic, you've got it. I said I would and I won't let you down. But it'll take time.'

'We don't have long.' Sharon admired her ring artfully. 'You'd better get working on it.'

Peggy was cool when Grant and Sharon announced their engagement, barely managing a stiff 'congratulations'. Grant was irked. It was the first time in his life he'd felt this way about a woman. He didn't give a damn about what other people thought – everybody had been quick to voice an opinion once they saw Sharon's ring – but his mother's approval was important. Sharon, generously, put it down to Peggy being distracted by Sam and Ricky's forthcoming nuptials – after a council of war with the Butchers, it had been agreed that the runaways should have their marriage blessed in Walford – but Grant took his mother's slight personally.

Peggy Mitchell was a calculating woman who had learned to wise up to life early. She was not sentimental, but she cared more than she let show. Knowing that Grant would present problems for any woman who took him on, her concern was whether Sharon was up to the job. Almost as important was whether she would do credit to the name Mitchell. Family meant everything in her book.

She took the opportunity to interrogate Sharon behind Grant's back. Calling round at the flat she invited herself in for a cup of tea and went straight for the kill. 'There's no flies on you, eh, Sharon?'

'What do you mean?'

'Don't get me wrong.' Peggy sat down, balancing her cup and saucer. 'I like a woman who knows what she wants.'

'Sorry?'

'You managed to sell the flat and still live here.'

'Sugar?' Sharon decided to play it Peggy's way.

'No thanks.' Peggy got up and walked around the room, picking up ornaments and inspecting shelves. 'It's very cosy. Specially now you two are shacked up together.' Sharon eyed her suspiciously, wondering what was coming next. 'Tell me about yourself,' Peggy said suddenly, taking her by surprise. 'If you're going to be my daughter-in-law, we'd better get to know each other.' Sharon blinked nervously. 'It's alright,' Peggy continued, slightly more friendly. 'I don't bite. At least, not where it shows.' Fortunately, Grant arrived back before Sharon had to find a place to start.

Phil's reaction was less obtrusive. Having been initially mistrustful of Sharon, she had gone up in his estimation with her stand against Eddie. To his mind it was a public declaration of commitment to Grant that boded well. His brother needed a wife who would fight his corner. Sharon, Phil decided, had obviously taken their earlier conversation to heart.

His conversion was not entirely unselfish. He had always been there for Grant and always would be, but it was a relief to relinquish some of the responsibility. Of late, Phil had been feeling weighed down by worries about Grant's nightmares, Eddie's beating, the court case, the police raid, the Ricky and Sam debacle. Now that the CPS had dropped the charges – Marcus Christie had just confirmed it – he was beginning to feel like picking up the threads of his own life again. Newly divorced Kathy Beale had been showing some interest and Phil was hopeful it might develop into something more.

'What happened to you last night?' Sharon asked Michelle, grinning saucily. She was on her way to catch a Tube to go up West and ran into Michelle in the market. The Square was still humming with gossip from the previous night; Rachel had thrown a surprise party for Michelle's birthday which had resulted in some interesting pairings. Phil, after some encouragement from Grant, had danced with Kathy Beale and Michelle had been spotted creeping upstairs with Clyde Tavernier, a young black single father who worked at the Vic.

'Don't know what you mean,' Michelle said, playing dumb.

'Yes, you do. I saw you two go off. Deserting your own party! It must have been really urgent.'

Michelle had the grace to blush. 'Yeah, well, he and Phil and Grant were going on about me and Rachel bein' gay. I thought I'd better prove him wrong.'

'So long as you had fun.'

'Yeah.' Michelle considered. 'We did, actually. And you can wipe that smile off your face. I think there could be something in it. Clyde's got Kofi; he knows how hard it can be bringing a kid up on your own. Anyway, gotta go.' Michelle beat a hasty retreat. 'Catch you later, alright?'

Sharon had only gone a few more paces down the road when she saw Eddie's father, John Royle, washing the windows outside the Vic. 'Sharon!' He waved her over.

'I thought I was public enemy number one.'

'Not with me. Though I'm the mug that's been roped in to do your job. No hard feelings, eh?'

'Nice of you to say so, John,' Sharon replied, adding, deliberately, 'Don't worry – it won't be for long.'

John, apparently missing the dig, said, 'You're right, to be sure, the way Eddie's losing punters. There's an atmosphere in there you could cut with a knife. I've told him meself to take you back – half of 'em don't want him to serve them now; I have a queue my end o' the bar and he's standing there all alone with a face like a wet weekend.'

'Not Mr Popular then.'

John pulled a wry face. 'He's still talking about changing the pub's name. And refurbishments. That's not won him any friends by all accounts. I keep telling him, if it ain't broke … Well, you know what he's like. Stubborn as a mule.'

'That makes two of us,' Sharon said. 'And I happen to like the Vic the way it is. He hasn't heard the last of me, you can tell him that.'

She went on her way, more determined than ever to see her plan through. Inspired by Michelle's earlier comment, she had been having talks with a union representative who confirmed she had a good case for claiming unfair dismissal. The machinery was in motion and Eddie had been summoned to attend an industrial tribunal. The case came up in ten days' time. Meanwhile, she had a wedding to organize, hence the trip up West. It was time for some *serious* shopping.

When Grant saw the pile of holiday brochures Sharon had come back with, the reality of his romantic impulse started to hit home.

'This is going to cost, big time,' he complained, as Sharon enthused about wedding dresses, bridesmaids' outfits, a champagne reception and an exotic honeymoon.

'You get what you pay for,' she replied defensively. 'The average wedding — *average* — costs over ten grand these days. Anyway, I don't want some cheapskate affair, all sausage rolls and Asti Spumante. I want the works.'

Grant, seeing how much it meant to her, gave in. 'Alright, princess. If that's what you want …'

'Do you know what you just called me?' Sharon asked softly, sitting up.

'Ye — es.' What had he done this time?

'Princess. That's what me dad used to call me. His little princess.' He saw a tear glisten in her eye.

'And now you're my little princess.' He kissed her again, sweetly, on the lips and she wrapped her arms round him, resting her head on his shoulder.

'You know, until you came along, he was the only really important man in my life. All the others, the boyfriends — well, they felt like they were just passing through. None of them ever came close to Den. I looked up to him like he was some kind of god. And he treated me like I was so special …' Grant felt her give a sob and held her tighter. 'I just wish he could be here to see me married,' Sharon whispered. 'He would have been so proud.' She raised her head and looked at Grant with mascara-smudged eyes. 'Let's make it a wedding to remember, Grant. For Den.'

CHAPTER SEVEN

Grant didn't need to be a genius to guess where Sharon wanted to go for their honeymoon: not only had a luxury beach hotel in Mauritius been circled in heavy red pen in one of the brochures, but she had been talking about dieting to fit in to her new bikini.

'I shouldn't bother, it'll be too cold in Clacton,' he said, enjoying winding her up. 'Anyway, you're lovely the way you are. Shapely – just like Marilyn Monroe – that's the way I like my women.'

'Get out of it! Seriously, have you had any ideas?'

'Yeah,' he remarked, po-faced. 'Funny but one of them just jumped right out of the page at me. Bit pricey, mind.' That, Grant thought, was an understatement. He'd need a bank job – let alone a bank loan – to pay for it. Still, he'd find the money. Somehow.

After he'd gone over the accounts with Phil that lunchtime, Grant was beginning to revise his plans. Business had been slow and they were ticking over on the bare minimum. It was scarcely enough to keep the garage going, and certainly wouldn't fund Walford's wedding of the year. There was only one solution: put the date back and start saving. When he told Sharon, expecting her to go ballistic, she was understanding, which made him feel even worse.

'Of course I'm disappointed, but what matters is we get married, not how much it costs.'

'No, you're gonna have it all, posh wedding, flash honeymoon. It's just it may take a bit longer to get it sorted.'

'Grant.' Sharon hugged him. 'Forget what I said earlier. I was being sentimental, getting carried away. It's feelings that matter in the end.'

'And I feel,' he said, pulling her close, 'that I want to give you the best. Okay?'

'I won't argue with that,' she replied, smiling.

'Pint please. And a whisky chaser,' Pete Beale ordered, leaning against the bar. He sank half his bitter in one draught and let out a long, satisfied sigh.

'You look done in.' Arthur Fowler, who was having a drink in the Vic with Pauline and Michelle, clapped him on the back. 'What have you been up to?'

'Helping Dot with Nick.' Pete took another large glug. 'She twisted me arm, said she needed a strong bloke to help her with this programme they've got him on. Keep him under lock and key in his bedroom, see he don't buy no more heroin. What does she call it?'

'Tough love,' interrupted Michelle. 'Sounds like the story of my life.' Pauline shot her a look. 'It's okay Mum, that wasn't a crack,' Michelle said, reading it. 'I'm just worried about Sharon. They should be back from the tribunal by now.'

'It was bloody tough on *me*, I can tell you that,' Pete continued. 'Nick was in a right old state, rantin' and swearin'. I knew he had it stashed away somewhere. Found it in his old teddy bear. He went berserk.'

'Well I think Dot's mad to be having anything to do with him,' Pauline pronounced, downing the rest of her gin and tonic. At that moment, the door opened and Sharon and Eddie entered, both dressed in smart suits. The pub fell silent. Eddie, ignoring everyone, went behind the bar and disappeared upstairs. Sharon walked over to the Fowlers and Pete, smiling broadly. 'What are you all drinking?' she asked. 'I'm celebrating.'

It turned out to be a hollow victory. Eddie refused to reinstate Sharon, saying he would rather pay her the compensation the tribunal had specified instead. She was even more upset when she saw the 'Queen Victoria' sign being taken down.

'I can't believe he's actually doing it. It's like he wants to hurt me personally,' she sobbed to Grant.

The regulars, who had gathered in a small crowd outside, were equally angry.

'You alright, treacle?' Pete asked, putting his arm around Sharon. He gave her a squeeze. 'It'll always be the Vic to me, whatever that bent-nosed copper calls it.'

Arthur nodded sadly. 'But it won't be the same without Sharon. There's been a Watts in that pub for as long as I can remember.'

Grant listened to the talk tight-lipped. When the others had gone he had a word with the workman Eddie had paid to remove the letters and soon had them up in the Arches.

'You're gonna want them back soon, anyway,' he pointed out to Sharon, thinking she'd be pleased with his surprise.

'It's – it's a lovely thought, Grant,' she said haltingly.

'But?'

'I'm not sure I want to be reminded of the Vic. The only thing to do now is move away from here, start again, go for a pub somewhere else.'

'You're just upset. You don't mean that.'

'Yes, I do.'

Grant's intuition proved to be right. After a couple of days looking at other pubs, Sharon had changed her mind. She was obsessed with getting the Vic back. Her relationship with the place seemed odd to Grant, who had never felt a particular affection for any of his homes. It occurred to him that it was almost as if she was in love – which left him playing second fiddle to a boozer. But she hadn't given him any choice. Sharon and the Vic came as a package; to get her, he had to get the pub. Had it been a man, he would have known how to sort it, but you couldn't knock the stuffing out of bricks and mortar.

'I suppose we should have seen this coming.' Sharon was still chuntering about Eddie's plans for the Vic when Grant got back for tea. 'Eddie's just out for number one and he doesn't care who he upsets. He doesn't care about this community, he doesn't care about its traditions, he doesn't respect values or feelings.' She was in full flow now, eyes flashing. 'People stick together round here. But not Eddie. He's a nasty, vindictive piece of work, just as likely to grass you up as serve you a pint. More likely, probably, given his track record. It weren't no coincidence the Arches got raided on a Wednesday.'

'He knew it was our delivery day?' The Mitchells had an arrangement with a middle man, who delivered a new package of stolen number plates every week. 'Are you saying it was Eddie who tipped off the old bill?'

'Well, um, I …' Sharon stammered, realizing she'd said too much.

'Why didn't you tell me?' Grant demanded fiercely, taking hold of her by the shoulders. 'I can't believe you've been covering for that bastard all this time. Does Phil know?'

'No,' Sharon breathed, terrified by the fury distorting his features. Grant turned on his heel. 'I couldn't say anything because …' The door slammed. 'Because I was afraid you'd react like this,' she whispered.

Sharon stayed in all evening, waiting for Grant to return, flicking the television from channel to channel, unable to concentrate. By nine o'clock she had emptied his congealed meal into the bin. By ten o'clock she had hoovered and dusted everywhere and scrubbed the kitchen floor. At eleven o'clock she started pacing the room. When a police car's wail pierced the quiet half an hour later she felt her worst nightmare was about to come true. Full of foreboding, she went outside.

A second patrol car had joined the first one and was parked, lights flashing, opposite the Vic. The garden in the middle of the Square was being sectioned off with fluorescent yellow tape and a police officer was asking people to stand back. Most of the residents had come out and were craning their necks to see what was going on.

Sharon pushed her way to the front of the crowd. 'What's happened?' she asked Dot Cotton.

Dot turned to her with huge eyes. 'It's Eddie Royle. 'E's been stabbed.' She drew hard on the cigarette trembling in her hand. 'I found 'im.'

'Is he ...'

Dot shuddered. 'Yes, Sharon. 'E's passed on. No one but the good Lord can 'elp 'im now. We've all gotta pray for 'is soul.'

Sharon gasped. This wasn't real. Eddie – dead. 'Did you see who did it?' she asked, realizing she was shaking too.

'No.' Dot looked over her shoulder furtively at Clyde Tavernier, who was being interviewed by another policeman. 'But I saw someone runnin' away.'

Sharon scanned the square for Grant but he was nowhere to be seen. Neither was Phil. She noticed the Fowlers glancing in her direction and heard Pauline say loudly, 'I can't see them Mitchells here. 'Course, we all know what a temper Grant's got. It wouldn't surprise me if he was behind this.'

A man in a sports jacket who was obviously the detective in charge went over to them. Sharon made herself scarce.

Predictably, the police arrived on her doorstep early the next morning. Sharon, who had been up all night waiting for Grant to return, greeted them in rumpled clothes, her face drawn.

'DCI Chapman and DC Bedford, Walford Police. Are you Sharon Watts?'

'Yeah.'

'We understand Grant Mitchell lives with you.'

'He's my fiancé.'

'Is he in?' The female detective, Chapman, was doing all the talking.

'No.'

'Rough night, Miss Watts? You look tired. Not worried about him, are you?'

'Look, if you've come round to insult me ...' Sharon flared.

'No,' Chapman said grimly. 'We've come round to ask him some very serious questions about his whereabouts yesterday evening.' She pushed open the door, which Sharon had been holding half-shut. 'We'll wait, if you don't mind.'

An unsuspecting Phil and Grant came back fifteen minutes later and were taken away again immediately to the police station. Sharon, unable to get any news, was going frantic, not helped by an unsympathetic Michelle who came over and gave her the 'I told you so' routine.

It was evening by the time Phil turned up, alone. They had been interviewed separately and all he could tell Sharon was that Grant was still being held for questioning. She was immediately suspicious.

'So where on earth were you both last night? I've been doing my nut in here. As soon as I heard about Eddie ...' Sharon didn't need to spell it out.

'We had a few beers in another boozer, went on to a nightclub, ended up at a mate's. Grant wanted to let off steam; it was the safest way to do it. I've given the old bill some names; they're checking out witnesses.'

'So it'll be alright?'

'Should be, yeah.'

'But if you've got witnesses, Phil ...'

He shrugged. 'Maybe they're taking their time about finding them, stringing things out.' Seeing Sharon gnawing her nails, he dropped his defensive tone. 'Look, don't worry. They can only keep him so long without charging him.'

'And what if they do? Charge him.'

'They can't, can they,' Phil replied wearily.

'Why not?'

'Because he didn't do it, that's why not.'

'Then why are they keeping him?'

She got her answer the next morning when Phil's solicitor rang. Grant had been arrested and formally charged with the murder of Eddie Royle.

'I just don't understand,' Sharon said, as Phil drove them to the police station to meet Marcus Christie. 'How could they let you go and arrest him when you were together all night. It just don't make sense.'

Phil looked awkward. 'Grant went off on his own for a couple of hours,' he said, keeping his eyes on the road. 'He said he had something on. I don't know where.'

Grant sat slumped in the police cell, head in his hands. The cell smelt strongly of disinfectant, which just about overpowered a lingering smell of urine, but it was a close contest. It made him feel sick. You're going soft, he told himself, you've been in far worse situations in the army. Felt-tipped graffiti covered the walls, continuing an obscene dialogue between the cell's past occupants. Reading it afforded Grant a brief distraction from his jumbled thoughts. Underlying it all, the nagging fear that this time he might go down, that a cell and barred windows might become an everyday reality, sat in his stomach like lead.

The woman DCI, Chapman, was determined to pin the murder on him. She had been grilling him for two days, trying to catch him out any way she could, goading him into losing his temper by suggesting that Eddie and Sharon had been having a fling. Grant had nearly lost it but Marcus Christie had cut in smoothly and stopped him. Afterwards he had given him a lecture about playing into their hands and told him to relax. It was easier said than done. Grant's usual confidence had been eroded by the interrogation and he was as tense as a coiled spring. Eventually Chapman had called a halt and he had been taken down to a holding cell while they checked out his alibi.

He had been stewing there for five hours now, and there was still no news. Chapman was going to stitch him up, he was sure of it. A key sounded in the heavy metal door and he looked up to see Chapman, accompanied by Marcus Christie.

'You're free to go. For the time being,' the DCI said in a clipped voice. She did not seem happy about it.

Christie extended an arm. 'Your witness has confirmed your story, Grant. The charges have been dropped. Phillip's waiting for you outside.'

★

Sharon was asleep on the sofa when Grant got back to the flat. He had told Christie to send her home when he learned she was at the station with Phil. He didn't want her exposed to all that. He knelt down beside her, looking at her peaceful face, and caressed her hair. Sharon opened her eyes.

'Grant.' She sat up and threw her arms around his neck. 'Oh Grant. I was so frightened.'

'Hey,' he said softly, 'It's alright. I'm home now.'

'But I didn't know what was happening. No one would tell me anything ...'

'They wouldn't tell me anything, either,' Grant said bitterly.

'But you're back?'

'What does it look like?' He smiled at her, wiping a tear away from her cheek with his thumb. 'They said they'd be in touch. It's just sour grapes. They ain't got anything on me.'

'They did believe you, though, in the end?'

'Must have done. Mind you, they even had me believing it after a while.'

Sharon's laugh sounded a little strained. 'Phil said you got split up last night.'

'Oh, yeah ...' Grant dug into his pocket and drew out a large wad of cash, which he put on the coffee table. 'For you. Couple of bridesmaid's dresses and a few bottles of champagne.'

'Oh.'

'You don't look too pleased.'

''Course I am,' she said, not meeting his eyes. 'So that's where you went, then? To collect some money?'

'Yeah. I did a private welding job, got paid in cash.'

'You were nowhere near the Square when it happened?'

'No, thank God. If I had of been ...' Grant stopped and stared at Sharon intently. 'What's all this about? All these questions?'

'I just wondered.'

'No kidding. It must be catching. I've been shut up in a room for two days with a woman who wanted to know where

I was when Eddie was killed, an' all …'

'Meaning?'

'Meaning I expected it from her. She was a copper.' Sharon was staring at the floor, twisting her ring round and round on her finger. Realization suddenly dawned on Grant. 'You thought I might have done it, didn't you?'

'No,' she replied defiantly, still not looking up.

'So why the third degree?'

'I wasn't. I was just … worried. After what happened last time, with Eddie …'

Grant stood up, breathing fast. 'I don't believe this. You really think that I might have done it. Actually killed Eddie Royle.' His world seemed to be falling apart around his ears. Thinking about Sharon was what had kept him going in the police station when they had hammered on and on trying to make him confess. She was the one, true, good thing to have happened to him in years, and now even she doubted him.

'I didn't say that.'

'Yeah, but you meant it. Come on, Sharon, admit it.'

She was silent for a moment. Then, in a quiet voice, she said, 'You nearly killed him before.'

'Rubbish.'

'I saw you.'

Stalemate. Grant tried another tack. 'You know, this would be funny if it weren't so tragic.' He sat down again, leaning his head back against the sofa, and closed his eyes.

Sharon remained standing. 'How am I supposed to understand anything when you won't talk to me?' she demanded.

'What are we doing now?'

'No, I mean *really* talk.'

Grant sighed and sat upright, folding his arms. 'Alright, let's really talk. What do you want to *really* talk about?'

'Oh, don't bother.' Sharon stormed off to the kitchen.

Grant, realizing he was acting like an idiot, got up and followed her. 'I'm sorry,' he said, gruff.

She swivelled round. 'You know what's frightening? We're

supposed to be getting married and I don't know the first thing about you. Oh, I know how many sugars you like in your tea, how you like your shirts ironed, but that's not what I mean.'

'What, then?'

She breathed in deeply, trying to summon up courage. 'You still haven't told me what happened that night with Eddie.'

'I've told you. I just go a bit wild sometimes.'

'Yes but what you haven't told me is ...' She paused for a second. 'Why?'

Grant's face took on the shuttered expression she had seen him wear so often. 'You see, you can't even be honest with yourself, never mind with me.'

'Just leave it, Sharon, alright?' It was what he always said. But this time she was determined to see it through.

'No. I'm fed up with leaving it, papering over the cracks, pretending everything's alright. Because it's not. Now we either face that or we've got nowhere left to go ...'

He did not reply.

'It was in the army, wasn't it?' Sharon probed. Abruptly, Grant turned and walked away. She ran after him. 'Grant. Don't turn your back on me. Grant.' Grant carried on walking, heading for the front door. 'Look, Grant, I didn't mean to doubt you. I couldn't help it. There's a part of you I don't know anything about,' she sobbed, breathless. 'This will happen again and again ... until you help me understand what's the matter ...'

He swung round and grabbed her so fast she almost screamed.

'Look, I killed someone, alright? He was just a kid, sixteen. He was sat in some trench on the side of some godforsaken hill. All he wanted to do was give himself up and go home. I emptied a magazine into him. He was crying. He didn't even have a gun.' Grant's eyes bored into hers. 'Now do you understand?'

'You should have told me,' Sharon whispered.

'I've never told anyone before.'

'Except Phil?'

Grant relaxed his grip on her shoulders. 'Not even Phil.' He expected her to shrink away but instead she put a hand to his cheek and stroked it.

'Now you listen to me. What you did over there was different. Separate. You can't blame yourself ...'

Suddenly he wanted to talk about it, desperately. After all that time, it was such a relief to unload. 'We'd been chucking stuff at them all day, long range ... They were spots on the horizon. It was more like a funfair.' The explosion of rocket fire seemed to be filling his head. 'Afterwards we were told to go in and mop up. I'd never seen the enemy ... not up close before ... when I got there, I didn't think ... I just ...'

The fear and surprise on the soldier's face, just before he fell backwards in a rain of blood, was seared forever into his brain. 'I kept pumping bullets into his body ... even after he was dead ...'

'It's alright.' Sharon cradled his head. 'It wasn't your fault. It's what you were there for.'

'No, it wasn't,' he cried wretchedly. He pulled away and fumbled for a handkerchief. 'I was shipped home a week later. Out of the army within a month ...'

'And since then?'

'Sometimes, when I'm in the middle of something, I lose it ... I don't know what I'm doing ...'

'Like with Eddie?'

'Yes. I went into the pub and ...'

'I saw. It's alright. Now that I understand ...'

'No.' Grant's face was stony.

'What?'

'It's too late.'

Sharon was stunned. 'It can't be too late, Grant. I love you.'

'Think about it. If you could think for one minute that I might be capable of murdering someone, what kind of life would we have together?'

'Let's find out, shall we?' Sharon said, taking his hand.

CHAPTER EIGHT

'Take a gander at this.' Frank Butcher spread the *Walford Gazette* out on a table in front of him. Pauline Fowler and Kathy Beale, who had come into the café for a quick cup of tea, peered over his shoulder.

'What's Clyde Tavernier doing in the paper? Oh my gawd,' Pauline exclaimed.

'"Murder Suspect on the Run",' Kathy read out loud. '"Local boxing hero linked with pub landlord slaying".'

'Clyde? I thought they were trying to nail Grant,' said Ian Beale, who had been listening in. Ian, Kathy's son, was a hard-nosed young entrepreneur who ran his own catering business, called the Meal Machine. There was no love lost between Ian and Grant, but then there was no love lost between Ian and anybody.

'No, it says here Clyde's already been questioned by the police after another local man was released without being charged,' Pauline read on. She dropped the paper in disgust. 'If Sharon wants to swan around with a man with Grant's reputa-tion, that's up to her, but I don't want Michelle associating with a criminal. She's got little Vicki to think of, for heaven's sakes.'

'Come on, Pauline, we don't know for certain who did it. It might not be Clyde. You know what the police are like. He's black, that automatically makes him a suspect as far as they're concerned,' Kathy reminded her.

'Well, they must have their reasons,' Ian said. 'Somebody must have seen him.'

'Yes they did.' Dot Cotton had come in unnoticed and was standing behind them, clutching her handbag to her chest. 'It was my Nick. 'E saw 'im bending over the body with a knife.

Then 'e ran off. 'E weren't going to tell the police, but I made 'im. It was our Christian duty. Not that you get any thanks for doing it round 'ere.' She went out again, nose in the air.

Frank folded the paper. 'I don't like it. All this bad publicity, it ain't doing my business no good. There ain't been a sniff at the car lot all morning. And more to the point ...' he got up stiffly. 'You can't get a drink round here neither.'

The Vic was a forlorn sight with its doors shut and bolted and curtains drawn, as if the pub, too, was in mourning. John Royle, Eddie's father, had wanted nothing more to do with the place and had gone back home to Ireland. The brewery had put up a sign, 'Closed pending appointment of Temporary Licensee'.

It was the chance Sharon had been waiting for. Okay, so the timing wasn't great, she told herself, but she couldn't let that stand in her way. The Vic was hers by rights and there would never be a better opportunity. But when she went for the interview there turned out to be one major sticking point.

'How'd it go?' Grant enquired when Sharon got back, smartly attired in a suit that made the most of her assets. He caught her from behind and gave her a squeeze. 'I bet their tongues were hanging out. You look the business, you do. A right tasty landlady.'

'Get off me, Grant.' Sharon wriggled out of his grasp. 'For goodness sake, go and make yourself useful. Get the tea going or something.'

She stomped off into the bedroom. Grant followed her. 'What's up? Didn't it go well?' Sharon, who was taking pins out of her hair, did not reply. 'Sharon? Did they blow you out?' He hovered in the doorway. 'What did they say?'

Sharon put down her hairbrush and glared at him. 'It was going fine, just fine, if you want to know. I did my pitch, they liked it and I had it in the bag until one of them started asking questions about – how did he phrase it? – oh, yes, "the company I keep".'

'What's that got to do with them?' Grant asked, bristling.

'Well, for starters, they didn't think the magistrate would look too kindly on a landlady who was engaged to be married to the local hoodlum.'

Grant balled his fists. 'They ain't got nothing on me.'

Sharon sighed. 'Grant. You've got a name. You may not have a record, but word gets about.'

'So what have they said. "No"?'

'Not exactly. We agreed to compromise.' Sharon tipped her head forward, brushing her hair out. Grant couldn't see her face.

'How?'

'Well, you and I agreed to delay the wedding anyway, so putting it off for a bit longer won't harm things. Just 'til I get settled in, get the pub up and running again.' Grant was silent. 'And I said – well, I said you'd keep a low profile, keep out of trouble.' Sharon peered at him through a veil of blonde hair. 'You will, won't you, Grant? It's not just so as I can get the Vic. I can't stand going through any more nights of worry like the last few. I want you to go straight.'

To get Sharon off his back, Grant told her yes, a promise he had no intention of keeping. As far as he was concerned, to tell a Mitchell to pass up an opportunity to make a few grand without the taxman knowing was going against nature. He would just have to be more careful in future.

'She's got you where she wants you – by the short and curlies,' Phil warned over teabreak in the Arches several days later.

'That's what she thinks.'

'You're doin' everything she says, ain'tcha? Runnin' when she clicks her fingers? Seems like Sharon's got her priorities pretty well sorted.'

'You mean the Vic.'

'Yeah, I mean the Vic. Look, bruv. First she tells you to get her the boozer as a condition of marriage. Then, she tells you she can't marry you because it would stop her getting it. Spot the connection?'

Grant got up, annoyed that Phil had voiced the thoughts going on in his head. 'We're postponing it, that's all,' he said abruptly, stripping off his overalls and going out.

'Now where are you off to?' Phil sighed.

'To talk to Sharon.'

Sharon saw Grant coming from the window and came bounding out of the flat to greet him. 'Oh Grant, Grant, I'm so happy!' she cried, throwing her arms around his neck. 'The brewery has given me the temporary licence. The Vic's mine! Well, almost. Just got to convince the magistrate now.' She kissed him on the cheek. 'What's the matter? I thought you'd be pleased,' she said when he didn't respond.

'Why? You've got what *you* wanted. I'm surplus to requirements, aren't I?'

'No! I need you now more than ever.'

'What, to change barrels, kick out rowdies and pull the odd pint?'

'Yes. *No*! What is this, Grant? I thought we were in this together.'

Grant stared at her coldly. 'I'm beginning to think you're in this for all you can get.'

He stalked off and went down to the canal that ran behind the back of the houses at the far end of Albert Square. It was not a very picturesque stretch of water but it was peaceful and he could think there. Watching the sludgy brown water ripple with the occasional fish he felt himself calming. If Sharon was just using him to get the Vic, she'd have dumped him by now, he reasoned. She was single-minded when she wanted something. It was just that it left him feeling like a spare part. What he had to do was establish the upper hand. He got up from the bank and dusted his trousers down, smiling.

Sharon's worries about the magistrate proved to be un-founded. No mention was made of Grant and her application for the temporary licence was approved after the usual formalities. She returned to the Vic, jubilant, to find the old 'Queen Victoria' sign had been re-erected and a large crowd of regulars waiting outside the door. Grant was with them.

'Grant ... I didn't know whether ... thank you,' she whispered. 'It feels like I'm home. Like *we're* home.'

'Are you gonna open up or what?' Frank Butcher yelled. 'There's a man dyin' of thirst here.'

'And here,' Phil chorused, prompting Big Ron, Pete Beale and Arthur Fowler to join in too.

'Alright, alright.' Sharon turned to face them, beaming. 'I declare this pub officially open! And as your new landlady, let me say — first drinks are on the house!'

'Hold on, hold on.' Grant interrupted the cheers, barring the door with a muscular arm. His face was solemn. 'There's someone we forgot. Someone very important. You can't open until they get here.'

'What on earth are you playing at?' Sharon asked, mystified.

'Yeah, c'mon Grant, stop messing about,' Pauline Fowler shouted.

'I won't be long. Just hold them off for a couple of minutes.' So saying, Grant sprinted away in the direction of the flat, leaving the crowd booing and jeering. Sharon put up her hands helplessly.

She had taken a lot of flak by the time he jogged back round the corner bearing the stolen bust of Queen Victoria. 'Wouldn't be the same without royalty present,' he said, holding the bust aloft. Laughter broke out and everybody applauded.

'Can we go in now?' Sharon asked. 'They've been baying for my blood.'

'Ma'am, your subjects are revolting. Shall we proceed?' Grant said, mock-courteous. He carried the monarch across the threshold and placed her on the bar.

'Look at that,' Arthur Fowler spluttered, nudging Pete Beale. 'I'm sure she smiled.' Pete gave him a shove.

'Give this man a drink, treacle, before he sees pigs flying past.'

Michelle and Sharon had barely spoken since Eddie's murder. Normally, Sharon would have made an effort to mend fences, but she felt betrayed by her friend's sceptical attitude towards Grant. To her mind, it was up to Michelle to make the first move, but Michelle seemed to be preoccupied with other things. Sharon had heard, via Pauline, that Michelle had applied to the poly and had been accepted as a mature student. Rachel's influence again, Sharon noted sourly. She was missing Michelle more than she cared to admit.

Pauline, though, was more concerned about Clyde's influence. 'It doesn't look good, whichever way you cut it, 'im disappearing like that. I mean, she's his girlfriend, she's bound to get tarred with the same brush,' she complained over her gin and tonic. 'I've tried talking to her about it but she's so touchy … we ended up having a flaming row about it and I've scarcely seen her since.'

Several weeks passed, during which Sharon was too busy at the Vic to do anything about patching up her friendship. She and Michelle remained curt and uncommunicative, so it came as a complete shock when news reached her that Michelle and Clyde had been spotted driving off together with the children, Kofi and Vicki, in the back of a suitcase-laden car. Nick Cotton had seen them go and reported them to the police – Clyde had a reward on his head – and the Square was buzzing with excitement. When Sharon heard that the pair of them had been arrested at Portsmouth, her heart went out to Michelle. It could so easily have been her …

Clyde was charged with Eddie's murder and remanded in custody but Michelle was released without being charged. She returned to the Square and went straight to Rachel's, snubbing Pauline and Arthur, who had been going out of their minds with worry.

The next day, Michelle came round to the Vic. 'I won't beat

about the bush,' she said gruffly, 'I need a part-time job. I was wondering whether you had any shifts going here.' Grant, who was behind the bar, raised an eyebrow. Sharon shot him a look and he shrugged and went away.

'Take no notice. You know what he's like,' she whispered confidentially.

'Is Grant working here?'

'Only when I'm desperate. He's more of a hindrance than a help. Pat's full-time and there's a couple of casuals but I do need someone else.'

'So will you give me a go?'

'Got any experience?'

Michelle's mouth twitched. 'You know I have.'

'References?'

'I'll have to ask my old mate Sharon Watts. If she's still a mate, that is.'

'Criminal record?'

Michelle, who had started to relax, tensed again. 'Not as such,' she replied stonily. 'But my boyfriend's being held for a murder he didn't commit. Does that count?' She was about to leave when Sharon called her back.

'Michelle. So was mine.' They looked at each other warily.

'Okay, point taken,' Michelle said. 'I'm sorry, Sharon. Truly I am.'

'That's alright, you're forgiven.' Sharon grinned. 'When can you start?'

Grant's plan was simple. They had to buy the Vic. That would give him a proper stake in the place and put him on an equal footing with Sharon. At the moment he felt like a combination of pump man and lackey and he wasn't enjoying the experience. Sharon was completely focused on her work to the exclusion of everything else, including any talk of the wedding. Grant, who wasn't used to coming second in anything, had had enough. It was the only way to get through to her, he decided. If he got her the Vic, the thing she wanted most in the world, they could get on with building a life together, running the place side by side as husband and wife. Besides, he quite fancied being addressed as 'landlord'.

When he put the suggestion to her, Sharon was surprisingly reticent and refused to give him an answer until she had spoken to the brewery. She seemed to have been avoiding him all day, which was driving him wild.

'I'm gonna have it out with her tonight,' he told Phil as they worked together on a rush MOT job. 'Every time I bring up the subject she finds an excuse to change it.'

'Well, maybe she just don't wanna know,' Phil replied, his voice tinny under the bonnet.

'Then she's got a problem, hasn't she?' Grant said grimly.

'You sure you ain't the one with the problem? Pass us that spanner on the floor.'

'Meaning?'

Phil's head reared up from the car's engine. 'You don't think you're going over the top with this buying the pub caper? Quite apart from the fact it'll cost about two hundred and fifty grand and I can't see where you're gonna get your hands on that kind of dosh. There's more to life you know.'

'Not to me there ain't.' Grant's face was serious. 'Either she comes in with us and buys the pub or I've no choice but to finish with her.'

'Bit drastic.'

Grant hurled the spanner he had been holding onto the floor. 'Phil. That boozer is Sharon's entire existence. I don't get a look in these days. If she ain't willing to share it with me, I'll know exactly where I stand. And it's not gonna be on the sideline any more.'

'I see,' Phil said, nonchalant. 'Who's this "us"?'

It was midnight by the time Grant got Sharon alone. Even then she wouldn't sit down and insisted on washing up the glasses, causing Grant, who had been pacing up and down like a caged tiger, to snap, 'Will you leave that!'

'I've got to clean up ...'

'For God's sake, do it in the morning then.'

She turned round to face him, soapy hands dripping. Grant stopped pacing.

'Sharon. All you have to do is say "yes" and all your problems will be answered.' He looked at her searchingly, his eyes glowing. 'Don't you see? I can make it happen.'

'Yeah, but that's the problem. *I* want to make it happen. Me.'

'But you still will be. Me and Phil would just be giving you a helping hand, that's all.'

Sharon looked uncertain. 'Grant, it's not that I'm ungrateful, but I just don't ...'

'Okay,' he interrupted her. 'It's over.'

She was shocked. 'Are you serious?'

He threw up his hands. 'At last I'm getting through to you.'

'Alright,' she sighed. 'Answer me one question. What has buying this pub got to do with us? With our relationship?'

'It's got everything to do with it,' he shouted. 'Can't you see that I'm willing to sell my flat to give you what you want?' He paused, breathing rapidly. 'That I am willing to give up my home for you? Just to please you?'

'Alright, don't shout.' Sharon looked about her nervously.

'Well, I'm sorry,' Grant replied, controlling himself with difficulty, 'But I'm a little confused. I'm willing to give up everything I own for you. And you're telling me you don't want it. Or is it ...' he stared at her accusingly, 'that you don't want me?'

'Of course I want you. I love you.'

'I wish I could believe that.' Grant shook his head wearily.

Sharon, upset, gasped, 'I don't know what else to say, Grant.'

'Say "yes", or I'm walking out of that door and I'm walking out of your life. Well?'

She blinked at him, her face clouded with confusion. 'Alright, Grant, you win.'

★

'Isn't it going to be a bit crowded upstairs sharing with Grant and Phil?' Michelle quizzed Sharon when she told her the brewery had accepted their offer to purchase the freehold. The process had gone through amazingly quickly and she was still feeling a little stunned by the situation she now found herself in. 'You know what they say,' Michelle continued, "Two's company, three's …".'

'Yes, I know. But we ain't got much choice. Phil and Grant are both going to sell their flats so's we can put up a third each. Can't very well make my partners homeless, can I?' Sharon returned brightly. 'Anyway, Phil's pretty easy-going. I'm sure we'll get on alright. And it's not like it's gonna be a permanent arrangement; he's just giving us his money as a loan.'

'So, what does he get out of it? You gonna wash his socks and cook his tea an' all?' Michelle's face wore a wicked grin. 'Hope he don't expect any extras. You hear things about these threesomes …'

'You and your filthy mind.' Sharon swiped at her with a bar towel.

'They're very close, those two. Thick as thieves. Who knows what they might have in store for you?'

'Marriage, according to Phil.'

'What, bigamy?' Michelle's jaw dropped.

'No, silly. He gets all protective about his little brother. Told me now we've got this pub business settled I should make an honest man out of him. So to speak,' Sharon giggled.

'And what does Grant say?'

'Oh, he's as keen as mustard. Wants to bring the wedding forward again. To tell you the truth, I don't know whether I'm coming or going.'

'And what do you want?'

'What is this, twenty questions?'

'No. I'm serious. You mustn't let them railroad you into it if you're not ready.'

'Oh, 'Chelle.' Sharon sighed. 'I'm as ready as I'll ever be.'

CHAPTER NINE

Christmas was approaching fast and Albert Square was buzzing with preparations. The Turpin Road market traders, clad in an assortment of Santa hats and antler earmuffs, were doing a brisk trade. Even Grant could be heard entering into the festive spirit, letting rip with a few rousing choruses of 'Jingle Bells', albeit rather out of tune. The Vic was bursting with lunch-time drinkers – office workers on Christmas pub crawls – who got uproariously drunk and staggered out into the darkening December afternoons flushed with goodwill and brandy.

The celebratory atmosphere was heightened when Clyde Tavernier walked back into the Vic, a free man. Sharon imme-diately offered him his old job back, which he accepted. Thanks to Mark Fowler's successful attempts to track down a witness, Nick Cotton had been arrested for Eddie's murder. He had made a full confession, admitting that he had escaped from his room, desperate for a heroin fix, and had attacked Eddie who had tried to force him to return to the house. Eddie had been stabbed in the struggle and afterwards Nick had shinned up the drainpipe to his room. It was from there that he had spotted Clyde pick up the knife and decided to frame him.

By Christmas Eve, a towering Christmas tree had been erected in the garden in the middle of Albert Square. Sharon assumed that it had been Frank's idea – he had been talking about the need to improve the Square's image – but later on, when Grant asked everybody in the pub to step outside, she realized he was behind it. The glittering tree was strung with fairy lights spelling out the message, 'Happy Christmas Albert Square from all at the Queen Vic'. Standing beneath it, the Salvation Army band struck up 'Silent Night'. As the residents gathered round, joining in with the carol, Sharon felt a wonderful sense of completeness. She glanced at Grant and saw he was smiling at her.

'Happy Christmas, princess,' he whispered. She was too choked with tears to reply.

The harmony did not last long. Over breakfast on Boxing Day, Grant calmly announced that they were getting married. At eleven-thirty that morning. Sharon went ballistic.

'You've done what?!'

'I wanted it to be a surprise. I thought you'd like it.' Grant sounded injured.

'Like it?'

'Yeah. You. Me. Couple of witnesses ...'

'You plan our wedding without telling me and you thought I'd like it?' Sharon yelled, hardly letting him get a word in edgeways.

'... Twelve o'clock and it'll all be over ...'

'I don't believe this.'

'... I didn't want us to go through all the sort of stuff ...'

'You thought you'd marry me without even telling me!'

'... that people have to go through ...' Grant continued valiantly.

When Sharon built up a head of steam like this there was no stopping her.

'Grant, if two people decide to get married, both of them have to decide, not just one,' she spelt it out as if he was stupid.

'Both of us did decide.'

'Not on today we didn't.'

'What's the difference between now and a month's time?'

'A big difference!'

Grant sighed crossly. 'I don't see your problem.'

'That's just it!' Sharon screamed. 'You don't see my problem!' She stomped out of the kitchen and stood with her back to him, leaning her hands on the banister. They were both so engrossed in the argument that neither of them heard Phil slip in through the side door.

'Arranging this wasn't easy, you know. I mean, not many people get married on Boxing Day. I had to pull a load of strings,' Grant said, irked.

'Well, you've wasted your valuable time, then, haven't you?' Sharon snorted.

Phil came up the stairs, smiling cautiously. 'Morning.'

'And what's he doing here?' she added dangerously.

'What do you think? He's me best man.'

'Oh, great!'

At that moment there was a knock on the door.

'I'll get it,' Phil offered, grateful for the chance to escape. Grant followed Sharon back into the kitchen.

'You have no intention of marrying me. Is that right?' he demanded, squaring up to her.

'If you were any slower, Grant, I'd think you worked for British Rail.'

'And that's your final word?'

'That's my final word.'

'Right.' Grant stormed downstairs, almost knocking over the hairdresser Phil had just let in.

'Where can I plug this in?' she asked, brandishing a dryer.

'Better I don't tell you,' Grant snapped, striding out into the street.

A short time later Michelle had dropped round to see Sharon to escape the atmosphere at the Fowlers – she and Pauline were still on edge over the Clyde business and Arthur was sulking because the telly had broken – and found her moping in the kitchen. When Sharon explained about Grant's presumptuous wedding arrangements, Michelle seemed unfazed.

'So what time's it happening?'

'You don't think I'm going to go through with it, do you?' Sharon said, outraged.

'Why not?'

Sharon spread her hands. 'It's not what I wanted. I wanted to plan it properly – you know, the dress and a proper reception and all that. If I got married this morning it would make it as important as going to the Cash and Carry.'

'Does this mean it's off for good, then?'

'No. Why should it be?'

'I don't know. I just thought this might have messed things up, you know, permanently.'

There was a pause as Sharon considered this. 'I hope not.'

Michelle sat down at the kitchen table. 'Do you love him, Sharon?'

'Yeah.'

'And does he love you?'

'I think so.'

'And you want to marry him?'

'Yeah.'

'Then why don't you? If your only reason's going through all the preparations again, then I think you're mad.' She sat back and folded her arms.

'What?' Sharon couldn't believe her ears.

'Marry him, Sharon. Don't prat around. All the planning's not important. Anybody can do that. I did that … look where it got me.' Michelle thought briefly of Lofty, the man she'd jilted at the altar. 'What's important is that you love each other. That's all that matters.'

Sharon was touched by her friend's honesty. 'Why are you saying this? You don't even like Grant.'

'No … but I like you.' Michelle covered her hand. 'And I want you to be happy. And whatever I think about Grant, he's done what he's done because he loves you.'

When a despondent Grant went past the open doorway five minutes later he was alerted by the blast of a hairdryer.

'What are you doing?' he asked, looking between Sharon, Michelle and the long-suffering hairdresser.

'Having my hair done.' Sharon smiled sweetly. 'Well, if I'm getting married I thought you'd like me to look half-decent. And Michelle says she'll be my bridesmaid.'

★

For an impromptu wedding, there suddenly seemed to be a lot of guests. Sam and Ricky, having seen Phil dolled up in the street, had demanded to be allowed to come along too, and Arthur, Pete, Kathy, Frank and Mark, who had got wind of it at the last minute, had all scrummed down to the registry office as well. Grant and Phil were waiting at the front, Grant not daring to turn round. The only people missing were the bride and bridesmaid, a fact that the registrar, who kept glancing pointedly at his watch, seemed to be underlining. Grant felt suddenly sick with nerves. What if she doesn't show and I've made a fool of myself? he thought.

Phil glanced at him sideways. 'Relax, bruv, she'll be here.'

'She changed her mind once, what's to say she hasn't changed it back again?' he hissed, agitated.

'She won't have.'

At that moment there was the creak of a door opening. Phil glanced behind him and gave Grant a nod. Grant, realising he had been holding his breath, exhaled. Sharon, radiant in the new suit he had secretly bought her a few days earlier, appeared by his side. He took her hand and squeezed it.

'You look beautiful.' Sharon smiled up at him. This is it, he thought. This is really it. For once in my life I've done the right thing.

For a few short weeks, Grant and Sharon settled down to blissful domesticity, stealing kisses behind the bar, cuddles by the crisp boxes and even, on one, lust-mad occasion, a quickie in the cellar. But, once the heady honeymoon period was over, their perceptions of married life turned out to be rather different. Grant, seeing no reason to change his bachelor ways, invited Phil on a lads' night out.

'Aren't you forgetting something?' Phil reminded him mildly, as Grant enthused about playing snooker, going on to a club and the possibility of a late-night card game.

'No – what?' Grant looked nonplussed.

'Your wife.'

Grant paused. 'Sharon? Yeah, yeah. She'd love a night out.'

'That kind of night out?' Phil was not convinced.

Neither was Sharon when Grant turned up in the Vic. She had an entirely different evening planned.

'Grant, just the man!' she greeted him breezily. 'You and me, eight-thirty tonight, at Chez Jerome. Be there!'

'What's the matter, Grant?' enquired Clyde, who was bottling up. 'You look as sick as a parrot.'

Sharon cocked her head at him. 'Yeah, come on, Grant, out with it.'

'I've made other arrangements. With Phil. I was just coming to invite you along too,' Grant said lamely. Realising he was in a no-win situation, he added, 'I'll cancel.'

'Are you sure?'

'Look, I'd rather go to Chez whatever, alright?'

'I know it's not your Chicken Tikka or meat pie kind of place, but I thought we should try something different.'

'I bet there won't be any draught lager,' he grumped. 'Just don't expect me to eat snails.'

The evening was not a success. Grant, uncomfortable in a suit and feeling out of place, had been patronised by the wine waiter and left hungry by the chef. By the time they got back to the Vic he was in a foul mood.

'What's wrong?' asked Sharon, who had enjoyed herself.

'The place was a rip-off,' he growled, tearing into a packet of salted peanuts.

'It was *nouvelle cuisine*.'

'Exactly.'

'So?'

'If the soup had been as warm as the wine and the wine as old as the beef and the portions as large as the waitress, it would have been alright. It just wasn't my idea of fun, that's all.'

Sharon snuggled up to him. 'Oh? So what is, then?'

Grant, unusually, did not take the hint.

'Maybe we should have gone on somewhere else.'

'I thought you'd like to come home. Phil's out; we've got

the place to ourselves …' Grant still looked blank. '… so let's make the most of it,' she continued, nibbling his ear.

'If that's what you want.'

'Grant. What's happening here?' Sharon moved away, hurt.

'Not a lot.'

'I mean with us.'

He sighed. 'I'm just a bit tired, that's all.'

'Come on.' Sharon took his hand and led him towards the stairs. 'I'll give you a massage.'

'Let's hope those oysters do their job,' Grant muttered, following her reluctantly.

Half an hour later, Sharon felt the bedsprings move as Grant slid out of bed. Pretending to be asleep, she listened to him fumbling about in the dark, getting dressed and tying his shoes. Cursing softly as he trod on a creaky floorboard, he crept out and down the stairs. The side door clicked shut. Straining her ears, she heard his footsteps outside, accompanied by a jaunty whistle. She curled into a tight ball and squeezed her eyes tight shut, determined not to cry.

The next day things went from bad to worse. Phil, sensing an air of marital tension, popped into the bar just before lunch-time opening and announced he was going out again that evening, alone. Sharon, in turn, tried to mend the rift between herself and Grant by suggesting a cosy night in together.

'The day I want to put me feet up by the fire with a cup of cocoa you can shoot me,' Grant snarled, itching for a return match at the snooker hall with his mates.

'Don't tempt me,' Sharon retorted, stung.

Grant glared at her. 'I haven't changed, Sharon. I still like what I've always liked. What do you want: some drippy, bleedin'-heart new man from one of your glossy magazines? Someone who knows about fine wines and wild mushrooms and wears pink shirts and bow ties? Well, I ain't him. And if that's what you want …'

Sharon slammed a crate of mixers down on the bar. 'No,

Grant. That's not what I want. I just want to spend time with you. Is that such a crime?'

'We spend enough time together behind that bar. I need my own space.'

'To do what? Gamble? Set up dodgy deals? Get off with other women?' Sharon drew a deep breath. 'Your problem is, Grant, you want a doormat, not a wife.'

'Good night out?' Grant asked Phil the following morning as they worked together at the Arches. Phil had insisted Grant spend more time helping him; business was picking up and even with Ricky, who had proved to be a competent mechanic, he was having trouble keeping abreast of it.

Phil grunted. 'Not bad. Good night in?'

'What do you think?'

Phil straightened up, easing his back. 'I think you two are getting off on the wrong foot.'

Grant said nothing. They carried on working, the radio filling the silence between them.

'Here, I know what'd do it.' Phil leaned his forearms on a car roof, grinning across at his brother. 'Of course, you'd need to play your part. Shouldn't be too hard for you, though …'

'Go on.'

'Get her pregnant. That'd keep her quiet. She'd be only too happy to stay in and too knackered to give you grief about goin' out.'

'I like it,' Grant said.

When he brought up the subject with Sharon, she was completely thrown. Grant had never expressed a particular yearning to become a father before. The pub was busy and she was not in the mood to give it serious thought.

'Yeah, well, sometime, definitely,' she said, ringing up a round on the till. 'But I'm not available at the moment, as you can see.' She handed Pat Butcher her change. 'Let me think about it, Grant, eh?'

For Grant, that was as good as a yes. Totally smitten with the idea, he immediately started daydreaming about his kid, seeing them both down the North Bank at West Ham, the little lad in a bobble hat and scarf. He might even play for them one day. He might even play for England! Grant imagined himself sitting in the stands at Wembley watching his son run out onto the field and felt a lump in his throat. He would give him all the things that he, as a boy, had always wanted from his own father – love, security, encouragement, friendship – and maybe, just maybe, it would erase the bad memories.

Grant was so taken with the prospect of being a parent that it astonished him he hadn't thought of it before. He had never been committed enough to anybody, he reflected; before Sharon, his longest relationship had been with Jeanette, a nurse. It had lasted ten months, and even then he hadn't been entirely faithful to her. She was warm and funny and generous-natured and he couldn't hack that. One-night stands and brief affairs (there had been a couple of married women) required much less emotional involvement. As for having kids: that was something other people did.

Now, though, everything was different. Suddenly, it all seemed to fall into place. Him and Sharon, marriage, buying the Vic; it was all leading to one obvious conclusion. They should start a family. Out in the streets, walking Roly, the Vic's dog (originally Den's, he had been passed on to Sharon by John Royle), Grant found himself noticing toddlers in push-chairs for the first time. Stopping outside the shop, he peered into a pram and was met by a pair of startled blue eyes. He grinned. The baby watched him cautiously. Grant pulled a face and the baby smiled delightedly, kicking and gurgling. Just then its mother came out and gave Grant a filthy look.

'What do you think you're doing? Get away from my child, you pervert!'

'Sorry, sorry!' Grant backed off, alarmed. 'I wasn't doing anything. I was just saying hello.' Phil came round the corner in the nick of time.

'It's alright, love, I can vouch for him, he's harmless.' The woman, unconvinced, hurried away. 'What were you playing at?' Phil asked, scratching his head. 'Since when have you gone all gaga over babies?' An alarmed look spread across his face. 'Here, you haven't?'

'Haven't what?'

'You haven't got Sharon up the spout?'

'No,' Grant said, 'but I'm working on it.'

'You've only just married, mate. You don't want to start breeding yet.'

'It was your idea.'

'I was joking!' Phil said, exasperated. 'I can't believe you two. Especially Sharon. She's got to get that pub up and runnin'.'

'She can handle it.' Grant beamed. 'I reckon he might play for West Ham one day.'

Phil rolled his eyes. 'And he might not! He might be an axe murderer. He might be a ballet dancer. He might be a she.'

Grant seemed not to hear. 'He'll be special. I can feel it.'

'Give me strength! You don't bung the Almighty a fiver and get a fully-grown midfield genius. It doesn't work like that. You'll have years of nappies and screaming. You'll never be able to go out. I just don't see what your hurry is.'

Roly pulled on the leash, whining.

Grant moved off, shouting over his shoulder, 'It won't be like that for me and Sharon.'

'Like hell it won't,' Phil muttered.

When Grant broached the matter with Sharon again later, she did not share his enthusiasm. 'Is this a wind-up, or are you really serious?' She looked at him in the mirror as she applied her lipstick, getting ready for the evening shift.

'Of course I'm serious,' he retorted. 'What's wrong with now? We're both young, healthy ...'

Sharon swivelled round. 'I'll tell what's wrong with now. You may not have noticed, but pubs all over London are going to the wall ...'

'I'm not talking about pubs, I'm talking about kids,' Grant said, calm but determined. She gazed at him, trying to read his expression. She could hardly believe what she was hearing.

'I'm just starting to make my mark on this pub. You of all people know how much I wanted it.'

'So, we get a manager in.'

'You expect me to sit up all night washing nappies while some bloke runs my pub? No chance!'

'Alright, alright, we'll make some arrangements. I'm sure you can run a pub and bring up a kid at the same time.'

'Get real, Grant. Serve all day with some puking kid strapped to my back?'

Sharon felt herself beginning to panic. His earnestness freaked her out. This was a Grant she didn't know at all. It was almost as unsettling as the violent one. She saw the hurt and disappointment on his face and softened her tone.

'Grant, one day it'd be great to have kids with you. But I'm twenty-two years old. I've got a business to build. It's not the right time.'

'Other people manage it.' Grant, she could see, wasn't going to take no for an answer.

'End of conversation,' she said curtly, snapping her make-up bag shut and getting up. She went downstairs, her mind in a turmoil, putting on a bright smile as she walked into the bar. Clyde had opened up and several regulars were in already. Sharon looked around at the familiar walls, the tobacco-toasted ceiling, the old furniture. This was where she wanted to be. She was going to keep it a proper East-End local; no lunchtime strippers or video jukeboxes or revamps or special themes. That had been the secret of Den and Angie's success, and she was going to carry it on. Having children didn't enter into it. Not yet, anyway.

Grant, keeping an eye on the main chance, refused to give up his campaign. Two weeks later, when Sharon mentioned that she had to go round to the surgery to pick up some more contraceptive pills, he made his move.

'Don't,' he said gently, kissing her neck. Sharon, who had just staggered in with the shopping, was puzzled.

'Don't what?'

'Don't go back to the surgery,' he whispered, his lips brushing her ear. 'Don't get any more pills.' He kissed her again.

'Grant!' Sharon protested, laughing. He continued to plant kisses, whispering, 'In fact, don't go into the bar. Take the day off. Come upstairs with me. We don't have to try for a baby just yet but it won't do any harm to practise.'

She felt her body responding, despite herself, a fizzy feeling contradicting the cold voice of reason in her head.

'Grant ...'

'It's only because I love you, Sharon. That's all.' He held her close and she felt his heart beating rapidly. As he kissed her, his passion melted any last vestige of resistance she once had.

'Now tell me you'll come off the pill altogether,' Grant said softly as Sharon lay in his arms. She looked up at him.

'I'll come off the pill altogether.'

'What?' Grant hadn't expected her to be won round quite so easily.

'I said, I'll do it! *Now* will you stop nagging me?' Sharon got out of bed and pulled a dressing-gown around her, drawing the curtains back. 'Sex in the afternoon. How decadent. I hope you're not going to expect this all the time. It'll play havoc with my book-keeping.'

'You mean ...?' Grant still couldn't quite take it in.

'Yes!' she insisted, grinning. 'Yes. Anything for a quiet life.' He leapt out of bed and picked her up, whirling her around. 'Grant! Put me down!' she giggled. 'And for God's sake put some underpants on! Dot Cotton's out there with Ethel.'

Grant peered out of the window at the two women, who were conferring by the garden railings. Ethel had her pug dog tucked under one arm.

'I see she's got Willy with her.'

Sharon drew the curtains again smartly. 'So she won't want to see another one, will she?'

Having made such a momentous decision left Sharon feeling a little light-headed. Out in the Square, later, on her way to drop off a misdirected invoice at the café, she, too, started looking at people with babies with a different eye. She couldn't help noticing that the mothers – most of whom were sloppily dressed in leggings – seemed tired and cross and the babies red-faced and fractious. They did not make a very good advertisement for parenthood. She tried to convince herself it was an unrepresentative sample, but the little voice at the back of her head, which was once again making itself heard, said, 'If you believe that, you'll believe anything.' Sharon told it to shut up.

Rachel was behind the till in the café. She had been made redundant from the polytechnic and was working at the café until she found something else. Sharon was genuinely sympathetic.

'Sorry about your job. Michelle told me.'

'Thanks. Even though I could see it coming it was a bit of a blow.' Rachel glanced at the cover of the paperback she had been reading sneakily under the counter. 'Still, maybe it was just what I needed to kick me into doing something positive with my life.'

'Like what?'

'Write a book. I've had short stories published. I know I can do better than this rubbish.'

'Good for you! Go for it.'

'It's just the starving in the garret bit that comes first that I'm not looking forward to,' Rachel admitted. 'But it could be worse. I could be a single mum. At least I'm not in Michelle's position with a family to support.'

'Michelle's job isn't under threat!' Sharon said, defensive.

'I know. I'm just saying that children complicate the issue.'

'Yeah,' Sharon replied carefully, 'but I guess they have their compensations.'

Rachel laughed. 'Name one.'

'It's something to love.'

'Buy a hamster.'

Sharon pretended to be shocked. 'You *need* to be part of a family.'

'Okay, buy two and let them breed.'

'Oh, come on. The whole point is that a baby is part of you and part of the person you love.'

Rachel snorted. 'So what happens if you get all the bits of the other person you can't stand? You can divorce a partner; you're stuck with kids.'

Suddenly, Sharon wasn't finding their conversation so amusing.

'God, you really are cynical, aren't you?'

'No, I'm not saying people shouldn't want children – I quite like other people's kids – I'm just saying it's not for me, that's all.'

'But don't you ever feel, you know, the urge?'

Rachel considered, her dark eyes serious for a moment. 'Yes. Then I remind myself that the minute you have kids you stop being "I" and you become an "us" 'til the day one of you dies.' She smiled again. 'And then the urge just disappears.'

On her way back, Sharon hesitated outside the surgery. Doctor Legg passed her on his way in and she hailed him. 'Are you booked up this evening?'

'Pretty much so. Why? Is it urgent?'

'No, I just wanted to pick up a prescription, that's all. For my pill.'

'Well, in that case,' he began, ushering her down the steps, 'come on in now and I'll do it before the rush starts.'

CHAPTER TEN

''Ere, Grant, what's your game?' Phil cornered his brother in the pub. He knew he was up to something; Grant had asked for time off that afternoon but wouldn't say why and he had a shifty, closed-down look on his face that always spelled trouble.

'Nothing,' Grant said stonily. Phil knew he was lying.

Earlier, he had seen him talking to Steer and Keating, two ex-cons who had a reputation in the Docklands underworld. The Mitchell brothers kept on the periphery of it – Phil had never wanted to get in any deeper – but Grant liked to live dangerously. Just how dangerously was what Phil wanted to find out.

He knew Sharon was worried, too. She had heard Grant arranging something on the phone and had bent Phil's ear about it, but he was as much in the dark as she was. Phil was beginning to feel some sympathy for Sharon. He didn't think she'd have the staying power for a relationship with Grant, but she had proved him wrong. Grant, he thought, didn't know a good thing when he found it.

'Come on, this is me you're talking to. Your big brother. I can read you like a book.'

'So what's it say?'

'Eh?'

'The book.'

Phil drained his pint. 'I dunno. *The Heist*? Am I warm? That's what those two toerags are known for. You're not going in with them, are yer?'

Grant jutted his jaw. 'So what if I am?'

'For God's sake. You've got responsibilities. Sharon. This place. You're talking about starting a family, and now you're planning a hold-up. You can't carry on like you used to.'

'Like *we* used to.'

'Alright, like we used to. But them days are over. I've had enough brushes with the law recently.'

'Anyway, I can't get out of it,' Grant said sullenly. 'And I'm not going inside, I'm driving.'

'You're the getaway driver?' Phil slapped his forehead. 'Are you stark, staring bonkers? The old bill are onto you. They've already been down the Arches, asking questions. They know something's up.'

'I've seen 'em.'

'So what are you gonna do?'

'Shake 'em off somehow. I've got to do it. You know what Steer will do if I don't show?'

Phil sighed. 'I'll go.'

'But …'

'Don't bloody argue with me, Grant. You can't risk Sharon's life. You pull out, he'll come after her to get at you. I ain't got no one to worry about me. I'll go.' Reluctantly, Grant handed him the car keys.

When Phil heard the gunshot, his heart leapt. Grant hadn't said anything about shooters, he thought, wondering whether to drive off then and there. The door to the bookies opened and Steer ran out, followed by Keating, who was limping badly and dragging his leg. He half-collapsed on the pavement. Steer galloped over to the car, a bag under his arm.

'You can't just leave him there.' Phil, horrified, got out to rescue the injured man. When he heard furious revving behind him he realized, too late, that Steer had done a bunk, leaving the two of them to face the music. Cursing, he hooked Keating's arm around his neck and helped him down an alley.

The police were at the Vic within an hour, giving Grant a grilling. He took great pleasure in denying all knowledge, arms folded, chin up, giving them the eye.

'What is it with people like you?' Jackson, the DCI, snarled.

He looked around the pub, which had a smattering of afternoon drinkers. 'I'm not fooled by your cocky little act, not for one minute. You've got all this, but you can't stop dipping into what's not yours. It'll be a good old long stretch for armed robbery when we nail you. It might just teach you a lesson.' Sharon, who was making a show of tidying up behind the bar, froze.

Jackson got up to go just as Phil walked in through the door. 'Ah-ha. And here's Tweedledee. Bang on time, I see.'

Phil regarded him mildly. 'Do I know you?'

'You'll wish you didn't soon enough.'

Phil grimaced at his brother. 'Nice company you keep.'

'Cut the crap,' Jackson ordered. 'Where were you at 3.35 this afternoon?'

Frank Butcher, who was passing on his way to the bar, stopped to listen.

'We don't require an audience, thank you,' Jackson snapped.

'I'm sorry, officer. I presume you are a police officer, from the manner of your speaking?' Frank inclined his head, mock-courteous. Jackson, who was in plain clothes, went crimson. 'It's just that I couldn't help overhearing what you were asking my mate here,' Frank continued to bluff. 'And I thought I should tell you, in case you wanted to know, that he was upstairs with me and a couple of others watching the gee-gees. It was a good race. Favourite won. But don't they always?'

'Not always,' Jackson spat. 'Is this true, Mitchell?'

'Absolutely,' Phil replied.

'And you'll sign a witness statement to that effect?' He turned to Frank.

'Of course, officer. I'd be delighted to.' Frank winked at Phil behind Jackson's back, licked a finger and stroked the air. Phil got the message. He wondered what it was Frank wanted.

'So that's what you were up to. And Phil saved your neck. That copper knows.' Sharon had hauled Grant upstairs to give him a rocket.

'He doesn't know anything. He's just guessing.'

'You heard what he said.'

'Sharon, if he knew, he'd have banged somebody up by now. Anyway, what are you worried about? They're not after you.'

'You think you're so smart, don't you?' Sharon was shaking with rage.

'Don't start ...'

'You put everything I've ever wanted ... everything I've worked for ... you put it all at risk and you're telling me not to start ...'

'Oh, why don't you go and have a little lie down?' Grant said, heavily sarcastic. It was too much for Sharon. She took a swing at him, catching him on the upper arm. 'You pig! You absolute pig!'

'That's enough,' he warned, eyes flashing.

'No, it's not!' Sharon flew at him, arms flailing, trying to hurt Grant any way she could. 'It's not enough, it's not enough, it's not enough ...' she screamed, pummelling him. Grant caught hold of her wrists.

'Stop it.' Trapped in his iron grip, she gave up. Grant relaxed his hands and she wrenched herself away. Sobbing hysterically, she stumbled to the bathroom and locked the door. Grant left her to get on with it and went out.

When Grant returned it was gone eleven and the pub was closed. He let himself in through the back door and saw Sharon collecting ashtrays in the bar. She looked done in, he thought, watching her for a few seconds unobserved. He felt a stab of contrition.

'I'm sorry,' he said quietly, walking in. Sharon turned abruptly.

'That makes it alright, does it?'

'Just ease up, will you?'

She came up to face him. 'You still don't see it, do you? You don't see what I'm upset about.'

''Course I do. Tell you what, let's go out in the week, get Clyde and Michelle to cover for one night. We could do with a break, get us back on an even keel. Or we could go to a nice little restaurant …'

Sharon gave a hollow laugh. 'You really are incredible, Grant.'

'What?'

'You can't buy me. I would have thought you'd have known that by now.'

'I'm not.' Grant looked genuinely perplexed. 'I just thought it would be nice for the two of us to go out.'

'I don't want to go out.' Her face was grim. 'I've got things to think about.'

'What is there to think about?' he coaxed. 'I was stupid, I admit that, but everyone makes mistakes …'

'Mistakes? You call armed robbery a mistake?' Sharon was incredulous. 'Just get out of my sight! I've finished with you, Grant – finished.'

A week later, Sharon was still hostile and Grant, having tried chocolates, flowers and more apologies, had run out of inspiration.

'Why doncha try doin' something really special, something that makes a statement, tells her how committed you are?' Phil suggested over a teabreak at the Arches.

'She don't wanna know.'

'Look, she's pissed off and she's feeling hurt, but she ain't walked out, has she? You've gotta get in there, show her you care.' Grant shot him a look. It was unlike Phil to get so worked up about someone else's relationship. Phil had had a short-lived fling with a woman recently that had all gone pear-shaped when he found out she was married. Perhaps it had made him a bit touchy, Grant reflected.

'Got any ideas?' he asked.

'She's been on about getting upstairs redecorated, ain't she? You could do that.'

'Bruv, you're a genius.' Grant put down his mug and leapt up.

'Where are you goin'? That Peugeot's owner's coming back at five.'

Grant stepped out of his overalls. 'Tell Ricky to do it. I'm off to the DIY superstore.'

Ricky was no more help than Grant. He was upset about Sam, who had forgotten their first wedding anniversary. Not only that, but he'd caught a photographer taking shots of her in the Square for some photo love story for a teen magazine. After the last modelling fiasco, when Sam got set up by a sleazebag who had sold topless shots of her, he had put his foot down about her new career. Apparently, Sam hadn't taken any notice.

By the time Phil knocked off, he was gasping for a drink. Sharon looked up when he came into the Vic and smiled. She was more relaxed than he'd seen her all week.

'You've perked up a bit,' he remarked.

'Yeah, well, I think you might have had something to do with that,' she shouted above the din. 'It was a lovely idea. Grant's up there now with the paint-stripper. He admitted he couldn't take all the credit.'

'That's a first.' Phil pulled out a fiver. 'Well, here's to happy families. I'll have a pint please.'

'Put that away, this is on the house.' Sharon placed a foaming pint of bitter in front of him.

'What's going on here?' Phil asked, surveying the room. A large crowd was gathered around one of the tables, including Pete, Arthur, Kathy, Frank, Rachel and Mrs Hewitt, who was widely whispered to be Arthur Fowler's fancy woman. Pauline had gone to New Zealand to visit her sick brother, Kenny, and Mrs Hewitt had by all accounts got her claws stuck into Arthur in her absence. A burst of drunken laughter erupted from their table.

'Rachel's birthday,' Sharon explained. 'It's 'Chelle's coming up soon, an' all. I'm planning a surprise party for her here.'

★

Michelle's party was a sore point with Grant. He and Michelle had long ago acknowledged their mutual dislike but suffered each other for Sharon's sake. He thought Sharon did too much for her and resented their closeness. It was something he couldn't understand and it made him feel sidelined. Like today, he reflected, slopping paint on the wall vigorously and showering his T-shirt with specks. The two of them had been cackling like fishwives after Sharon had made a remark about them 'trying for a baby'. Michelle compared it with a school report – 'Must try harder' – which had hit Grant where it hurt. He couldn't understand why Sharon wasn't pregnant yet. He had never wanted something so badly, ever, and it wasn't happening. Each time they made love he found himself thinking, This is it. Surely this is it. But then she came on again and he felt a total failure. It was beginning to affect his ability to perform at all.

'How long's this going to go on? How long's it take to get a baby?' he said to Phil later. Phil had walked in on him and Sharon rowing – it was what they did best these days – and was giving him the third degree.

'You on about that again?' Phil asked, surprised.

'It's important. To me, anyway.'

'And Sharon?'

Grant sighed. 'Every time I bring it up she goes all weird on me.'

'Maybe you should shut up, then,' Phil replied bluntly.

'Why?'

'You're probably making her self-conscious. I mean, use your head. Girl's going to get embarrassed, you going on day and night about getting her in the club. How d'you know she ain't worried that she can't have kids? Ever thought about that?'

'You think that's it?'

'It might be.'

'So tell me, what should I do about it?'

'Relax. Don't give her a hard time. You're all wound up about it.' Phil slapped him on the back. 'Right, that's therapy over. Now are you going to shift your backside down the Arches or am I going to have to give you one almighty kick?'

Phil was right, Grant thought, as he worked. His brother had a knack like that – seeing through the garbage people spewed out and grasping the truth. There was only just over a year between the two of them but he had always looked up to Phil. Phil knew what to do. It was Phil who had saved his skin when they were little. Now here they were, grown men, and he was still doing it.

Grant went home glowing with optimism. Sharon was making a cup of tea in the kitchen when he got in. She was edgy and sharp with him, reprimanding him when he crept up on her.

'Don't be like that,' he said, trying to put his arms around her. She shrugged him off. 'Hey. I know I've been giving you a hard time but I'm here so say sorry, okay?' Sharon was silent, keeping her back to him. 'Sharon, I said sorry. That's not an easy thing for me to say.'

'I know,' she replied, half-relenting.

'If I've been going on too much about us having a kid …'

'You have been.'

'Yeah. I'm a bit insensitive, ain't I?'

'A bit. Especially when it comes to that.'

'Well, I'm not going to be like that any more. If it happens, great, if it doesn't then it'll just be one of those things. What really counts is you and me. Isn't it?' He brushed her cheek with his thumb, gazing at her raptly.

'Yeah, it is,' she said in a quiet voice.

'I'm not very good at saying what I really feel but what I really want to say is that I care for you more than I've ever cared for anybody else and I just need to know that you feel the same.' Sharon did not meet his eyes. 'Sharon?' he prompted. She looked up, forcing a smile to her lips.

'Yes, Grant. I feel exactly the same.'

The fact was, Sharon admitted to herself as she drank her tea, she didn't know how she felt about Grant these days. His temperament was more unpredictable than ever and after the business with the robbery she wasn't at all sure that she could trust him. Increasingly, she found herself turning to Phil when she needed someone to rely on. He was always there in the background, steady, unobtrusive, strong. And he knew how to deal with Grant. Just the thought of having a baby with Grant unnerved her. He was so immature himself at times that it felt as if she and Phil were the parents looking after a naughty kid.

'Penny for them?' Grant said, making Sharon jump. 'You were miles away.'

'Was I?' She fiddled with her teaspoon, wondering what to say. 'I was just thinking about Michelle's party, that's all.' Grant's face darkened.

'What is it with that woman?' he growled. 'What's she ever done for anybody?'

Sharon bit her lip. So much for Grant's attempt at Mr Nice Guy.

By the following evening, Grant's mood had got worse, aided and abetted by most of a bottle of gin. He had been drinking upstairs since mid-morning, refusing to help out with the party preparations and being abusive about Michelle to anyone who mentioned her name. Sharon had decided to let him get on with it, though she had demanded he show his face for her sake.

It had turned out to be a bad decision. Grant's presence was not exactly helping the party go with a swing – he had parked himself by the drinks, to which he was helping himself frequently, and wore an expression that forbade conversation of any sort. A space had formed around him, the other party-goers reading the message loud and clear. Grant surveyed the scene with annoyance and then announced, loudly, 'How lovely. What a charming little gathering.' A few people cast him wary glances and moved away slightly. Grant got unsteadily to his feet. 'All the no-hopers all together in one room. How very nice.'

'Grant!' Sharon said sharply. 'Behave yourself.'

'You talking to me?' Tight-lipped, Sharon turned her back and walked away.

'Don't you walk away from me!' he shouted, causing a momentary hush to fall on the room.

Phil hurried over. 'Come on, bruv, slow down, eh?'

Grant focused his eyes on him. 'Yeah, okay, sorry.' His outburst might have ended there, had Dot Cotton not complained to Phil, 'Can't you do something about him? He's spoiling Michelle's party.'

'Ah, get out of my face,' Grant said rudely, sending Dot scurrying away. Sharon looked helplessly at Michelle.

'I'm sorry, 'Chelle. I'm really sorry.'

'It's not your fault,' Michelle comforted her.

'I feel terrible. I don't know what to do. He's been drinking all day.'

Grant lurched over and gave Michelle a filthy look. 'What's going on, are you talking about me?'

'No,' denied Sharon.

'Yeah,' said Michelle.

He linked his arms round their necks, mock-affectionate. 'One of you ain't telling the truth. Surely not my darling wife?' Sharon looked away, dreading whatever was coming. Michelle, who was made of sterner stuff, shoved Grant off.

'Yeah, and you can take your hands off me, an' all.' By now you could hear a pin drop.

'Take my hands off you?' Grant feigned amazement. 'Well, that must be a first. Can't be too many blokes around Walford you've said that to.'

'Your mother drop you on your head at birth?'

'Yeah, what of it?'

'She should have dropped you a bit harder then.'

Phil and Clyde got to Grant just in time to stop him

throwing a punch at her, Phil steering him towards the door while an irate Clyde threatened to split his head open. Grant struggled free of them both and headed for the door, turning round to shout, 'Go to hell, the lot of you,' before stumbling out into the night. In the silence that followed, Sharon's muffled sobs were painfully audible.

Sharon checked her watch. Midnight. Yawning, she finished cashing up, feeling utterly wiped out. The party hadn't been a total disaster – Arthur Fowler and Pete Beale had instigated a drunken conga, which got everybody going – but she was embarrassed and ashamed by Grant's outburst. Why did he have to do these things? It was as if he had to destroy everything that was good, as if he couldn't help himself. But she was getting beyond the point of caring. Grant had tested her patience too much.

Predictably, he came back acting as if nothing had happened. 'Let's go to bed,' he said, swaying in the doorway. 'You never know, tonight may be the night you get pregnant.'

'I doubt it, somehow,' she returned scornfully, half to herself, but Grant picked up on it and came into the bar.

'What d'you mean? Don't you fancy me any more?' She refused to answer. 'You don't want my kid?' he persisted. Sharon slammed the till shut, still saying nothing. 'I'm right, aren't I? You don't want my baby.' Grant's face was stricken with paranoia. Sharon, unable to contain her anger, exploded.

'No, I don't! I wouldn't have a kid by you if you was the last man on earth. You're sick and crazy, that's what you are. You act like an animal. Think I want to bring another you into the world?'

Grant looked stunned. 'I'm sorry,' he said quietly.

'Oh, you're always sorry. I've had it with you and your "sorrys". And I've had it with you always going on about me having a kid,' Sharon ripped into him, unable to stop herself now. 'Well, it's not going to happen, and you know why? Because I've never stopped taking the pill, that's why. Because, deep down, I've always known what a pig and a boor and a flaming nutcase you was. So now you know, right?'

He stared at her as if he couldn't believe it, his face pale. Sharon, her blood up, stared back, breathing rapidly. Slowly, as if in a dream, she saw Grant reach behind him and grab a bottle. She saw the bottle arc hurling towards her, but still she didn't flinch. It was only when it smashed against the wall near her head that she screamed.

'Yeah, go on then, scream. I'll give you something to scream about ...'

He had another bottle in his hand and was coming towards her. Sharon fled into the hallway, just as it crashed past, making her scream again. He picked up a stool and swiped it across the bar, sending bottles and glasses flying, then set to work on the rest of the room with a terrifying ferocity. Pressing herself into a corner, Sharon sank to the floor, jamming her hands over her ears to try to block out the noise of the madman destroying her pub.

When Sharon finally dared to go down to the bar the following morning, the place looked as if it had been torn apart by a mob. Hardly one piece of furniture had survived undamaged and the floor was a sea of broken glass. Grant was on the phone, apparently trying to get a friend to come round and do repairs. He ignored Sharon completely. Phil, who had been out most of the night looking for his brother, not realizing he'd come back home, staggered in wearily. He stared at the mess in disbelief.

'Were we raided or summat?' One look at Grant's face gave him his answer. Phil decided not to push it.

The repairs took all day. Sharon, her nerves already torn to shreds by Grant's terrifying explosion of violence, was even more frazzled with all the hammering and banging. Gritting her teeth, she painted on a smile and bore the disruption with a touch of the old East-End Blitz spirit, covering up the truth from a concerned Michelle. Grant, whose temper had been deteriorating by the hour, disappeared again without saying where he was going. By late evening, he had still not returned. Phil wanted to come up with a contingency plan in case he returned drunk, but Sharon refused.

'No, Phil, this is between me and Grant.'

She was just about to get ready for bed when she heard a loud thump in the bar.

'Grant? Is that you? Grant?' There was no reply. Too ashamed, as always, she thought, descending the stairs cautiously in the dark. A cool breeze fanned her legs and she cursed softly, thinking he must have left the front door open. A pale finger of light from the street outside illuminated part of the hall, throwing the rest into deep shadow. It wasn't until she got to the bottom of the stairs that she saw the door had been knocked off its hinges and hung open, askew. Sharon froze, her heart pounding.

'Grant?' she tried to call again, but her tongue seemed to be stuck to the roof of her mouth and all that came out was a croak. A floorboard creaked behind her. As she turned, something hit her on the back of the head and she fell, the sound of shattered glass ringing in her ears.

CHAPTER ELEVEN

'Sharon? Sharon? Can you hear me? For God's sake, say something. Sharon!'

'Grant?' Sharon, dazed, opened her eyes, trying to focus through the fog of her headache. She was being cradled in strong arms. She felt his breath warm on her cheek, his fingers gently parting her hair.

'Sharon? Thank Christ. I thought you was a goner for a moment.' Sharon blinked. It was Phil.

'Don't move,' he ordered, as she struggled to sit up. 'You've got a nasty cut on your head. I'm going to call an ambulance.'

She touched her hair, feeling stickiness on her scalp, and remembered.

'No.'

'I ain't taking no notice. You're concussed.'

'No, Phil!' she repeated sharply. He held up his hand. 'How many fingers?'

'Er ...,' she screwed up her eyes, 'three'.

He hesitated, then said, 'Okay, okay.'

'Help me up, will you?'

Phil eased her to her feet, looking concerned. Suddenly, everything started to spin and the floor seemed to rear up to meet her. She heard a roaring in her ears and swayed.

'I've got you, it's alright.' Phil put a supportive arm around her shoulders and she clung to him until the roaring subsided.

'I'm fine now,' she lied, her body bathed in sweat.

'No, you ain't.'

'I just feel a little bit woozy, that's all. It'll pass.'

Phil sat her on the stairs, keeping his arm around her. He looked into her face, trying to read her eyes.

'Was it ...?' He swallowed. 'Was it ... Grant?'

'I don't know. It all happened so fast.'

'But *could* it have been?'

Sharon paused only slightly before replying. 'Of course not. You know Grant. He swore he'd never lay a finger on me and I believe him.' She returned his gaze steadily. 'I'm surprised at you, Phil.'

When Phil checked the bar he found the cash tills emptied and drew a sigh of relief. So it was a robbery after all. Despite Sharon's conviction that the break-in was nothing to do with Grant, he hadn't been so sure. These days he was beginning to feel like he didn't know his brother as well as he thought.

Phil kept close to Sharon's side all day, leaving Ricky in charge at the Arches. He managed to persuade her to see Dr Legg, who cleaned and dressed the wound, but could not dissuade her from opening up. The attack on Sharon rapidly became the talk of the Square, along with Grant's violent outburst at the party. Sharon, as usual, shrugged the speculation off, carrying on as if nothing had happened. Phil could only look at her in admiration.

'You're amazing, do you know that?' he said later, as they had a nightcap in the flat. 'You're so strong. The way you've got through today I'm impressed, I really am.'

Sharon, who was reclining on the sofa, eyes closed, said, without opening them, 'I couldn't have managed it without you, Phil.'

He chuckled. 'We made a good team behind that bar, eh?'

She smiled to herself. 'Yeah.'

Suddenly, there was a crash, making both of them sit bolt upright.

'Ssh.' Phil held a finger to his lips and went to the door. He waved her back when she tried to follow him.

'Stay here. It might be them again.' He stole across the landing, walking on the balls of his feet, and crept downstairs. Undeterred, Sharon followed him, picking up a weighty brass figurine first. Phil pushed open the door into the bar and shouted, 'Come on, show yerselves, you miserable bastards. We got your number and the cops are on their way.' Sharon held her breath. There was a bark and a scrabble of claws and Roly trotted across the carpet, the little bell on his collar tinkling. He sat down in front of them obediently and put his head on one side, gazing up with big liquid eyes. Phil turned to Sharon with a comical sigh of relief and they collapsed into each other's arms, laughing. This feels so good and safe, Sharon thought, fighting a momentary urge to lay her head on Phil's chest.

'I think he's got *our* number,' Phil joked, giving her a smile. 'We're both as nervy as kittens.' He continued to look at her, his expression tender.

'Yes,' Sharon whispered, pulling away, not quite sure why she was shaking.

Grant returned briefly the next day, but would not see Sharon. Phil, who'd had a visit from him at the Arches, broke the news to her as gently as he could, leaving out his brother's rant about Sharon's untrustworthiness and never wanting to have anything to do with her again. Sharon, he could see, was hurt enough. As far as Phil was concerned, Grant didn't deserve any sympathy. He'd warned him to lay off Sharon about having kids and Grant had carried on with all the sensitivity of a rhino on heat. No wonder Sharon had taken fright.

He was surprised she stuck with him, what with all the grief his brother had given her. Above and beyond the call of duty, that's what mum would call it, Phil thought, and then changed his mind. When he remembered what his dad had put her through, with his gambling and womanising and getting banged up for being drunk and disorderly ... besides, she would expect nothing less of Grant's wife. 'Families must stick together', that was her motto. Everyone, Phil thought, disgruntled, was expected to make allowances for Grant since he came out of the Army. Phil had put himself on the line for Grant enough times and he didn't mind doing it, but his loyalty was not proving as bottomless as he'd always thought.

Especially when he thought about Sharon.

When Phil went back to the Vic in the afternoon, Grant had still not shown up. Sharon was in pensive mood. She had dark rings under her eyes and was sitting on the sofa, her feet tucked under her, nursing a mug of tea.

'Look, I can try having another word with him, if I can find him,' Phil offered, wanting to do something to comfort her.

She turned a wan face to him. 'It's alright, Phil. He don't want to see me. We both know why. And, if I'm honest …' She bit her lip, hesitating a moment. '… If I'm *really* honest, I don't know whether I want to see him …'

Phil sipped his own tea, saying nothing. 'Me and Grant, we seem to be going off down different roads,' Sharon continued. 'We seem to want entirely different things these days. He wants a family; I want a successful pub. Maybe there isn't any point in trying to pretend we can make a go of it anymore.'

'Well, I want a successful pub, too. My life savings are tied up in this place,' Phil reminded her.

'I know.' She smiled suddenly. 'I won't let you down, Phil.'

'I ain't concerned on that score.' Phil got up to go. Standing in front of her, he said, softly, 'You should have a lie down. You look wrecked.'

'Thanks a lot,' Sharon yawned. 'It's nothing that a bit of slap won't take care of. Anyway, I can't relax. I'm too worried about him.'

'Come on.' Phil pulled her to her feet. 'You're done in. Go and get some shut-eye. I'll help out downstairs if it gets busy. And if he don't turn up by closing time, I'll trawl round his usual hiding places.' Sharon opened her mouth to protest, but Phil silenced her by kissing her on the lips, a fleeting, dry, affectionate kiss that was somehow not quite brotherly. 'Go,' he whispered sternly, 'or I'll take you there myself.'

By the next morning, the strain of waiting for Grant was beginning to show in both of them. Phil, who had been out half the night combing clubs and bars and snooker halls, was exhausted, and Sharon was pent-up and tearful. When Michelle came in, Sharon finally broke down.

'Oh, 'Chelle, he's not coming back,' she sobbed, inking her friend's white blouse with mascara. Michelle fixed them two stiff vodka and tonics and sat her down. 'Everyone told me I'd got a bad one and it looks like they were right,' Sharon sniffed, repairing the damage to her makeup with a tissue. 'I bet they're all having a good laugh now.'

'No one's laughing.' Michelle patted her arm. Sharon stared unhappily into her drink. 'He's been away before,' Michelle pointed out, trying to console her. 'It's just his way of dealing with things. He'll be back.'

'I'm not so sure. I really hurt him this time.'

'You didn't mean it. He'll see that.'

Sharon shook her head. 'He's a strange man.'

'I think I worked that one out for myself.'

'When he's good, he's really good. But when he's bad ...' She looked at Michelle with watery eyes.

'All blokes are like that,' Michelle replied, stoical.

'No, they're not. Not like Grant. I mean, when he feels good he really feels good, you know? He's so full of life and energy you could run a small town off him. He reminds me a lot of Dad in that respect.' Sharon smiled fondly for a moment.

Michelle was unconvinced. 'Grant and Den?'

'Yeah. Dad was no saint either ...'

'I remember,' Michelle said wryly.

'... but no one could say he didn't live his life to the full,' Sharon continued, missing Michelle's oblique reference to Vicki's father. 'And Grant's like that. He never sits still, he never reads a book, he can hardly get to the end of a film unless it's got exploding people in it, but I like him like that. I wouldn't want him any other way.' She traced a knot-hole in the table. 'He wasn't made to sit around quietly. He loves meeting people and having a laugh and being out there and doing it. He doesn't think much about life but he doesn't half live it.' Sharon's eyes glowed, her earlier doubts forgotten.

'Maybe that's the price you have to pay for loving a bloke like Grant,' Michelle suggested.

Sharon sighed. 'I'm not sure I like the sound of that.'

'Well, he's never gonna be the kind of bloke that's gonna be happy staying in and watching you iron his slippers, is he?'

'That's not what I want, either,' Sharon said slowly. She took another sip of her drink. 'The worse thing about Grant isn't that he has his bad times, it's that he can't share them with me.'

'Can't? Or won't?'

Sharon considered this. 'Can't, I think. It's like he goes into a dark tunnel and there's no following him in. And I think it's really dark in there, Michelle. Darker than anything I know. And I can't help him, that's the real problem.'

'Maybe it's just a matter of time, Sharon.'

'Time?' Sharon snorted. 'That's the question, isn't it?' She drained the rest of her drink. 'I just don't want it to end like this, all bitter and unspoken and horrible. I want to give this marriage a damn good go before I throw in the towel.'

Phil had been in a foul mood all day, banging about the workshop and taking his mixed feelings about his brother out on the hapless Ricky. When a careless bit of soldering resulted in him burning his hand, he flung the keys at Ricky, told him to lock up, and stomped back round the corner to the Vic. He was running his hand under the cold tap in the kitchen when he felt two muscular arms lock around his chest, holding him prisoner. Thrashing violently, he tried to shake his attacker off, but the arms were like steel pincers. Suddenly, they let him go and he swivelled round, ready to fight, only to find himself face to face with a grinning Grant.

'You stupid idiot!' he yelled, furious.

'I thought you'd be pleased,' Grant said, undaunted.

'Where the hell have you been?'

'What's the matter? What have you done?' Grant asked, noticing Phil's burnt hand for the first time.

'Just sit down and shut up,' Phil bawled, in a roar that would have done credit to a company sergeant–major. Grant sat. 'You've done some pretty stupid things in your life,' Phil began, pacing up and down, holding his throbbing hand. 'But I always stood by you, didn't I?'

'That's what brothers are for,' Grant said, as if it was a simple, unarguable fact.

'Some of them were stupid. And some of them were violent. But I always stood by you because I knew, underneath it all, you were basically a decent man.'

'Are you going to get to the point?' Grant retaliated, shaken at the severity of Phil's dressing down.

'Yeah, I'll get to the point.' Phil sat down opposite Grant, his face flushed and angry. 'The things you've been doing to Sharon … they're not the thing a decent man would do. You were selfish and cruel …'

'Go on.' Grant's eyes hardened.

'And you made me ashamed to be your brother,' Phil finished. He paused, looking at Grant, who stared back.

'You know what she did to me and you can say these things?' Grant was shocked.

'She was wrong. But you don't cut off someone's foot because they stepped on your toes.'

Grant looked a little shamefaced. 'I'm back, aren't I? I'll sort it out with her.'

'Until the next time.'

'What d'you mean by that?'

Phil got up. 'Maybe she'd be better off without you. Maybe you shouldn't come back at all. Because I don't think you're man enough for this marriage.'

Grant's mouth fell open, but before he could say anything, Sharon, who had appeared in the doorway, said, quietly, 'I think that's for me to decide, Phil, not you.' She came into the room and put her shopping down on the table. 'I'd like to speak to Grant in private, please.'

All the time Grant had been roaming the streets, hanging out in dives and dossing down with mates, one thought had been hammering through his mind. She made me think it was my fault and it wasn't. When Sharon had failed to conceive, the spectre of his own sterility had made him impotent, turning his desperation to have a child into something even more significant: a desperate need to prove himself as a man. The more he'd tried, the worse it had become. Then Sharon had started making excuses, avoiding having sex, and he knew she was getting fed up with him too. The frustration had reached boiling point the night of Michelle's party. When Sharon let slip the truth about the pill, the knowledge that he'd been so humiliated – *for nothing* – had pushed him over the edge. Once again he had found himself lost in the dark no-man's-land where his rage always took him, a dangerous, wild terrain lit only by vivid bursts of tracer-fire anger. There was only one law of survival in this remote place: kill or be killed. Going there frightened him, but coming out frightened him almost more. After a blackout, he never knew what he had done.

Grant couldn't explain it to Sharon. He couldn't put it into words for anyone. But she didn't seem interested in explanations, or where he'd been, or why.

'That's not the point,' she said, when Phil had left them alone. 'I can't live like this, Grant. Waking up and feeling sick in the stomach because you might not be lying next to me.'

'You want out?'

She drew a deep breath. 'I'm saying that the next time we have a problem or something happens, we face it together. No more running away.'

'What about the baby? What about the pill?'

'We'll talk about it. We'll work something out. Just don't run away on me again, Grant, 'cos that'll be the last time you do. Have we got a deal?' she asked calmly.

'Yeah,' he replied, 'we've got a deal.'

Bathed, shaved and in clean clothes, Grant came into the lounge to announce to Phil and Sharon that he had turned over a new leaf. Top of his agenda was to cook them both a meal. Phil raised his eyebrows – Grant's repertoire did not extend much beyond beans on toast – although when Grant was out of earshot he asked Sharon sarcastically whether any of her cook books had recipes for humble pie.

Grant's transformation into apron-clad new man did not last long. The following day he offered to take Sharon for a Chinese meal, then blew her out at the last minute to go on a stag night. He went out drinking at lunchtime without telling her, leaving the Vic short-staffed, and then tried to make it up to her with a cheap charm bracelet he'd bought in the market on the way back. Sharon, depressed at seeing his old pattern of behaviour repeat itself so soon, barely bothered to protest. It was Phil, who found himself increasingly stepping into Grant's shoes to help Sharon out behind the bar and around the flat, who grew angry at the way he was taking his wife for granted.

Since Phil's kiss, Sharon had found herself thinking more and more about her brother-in-law. Just the brief brush of his lips had excited her more than sex with Grant had for a while now. Their warm pressure had seemed to suggest there was more, if she wanted it. He had not said or done anything since, but she could sense a buzz between them whenever they were together.

Sometimes, when she was working behind the bar, she would know Phil was looking at her, without even glancing up. Then she would have to check and his face would crease into a secret smile when their eyes met. Once, when the Vic had a sudden powercut, they shared a moment together in the fuse cupboard and his physical proximity made her feel weak with longing. His face was so close that she felt sure he was going to kiss her again but just as she leaned hesitantly towards him the lights came back on. They sprang apart guiltily, causing Michelle, who had come to see if they needed a hand, to become very suspicious indeed.

Despite the strength of her attraction to Phil, Sharon had no intention of it being anything more than a fantasy safely inside her own head. To act on it would be to play not so much with fire as with an inferno. She had, after all, witnessed what Grant did to Eddie – and that was just for making a pass. But when Grant himself stopped out all night, returning in the morning with a wilted bunch of carnations and a beery kiss, still expecting to get his 'conjugals', as he put it, she began to think again.

After a row, in which she accused him of sleeping with another woman and he hurled insults and a beer glass at her, Grant stormed off leaving Sharon trembling and upset. Vulnerable to the slightest show of affection, she found herself opening up to Phil. He helped her lock up and then poured them both a large whisky.

'Come on, get this down you.' Phil passed her a glass. Sharon took a gulp, feeling its warmth lick her throat.

'Better?' he enquired, looking at her solicitously.

'Yeah.' She took another swallow and, emboldened, added, 'You always seem to come to my rescue these days.'

Phil grinned. 'Hear that stamping noise outside? That's me white charger. I left me armour at the door; thought it might dent the furniture.'

Sharon smiled back over the rim of her glass. 'So what made me pick the black knight, then?'

'You tell me.'

'I don't know,' she said softly. 'But I do know that I keep thinking I made the wrong choice. I should be with his brother.'

'D'you mean that?' He put his hands on her shoulders, gazing deep into her eyes.

'Yes, I do,' Sharon breathed.

'Oh, Sharon.' Phil pulled her to him, devouring her with his kiss. Sharon, past caring about the consequences, gave herself up to him entirely, her whole body aching for his touch. When they got to the bedroom door, neither of them hesitated for a moment.

CHAPTER TWELVE

Grant's old schoolmate, Nigel, was the one who brought it home to him about Sharon. The two of them had gone out to a club, planning on getting well and truly ratted, and Grant ended up pouring his heart out.

'Well, all I can say is, I wish I was half as lucky as you, Grant – not that I ever have been,' Nigel shouted above the music.

As usual, none of the girls gyrating on the dancefloor had given him a second glance, or, if they had, it was generally to nudge their friends and giggle. With his shaggy curls, shambling gait and penchant for wearing loud shirts with clashing ties, Nigel was no one's idea of a dreamboat. He was, however, Grant's oldest and truest friend, and had seen him through many a crisis during and since their playground days. Nigel had announced his intention of settling in Walford and Grant was chuffed. Sometimes he felt almost closer to him than Phil. Especially recently.

'I think you're mad to give Sharon the runaround. I'd be home every night if it was me,' Nigel continued, enthusiastic. 'She's gorgeous, sexy, funny, sweet-natured, kind ...' He gave Grant a huge grin. 'Here, if you really don't want her, can I have her? Sounds like we've got a lot in common. I like soppy films. I get on with Michelle. I even like French food. Well, French fries, anyway.'

Grant couldn't help laughing, despite himself. 'Nige, you've got no chance.'

Nigel looked downcast. 'Really?'

'Really. Not if you want to stay mates with me, that is.' Grant got up and slapped him on the back. 'I'm off home to face the music.'

*

'So where do we go from here?' Phil swilled the dregs of his whisky around in the bottom of his glass, then drained it. Sharon did not answer.

The full impact of what they had done upstairs was still sinking in. Afterwards, she had suggested a nightcap in the bar in an attempt to normalize the situation. It wasn't working. When she looked at Phil she no longer saw a platonic brother-in-law but a passionate lover. Suddenly, the tables had turned completely.

Phil reached out and took her hand, turning it over in his large, work-roughened palm. 'Such beautiful hands,' he said, lifting it to his mouth and kissing her fingers one by one. 'In fact …' he put his arms around her neck, gazing into her eyes, 'you're beautiful all over. I didn't appreciate quite how much until just now.'

Sharon squirmed. 'Phil.'

'Well, you are, take it from me.' He smiled at her. 'You haven't answered my question.'

'That's because I don't know what to say.'

'It's easy.' In the dim light of the bar, his face grew suddenly serious. 'I love you.'

She felt a shiver run down her spine. 'Is that what you want me to say?'

'Only if it's true. It is for me.' He stroked her cheek gently. 'I want you to say you'll leave Grant and come away with me.'

Sharon's mouth fell open. 'Phil, I don't … I can't … I – I – I didn't think you felt *that* way about me.'

'I've been wanting you like crazy for weeks. You knew that, didn't you? Those looks you gave me. The little touches. The electricity between us. You felt it, you must have.'

'Yes, of course I did. But somehow it wasn't real. I didn't think it would really happen. And now …'

Phil stood up abruptly. 'So you were just leading me on? You know what they call women like you?' His eyes blazed with anger.

'No!' Sharon protested, pulling him back into his seat. 'No, it was nothing like that. It's just that it's all so sudden. I'm still in shock. I need a while for it to sink in before I can make up my mind about what we do next. That's all.'

She kissed him reassuringly.

Phil relaxed again. 'Okay.'

Sharon checked her watch. 'I'd better go and tidy up a bit in the bedroom, in case …' He nodded, understanding.

She went upstairs, head in a whirl. Her fantasies had always stopped at the point when she and Phil made love. How the story progressed after that had never crossed her mind. They all had a share in the Vic; she and Phil couldn't just run off and leave it. Even if she wanted to. Which she didn't, Sharon reflected, straightening the duvet. The Vic was the one thing in her life she would always be faithful to, whatever she did with her men. She plumped up the pillows and was about to switch off the light when the door opened and Grant walked in.

'That's what I like to see – ready for action,' he said, embracing her.

'What the hell do you think you're playing at?' Sharon erupted.

'Sssh.' He kissed her forcefully, a deep, probing kiss that left her struggling to draw breath.

'For God's sake, get off, Grant, you pig!' Sharon tried to push him away but Grant would not let go.

'No more fighting,' he said. 'From now on it's gonna be different.' He stroked her hair. 'I love you Sharon.'

'Don't give me that,' she snorted. 'Another – what, twelve hours? Twenty-four, max, and you'll be off again. What kind of a mug do you think I am, Grant?'

He stared at her, his expression intense, and for the first time she noticed that he had tears in his eyes.

'I'm sorry for leaving you like that. I know you hate it. I won't do it again, I promise.' He tipped her chin up and gazed into her face as if trying to read her thoughts. 'I'll do anything to patch this up, Sharon, anything you say. Just don't freeze me out, please.' Sharon looked away, unable to meet his eyes. 'We were so good before, weren't we?' Grant pleaded. 'Before all this baby stuff. Let's go back to then, start afresh.'

Sharon looked past him at the doorpost, which still bore the pencil marks where Den had marked off her height as a girl. The memory made her smile. She saw her young self, all pigtails and puppy fat, demanding, 'How much have I grown, Daddy, how much have I grown?' and Den, laughing, going, 'This much', putting his arm up high. Well, you're a big girl now, Sharon thought. You've got to live in the real world, not some silly fantasy. She turned back to Grant, deciding.

'This is absolutely your last chance.'

'You won't regret it.' He slipped off her silky dressing gown and pulled down the straps of her slip. 'I'm going to prove to you just how good I can be.'

Sharon, numb, closed her eyes and let him take her, hoping to God he couldn't smell his brother on her skin.

Phil did not need to be told Sharon's answer. He had heard Grant come in through the back door and go straight upstairs. He had heard the row that followed. Then he heard it go quiet and waited, holding his breath. Sharon did not come down. Phil poured himself more whisky. Later, much later, when he had drunk enough to obliterate the pain, he went up to his lonely bed, stumbling past Sharon and Grant's closed bedroom door. All he could hear now was the soft, regular breathing of two people sleeping. The thought of Sharon wrapped in Grant's arms was almost more than he could bear.

Living with her decision became a nightmare for Sharon. The tension between her and Grant was tearing her apart. Unable to sleep, she drifted through the days pale and exhausted. Michelle thought Grant was taking his fists to her and tackled Sharon on the subject, but for once Sharon did not open up, even to her. Finally, the strain became too much to bear. With shaking hands, Sharon dialled the Arches.

'Tell Grant I want to see him,' she said, when Phil

answered. 'Now.' She sat down on an upturned crate, her legs suddenly weak, and waited.

But it was Phil who turned up, not Grant. 'You're going to do it, aren't you? You're going to tell him …' His voice interrupted Sharon's thoughts as she sat in the Vic yard staring at the dust dancing in a shaft of sunlight. She nodded, refusing to look at him.

'*Why*?' he demanded, furious.

'I've got to do something, Phil. I'm going half out of my mind. I can't carry on pretending …'

'Pretending what?'

'That I still love him.'

'But you don't have to pretend,' he said sarcastically. 'You do still love him. That's what you said. He told me. Pleased as Punch about it, he was.'

'Yeah. That's what I said,' Sharon repeated dully. She dared to look at him for a second, then dropped her gaze.

'What we done, Sharon … you can't undo the past,' Phil said, more gently.

'Would you want to?'

'That's not the point.'

'Would you want to?' she insisted. 'Do you wish we hadn't slept together?' Phil looked at her, shaking his head. 'The other night you said you loved me,' Sharon reminded him.

'You made your choice. And you chose Grant. So there ain't much use telling him anything different, is there?' Phil turned on his heel, almost colliding with Grant.

'Sharon?' He saw the tears in her eyes and came closer. 'You alright? What's the matter?'

'I feel terrible. I've got a splitting headache,' she lied, brushing past him. 'Can you cover for me for a while? I've got to go and lie down.'

Sharon seemed to have recovered by the evening, though Grant wasn't too keen on her working. He was concerned about Phil, too – he'd been silent all day and was walking around with a face like thunder.

'I wish you'd try and talk to him,' he said to Sharon, as they stood behind the bar.

'Me? Why?'

'You've seen him. There's obviously something on his mind. I don't know what it is. I think it's a woman, but I can't be sure. He won't tell me what's up – just bites my head off. But perhaps he'll tell you.' Grant put away a glass. 'I don't suppose you've got any idea what it might be? Or who?'

'No,' she replied, moving off down the bar to serve Ricky and Sam. 'Why should I?'

Grant sighed and went over to serve Nigel and Dot Cotton, with whom he had put in a word suggesting Nigel as a potential lodger. Nigel was confident of winding her round his little finger, but Grant had his doubts. Especially when he heard the grilling Dot was giving him.

'No dirty underwear to be left soaking in basin or bath,' began Dot, reading from a long list.

'We talked about that.'

'And no washing up to be left in the kitchen sink.'

'And that,' Nigel sighed.

'Number three. No playing of loud music after the hour of ten o'clock,' Dot pronounced, taking no notice of him.

Nigel ran his hand through his Kevin Keegan curls. 'I'm not a teenager, Mrs Cotton …'

'Number four, no entertaining of female guests.'

'But Mrs Cotton …'

'Let me finish,' Dot said, batting him down. 'No entertaining of female friends without prior arrangement. That's fair, isn't it?' Nigel looked doubtful. 'Give me a chance to get out of your way,' she whispered loudly. Nigel still didn't look convinced. Dot sallied on, 'Number five, no overnight visitors.'

'What, never?'

'Never.'

'Not even in exceptional circumstances?' Nigel was clearly

desperate now.

Dot arched her eyebrows. 'What sort of exceptional circumstances was you thinking of?'

'Er …' Nigel looked around wildly, hoping for inspiration. 'Well, say I had a friend round for a meal and they missed the last bus home?'

'Would that be a female friend or a male friend?' Dot enquired graciously.

'Either.'

'They could always catch the night bus.'

Nigel gulped. 'They don't come along very often.'

She considered this. 'Well, if it was an emergency, I suppose they could sleep on your floor.'

He smiled broadly. 'That's what I wanted to hear.'

'Unless it was a female friend, in which case I could probably make space on my floor.' Having got to the last of her commandments, Dot put her list in her handbag and snapped it shut. 'I'll have a tomato juice, please. I'll be over there.'

Grant, who had been earwigging, leaned over the bar and said, 'Still eating out of your hand is she?'

That night, Sharon moved out of their bed and into the spare room. She claimed she didn't want to disturb Grant, saying her insomnia made her restless, but Grant didn't buy that. He always slept right through it. There's only one other thing it could be, Grant reasoned, as he lay staring up at the ceiling. The thought of it made him break out into a cold sweat. She must have another bloke. It would fit in. Every time he touched her recently, she had pulled away, making excuses. She was moody, tearful, tired. He turned over and smashed his fist into the pillow, hitting it with such force that it burst. Watching the goosedown stuffing float to the floor like snowflakes, he felt an icy rage descend. *If Sharon is seeing anyone else, I'll kill him*, he vowed. *And then I'll kill her.*

Phil couldn't stand the situation with the three of them at the

Vic any more than Sharon. Eating breakfast together, sharing a bathroom, watching TV, all the things they had done before, were fraught with tension. Whenever they were alone in a room together, he didn't know whether to run out or sweep her into his arms. There had been times when he'd had the opportunity to do the latter, but he didn't know what was going on with her any more. From her hollow eyes and haunted face he knew she wasn't happy, but he felt powerless to intervene. Their guilty secret weighed down on him heavily. As much as he wanted to be with Sharon, he did not want to betray his brother. It was a condition of the pact they had made as boys and neither of them had ever broken it. The pact had been sworn in blood. Then, Phil had saved Grant's life. If Grant knew he was sleeping with Sharon, Phil did not think he would stop to remember that.

There was only one solution: he was going to have to move out of the Vic. Then, at least, he wouldn't have to undergo the temptation and the torture of being with Sharon every day. When, later that morning, Ricky and Sam were evicted from the squat – which they had shared with Mark Fowler and the troublemaking Mandy – Phil took his opportunity. Angry at having found their sister out on the street, he suggested the pair of them move in to the Vic and take his room. An unusually magnanimous Grant scuppered Phil's plan by insisting there was room enough for all of them. Clocking the panic in his brother's eyes as he pleaded with him to stay, Phil realized Grant needed him to be there as much as he needed to go. Ironically, it was for the same reason.

'Look, Sharon, I know something's up.' Michelle leaned her elbows on the bar. 'You're as miserable as sin and it's been going on for far too long. I hate seeing you like this. When are you going to tell me what it's all about?'

Sharon, who was busy shining the tables with polish, froze. ''Chelle, I can't. It's got too big, too complicated …'

Michelle came over and pulled up a chair. Whisking the

duster out of Sharon's hand she said, 'Well, start small then. What are we talking about?'

Sharon hesitated, glancing over her shoulder. 'It's Phil.'

'Phil?' Michelle looked puzzled. 'You're always going on about Phil. I thought Grant was the problem.'

'Yes. No. I mean, they both are.'

Michelle cocked her head. 'Are you saying what I think you're saying?'

'Might be. Depends on how vivid your imagination is.' Sharon smiled feebly.

'Ain't we had this conversation before? When Phil moved in? You're not ... not with both of them?'

Sharon screeched with laughter, the absurd idea releasing her pent-up emotions. 'No!' She mopped her eyes, then became more serious. 'But I did sleep with Phil, once. And now I can't get him out of my head.'

'I don't believe you just said that,' Michelle said, goggling.

'It's true.'

'This calls for a drink. May I?' Michelle poured them both doubles and brought them back. 'What are you going to do?'

'I don't know. I thought I'd made me mind up to stick with Grant, but it's hopeless ...' Sharon knocked back her gin. 'I've tried to feel guilty, 'Chelle. I've tried to forget all about it. But I can't.'

'What on earth are you trying to do, Sharon? Commit ritual suicide? You know Grant's gonna carve you into little pieces when he finds out. And I doubt there'll be much of Phil left either by the time he's finished.' Michelle slammed down her glass. 'For crying out loud, wake up, Sharon! You're in way over your head.'

Sharon, hurt, retaliated. 'You're not exactly whiter-than-white yourself, are you? It was my dad you slept with on this very carpet, I seem to recall.'

'Den wasn't violent. I'm not preaching morals, here, Sharon, I'm talking common sense.'

'Well, it's too late for that.'

'No, it's not. Nip it in the bud right now.'

'It's not that easy.' Sharon buried her face in her hands. 'I know it's dangerous, but it's out of my control. I can't just switch it off. I love him.'

'Oh, Sharon.' Michelle proffered a hankie. 'You're my friend and I don't want to lose you. But if you really want Phil, you know there's only one option, don't you? You'll have to leave Walford behind for good.'

22 October 1992 was going to be a red-letter day, Sharon decided, waking up and stretching. She had spent most of the night tossing and turning and had come to a decision. This time, she knew it was the right one.

A knock on the door interrupted her thoughts.

'Morning, birthday girl.' Grant brought her breakfast in on a tray, together with a pile of cards and a couple of wrapped parcels. Sharon opened them and found a gold chain from Grant and a box of chocolates from Phil, who was obviously downplaying his affection.

'Thanks,' she said, kissing him politely on the cheek. Grant beamed. 'That's not all. I'm taking you out later. Have your gladrags on for eight.'

Sharon did not have a chance to talk to Phil all day. By the time evening came round, she was as tense as a coiled spring and convinced he was avoiding her. Praying Grant hadn't booked them a candlelit dinner for two, she was delighted when he escorted her to Michelle's and she found the whole of Albert Square waiting to celebrate her twenty-third birthday with a surprise party. She was even more delighted to see Phil there, although he seemed agitated and answered her questions about his earlier whereabouts in words of one syllable.

When Grant disappeared, apparently to get more drinks, Sharon seized the opportunity to get Phil alone and, observing him go outside, followed him.

'Phil, wait!' she called softly, as he strode across the road towards the Vic. He swung round, startled.

'Sharon! Why ain'tcha at the party?'

'Because I want to be with you.' She looked at him steadily. 'For ever.'

He dropped his eyes. 'It's too late, Sharon. You made your bed. You gotta lie in it.'

'I lie in an empty bed in the spare room, Phil. You know that. But in my dreams you're there, too.'

'Leave it out.' He glanced around nervously. 'I'm not prepared to be second-best, Sharon. You tried one brand of Mitchell and he didn't suit so now you think you'll try the other version. No thanks.'

'Phil ... ?'

He waved her away. 'Go back to your mates. It's over between us.' Sharon, cut to the quick, ran into the empty Vic, sobbing.

The pub had been closed early for the party and she felt suddenly, desperately alone. A sharp bark from upstairs reminded her that Roly had been locked in the kitchen. Sharon took him into the lounge and buried her face in his curls. He licked her face anxiously, stubby powder-puff tail beating the table, then ran to the door, whining. Sharon, who was crying as if her heart would break, did not register the fuss he was making until she smelled the smoke. But by then it was too late. Coming out onto the landing, she saw a bright orange glow dancing on the wall of the staircase and realized, to her horror, the bar was alight. The roar of the flames was terrifyingly loud and thick, acrid smoke was billowing towards her, making it impossible to see down the stairs. Coughing violently, she wetted a teatowel to hold over her face and stumbled back into the lounge, slamming the door. As she did so, there was an almighty explosion down below and the sound of glass shattering. Spluttering, she ran to the window and threw it open, gulping the cold night air. People were already beginning to gather below. She saw their wondering faces and screamed with all the breath left in her body.

'For God's sake, help me, somebody! I'm trapped!'

CHAPTER THIRTEEN

A fire crew arrived on the scene within minutes – the longest minutes of Grant's life. He tried to climb the ladder himself to get Sharon, but Phil hauled him off, shouting at him to let the professionals do their job. Sharon, suffering from smoke inhalation, was whipped away in a waiting ambulance, accompanied by a frantic Grant. Phil, who had caught her eye just before they slipped the oxygen mask on, could only stand and watch helplessly as the flashing blue light vanished from view, a rescued Roly whimpering at his heels.

For Sharon, although the effects of the smoke were bad, the psychological scars went far deeper. She was scared to return to the gutted pub – her sleep was racked with nightmares about being trapped in the blazing building – and the thought of her home reduced to a charred mess had sent her into a depression.

When Grant visited her in the hospital the next day she was weak and weepy and refused to believe his lie that all the Vic needed was a coat of paint.

'First I lost my dad. Then my mum disappeared. The only thing that ever stayed the same was the pub.'

'It's still the same,' Grant said, trying to reassure her.

'No it ain't. It ain't ever going to be the same, is it? It's ruined.' Sharon turned her face away, tears soaking her pillow. 'I've got nothing left, now. Not a thing.'

'You've still got me.'

She shut her eyes. 'I've got nothing.'

Grant took Sharon away to the seaside to recuperate while Phil, Michelle and Clyde oversaw the refurbishments at the

Vic, but there was still a lot of work to be done by the time they got back. Sharon took one look at the bar and went upstairs without saying a word.

Michelle followed her. 'How was the trip?'

'Good.'

'And you're fully recovered?'

'Yeah, hundred per cent.' Sharon stroked the singed wallpaper with a fingertip. 'Grant keeps saying it'll be better 'cos we can get the place done up how we want, but I liked it just the way it was.'

'So did I,' Michelle agreed, following her into the living-room. 'How are things with Grant?' she added casually.

'Okay.'

'Well, that's something. And what about Phil?'

Sharon turned to her. 'What about him?'

'You know.'

'It's over. It was stupid of me. It was just one of those things.' Michelle looked sceptical.

'Are you sure?'

'Yeah ... I've had time enough to think, walking along windy beaches for a week.'

'And it's what you want?'

Sharon closed the magazine. 'No. It's what Phil wants. So who am I to argue?' She gestured towards the smoke–damaged ceiling. 'I'll just carry on living with Grant in this imitation bonfire. Why not? What else can I do?'

'We could go out tonight.'

When Grant heard about Sharon and Michelle's plans, he was immediately mistrustful. He had been counting on spending the evening making things up with Sharon. She hadn't been responsive in Brighton, but he had hopes that once they were back home ... The fact that they were going to the college to see a band made him even more paranoid. The word 'student' was enough to make his hackles rise – and that was on a good day. On a bad day, he ate them for breakfast.

He was even less happy when Sharon appeared, dressed in a short, tight, hot-pink skirt, low-cut blouse and high heels, and more makeup than she'd managed to put on all week when they were away. She kissed him on the cheek and tottered out with Michelle, leaving Grant muttering into his beer about standards slipping and the country going down the pan.

'What you on about?' asked Phil, who was helping Clyde out behind the makeshift bar.

'Society … relationships … they're all wrong these days.'

'I don't think the break did you any good. Sounds like the air got to your brain,' Phil laughed.

Grant got up, his shoulders hunched, and regarded him balefully. 'I know what I'm talking about … a bit of respect, that's all I ask.'

Phil stopped laughing. When Grant started talking about wanting respect, there was always, always trouble.

By one o'clock in the morning, the girls had not returned. Grant, who had been waiting up in the living-room in the dark, imagining every possible scenario − each one of which involved Sharon and a shaggy-haired student − suddenly determined to take action.

Knocking up a bemused Clyde, he headed for his car. 'Where are we going?' Clyde panted, running to catch up and trying to pull on a sweatshirt at the same time.

'The naffin' college,' Grant snarled, gunning the engine.

There was a security guard on the gate at the halls of residence. Clyde assumed Grant would give up then and there, but Grant was in *Terminator* mode, unstoppable. Getting out of the car, he stole along the outside of the perimeter wall, Clyde creeping nervously in his shadow.

When they reached an unlit section, Grant flexed his muscles and glanced quickly about. 'Right. Give us a bunk up.' Sitting on top of the wall, he pulled Clyde up after him.

'We don't even know if they're in there,' Clyde protested, worried about being caught.

'Somebody will know where they've gone.'

'It's two o'clock now. They'll all be asleep.'

'Then we'll have to wake them up.'

Inside the first block they came across a girl in a dressing-gown shuffling along the corridor carrying a hot-waterbottle.

'Oi!' Grant was in no mood for niceties. 'I'm looking for someone.'

'What?' the girl peered sleepily at them through her fringe.

'She's small, blonde, short skirt, high heels … friend of Michelle Fowler's.'

'Oh, yeah.' The student laughed knowingly, her tone mocking. 'Couldn't miss *her*. Stood out like a neon sign.'

'Well?'

'Try Christian James. She was with him earlier. Next floor up. His name's on the door.'

The first time, Grant knocked. When there was no answer, he thumped the door with his fist. The third time, he kicked it, making the door shake. Finally, he stood back against the corridor wall and, with a bellow of rage, slammed into the it, busting the lock. The door flew open, revealing a darkened room. Grant flicked on the light switch. There, in the single bed, was Michelle with a dark-haired youth. She pulled the sheet up under her chin, glowering at Grant defiantly, but when Clyde appeared from behind him, she blanched.

'Where's Sharon?' Grant thundered.

'Well, she clearly isn't here, is she? So why don't you leave us alone?' the student retorted. 'And who the hell do you think you are, anyway, barging in like that?'

'I'm her boyfriend. Or I *was* …' Clyde looked at Michelle with disgust.

'Leave her alone. I could call security …'

'Don't even think about it.' Clyde bunched his fist. 'You'll be mincemeat way before then.'

'Jack … forget it.' Michelle laid a restraining hand on his arm.

'Yeah, you heard what she said. You ain't exactly in a position to argue, are yer?' Grant thrust his face at them. 'Neither of you,' he continued, looking between them menacingly. 'So come on, then. Tell me. Where is she, the slut? Which of your greasy little cronies is she doing it with?'

'She ain't "doing it" with anyone,' Michelle protested.

'You do surprise me.' Grant held her jaw between iron fingers, forcing her to look up at him. 'Thing is, I heard different. Practically advertising it, that's what I heard.'

'Let me go.' Michelle struggled, but Grant gripped her face harder. 'You're hurting me. Ow! Let me go, Grant!'

Grant had her nose to nose with him. 'Not until you tell me.'

Michelle started to scream, 'Somebody help ...' but he clamped a hand over her mouth.

'She's in the rec room with the others,' Jack intervened, frightened. Grant let go.

'There you are.' Sharon dispensed the remainder of her smuggled-out gin bottle into Christian's glass.

'That's favouritism. What about the rest of us?' Nick, one of the other students, moaned.

'Sorry. All gone.' She held the bottle upside-down. 'And anyway, Christian's been nicest to me.'

'Not as nice as I want to be.' Christian, a tall, blonde, athletic hunk, put his arm round her neck and tried to kiss her. Sharon, giggling, pushed him away.

'Hey, I'm a married woman. People will talk.'

'Spoilsport. I don't give up that easily, you know. What's your old man like, anyway?'

'What do you want to know for?'

'Is he big?'

'He's not small.'

'But he doesn't object to you being here?'

'He doesn't know.'

A few seconds later, Grant exploded into the room, homing

in on Christian like a guided missile and smashing him against the snooker table.

It took four students and Sharon to prise Grant off Christian, and the furore woke up most of the corridor.

'This is why I cannot stand your behaviour – your stupid, jealous, violent temper!' Sharon yelled as Grant, rolling his eyes, tried to take another poke at Christian.

An audience was gathering around them, students pouring into the rec room and lining the walls as if Sharon and Grant were putting on some sort of bizarre, late-night improvised theatre.

'What about your behaviour? What about what *I* have to put up with? You, behaving like a complete and utter tart, an East-End slag desperate for whatever piece of trash she can pick up?' Grant cast a murderous look at Christian, who was still in a daze.

'How dare you!' Sharon went to slap him, but Grant caught her arm. She shook him off. 'It's one rule for you and another rule for me, isn't it? It's perfectly okay for you to disappear all night doing God-knows-what. But if I'm not back by eleven there's hell to pay. You're a chauvinist and a bully!'

Someone cheered, causing Grant to swing round. The crowd surged back suddenly.

'Come on,' he barked. 'We ain't staying here.'

Sharon didn't budge. 'Oh, no. If you're gonna hit me, I want witnesses.'

'Don't tempt me.' Grant hooked her arm under his and half-dragged, half-carried her out.

'Grant … we were just talking. We weren't doing anything,' Sharon pleaded, her bravado disappearing as he frogmarched her down the corridor.

'D'you think I don't know what you're up to?' Grant stopped, pinning her against the wall. 'You're obviously gagging for it. So who's the lucky man if it ain't that wally?'

'There isn't one.'

'How do I know?'

'There isn't. You'll just have to trust me on that.' Sharon wiped her wet cheeks with the back of her hand. 'Where's Michelle?' she ventured at last.

'Oh, so we're back to her, now, are we?' Grant grimaced. 'Well at least I know what she's up to. We caught her on the job.'

Michelle was sitting outside on a bench with Clyde. Clyde had his head in his hands. She had managed to prevent him hitting Jack, who had fled from the room in his underpants, but in the row that followed they had said things to each other that couldn't be unsaid. Now there seemed nothing else left to say.

Grant and Sharon were silhouetted against the lights of the hall, many of which were still blazing thanks to the disturbance. Grant had Sharon by the shoulders and was shouting,

'Do you know what I've gone through, for you? All the things I've done – for you? To make you happy? To buy you that blasted pub? I've got involved with robberies. I've got meself arrested for murder. I've got the insurance pay-out for the Vic …'

'You what?' Sharon said quietly. She stared at Grant. He stared back, challenging her. 'I thought you said the fire was caused by travellers? Are you telling me you started it deliberately? The fire that nearly killed me and almost destroyed my home?'

'Yeah. But I did it because …'

'I don't want to hear!' Sharon threw up her hands. 'Just don't ever come anywhere near me again.'

Michelle stood up and waved her over. They took in each other's situations at once. Linking arms, they walked off together, leaving Grant and Clyde alone.

'Well,' Sharon said, giving Michelle's arm a squeeze. 'It's just you and me again, gal. We must do this again sometime.'

★

After that, the atmosphere in the Vic was almost as icy as the wintry weather outside. With Michelle and Clyde not talking, Sharon and Grant at loggerheads and a morose Phil trying to keep out of Sharon's way, not even the pub's grand reopening could lift their spirits. Finally, Grant, wound up by Sharon ignoring him, could take it no more.

'I'm sick of this,' he raged to Phil over a lunchtime pint. 'I want it sorted, one way or the other.'

'Just calm down, will yer?'

'And I'm sick of you telling me what I should and shouldn't do,' Grant rounded on him. 'Ain't it about time you started sticking up for me?'

'All I'm saying is you don't want to make things worse, that's all. It's got nothing to do with taking sides.'

'That's a joke,' Grant snorted. 'How much worse can it get?'

'That's because every time you've had a chance to sort things out, you've gone at it like a bull in a china shop. You've got to give things time to settle down ...'

'And if they don't ...?'

'Then at least you can say it wasn't down to you,' Phil replied, squinting into the middle distance.

'The way she is at the minute, I'm not even sure I want her any more.'

Phil, seeing Grant's anger was really a mask for his despair, felt even guiltier. 'You don't mean that.'

'Don't I?' Grant looked up at him and for a moment Phil saw his small brother again, vulnerable and afraid, lashing out before he himself got hit even harder. 'I've just had enough, Phil.'

What have I done? Phil thought, torn apart inside by living a double lie. We're all of us miserable and it's my fault and I don't know how to right it.

The showdown happened an hour later outside the Vic, when Sharon, who had been out all day, returned to the pub in a black cab.

'Where have you been?' demanded Grant, tanked up after his lunchtime session.

'None of your business.' She went to walk past him, but he put an arm out to stop her.

'I asked you a question …'

'And I told you …'

'You're my wife!' Grant shouted, loud enough to draw the attention of several of the market traders.

'Not any more I'm not,' Sharon returned grimly.

'You what?'

'You heard. Now move out of my way, Grant. It's over. Finished.'

Phil, as usual, restrained his brother. 'Come on, Grant, let her in …'

Grant stepped aside reluctantly, but as she went to cross over the threshold he announced, 'I think you've forgotten something.'

'And what would that be?' Sharon replied, haughty.

'Two-thirds of this place is in mine and Phil's name. You want to be single again, you better find a job as well, because as of now the Vic is up for sale.'

It would be easier – and more rewarding – to work as a peace-maker for the United Nations, thought Phil, trying to negotiate a compromise between Grant and Sharon. At least he'd be given a flak jacket. Trying to dodge the abuse being hurled about the Vic was wearing him down. It took several days of heated discussions, but finally Grant agreed to think things over for a month and make a decision after Christmas.

'That's the best I can do,' Phil told Sharon. 'With any luck it'll all blow over and he'll let it drop.'

'And what about us? Where do we fit into this, Phil?'

'Leave it, Sharon,' he said sharply. 'I ain't gonna talk about it.'

By Christmas Eve, Walford was once again in seasonal overdrive. The market was awash with novelty Christmas toys, including a consignment of suspiciously cheap electronic games and a positively indecent flashing Santa. A distracted Dot Cotton, preoccupied with Nick's forthcoming murder trial, marshalled her carol singers (including a reluctant Nigel) for a concert in the Square. Meanwhile, a department-store Santa got drunk in the Vic and was punched by Pat Butcher when he turned nasty in the back of her cab. Grant, likewise, got into the Christmas spirit by picking a fight with a rowdy punter, prompting Phil to pack him off to Scotland on his annual fishing trip to cool his heels.

Pre-Christmas tension had also affected the Fowler household. Michelle, who was secretly missing Clyde, also had to fend off the advances of Jack, who had been pestering her since the college debacle. Pauline and Arthur were barely on speaking terms over Mrs Hewitt, a relationship Arthur was being tempted to consummate while Pauline was out singing 'Silent Night'. Pete Beale, Pauline's twin, was seething about Kathy going off on a winter break to Tenerife with 'Tricky Dicky', the slimy market inspector. The only person who actually seemed to be enjoying himself was Ian Beale, who had undergone a Scrooge-like transformation after a clandestine meeting with the ghost of Christmas past, in his case, his ex-wife Cindy, who had run off two years earlier and was now single again.

Thanks to the mulled wine laid on for the carol singers, the revels at the Vic were in full swing. Nigel had just launched into an impromptu rendition of 'The Wombling Song' when a telephone call brought shattering news. Pat Butcher had been arrested by the police for drunk-driving after knocking down a teenage girl in her cab. The girl was seriously ill in hospital and Pat was being held in the cells. Frank rushed off to the station, a worried man. After that, the festivities were more subdued.

With Grant out of the way, Sharon and Phil found themselves thrown together again. At first, the atmosphere was strained, and with the Vic busy, it was several days before they relaxed and opened up to each other.

It was Phil who eventually took the initiative, one night after closing.

'Go and sit down, you're all in,' he ordered, noticing Sharon's exhausted face. 'I'll be up in a minute.'

'Thanks.' She went upstairs and collapsed wearily on the sofa, closing her eyes. She was just starting to drift off when she heard Phil's measured tread on the landing, followed by the soft 'pop' of a wine bottle being uncorked.

'Mmmm, my favourite sound,' she said, as Phil handed her a glass of red wine. She took a sip. 'This is the good stuff.'

'You deserve the best.' He sat beside her and raised his glass. 'To us.'

Sharon regarded him warily. 'Do you really mean that?'

He put his arm around her. 'Yes, I really do.'

She clinked her glass against his. 'I'll drink to that.'

They sat without talking, Sharon's head on Phil's shoulder, listening to the Diana Ross CD he had put on. 'Are you trying to tell me something?' Sharon asked quietly.

'Like what?' He stroked her cheek with a finger, making her quiver.

'"We don't have tomorrow. But we had yesterday",' she said, quoting the lyrics.

Phil laughed. 'That wasn't intentional. I just like the music.' He pulled her closer.

'It's smoochy.' Sharon gazed into his eyes, trying to read what was going on behind them. 'We make a good team, you and me, don't we?'

'Yeah, we do,' he whispered, kissing her, a long, lingering kiss that set her senses on fire.

'Shall we ...?' Sharon was just about to suggest they moved to the bedroom when the back door slammed and heavy footsteps stomped up the stairs. They sprang apart guiltily just as Ricky burst into the room, pie-eyed and ranting, 'Sam's going off for the weekend to a poncy house in the country with some toffee-nosed photographer.'

'On a shoot?' Phil asked, apparently unruffled by the intrusion.

'Yeah.'

'So why is that a problem?'

'Well you know. When the cat's away an' all that ...' Ricky said lamely.

'Ricky, it's the mice that play. The ones left behind.'

Ricky furrowed his brow. 'Why are you laughing?'

'I don't know, Ricky, mate. I really don't know.'

An hour or so later, Phil, clad only in a pair of boxer shorts, was about to open Sharon's bedroom door when Ricky bumped into him on the landing.

'Er ... Sharon wasn't feeling too hot, I'm just checking to see if she wants anything,' Phil lied, cursing Ricky's timing. Clearly his relationship with Sharon was fated.

Nothing had been resolved by the time Grant got back, to Sharon's frustration. The snatched moments of intimacy she had shared with Phil made her all the more determined to be with him, but he was dragging his feet over making a commitment, racked with guilt at betraying his brother.

Grant returned in bullish mood, his mind made up about the Vic and his marriage.

'So what's the plan?' Phil asked over tea in the café.

'Sharon goes.'

'Just like that?'

'I'm not offering her any choice.'

Phil sighed. 'The Vic's her home.'

'If she won't go, we put the pub on the market and sell up. There's no future in us staying together.' Grant set his jaw.

'Look, don't you think you should talk about it . . .'

Grant got up. 'We're past that, bruv. Well past that. Just tell her to be in the Vic at three o'clock this afternoon. We're going to have a board meeting.'

★

When Phil warned Sharon about Grant's scheme, she did not appear shocked. She did, however, put one over on him. Up until then, he hadn't witnessed her hard streak, so when she said, 'I'll do whatever it takes to keep the Vic,' he wasn't prepared for what came next.

'I don't see what you can do,' he faltered. 'I mean, if I could think of anything to persuade him …'

'Oh, come on, Phil. Without your money we couldn't have bought this place. Just tell him you want to keep it.'

She looked at him, unsmiling. 'If you don't, I may have to tell him about us.'

'You wouldn't.'

'I want this pub, Phil.'

At the board meeting, Grant and Sharon slugged it out, both determined not to give an inch.

'Alright,' Grant announced at last. 'Phil's got a share in this place, let's have a bit of democracy.' He turned to Phil, who was sitting opposite Sharon. 'If my ex-wife won't sell to us, should awe put the pub on the market or not?'

'Phil?' Sharon said confidently, lifting her chin.

'Looks like you've got the deciding vote, mate.' Grant looked at his brother, equally confident. Phil hesitated. 'Well?' Grant pressed.

Unable to meet Sharon's eyes, Phil called her bluff. 'I think we should sell the Vic.'

CHAPTER FOURTEEN

When it came to the crunch, Sharon couldn't do it. Telling Grant about her and Phil wouldn't achieve anything, she decided. Not now. With the Mitchell brothers closing ranks it was obvious where Phil's loyalties lay. Defeated, she packed her bags and headed off to Angie's to lick her wounds in the Florida sunshine, leaving Clyde in charge of the Vic.

For Clyde, the responsibility was a mixed blessing. It gave him something to occupy his mind after the shock news that Nick Cotton had been found not guilty of Eddie's murder – *he* wouldn't have got off, Clyde thought bitterly – but Grant's jibes were beginning to get to him. Grant had taken advantage of Sharon's absence to fill the pub with his disreputable mates, drinking and playing card games after hours. And as if that wasn't enough, Jack was hanging around and making a nuisance of himself. Clyde could tell Michelle wasn't interested but Jack was too thick-skinned to take the hint.

Things came to a head after one particularly rowdy late-night gambling session orchestrated by Grant, which was now drawing a sizeable crowd of East-End wideboys. Clyde, who had opposed the lock-in, walked out. The following day he rang Sharon in the States to tell her the Mitchells were turning the Vic into a dive.

'I'll get the next flight home,' she promised.

Sharon walked back into the middle of a crisis. Police cars were parked outside the Fowlers and Michelle was hysterical with fear: Vicki had been abducted from school and Jack was suspected. An incident room had been set up and Michelle was to make a televised appeal. Watching her plead for her child's life was more than Sharon could bear. Little Vicki was her half-sister. When she looked into her face she saw Den's eyes. If anything had happened to her ...

After twenty achingly long hours, during which the whole of Albert Square joined in the search, Vicki was found, safe and well. She had been taken by a woman who had lost a daughter of her own and, far from being ill-treated, had been showered with gifts and toys. Jack, who had nothing to do with it, turned nasty and was tormenting Michelle with abusive phone calls. Michelle went to pieces and Sharon had to postpone sorting out the Vic to stay with her friend. It was several days later before she walked into the bar, ready to take on Grant.

The first thing she did was to reinstate Clyde.

'You can't do that. I sacked him,' Grant seethed.

Sharon gestured to the doorway. 'Whose name is it above the door? Mine. I am the licensee of this pub and I decide about staffing.' Taking in a gang of skinheads who were swearing and monopolising the juke-box, she added, 'And I decide who can and cannot drink in this pub. So you can tell your mates that as of now they're barred.'

Turning on her heel, she went upstairs with her bags. Grant pounded up the stairs after her.

'Sharon!' He caught her roughly by the arm and bundled her into the kitchen. 'I am going to make this easy for you.' His eyes glinted dangerously. 'Easy if you make the right choice, that is.'

'Are you threatening me?'

'I haven't even started. Sit down.' He pushed her onto a chair. 'Now. You can keep out of my way 'til we sell this gaff and we'll all get along fine. Or ...' he cracked his knuckles, his stare cold, '... you can carry on the way you're going. In which case, things aren't gonna be much fun round here. For you, anyway.'

Sharon, quaking inside but determined not to be bullied, retaliated. 'I ain't going to stand by and watch you run this pub into the ground, if that's what you want.'

'What I want? Since when have you ever bothered about what I want? You've never really cared for me, have you?' He smashed his fist down on the table, sending crockery flying and spilling a carton of milk all over the floor. 'You've only been interested in one thing all along. You were even prepared to marry me for it. It's always been the Vic, hasn't it, Sharon?' He hauled her to her feet by her lapels, holding her close to his face. 'Go on, tell me I'm wrong,' he hissed. 'Tell me that you loved me, not this fleapit. Well?' He shook her hard.

'Grant!' Sharon struggled to get free. There was a ripping noise as her lapel tore but Grant refused to let go.

'I'm waiting.'

A wave of anger rose inside her. 'You were right the first time. There was never any contest, Grant.' She laughed derisively at him. 'The Vic wins hands down.'

Grant's face contorted with fury. 'You bitch,' he spat, his eyes narrowing. 'You bloody little bitch.' With an effort, Sharon managed to wrench herself free, leaving the lapel in Grant's hand. She wasn't fast enough. Grant's fist seemed to come out of nowhere, the force of his punch sending her crashing to the ground. She lay, face-down, in a puddle of milk, too numb even to cry.

Sharon did her best to disguise the bruising with makeup, but Michelle spotted it almost straight away.

'What have you done to your face?' she asked when she came into the pub. Sharon kept her head lowered. 'Nothing. It's always been like this.'

'How many years have I known you?'

'Too many.'

'Well, then, don't treat me like an idiot – and a blind one at that. How'd you get that bruise?'

'I slipped.' She went off to pick up some glasses, leaving Michelle and Clyde speculating.

'I'm not sure how you slip head first,' Clyde said, watching Sharon. 'But that looks like the work of a good right hand.'

When Michelle pressed her on the subject, Sharon stuck to her story. 'Alright, then, I'll go and ask Grant and Phil, see what they have to say about it,' Michelle threatened.

''Chelle, please.' Sharon, who had said nothing to Phil, glanced around nervously. 'If I tell you what happened, will you promise to drop it?' Michelle nodded. Sharon drew a deep breath. 'We had a bit of a row about this place. Things got a bit heated and ...'

'... And Grant hit you?'

'Yeah.'

'I'll kill him!'

'But you said ...'

'I lied.'

''Chelle, don't, please,' Sharon begged. 'It was just one of those things.'

Michelle's eyebrows shot up.

'So it gives him the right to land you one?'

'It won't happen again.'

'How do you know?'

'He might be a lot of things but he doesn't get off on beating women up.'

'Well then maybe he's changing,' Michelle said, scathing.

'No ... it was a one-off, I know,' Sharon insisted. It sounded to Michelle as if she was trying too hard to convince herself.

After Grant's vicious opening salvo, he waged a war of attrition against Sharon, humiliating her in front of the customers and goading her in private.

'Are you going to work dressed like that?' he asked that evening, as she came into the living room to pick up change for the tills. 'I think you should wear something less tarty. I don't want my pub to be known as a sleaze pit.' Sharon gritted her teeth. 'As co-owner of this place, I have a say in the way the staff dress,' Grant continued. 'Have you looked at yourself lately? You're getting a bit past it for the dolly-bird image.'

'Drop dead.'

'I just want my pub to be run properly ...'

'It's my pub ...'

'... *our* pub then ... and you wearing this ... and this ... and this ...' He walked round her, flicking her clothes, 'what do you think you are, eh?'

'Just leave me alone.'

'You want this pub to be successful, don't you?' Grant sneered. 'Well, I'm only trying to help.'

'Please, Grant ...'

'Oh, "please" is it, now?' Grant continued to circle Sharon. 'Let's get on with our lives.'

'You're missing something here, Sharon.' Grant stopped, looking her up and down disparagingly. 'As things stand, your life is mine and mine is yours ... that is until one of us decides enough is enough.' He recommenced his prowling, flicking at her clothes and hair again, repeating, 'Had enough, yet, Sharon, had enough yet?' She attempted to dodge past him but he snatched the bags of change out of her hands and emptied them on the floor. Trying desperately to hold back her tears, Sharon scrabbled around picking up the money.

'I want you to do me a favour ... when you've had enough, let me know.'

Grant kicked a pile of coins across the floor, sending them spinning under the sofa.

'I've had enough,' Sharon whispered into the carpet.

'Good.'

'But I'm not going to give in. Not to you.' Sharon stood up with as much dignity as she could muster and walked to her room. Once inside, she broke down and howled.

Phil had suspected something was up − Sharon had been avoiding him all day and Grant was in a filthy mood − and when he saw Sharon's face, he quickly realized what it was. Sharon, still protesting that she'd slipped, ran down the stairs after him as he swept into the bar and collared Grant.

'I want a word with you. Outside.' Grant shrugged and

followed Phil out into the Square.

'Answer me yes or no. Did you hit Sharon?' Phil barked, swinging round to face his brother.

'What has she been saying?'

'Yes or no?'

'I'll kill her,' Grant exploded. Phil grabbed him and threw him against the wall. Grant, off-balance and taken by surprise, offered no resistance.

'Yes or no?' Phil snarled. Grant squirmed.

'Yes.'

'You ...' Phil drew back his fist.

'Come on, come on, hit me ... you remember how he used to do it, eh?' Grant taunted him. 'Nothing like turning into your old man, is there? But just remember – I'm your brother.'

'You hit her,' Phil said, holding off.

'She's my wife. She was asking for it.'

Phil, incensed, lunged at Grant again, but this time he was ready and fended him off.

'Alright, alright, I shouldn't have done it. I got carried away.'

'You what?'

'I'm not just going to stand back and let her win. This place is as much mine as hers and I do what I want.'

'And I'm telling you, you don't.'

'I don't see what it's got to do with you,' Grant said defiantly. 'Why this big concern for Sharon?'

Phil hesitated. 'It's not a big concern.'

'Seems that way to me.'

'You were out of order.'

Grant, sensing a new tension in his brother, insisted, 'Sure there's nothing else kicking around here?'

'Like what?'

'I don't know. You tell me.' Grant squared his shoulders. 'Come on, let's get this out in the open. What else is there?'

Phil was thrown, his head full of conflicting emotions. I'm not ready. I haven't prepared him. I don't know what words to use. What will Sharon say? It would be such a relief ...

'You want to know?' he said, at last.

Grant looked at him oddly. 'Yeah, I want to know.'

Three little words, that's all it would take, Phil thought. Three tiny words. 'I love Sharon'. It would be so easy ...

'Come on, then, spit it out, what else is there?' Grant demanded.

Phil opened his mouth to speak, but before he could say anything the door of the pub opened and Sharon came out. She looked between them, her eyes fearful, and Phil knew then that he couldn't go through with it for her sake. After what Grant had done to Sharon already, there was no knowing how he would react.

'Nothing,' he said quietly.

'What?'

'It's nothing.' Phil walked away, heading for the Arches. Grant turned to Sharon and gave her a triumphant smile. It was the smile of a man who scented victory.

The film was a bad action movie he'd seen a hundred times. Grant tore the ring-pull off another can from the dwindling six-pack beside him and tried to catch the girly chatter coming from the kitchen. He knew Michelle had come up to keep an eye on him. She had had a go at him in the bar earlier and now she was hanging about spying on him – and no doubt, bad-mouthing him – in his own home. She obviously thought of herself as Sharon's minder, he thought, riled. Michelle had always been a thorn in his side. It was time he showed her who was boss. He got up and went to the kitchen.

'Talking about me?' Grant eyed Sharon and Michelle, who were sitting at the table with coffee mugs.

'Yeah, that's what you want, isn't it?' Sharon retorted, brave now that Michelle was there. 'I've just been telling 'Chelle how happy I am here. After all, it's not everyone who can claim to have their own personal maniac.' Michelle sniggered. Grant felt his skin flush, the way it always did before blind rage took over.

'What are you laughing at?'

'You.'

'Oh, yeah ... He started to approach her but she wasn't fazed.

'Yeah.'

'Leave off her, Grant,' Sharon said, pushing her chair back hastily.

'She wants to get involved.'

Michelle stood up too, facing him. 'Want to take a pop at me, do you? Go on, then. You like that, don't you? Hitting women.' She stared back, challenging him. Sharon tried to get between them.

'This is between you and me, Grant — not 'Chelle.'

'Alright. Me and you. Fine. How are we going to sort this, Sharon? Come on?' He dropped his glare from Michelle to Sharon, eyeballing her, unblinking. It was a trick he used to frighten off difficult customers — something he'd learned in the army — but Sharon wasn't scared.

'Easy. You open that window and jump.'

Her sarcasm stung him almost to madness. The pulse in his ears was hammering wildly, a driving internal rhythm that blotted out everything but his anger. Grant grabbed hold of Sharon and forced her backwards, towards the window.

'Me? I don't think so. If anybody is jumping, it's going to be you.' Dimly, he registered Michelle attempting to yank him off and swung round. He gave her an almighty shove, sending her reeling across the kitchen.

'You animal,' Sharon yelled, trying to get to Michelle, but Grant was too quick for her.

'You want somebody to jump ... well, go on ... I'll help you.' He pressed her against the window with one hand, the other on the catch, ready to throw it open. Sharon flailed but he had her in an iron grip.

'Come on, then, throw me out,' she dared him. 'If you hate me that much, do it, Grant.'

'Is that what you want? Is that what you really want?' He

opened the catch. A breeze lifted Sharon's hair and he saw apprehension in her eyes.

'You shouldn't do this to me … you shouldn't do this to me,' he roared, pushing against her. Blackness was crowding in on him, the street lights outside receding to fuzzy dots. Sharon screamed in his ear, 'I'm doing nothing, Grant. It's you … not me,' and suddenly, as if a plug had been pulled, the drumbeat of blood ceased.

When the police arrived it didn't take Grant long to figure out that Michelle must have slipped out and shopped him. The female officer insisted on speaking to Sharon alone and led her out of Grant's hearing to the corridor behind the bar. Grant tried to follow, but the male officer put his arm out in front of him.

'What's she talking about?' Grant strained his neck. 'This is my gaff, I have a right to know what's going on.'

He edged forwards and made a headlong dive for the bar, vaulting up on to it and swinging his legs over. The female officer was giving Sharon a card. Grant whipped it out of her hand. 'Domestic violence!' he read, becoming enraged again. 'Are you saying I've been beating up my wife?'

'We're not saying anything …' she began.

The other police officer came round the bar after Grant. 'So how did she get that bruise on her face?'

'Mind your own business.'

The woman turned to Sharon. 'Are you sure you're alright, love?'

Grant scowled. 'Get out.'

'We'll go when we're satisfied your wife is safe,' her colleague said.

'You'll go now.' Grant propelled him back into the bar, Sharon and Michelle, who had been hovering nearby, trying to haul him off. In the melee, Grant lashed out with his fist and caught Michelle a blow to the face. She crumpled to the floor with a cry. The policeman reached for his truncheon but Grant was ready for him, knocking it out of his hand and ramming him across a table. The female officer radioed for backup, but by the time it arrived Grant had given her a bloody nose and the injured policeman was moaning on the floor. It took five more uniforms to get Grant under control.

Sharon, her arm supporting Michelle, staggered out of the Vic in time to see him being manhandled, still bellowing, into the van. An ambulance was also parked outside and the WPC, a handkerchief over her streaming nose, was directing the paramedics into the Vic. Sharon realized she was shaking uncontrollably. She looked at Michelle's puffy face — her eye was closing rapidly — and they threw their arms round each other.

'Oh, 'Chelle,' Sharon said, through chattering teeth, 'This morning I told Grant the only way he'd ever get me out of the Vic was in a wooden box. He very nearly succeeded.'

CHAPTER FIFTEEN

Phil put the phone down from speaking to Marcus Christie, his face clouded.

'Bad news?' Sharon touched his arm gently.

'That copper Grant had a go at — he's got a back injury. Christie reckons they'll charge Grant with GBH.'

'Would ... that would mean prison?'

Phil nodded. Sharon, unable to think of anything to comfort him, sat down on the stairs. Phil was doing his utmost to get Grant out — he was going to the hearing later — but Sharon couldn't face it. She knew how Grant would take her absence, but the thought of having him back in the Vic terrified her. Phil had made it clear he had to stand by his brother and wanted Sharon to attend the hearing to create an impression with the magistrate.

Sharon had refused. 'He got himself into this.'

In the event, the police opposed bail and Grant was remanded in custody. Sharon, left alone again with Phil, felt her spirits rising. With Grant out of the way, they might have a future. She knew how she felt about Phil, but Phil's feelings were harder to read. His loyalties were split down the middle: one minute he was at Grant's throat, defending her; the next, he expected her to stick up for Grant in court. Well, this time, she decided, he would have to choose, once and for all.

'Do you realize it's been four months since ... ?' she began, as they cleared up after closing time.

'Since the last time we were left together to run this place? Yeah, I know. We've been here before, ain't we?'

'Yes.' Sharon felt herself blushing. Phil put a stack of glasses on the bar and came round to where she was washing up. 'Except that, this time, Ricky ain't in the way.'

'No.'

'Which reminds me ...' He slid his arms around her waist. 'We've got some unfinished business.' He kissed her throat, sending a shiver of pleasure through her. 'I've been thinking about you all day.'

'What about me?' Sharon asked breathlessly.

'Everything about you,' he whispered, his lips brushing her neck, 'though it's been such a long time, it was hard to remember all the details.' She felt his body press against her and leaned back into his embrace.

'Do you want a refresher course?' she murmured. Phil slid his hand inside her blouse. 'Yes. Right now.'

One thing marred Phil and Sharon's new-found bliss: the thought of telling Grant. Both agreed it had to be done before their relationship could go public, but neither of them wanted to do it. Their secret was beginning to create tension between them. Phil longed to be demonstrative but Sharon turned into a different person at work, recoiling from his clandestine touches and blanking him with her landlady act.

One lunchtime, annoyed at Sharon for continuing to drag her heels over Grant, Phil let rip. 'You know, I've about had it with all of this.'

Sharon flinched. 'You mean *me*?'

'No, I mean all this sneaking around. Watching what we say and what we do, as if we'd committed some sort of crime or something.' He looked at her searchingly. 'None of this is necessary, Sharon. Not if we tell Grant.'

'We can't,' she replied, a little too quickly for Phil's liking.

'Why not? Give me one good reason.' Sharon did not answer.

Michelle was sympathetic when Sharon went round to see her for advice. 'I wouldn't want to be you, telling Grant you'd been having a scene with his brother.'

'No.' Sharon studied the papers and books spread out on

the kitchen table – Michelle was struggling with an essay – and picked up a pencil. Doodling on a notepad, she admitted, 'I just don't know if I can do it.'

Michelle got up to make them both coffee. 'I'm not surprised. But it's best you do it while he's safely inside, that way at least he can't get at you.' She touched her eye self-consciously, which still bore the faint discolouration of a shiner.

'No,' Sharon corrected her, 'I mean I don't know if I can *do* it.'

Michelle almost dropped the mugs she was getting out of the cupboard. 'What do you mean, at all?' Sharon nodded. 'You're joking, aren't you? You can't bottle out now, not after all this time and everything that's happened.'

Sharon gave her a rueful smile. 'Can't I?'

'And do what instead?'

'Dunno. Go back to the way we were before.'

'What, you and Grant ...?' Michelle stared at her, disbelieving. 'For months, you've been telling me you're in love with Phil.'

'Yeah, but ...'

'Well, either you are or you ain't.'

'I am, but you see ...'

'And Phil loves you,' Michelle persisted, trying to hammer out the logic in Sharon's unfathomable argument.

'So he says.'

'Oh, come on, Sharon, it's obvious. I'm just surprised everyone else hasn't noticed.' Michelle paused, letting this sink in. 'So, the two of you love each other, right? But you're still married to Grant. And yes, he's going to go ape when you tell him, but it's got to be done because with Phil you know you've got the chance of real happiness.'

'Yeah, I have.' Sharon sounded convinced now.

'Well, then, grab it with both hands.' Michelle plonked herself down beside Sharon. 'I shouldn't have to tell you this, you've told me enough times. What's the matter with you?'

'I only wish I knew.'

*

Instead of going straight back to the Vic, Sharon sat down on the bench in the garden in the middle of the Square. She knew she should be inside, helping Phil — with Grant gone, they were frantic, and Phil had the Arches to run as well — but she couldn't face him just yet. Through the railings that surrounded the garden, she saw Ian Beale, who had been reunited with Cindy, pushing baby Steven in his buggy. Sharon disliked Cindy intensely — she was the one that had run off with her ex-boyfriend, Wicksy — but the fact that Ian had taken her back, despite the torment Cindy had put him through, made her think. Two people whose marriage had been smashed apart had made another go of it. It did happen …

Sharon gave herself a little shake. This was Grant she was thinking about; violent madman Grant. The Grant who had beaten Eddie half to death, injured a policeman, hit her and her best friend and almost thrown her out of a window. Michelle was right to ask what the matter was. But that was only one side of Grant.

It was Nigel who had made her remember Grant's other qualities. He had been pressing her to go with him when he next went to visit, telling her Grant was in a bad way. His words had been echoing in her head all day:

'He's not such a bad bloke really, is he, Sharon? He's got his good side. And he ain't as tough as he likes to make out …'

In her heart of hearts, Sharon knew that her life with Phil was a fantasy. That was why she had put off telling Grant. Grant behind bars was reality. Once she walked into the prison visiting room, the bubble of happiness she had been floating in with Phil would pop and Grant's pain and anger and suffering would dispel all the froth. Perhaps for ever. She did not want to risk that.

Nigel's concern for Grant had hit home.

'I reckon if he's in there any longer, he'll crack up. What if he does something silly? Tries to top himself or something?'

She would go, Sharon decided, without telling Phil; come

up with some excuse about going shopping up West. Otherwise, he'd want her to make a clean breast of it to Grant, and she couldn't do that. Not yet.

Nigel hadn't made Grant any promises, but nonetheless, Grant couldn't help hoping. He sat at a table, waiting, head bowed, trying to tune out the chatter at other tables, the wailing of overtired babies, girlfriends moaning, screws giving orders. When Sharon walked into the visiting room, he noticed other inmates' heads swivel and knew without even looking up that she had arrived.

She sat down opposite him, looking classy and composed, her face a carefully made-up mask.

'Hi.'

'Hi,' he said softly. Sharon shot him a quick glance and looked away again. Grant waited for her to say something — anything, even a torrent of abuse — but she was silent, keeping her eyes glued to the table.

Conscious of his baggy prison clothes and haggard face, Grant joked, 'I look that good, do I?'

She smiled faintly then, shaking her head. 'You look okay.'

Grant dropped the jocular pretence. 'Only I'm not.'

'So how are you. Really?'

'Bad.'

'Well, it won't be for ever. You won't be here that long.' If she was trying to cheer him up, she was not succeeding, Grant thought. He shot her a resentful look.

'Easy for you to say. I don't know how long it's gonna be. The old bill are trying to stitch me up.'

'What for? The fire?'

'Keep your voice down,' he hissed. 'Yeah, among other things. "Enquiries regarding further offences". It's a load of bull. They've got nothing to go on. But that's why I can't get bail.'

'I see,' Sharon said frostily. She might as well have said, 'I told you so'.

Grant sighed. 'No, you don't.' He put his head in his hands.

'Grant . . . ?' Suddenly, Sharon's tone was tender. 'Talk to me. Tell me about it.'

He looked up at her with bloodshot eyes. 'I'm stuck in a cell with two blokes, one of 'em a headcase, the other, a sad old man who thinks he's John the Baptist. Every time the cell door slams shut, I break out in a sweat. Every time I wake up I think the walls are closing in on me. That's what it's like.'

Sharon, taken aback at his sudden intensity, did not know what to say. Grant hung his head again.

He was silent for a long time, then said wretchedly, 'That's not what I meant to tell you. What I should have said was I'm glad you've come, though I didn't think you would.'

'Well, here I am.'

'Yes, here you are.' Grant paused. There was something he had to get off his chest. He took a deep breath. 'I was a bastard to you, wasn't I? I can't blame you for wanting rid of me. I had my chance and I messed it up, like I always do. But I am glad that you came, 'cos I wanted to tell you I'm sorry.'

He heard a sob and lifted his head. 'Don't. Please, Sharon, don't. Don't cry.' The sight of her tears moved him almost to tears himself. Did it mean she still loved him? Tentatively, he reached out and touched her hand, but she withdrew it immediately. He made no comment as she mopped her eyes and patched up her make-up, trying to bite back the question that had been eating at him since he'd been banged up. But still he couldn't stop himself.

'So, have you got yourself another bloke, yet?'

She looked up from repairing her mascara, a startled expression on her face. To Grant, it was confirmation enough.

'So, who is he? Anyone I know?'

'I haven't got another bloke.'

'That's not what your eyes just said.'

'I was just kind of surprised at you asking, that's all.'

'And it's none of my business even if you have, right? Now we're separated and all that?'

'Right.'

Grant studied her familiar features, the long eyelashes, up-tilted nose, rosebud lips. 'You're looking really good.'

'Thanks.'

'I think about you a lot. I know I shouldn't. But it's the only thing that keeps me sane. Especially at night.' He gave her a twisted smile. 'It's a lovely place, this, at night. You'd think it'd be quiet, wouldn't you?'

'Isn't it?'

'There's John the Baptist gnashing his teeth. There's always someone kicking the doors or shouting. Oh, yeah, it's real peaceful here, a real rest cure.'

She looked at him with compassion, then replaced her hand on the table, sliding it across to cover his. Grant caressed it as if it was the most precious gift in the world.

'I miss you so much,' he whispered in a choked voice. Sharon, saying nothing, squeezed his hand.

Sharon's shopping trip seemed to have worn her out, Phil thought. She had come home exhausted and had gone straight upstairs to lie down, leaving him regretting having rowed with her earlier about taking the time off. The sight of her wan face made him reflect guiltily that the strain of their situation must be hitting her harder than he had realized.

Later, when he found out the truth about Sharon's whereabouts that afternoon – Nigel had blabbed over a pint, assuming he knew – Phil's concern changed rapidly to anger. If Sharon wasn't playing straight with him, it could only mean one thing. She still wanted Grant. He couldn't believe it possible, after all Grant had put her through ... What had his brother got that he hadn't? Grant had always pulled the birds and Phil had been more or less happy to trail in his wake, but this time, it was different. Grant did not deserve Sharon.

Jealousy made him more and more paranoid as the evening wore on. Unlike the explosive Grant, Phil was a slow burner. He had wrestled his conscience long and hard before finally committing himself to Sharon. He knew he was taking from Grant the one thing he would kill for, and still he was prepared to take the risk. Now it looked as if Sharon was going to throw it all back in his face without so much as a nod to the sacrifices he had been prepared to make. The thought made Phil sick to his stomach.

He waited until after closing to confront her. Sharon, sensing something was wrong, asked hesitantly, 'Do you want to talk?'

'It's a bit late for that, innit?' Phil flung himself down on a corner seat, a bottle of beer in his hand. 'Don't bother making excuses, Nige told me where you've really been.'

Sharon looked guilty. 'I'm sorry, Phil. I was going to tell you, but I never got a moment.'

'Yeah, yeah.' Phil poured his beer, drinking half of it in one go. 'So, how is he?'

'He's in a bad way.'

'And you felt sorry for him, right? I bet he laid it on with a trowel, didn't he? "How Badly I'm Suffering" by Grant Mitchell. I know that one. I've seen him pull it a million times.'

'Well, he is suffering,' Sharon said nervously.

Phil slammed the bottle down, slopping beer on the table. 'Do you think I'm not?' Sharon cringed, as if expecting him to attack her, but Phil only said, 'Why d'you do it, Sharon? Eh? Tell me why.'

'Well, I thought …'

'You thought what?'

'I thought maybe …'

'Maybe *what*?' Phil shouted, his face flushed.

'I thought maybe I'd be able to tell him about you and me,' Sharon lied desperately.

'And did you?'

She drew a shaky breath. 'No.'

'Why not? Why didn't you tell him?' Phil leaned towards her, eyes blazing.

Sharon blinked, trying to hold back tears. 'I don't know.'

'And you expect me to believe that? I mean, you've been lying through your teeth to me and you expect me to believe you now?'

'When it came to it, I couldn't! I just couldn't!'

'You mean you still fancy him, is that it? One look at Grant doing his poor-pathetic-caged-animal routine and you forget everything that's gone on between us, is that it?'

'No! No it isn't, I swear.'

'Okay,' he said, calming. 'Prove it.'

'What do you mean?' Sharon asked tremulously.

'Go back to the nick tomorrow and do what you say you were gonna do. Tell Grant it's over between you and him and that you're with me now. Understood?'

Having backed herself into a corner, Sharon had no option but to agree. She went on up to bed alone, leaving Phil drinking in the bar. Sleep was impossible. Only a few days ago she had been so certain that a life with Phil was what she wanted. But now …

She tossed and turned in bed, straining her ears. From downstairs, there was the crash of a glass being thrown. For a moment she considered locking the bedroom door, then thought better of it. Locking Phil out would only make matters worse. She got out of bed and drew the curtains, looking out on the darkened Square. What's wrong with me?, she asked herself. Just that morning, she and Phil had made love. He had brought her tea and kissed her and they had been happy. She thought she could wrap herself in that happiness, like an invisible cloak, and it would protect her from feeling anything for Grant ever again. But she had been wrong. Seeing Grant so defeated had thrown her completely. I'm back at the beginning, she thought. I don't know what I want any more. Or who.

The next day, Phil changed his tune. Marching Sharon out back, he announced harshly, 'Since I can't trust you to tell him yourself, I've come to a decision. I'll go.' Sharon opened her mouth to object, but he held his hand up, silencing her. 'You've had it your way far too long, Sharon. Grant's my brother, he's got a right to hear it from me. Once he knows about us, we can all start our lives afresh.' He touched her cheek gently, adding in a softer voice, 'I've got to do it, Sharon. It's our only chance of happiness.'

'It'll break him, Phil. I know it will. You can't tell him, not while he's like this.'

Phil grimaced. 'He's survived worse. And I should know.' He held her by the shoulders. 'Look at me, Sharon. Do you really want to wait 'til he's out before we tell him? 'Cos frankly, I don't fancy our chances.'

'Then maybe we shouldn't tell him at all. Carry on as we were.'

'Skulking behind his back? Having a quick one when he's out? Is that the kind of relationship you want?' Phil shook his head. 'Oh no. We're in far too deep for that. This way, it's final.'

A phone call from Marcus Christie pre-empted Phil's prison visit with news that the charges against Grant had been dropped. He had been released that morning. The atmosphere in the Vic was wired; as news spread that Grant was coming home, Frank Butcher came into the pub to announce that Pat had been sent down. The teenager she had knocked over died and Pat had received a six-month sentence. After seeing what prison had done to Grant in six weeks, Sharon was sympathetic, but she had her own worries to contend with. As the day went on with no sign of Grant, she and Phil grew increasingly tense. It was evening before they got word: Grant phoned from down by the docks, asking Phil to meet him there.

'What are you going to do?' Sharon asked anxiously. Phil reached for his car keys.

'Tell him. Everything.'

CHAPTER SIXTEEN

Phil and Grant looked at each other without speaking. In the failing evening light Grant's face was grey and drawn. He had huge dark circles under his eyes and several days' growth of stubble. His T-shirt, which normally stretched tight across his barrel chest, hung on him loosely. Grant seemed to have faded, thought Phil, momentarily shocked at how much smaller and thinner he appeared. He felt a stab of protectiveness, seeing once again the unhappy, vulnerable little brother he had once fought to protect. Suddenly, Grant stepped forward and hugged Phil, clinging to him fiercely for a second. Then he let go and stood back, still silent.

'Where've you been?' Phil asked.

'Walking.'

'You should have let me know.' Grant did not move or respond. Phil had never seen him so subdued. 'Bad, was it?' he said, after a pause.

'It's just the time, you've got all that time.' A flicker of emotion showed in Grant's eyes. Phil steeled himself. 'We need to talk.'

'Yeah.' Phil glanced at him sharply. Did Grant have any idea …?

Grant picked up his bag and started walking, staring out across the Thames. The docks had been prettified and yuppified since the old days, the crumbling old wharves torn down or converted into executive offices, their doorways and windows and gates picked out in bright primary coloured lights. Behind them, a train rattled past on the Docklands Light Railway, taking a new breed of East-Enders home to their frozen ready meals in their minimalist lofts. Docklands was becoming a toy town, thought Grant. It didn't feel real any longer.

'I remember coming down here with the old man,' he said. 'He'd just sit for hours, looking at the boats. A lot different from now.'

'Yeah.' Phil decided to let Grant talk. 'So do I.'

'He always seemed to have a fag hanging out of the corner of his mouth. You wouldn't get a fighter smoking these days.'

'No.'

'It didn't seem to affect him, though.' Grant paused. 'I – I wish he was still alive. In spite of ... everything.'

'Yeah, so do I.' Phil gazed at the lights reflected in the dark water, thinking about their dad. He hadn't always been a monster. Yes, back when they were young. Later though, when they were in their teens, he had lost his power to hurt them. For a time there had been equality between them, but he was already going downhill with the drinking and gambling. Then the cancer got him and he died, a withered, bewildered man, a husk of the boxer in his prime. They were 26 and 28 years old at the time and had both genuinely mourned him.

'He'd know what to do,' Grant added suddenly.

'About what?'

'You know.'

Phil's mouth went dry. 'Let's go on a bit, shall we?'

They walked in silence. Night had fallen and the path was in deep shadow. Phil tripped on an empty cider bottle and cursed. He kicked it, sending it spinning into the river. Ahead, two makeshift braziers were burning brightly. They stopped to warm themselves. A tramp, who was huddled under a blanket nearby, muttered an argumentative dialogue to himself. He seemed not to notice them. Phil was glad of the dark. It helped that Grant couldn't read the guilt on his face.

Phil cleared his throat. 'Look, Grant ...'

'We're in a mess,' Grant interrupted him. 'Our lives are in a mess.'

'That's what I've got to talk to you about.'

'Yeah.'

'You got to listen to me, Grant. Hear me out ...'

'I know where we should go.' Grant leapt up off the plastic crate he had been sitting on. He was obviously not listening to Phil. Or perhaps he was, thought Phil, but he didn't want to hear? He had no choice but to play it Grant's way.

'What?' Phil said, getting up and following him.

'Where did you park the car?'

'Back up by the bridge.'

'Well, come on, then.'

'But ...'

'Come on,' Grant said, impatiently. 'I'll drive.'

Grant parked the car outside a block of mostly derelict flats.

'You can't leave it here. We won't have any wheels left,' Phil protested, 'and that's if we're lucky.'

Grant took no notice. 'Bring the beers.'

They climbed the stairs, which were littered with cans and rubbish and stank of urine. Phil skirted a syringe. 'This place is the pits, Grant. Whaddya want to come back here for?'

Grant, continuing to climb, replied, 'It's the nearest thing to home that I've got right now.'

They stopped outside a door on the fifth floor. It hung from one hinge and the lock had been smashed in, leaving a hole in the cheap plywood. Phil and Grant exchanged glances. Grant pushed on the door and went in. The flat was empty and deserted, although it had obviously been used by dossers or junkies; the mantelpiece where the carriage clock and the family photos had once been proudly displayed now held a row of bottles and crumpled cigarette packets. Grant put his hands in his pockets and looked around. The floor was thick with dust and the windows smeared and dirty. The place smelt of mice. They'd never had mice when they lived there. No mouse would have dared to broach Peggy Mitchell's threshold. Above the fireplace, there were patches of bare wall where the plaster had come away. What used to hang there? Grant asked himself, then remembered with a shudder. It was a framed black and white photograph of his father in the ring, his arms held aloft in triumph. You could just make out his defeated opponent on the floor behind him. As a boy, he had always felt sorry for that man, lying slumped in his father's shadow.

Phil, watching Grant's face, pulled open a can of lager and passed it to him, then opened one for himself. He still wasn't sure what Grant's agenda was, or how he was going to tell him. Grant knocked half of it back in one go.

'Aaahh. I ain't had one of these for a long time.'

'Better?'

He grimaced. 'I'll tell you when.'

They went into their old bedroom, both of them amazed at how tiny the room looked.

'Your bed was there.' Grant pointed.

'No, it wasn't.'

'Yes, it was.'

'It was here,' Phil indicated.

'It couldn't have been.'

'Yes, it was,' he said patiently, 'because I was next to the door. Remember?'

It looked as if Grant wanted to argue the toss, but then he backed down. 'Alright, it might have been.' He prodded the rotten skirting board with his foot. 'We've come a long way.'

'Yeah.'

Grant paused. 'Mum didn't find out, did she?' Phil shook his head. 'No. Been any longer, she might have had to know.'

'The old bill were paying me back. For all the times they haven't managed to send me down.'

'That's the name of the game.'

'I wish now I'd have been caught when I was a kid,' Grant said suddenly.

'Eh?'

'I don't want to go back in there again. But I might have got used to it if I'd have been a kid.' Grant was silent for a moment. 'No.' he went on, 'It's not for me. They're all losers in there, Phil, all of 'em.'

'It was only six weeks.'

'Six weeks too many. I was stupid. If I hadn't lost my rag ...'

Phil sat down on the floor, his back to the wall. 'Which time are we talking about here?'

'That's it, isn't it? Every time something doesn't go my way, I go off the deep end.' Grant sat down too, leaning his head back against the wall and shutting his eyes.

Phil traced a pattern in the dust. 'That about sums it up.'

Grant was quiet for a while, then he said, softly, 'Why did she ever marry me?' Phil, who had been thinking of Sharon too, looked up, unnerved. 'I wouldn't have married me,' Grant continued, as if he was talking to himself.

'The thought had crossed my mind,' Phil said, dry.

Grant snapped open his eyes. 'How is she?'

'Alright.'

'I hit her ... how could I have done that?'

'You tell me.'

'I must have been crazy. Does she hate me?'

'No.'

'She should do.'

Phil sighed. 'She doesn't hate you, Grant.'

'I hit her!' Grant repeated, punishing himself.

'It's over now.'

'No, it's not. She'll never forget that. The only thing that's over is me and Sharon.' He looked at Phil as if pleading with him to deny it.

Tell him, tell him the truth, now, the voice in Phil's head insisted. He took a swig of his beer. Not yet. Soon. But not yet. Grant hadn't opened up to him like this in a long, long time. And once Phil had told him about his relationship with Sharon, he might never talk to him again. He wanted to hold on to the last precious hours together for just a little longer.

They sat in the dark room, drinking and talking, working their way through the two six-packs. Grant showed no sign of wanting to return to the Vic, and Phil didn't press it. If he waited until Grant was really drunk, he might not react so badly. On the other hand, he could take it even worse, in which case at least his reaction time would be slowed by the booze. But then again, Phil reflected, if Grant could wreck a pub and beat up a copper after drinking gin all day, there probably wasn't much hope for him either way. He couldn't put it off any longer. He was just going to have to brace himself for whatever happened.

'Listen ...' he began,

But Grant was in full flow now. 'I used to wake up in the middle of the night ... and I'd think she was there, lying in my arms, her head on my chest ... and I'd be holding her gently ... she'd be sleeping like a child ... and I'd just reach out to stroke her hair ... but that will never happen, ever ...' His voice started to break. 'I got it all wrong ... everything.'

'Grant, listen to me.'

Grant raised his head, his eyes gleaming with tears. 'What's she said?'

'Nothing. She hasn't said anything.'

He drew a breath, calming himself. Wiping his wet cheeks with the back of his hand, he asked, 'How's the pub?'

'What?' Phil was taken aback.

'How's it doing?'

'Same as always.'

'So she's pleased?'

'Yeah ... I suppose so,' he said reluctantly.

'Good.'

'It hasn't sold yet.'

'Right. I'm going to take it off the market.'

'I thought you wanted out?'

'Not really.' Illuminated by the pale moonlight filtering through the filthy window, Grant's face was wistful. 'I just wanted to make her beg me to come back.'

'What's that got to do with the pub?'

'That's how you get to Sharon. Through the Vic. I tried to bully her with it. If I had any brains, I would have realized it was a waste of time.'

'But if Sharon won't have you back ...?'

'We'll move out. She can run it how she likes,' Grant said. Phil swallowed. 'That's not how it's gonna be.'

'We'll get a flat together.' Grant still wasn't listening.

'No, Grant,' Phil said, with force.

Grant looked at him as if he'd suddenly noticed his brother. 'I thought you'd want to.'

'I'm staying at the Vic.'

'Why?'

'I ...' Phil paused, a long, long pause. 'I just am. Sharon needs someone ...' Grant was staring at him intently. 'Someone to take the deliveries and things ...' Phil continued, bottling out. 'I said I'd do it.'

'She can find someone else to do that,' Grant said confidently. 'There'll be plenty of takers for a tenner.' He sighed heavily. 'That's why I wanted to re-enlist. Because it was simpler. Simpler than staying and coping with all the things I feel about Sharon.'

'Well, you can't do that now, bruv. You've got to face up to it. It's over.'

'I know,' Grant buried his head in his arms. 'And I don't know what I'm going to do. I'll always, always love her ...' His voice dropped, so that Phil could hardly hear what he was saying. 'I don't know if I can live without her. I've been so stupid ... so stupid.' He turned his head on one side, resting it on his knees, like a small boy hunched in a corner. 'I hate myself. I could have had everything ... everything.' Phil caught his eye and looked away. He couldn't do it. Not because he was frightened of Grant. He wasn't, not any more, not of this beaten, miserable, lonely man with a heart full of pain and regrets. He couldn't tell Grant about himself and Sharon because he just could not be that cruel.

Grant fell asleep, curled up on the floor using his holdall for a pillow. Phil, who found the bare boards too uncomfortable to sleep on, stayed awake, watching over his brother. It seemed appropriate, somehow. How many nights had he sat up, wide awake, in this room, doing the same thing? he asked himself. Waiting for their father to come home, drunk; hearing him swear at their mum through the thin walls? Waiting, too, for the doorknob to turn and their father to enter the room, stinking of booze and shouting, 'Where is 'e, the little toerag?'

He had always picked on Grant, the youngest. It was almost with a shock that Phil remembered how weak and skinny Grant used to be, all bony ankles and stick-like arms. He wasn't a bruiser, like Phil. And he wasn't hard, either; he was a gentle kid. He had built himself up over the years, getting into kung fu and body-building. The physical strength and aggression was something he'd had to acquire, to fight back, when their dad used him as a punchbag. The day when Grant, aged 14, slung him a good right hook, splitting his lip and chipping a tooth, was the day he finally stopped hitting him.

Eric, their father, had never referred to or apologised for the physical abuse he meted out, even when they were older. Phil presumed he must have rationalized it in his mind; he was always going on about 'toughening them up'. Beatings weren't uncommon in the East End in those days; there was no political correctness about slapping your kids or taking a belt to them. Peggy had never mentioned it either, except by way of her oft-repeated homily, 'It was my job to bring you up and your father's job to discipline you'. Phil wasn't sure to this day whether she really didn't know or whether she had turned a blind eye out of fear.

It had started when they were much younger, six or seven, Phil couldn't remember when, exactly. Looking back, he realized that it was when their dad's boxing career was on the ropes. Eric had been promoted as a local hero, an East-End champion in the making. It was when he started losing matches that he took it out on his sons. As his career declined, the punishment they received went up. At first, it was mock-sporting, a means for venting his frustrations and disappoint-ment. Eric would take them down to the gym and bully them into bouts with him, shouting, 'Fists up! Guard yourself! Watch me! There. You weren't watching properly, were you?' Phil closed his eyes, wincing, as he recalled the smacks round the head, being knocked to the floor, getting up, winded and dizzy, only to be knocked down again.

When their father's drinking began spiralling out of control, the beatings moved into a different league. This time, there was no half-hearted pretence; he would come home, yank Grant out of bed and lay into him. One night, he knocked Grant unconscious. Phil, too terrified to raise the alarm, had sat and held Grant's hand, not knowing whether he was dead or alive. When Grant came round, they made a secret pact, which they signed in pencils dipped in blood from Grant's head wound. Phil still had the slip of paper tucked away at home in a shoebox. The childish scrawl read: 'We swear to protect each other, no matter what'. The next time it happened, Phil had stood in front of his brother and taken the beating for him.

It was light outside. Phil, who had fallen asleep after all, sat up and stretched, easing his stiff back. He shook Grant.

'Where ...?' He blinked. 'God, I thought I was back there, for a minute, in that cell. Those bare walls ...'

'Yeah, well, this place is only fit for the condemned.' Phil grabbed hold of his arm and pulled him to his feet. 'Come on. Let's get out of here, leave the ghosts behind.'

'Ghosts? You're kidding me. What did you see, dad walking through the wall?' Grant grinned.

'Something like that.' Phil dusted himself down. 'First stop, find a caff. One that does big greasy fry-ups and strong tea.'

'Then what? I don't think I can cope with seeing her, Phil ...'

'Then,' Phil said firmly, 'you and I are going home to face the music.'

Lunchtime at the Vic had been fairly quiet. It was just as well, really, reflected Sharon. The state she was in, she couldn't have coped with a rush. She had heard nothing from Phil since he left the day before and had been worrying herself sick.

'I'll kill him, putting me through all this,' she said to Michelle, who knew about the meeting down by the docks.

'If he ain't dead already,' Michelle remarked. It had not helped Sharon's nerves, which were stretched to breaking point.

She was just wondering when she should start phoning the hospitals when the door opened and Grant walked in, closely followed by Phil. Phil caught her eye and shook his head fractionally. Suddenly, Sharon felt as if she could breathe again.

'Hi,' Grant said quietly. He looked like a completely different person. It wasn't just that he was hollow-cheeked and tired, or that he had lost weight. Everything about his demeanour was different. There was no swagger, no belligerent stance, no challenging stare, no tip of the chin. For a second, she hardly recognized him.

'Hi,' she said eventually, finding her voice.

'You look good,' he said. She almost smiled. The last time she had worn her pink suit he had called her a tart. Normally, the observation would have prompted a sarky comment, but she simply said, 'Thanks.'

'I'll go and smarten up, give you a hand.' He shouldered his bag and went upstairs.

Phil came round the bar and Sharon pulled him to one side. 'What happened? Why didn't you ring? I've been going out of my mind.'

'I couldn't.'

'Where've you been?'

'Talking.'

'All night?'

'Most of it,' Phil said wearily. 'He's changed, Sharon.'

'That won't last.'

'He's talking of moving out ... leaving you to it.'

'How much for?' she asked cynically.

'Nothing.'

She pursed her lips. 'He's trying something.'

'I don't think so. Look, I'm knackered. I'm going to get some shut-eye.' He started to walk away, but Sharon called him back. 'Phil. Why didn't you tell him?'

Without turning round, Phil replied, 'He's still in love with you.'

Several weeks went by, during which Sharon, Grant and Phil co-existed in the flat above the Vic, trying not to tread on each other's toes and skirting around potential flashpoints. Grant remained uncharacteristically subdued; he was polite, helpful and considerate, causing Ian Beale to remark sarcastically that he must have had a lobotomy while he was inside. Sharon, too, was suspicious of Grant's overnight transformation into a 'new man', but when she caught him vacuuming the living-room carpet, even she was impressed.

She and Grant had kept their distance, sleeping in separate rooms and living separate lives. Phil, unable to tear himself away from Sharon and equally unable to tell Grant, once again hovered on the sidelines.

It took a paras reunion to convince Sharon that the change in Grant was real. One of Grant's army mates, Chris, had turned up at the Vic, and Grant had arranged a get-together that evening. Sharon expected it to be a big, boozy lads' night out at a club or a strip joint or a seedy bar. However, when she caught up with them – Grant had left some photos behind at the Vic that he'd had copied especially for Chris – she saw the two of them sitting quietly together at a corner table in an Indian restaurant. Telling the waiter to give the photos to Grant, she slipped away again before he spotted her.

'Why didn't you come over?' Grant asked, when he got back.

Sharon, who was in the living-room with her feet up, said, 'You looked like what you were saying was private.'

Grant grimaced. 'Chris did most of the talking.' He went as if to go, assuming she wanted to be left in peace, but Sharon said, 'Grant. Sit down a minute.' He glanced at her, trying to read her expression, then sat down on the other end of the sofa. 'So, not a great evening, then?' Sharon continued.

'I've had better. He was really down.'

'Why? What's happened?'

'Everything. He's got no job, his wife's left him, taken the kids, his life's fallen apart.'

'Why did she leave him?'

Guardedly, Grant met her eyes. 'Because he hit her.' He paused, then added, vehemently, 'The trouble with Chris is, he doesn't see that any of it's his own fault. Spent all night blaming the army, blaming his wife, blaming Social Services ...'

He stopped suddenly, catching sight of an oddly sad expression on Sharon's face. 'Look, you must be tired.'

'No, go on.'

'You don't have to sit and listen to all of this.'

'I know I don't, but I want to, alright?'

Grant got up and paced around the room. 'I can't believe how he's gone downhill. He's seeing a shrink, now, has to go to a day centre, because he's disturbed.' He fidgeted with an ornament on the sideboard, turning it over distractedly. 'He was a brilliant bloke, Sharon. And now he's just some lonely nutter in a bedsit in Walthamstow.'

Sharon, seeing how upset Grant was, didn't know how to comfort him. 'You can't let it get to you, Grant ...'

'Why not?' he replied wretchedly. 'What's the difference between him and me? We're just two sad blokes making a mess of everything we touch.'

'You're not like that.'

'I'm scared, Sharon. I'm scared,' Grant confessed, his voice cracking. 'I'm no different to Chris. What's to stop me ending up the same?'

''Cos you're not the same.'

'And what makes me so different, eh? Chris ends up beating up his wife and I end up smashing you in the face?'

Sharon was silent.

'Yeah, you've got no clever answer for that one, have you?'

'Grant.' Sharon got up off the sofa and went towards him. 'You're not like this Chris bloke. You said it yourself. He keeps blaming everyone else; you keep blaming yourself. That's the difference.'

Grant turned away abruptly, dashing his hand to his eyes. When she put out a hand to him, he motioned her away. Sharon made a decision. 'Grant, look at me.'

But he kept his back to her, staring out of the window at the Square.

'How can I blame anyone else for what happened? I hit you, Sharon. You're my wife and I hit you. And I can't even say I'm sorry, can I. That's what blokes who hit their wives do. They hit them, then they say sorry, then they hit them again.'

'Are you sorry?' she asked softly.

'Do you really have to ask that?' His voice was bitter.

'I know you've said it before. But I think I need to hear you say it now.'

'What for?'

'Just say it, will you?'

'I'm sorry,' Grant said, breaking down, his shoulders heaving. 'I'm sorry, I'm sorry ...'

Sharon turned him round to face her. 'You don't have to tell me you won't do it again. I believe you. And that's what matters.'

'I won't, I won't.'

'Come here.' She put her arms around him and they stood, trembling, in the embrace, Sharon close to tears herself now. She pulled away from him, taking his face in her hands. 'I want us to try again. I want our marriage to work. Starting now.'

'It's too late,' he whispered, shaking his head.

'Funny, that's what I thought, too. But I don't any more.' She kissed him tenderly on the lips and gradually, slowly, he responded. They were so engrossed in each other that neither of them noticed Phil in the doorway, looking on with a face like death.

Sharon (Letitia Dean) and Grant Mitchell (Ross Kemp) during the better days of their stormy relationship.

TOP LEFT: Torn between two brothers: Sharon (Letitia Dean) with brothers Grant (left) and Phil Mitchell (Ross Kemp and Steve McFadden).

TOP RIGHT: Grant's mood swings put his marriage to Sharon in jeopardy.

LEFT, BOTTOM: The Mitchell brothers – bound by a childhood pact; threatened by Phil's betrayal. When Phil has an affair with Sharon, their blood ties are almost severed for good.

ABOVE: Grant on remand in prison for GBH. Meanwhile at the Vic, Phil and Sharon are taking advantage of his absence.

TOP LEFT: Grant, behind the bar at the Vic.

TOP RIGHT: Phil and Grant Mitchell – the brothers who stick together through thick and thin.

BOTTOM: Peggy Mitchell (Barbara Windsor) with her boys.

A new start? Tiffany (Martine McCutcheon) and Grant on the day of their Blessing.

TOP: Sharon, past caring about the consequences, gives herself up to Phil entirely.

BOTTOM: Grant and Michelle (Susan Tully), Sharon's best friend, share confidences and end up spending the night together after years of animosity.

TOP: Grant with Lorraine Wicks (Jacqueline Leonard). Lorraine is different to any other woman Grant has ever fancied before.

BOTTOM: Unintentional revenge: Grant and his brother's wife Kathy (Gillian Taylforth), brought closer by their concern for Phil, can no longer hide their feelings for each other.

Tiffany and Grant with baby Courtney. Finally, Grant's longing to be a father has been fulfilled – but will Tiff and Courtney stick around?

CHAPTER SEVENTEEN

The following year saw a lot of changes in the Square. Sharon and Grant had settled back into married life, although her resolution was tested to the limit when a so-called army 'pal' of Grant's, Dougie Briggs, flipped out and laid siege to the Vic with a sawn-off shotgun. Grant had rated Dougie a 'top man' and had even allowed himself to be talked into planning a supermarket robbery with him. Too late, he discovered from another ex-para that Dougie had turned into a maniac and was wanted by the police for rape and murder. By the time Grant arrived at the Vic, Dougie had attempted to assault Sharon and would have shot Grant, had Sharon not thrown herself in front of him. In the ensuing struggle Michelle got shot in the leg. Despite the fact that she was bleeding badly, Grant insisted it would be quickest to drive her to hospital – a ruse to prevent the police being alerted. When Sharon heard him putting pressure on the injured Michelle not to talk, she was disgusted with him. The incident shook her faith in Grant's judgement, and it took a while for things to settle down between them again. As for Michelle, her hatred of Grant, who she did not shop for Sharon's sake, increased ten-fold.

Phil, unable to bear living with Grant and Sharon, had moved out of the Vic into Grant's old flat. In a moment of ill judgement he had allowed himself to be talked into a marriage of convenience to Nadia, a Romanian refugee. Following a romantic trip to Paris, he became involved with Kathy Beale, who later moved in with him. After Phil proposed to Kathy (much to Sharon's consternation), Nadia reappeared on the scene to cause difficulties, but was eventually seen off by Grant.

*

Other relationships had also had their ups and downs. Cindy and Ian Beale were overwhelmed when she gave birth to twins prematurely. But it wasn't long before Cindy was up to her old tricks, conducting an affair with Matt, a young swimming-pool attendant. Pauline and Arthur, who split up over Arthur's affair with Mrs Hewitt, were finally reconciled, although Pauline was briefly tempted to have a fling of her own with a singing idol from her youth, Danny Taurus. Michelle had begun a relationship with her tutor, Geoff Barnes, and had graduated from the poly with a Third. Pauline and Arthur were enormously proud of their daughter's academic achievement but less approving of Geoff, who was older than Arthur.

The Fowler family were also reeling from a tragedy: Pete Beale, Pauline's twin, had run off to New Zealand with Rose, the new love of his life, only to be killed in a car accident that looked suspiciously like the work of mobsters. Pauline was devastated. Mark had taken over Pete's market stall, keeping it in the family, but it saddened him to think he would never be able to pass the business on to a son. Mark was HIV positive, a fact known only to the family. Gill, his wife, had died of AIDS a couple of years before, shortly after they had got married. Though Mark was well, he could not envisage any woman wanting to commit herself to him with such a future.

The Butchers had also had a bad year. Pat had been released from prison but found it hard to readjust to family life. Ricky, who had separated from Sam – she had gone off to pursue a modelling career – was living with them again, as was Janine, Frank's young daughter. Frank had struggled to keep their two businesses afloat while Pat was inside, but in the end the cab company had lost out to a rival firm and the car lot was barely ticking over. Desperate for cash, he called in a long-overdue favour from Phil Mitchell, getting him to set fire to the car lot in order to claim the insurance. A homeless boy, who was sleeping in one of the cars, was killed and Frank, tormented by guilt, disappeared. Pat was left to pick up the pieces.

Pat's eldest son, David Wicks (from her first marriage to

Pete Beale) had recently turned up in Walford and was keen to revive the car lot, but so far he had been more of a hindrance than a help. Not only was he in debt, but he was on the run from the CSA for avoiding maintenance payments to a wife and two children Pat didn't even know existed. He had already succeeded in rubbing people up the wrong way: Grant had decked him for coming on to Sharon, landing David in hospital, and there was tension, too, between David and Carol Jackson, who had moved into Dot's old house with her husband Alan and brood of four children. It was only when David started flirting with the eldest, a stunning redhead called Bianca, that Carol blurted out the truth to Pat: Bianca was David's own daughter, the product of a brief teenage liaison. David had problems accepting the news. He was still attracted to Bianca and deeply jealous of her relationship with Ricky, who was now working with him at the car lot.

The happiest man in the Square was undoubtedly Nigel, who had found the woman of his dreams, a divorcee named Debbie. He was even more ecstatic when she finally agreed to marry him. Unfortunately, there was a problem, in the shape of a violent ex-husband, Liam, who wanted custody of their daughter, Clare. Liam was threatening to disrupt their big day, but Grant extended his best man's duties to dealing with him, leaving Liam trussed up in the Arches until it was over.

By the autumn, preparations for the next Walford wedding – Kathy and Phil's – were also underway. Despite having made a commitment to Grant, Sharon found herself increasingly upset at the prospect of Phil getting married. She took it out on Grant, who put her moodiness down to 'women's problems'. Michelle, who knew the real reason, pleaded with Sharon to give it up, but Sharon was obsessed. The next day, on the pretext of visiting Michelle, she turned up on Phil's doorstep.

'Sharon,' he exclaimed, blinking with surprise.

'Are you alone?'

'Well, yes …'

She stepped inside. 'We've got to talk.'

'What about?' He shut the door hastily.

'Us.'

'Sharon, there is no "us". You chose Grant, remember?'

'I know. But there's still … history, isn't there? We can't pretend it never happened. I can't anyway.'

Phil led her through to the living-room. 'Look, I really don't know why you're here. We've moved on, both of us. It don't do any good to keep raking up the past.'

'You might at least have told me first! But oh no. I had to walk into the Vic and find Kathy flashing her engagement ring at all and sundry. How do you think that made me feel?'

'Well, what makes you think you deserve special treatment?' Phil shouted back. 'You didn't exactly give me any, did yer? I had to find you snogging Grant, that's how I knew what you'd decided.'

They glared at each other, breathing fast. 'I'm sorry,' Sharon said, eventually, dropping her eyes. 'I'm sorry you found out that way. I didn't want you to get hurt.'

'But I was,' Phil said softly. 'And it's lasted a long, long time.'

She looked up at him. 'Does it still hurt?'

'What do you think?'

'I – I don't know what to think. Seeing you with Kathy, it makes me feel so eaten up inside …'

'I thought you were happy now.'

'I am. Sometimes.' Sharon smiled faintly. 'Grant's making an effort and I'm content, just chugging along. Then, sometimes, it all catches up with me and I wish I was with you.' She studied Phil's face. 'I can't help it, Phil. I still love you.'

He flushed angrily. 'You do my head in Sharon, d'you know that? You want me when I'm spoken for and not when I'm free. Is that it? Why play games with me now, when I've sorted my life out at last? God knows, it's taken me long enough. What the hell goes on in that perverted little brain of yours?'

'It isn't a game, I'm trying to be honest with you, that's all,' she sobbed.

'And I suppose you've been this honest with Grant?'

There was a long silence. 'No,' Sharon said in a small voice.

Phil sighed, his anger draining away. 'Go home, Sharon. Forget about us.'

'Yes. I'm sorry. I shouldn't have come.' Sharon turned to leave, then turned back to him again. 'Goodbye, Phil.'

Impulsively, she leaned forward and kissed him on the lips. It was the briefest of brushes, but it ignited a spark of passion that Phil had been fighting to resist.

'See you,' Sharon said, turning to go once more. But Phil caught hold of her arm and pulled her close forcefully.

'Oh, Sharon,' he groaned, devouring her with his kisses.

It was some time before they spoke again. Undoing his shirt with trembling fingers, Sharon whispered, 'What time do you expect Kathy back?'

The mention of Kathy's name worked like a bucket of cold water on Phil, who suddenly came to his senses. 'Soon,' he said, breaking away and rebuttoning his shirt. 'Look, Sharon, this is crazy. I love Kathy. I ain't gonna risk my marriage for a quickie just because you're in the mood.'

'A quickie?' Sharon was mortified. 'Phil, I'm not here for sex. We love each other.'

'No. I love Kathy. You just want your cake and eat it,' he cut in tersely. 'Now get out.' He gave her a little push towards the door. 'And don't come back.' It was a humiliated and chastened Sharon who returned to the Vic.

After the shock of Phil's rejection, Sharon kept out of his way. As the weeks went by she was more able to put the situation in perspective and made a determined effort to concentrate on her relationship with Grant instead. Nonetheless, she was horrified when she learned that Grant, in a fit of enthusiasm, had arranged a huge party for 22 October, a double celebration to mark her birthday and Phil and Kathy's engagement. Unable to say anything without arousing suspicion, she gritted her teeth and said, 'That's a lovely idea.'

'Yeah.' Grant looked chuffed. 'Kathy suggested it. I thought you'd be pleased.'

I'm ecstatic, thought Sharon. I bet Phil is as well. At least she had one thing to look forward to, she consoled herself. Michelle was coming over the following evening for a good old natter. It was a long time since they'd had a chat that hadn't been charged with tension. Until recently, they had hardly been on speaking terms at all after Sharon revealed to Vicki that she was her half-sister. Fortunately, Michelle had forgiven her, although she had been disapproving about Sharon going to see Phil. As far as Michelle was concerned, the Mitchell brothers were trouble with a capital 'T'.

The official reason for the girls' night in was so that Michelle could interview Sharon for a book Geoff was writing.

'What's the social and economic importance of East-End women got to do with me?' Sharon asked, when Michelle told her about the project.

'You've grown up here, seen things change ...'

'Hey, I'm not that old!'

'Well, you know what I mean. Geoff seems to think you're ideal material, having your own business, an' all.'

'And it'll all go in a book?' Michelle nodded. 'Better keep it clean then,' Sharon giggled. 'Else Geoff'll be having hot flushes editing it.' The two of them shrieked with laughter.

Michelle, po-faced, mimicked Geoff. 'He said, "This is a text book, not a Jeffrey Archer novel".'

'Little does he know,' Sharon said. 'He could have a bestseller on his hands.'

'In that case,' Michelle grinned, 'we'd better skip the whole of the section on early adulthood.'

The next night, the Vic was full. Sharon had booked a drag act, Dolly Davenport, who was going down a storm, keeping the Vic's bar staff, Grant, Steve and Binnie, fully occupied. Sharon and Michelle had retired to the living-room upstairs, equipped with a cassette player, a stack of tapes and three bottles of wine.

'Essential for in-depth research,' Michelle said, uncorking the first and pouring Sharon a glass.

The interview started off with a well-intentioned Michelle sticking to Geoff's list of questions, but by the third bottle they were sprawled on the floor, reminiscing and giggling helplessly.

'... yeah, but what about Duncan, the randy vicar?' Michelle asked, prompting another gale of laughter from Sharon.

'Oh, don't ... he was lovely. He wanted to marry me.'

'What? To someone else?'

'No, he meant it ...'

'Oh, yeah. Sharon Watts, the vicar's wife. I can just see it.'

'I could have been!' Sharon protested.

'You?'

'Why not?'

'Bit of a jump, innit? To Grant Mitchell from the vicar? Talk about opposite ends of the evolutionary scale.'

'Here, Grant's been good to me.' Sharon propped herself up on one elbow. 'He loved me enough to give me the things I wanted. He knew how important this place was to me. And anyway, what about you?'

'What about me?'

'There was Danny, the computer bloke. Poor old Lofty. And now Geoff. Is he the one?'

Michelle leaned over and spoke pointedly into the microphone, which was resting on the floor between them. 'Yes. A fine figure of a man. He is the love of my life. Oh ... it's gone off.' She examined the machine.

'We haven't got to do all that again, have we?' Sharon said.

'No, we went off the rails a bit there anyway. Hang on while I put in a new tape.' She ripped open a new packet. 'Okay, we're rolling. Where were we?' She studied her list. '"How you perceived the world about you as an adolescent."'

They talked about Den and Angie and life at the Vic, but inevitably, as more wine was drunk, the conversation veered back towards Grant.

'I can't understand you, sometimes, Sharon.' Michelle put her hands behind her head, staring foggily up at the ceiling. 'What the big attraction is. I mean, after everything that's happened ...'

'I know. But I want Grant now more than ever. Oh, I know he's no angel and things haven't always been as good as they are now, but he's always there for me and I know that, whatever else happens in my life, he'll always be there. And that's important.' Michelle was silent. 'Oh, I know you don't like him, but you don't know him like I do. All you see is what he shows everyone else. But he's different with me. Gentler.'

'Okay. I'll buy that. But what about the other side, the side that beats people up? The side that hurts people?'

'But that's just it.' Sharon rolled back onto her stomach, squinting at Michelle. 'Most of that is because of me. Eddie Royle, David Wicks ... Alright, so maybe he went too far, but that doesn't change the fact he was doing it for me.'

Michelle snorted. 'I'm sorry, but you can't tell me he's the perfect man when we both know he isn't.'

'I'm not saying he's perfect ... but he's perfect for me.'

'What about Phil?'

'What about him?'

'You slept with him, remember? Grant's brother.'

'Phil was different.'

'Why?'

'He just was. Oh, I didn't know that the first time ... it was just lust, I wanted him. I mean, one minute I was looking at him, then the next we were ripping each other's clothes off.'

'And after?'

Sharon considered. 'Well, it was like Phil was the nice side of Grant. I think that's why I fell in love with him. I even thought things would work out, once ... when Grant was in prison and me and Phil were together all the time.'

Michelle shook her head. 'Phil must have had some front. Sleeping with his brother's wife, in the same bed.'

'No, Michelle, I don't think either of us thought of it that way.'

'And what about now? It's definitely finished?'

'Yeah.'

'You sure?'

'Yeah.' Sharon turned the wine glass in her hand, pausing for a moment. 'It wasn't,' she admitted. 'There was all that stuff over the engagement, when I just wanted to curl up and die.' She was silent again, then she added, 'But that's past now.'

'What about when you went over to see him at the flat, when Kathy was out?' Sharon looked sheepish. Michelle grinned. 'I know you weren't just over there to wish him luck.'

'I just wanted to find out if there was anything still there.'

'Was there?'

'Well, I'd only been in there five minutes and we were all over each other again … it was like the first time all over again.'

Michelle's jaw dropped. 'You said you didn't sleep with him.'

'No, but we could have done.' At that moment the door burst open and Dolly Davenport strode in, all legs and glitter.

'Sorry girls. I was looking for the little boys' room.'

'Straight ahead,' Sharon managed to utter, aghast. 'You don't think he heard, do you?' she said, after Dolly waltzed off.

''Course not. Me heart went though,' Michelle admitted.

'Yours did?' Sharon fanned herself. 'That thing ain't still going, is it?' She peered at the cassette player. Michelle crawled over to inspect it.

'No, it went off ages ago.'

'Thank gawd for that.'

'Sounds like you had fun,' Grant said, watching Geoff escort a giggling Michelle away.

'Yeah, it was brilliant.'

'Right, well, I'd better finish up downstairs …'

He turned to go but Sharon called, 'No, wait. Come here.' She beckoned him over. 'I want you to take me to bed.'

'Well, you're the boss.' Grant smiled wryly.

'No I'm not, you are.' She put her arms around his neck and kissed him tenderly. 'I really love you.'

He indulged her drunken state. 'And I really love you.'

'No, Grant, you don't understand. I really love you,' Sharon insisted.

'Thanks very much.' He touched her gently on the nose. 'So what's brought all this on?'

'I just want to tell you that everything's gonna be alright and that nothing's ever going to come between us ... Ever.'

When Steve, the live-in barman, came down the following morning he fully expected Grant to give him a bollocking. He had slept in after the revels of the drag night and knew there would be a mess to clear up. He burst into the bar, only to freeze in embarrassment as he came across Grant and Sharon, still in their night clothes, locked in a clinch which seemed to involve a prolonged examination of each other's dental work.

'Sorry, sorry ...' Steve was about to back out of the room, when Grant greeted him genially.

'S'alright, Steve, we've only just got up ourselves.'

'Yeah, I know, but I overslept.'

'Don't worry about it, mate.' Grant smiled, pulling Steve up short. 'Relax. I'm making coffee. Do you want some?'

'Eh?'

'Coffee,' Grant said patiently. 'Would you like one?'

'Er, yes.'

'I'll bring it through.' Grant slapped him on the back and disappeared. Steve, dumbfounded, looked at Sharon.

'Is he trying to poison me?'

'Put it this way, Steve, I don't think there'll be a better time to ask him for a payrise,' Sharon replied, smirking contentedly.

Grant's benevolent landlord routine had everybody fazed. By lunchtime he was the life and soul of the party, cracking jokes with the regulars.

'He's been like this all morning. I reckon that drag act unhinged his mind,' Steve hissed.

David Wicks, who was drinking at the bar, regarded Grant sourly. 'I always said it wouldn't take much.'

Even Sharon was driven to remark, 'Christmas come early has it?', which prompted Grant to squeeze her into the far corner of the bar and whisper, 'Did I ever tell you the one about Little Red Riding Hood?'

'Yes.' Sharon yawned. 'Several times.'

'Did you ever hear that I think you're beautiful?'

She looked at him with a smile. 'Not recently.'

'Well, you are.' He touched her cheek gently. 'We're good together, aren't we?'

'Yeah,' she agreed, smiling. 'Sometimes.'

Later that afternoon, Grant took a break upstairs, urged on by Sharon, who hinted that she might come up and join him for their own private happy hour in bed. Pottering around the living-room, he decided to put on some music, and rifled through their stack of cassettes. Nothing took his fancy. There was a tape already in the machine and he pressed 'play' to see what it was. It clicked off immediately, so he turned it over and tried again. The sound of Sharon laughing drunkenly to some comment of Michelle's startled him initially, then he realized what it was. Amused, he listened to her discussing her adolescence. Settling down on the sofa, he put his feet up and listened, fascinated at this insight into her character. When Steve stuck his head round the door, half an hour later, he found Grant relaxed and chuckling, which further spooked him.

'Er, Sharon said I could take an hour off,' he said cautiously.

'Yeah, go on, mate. I'm going down myself in a minute.' Grant got up and pressed 'stop'.

'Catch you later.' Steve disappeared before Grant could change his mind. Grant got as far as the door before he remembered the tape and went back to the cassette player to retrieve it. Smiling, he tucked it into his breast pocket. It would be something to entertain him in the car, he thought.

CHAPTER EIGHTEEN

'Someone like you should never wear clothes.' Grant nuzzled Sharon's neck as she stood in her bra and knickers in front of a full-length mirror, trying to decide which dress to wear.

'That'd be a surprise for them all down in the bar.' Sharon held another outfit up.

'We'll make it a nudist bar. The East End's crying out for one.'

She giggled. 'You're mad, you are.'

'But that's why you like me,' he breathed, fondling her.

Sharon swatted him away. 'Get off! I have to get back downstairs. Grant retreated, grinning. 'Whichever you wear, I know you'll look stunning tonight. You put every other woman in the shade.' He blew her a kiss and went out, leaving Sharon smiling happily to herself. All of a sudden she felt like a giddy sixteen-year-old going on a first date, not a married woman who had just that day turned twenty-five. Things were so good between her and Grant now, it made the lows of their past seem a distant memory. To think I nearly chucked him for Phil, she reflected more soberly. I must have needed my head examining. It's always been Grant ...

She held up the gold necklace he had given her that morning and fastened it round her neck, staring at her reflection in the mirror. Sometimes I don't know who you are, she thought. Only a few weeks ago you threw yourself at Phil. You were lucky he said no. What's the matter with you, girl? Have you got a death-wish or something?

Later that evening, Grant and Sharon went out for a romantic meal – the party was the following night – although they didn't stop for dessert. Unable to keep their hands off each other, they hailed a cab home and went straight upstairs.

'Come here and let me ravish you.' Grant swept her into his arms. Cuddling her close, he whispered, 'I don't suppose anyone can be as lucky as me.'

'Or as me,' she replied, melting.

He looked at her, suddenly more serious. 'You mean that?' Sharon nodded. 'Why?'

'You know why.'

'Because you've got your own pub?'

'No. You know why.'

'I want you to tell me.'

'Because I've got you.' She kissed him lingeringly.

'You really make me really happy, you know that?'

'Do I?'

'Never thought anyone could do that. I used to be a miserable sod. But now ... I'm almost completely happy.'

She raised an eyebrow. 'Almost?'

'Well, ninety-eight-and-a-half per cent happy.'

'So where am I going wrong?' She kissed him.

'You know what I'm trying to say.' They looked into each other's eyes.

'Maybe,' Sharon admitted eventually.

'Maybe you understand, or maybe you will?'

'Maybe I know what you're trying to say.'

They embraced again, then Grant begged, 'Please, Sharon ... I want us to have a baby.' He kissed her hungrily. 'Please say you do, because I want you to. Don't you want that, Sharon? I want you to. I want you to so much.'

She kissed him back fervently. 'Yes,' she whispered. 'Yes. I want a baby too.'

Phil and Kathy turned up at the Vic in high spirits the next day. His decree absolute had arrived in the post and they were celebrating the fact that he was officially a free man again.

'But not for long,' Kathy added, hugging him.

Phil glanced at Sharon standing behind the bar wearing an

inscrutable expression. 'No, not for long,' he agreed.

'Congratulations, both of you,' Sharon said, slightly coolly, moving off to serve another customer. Kathy clinked glasses with Phil.

'To a winning team, eh?'

Phil raised his glass. 'I'll drink to that.'

Grant bounded over, beaming. 'All ready for tonight, bruv?'

'Ready as I'll ever be.'

Kathy tugged Phil's arm. 'Hey! We ain't even in the church yet. You ain't getting cold feet, are yer?'

Phil patted her hand reassuringly. 'How could I be? I'm going to marry the most beautiful woman in Walford.'

'Er.' Grant cleared his throat. 'I hate to disappoint you, Phil, but she's already spoken for.' He looked along the bar at Sharon, who registered his gaze and smiled.

'Let's agree to disagree on that one,' Phil said tactfully, mindful of Kathy.

'What? You don't think Sharon's beautiful? Are you insulting my wife?' Grant threatened, mock-aggressive. He punched Phil playfully. 'I'll see you later – outside.'

The party was in full swing. Everybody in the Square was there, having a good time and dancing. Only a few seemed to be lacking in party spirit: Bianca's friend, Natalie, who fancied Phil, was looking on despondently; Pauline, who still thought of Kathy as Pete's wife, was whinging to Auntie Nellie, and Michelle, who was trying to keep an eye on Sharon, was being terse with Geoff.

Eventually she went over to her, leaving Geoff with Mark and his new girlfriend, Ruth, a Scottish girl he had met recently while visiting a friend at a hospice.

'Are you okay?' Michelle hissed, dragging Sharon into a corner.

'Yes, I'm fine.'

'What about Phil?'

'You'll have to ask him.'

'No,' Michelle said, exasperated. 'I mean, are you alright about him — and Kathy? Seeing them here together?'

Sharon looked across at Phil and Kathy, who were dancing. He had his arms around her, even though it wasn't a slow number, and they were smooching in the middle of the bopping crowd. 'Yes,' she said slowly, 'I'm fine.'

Grant pushed his way through the dancers and tapped on Sharon's shoulder, making her jump violently. 'There's a problem with the barrel,' he shouted above the noise. 'It's the last one. We gotta keep this lot happy, so I'm gonna nip over to the Three Feathers and borrow one off Dave. I won't be long.'

'Okay.' Sharon took his face between her hands and kissed him. 'Hurry home. It's my party, too, remember.'

Grant drove off to get the beer, thinking about Sharon. He had been on cloud nine ever since she'd agreed to try for a baby. It was like the last little bit of a jigsaw had finally slotted into place, he thought. With Sharon by his side and a kid of his own, his life would be complete. He was sure that they'd have no problems conceiving one; they'd done enough practising recently, that was for sure. With any luck they might have an announcement to make at Christmas. Grant smiled to himself, remembering what Sharon said about him on Michelle's tape. He'd been listening to it on the way to the Cash and Carry a week or so ago, but the machine had mangled it and Phil had had to sort the stereo out. Grant groped for the 'play' button. As he drew up outside the Three Feathers, he heard Sharon say, 'I want Grant now more than ever.' He switched off the engine and leaned his head back, closing his eyes for a second. Never in my entire life have I been as happy as I am now, he thought. It's like a dream. Any minute now I'll wake up. He gave himself a shake and went into the pub to fetch the barrel.

Distracted by having to take a diversion, caused by some roadworks, Grant did not put the tape back on again until he had almost got back to the Vic. He frowned as he listened to

Michelle rubbishing him, his face relaxing when he heard Sharon respond, 'I'm not saying he's perfect … but he's perfect for me.' Grant was just about to switch the ignition off, when Michelle's voice prompted, 'What about Phil?' He kept the engine running, curious.

'What about him?' Sharon replied.

'You slept with him, remember? Grant's brother.'

'Phil was different.'

'Why?'

'He just was. Oh, I didn't know that the first time … it was just lust, I wanted him. I mean, one minute I was looking at him, then the next we were ripping each other's clothes off.'

Grant listened, but he could not take it in. It was as if they were talking about two different people, total strangers. He pressed 'rewind', again and again, hearing Sharon say, '… ripping each other's clothes off …', '… ripping each other's clothes off …', '… ripping each other's clothes off …', until the image of his wife and his brother, naked, screwing, was seared into his brain as if with a red-hot poker. Tears fell silently from his eyes, although he was not aware of crying. He felt nothing at all. It was as if all the rage and fury and emotion that would normally take over him had imploded and been absorbed back into his body, into his very blood cells.

In the Vic, everyone had formed a circle around Carol and Alan Jackson, who were putting on an impressive display of jiving to a fast rock 'n' roll number.

'Sharon, this is brilliant, it really is,' Kathy said, glowing.

A large cake, iced with 'Congratulations', had just been produced and she and Phil had cut it, to much clapping and cheering. Sharon smiled warmly. 'Thanks.'

'Where's Grant?' Phil asked, looking around.

Sharon glanced at her watch. 'I dunno. He should have been back ages ago. I hope he's alright.'

A few seconds later, Grant walked in, unnoticed, threading his way through the applauding onlookers and going up to the deck of the mobile disco. Suddenly, the music stopped, causing everyone to groan. Grant, expressionless, looked at the assembled company, then pushed a button on the tape deck.

With a dreadful clarity, Michelle's voice rang out. 'What about Phil?' Sharon, the colour draining from her face, darted a glance at Michelle. They stared at each other helplessly, while people around them laughed, thinking this was some kind of party piece.

'You slept with him, remember?' Michelle's voice continued. The pub fell silent. The tape continued to roll. Everybody stood stock-still, some with glasses half-way to their mouths, as Sharon talked unguardedly about her lust for Phil, including her admission that she'd been round to see him recently. Sharon cringed as she heard herself say, 'I'd only been in there five minutes and we were all over each other again.'

Then Michelle's prompt: 'You said you didn't sleep with him.'

'No, but we could have done.' The tape had recorded Sharon's entire confession. The bar remained deathly quiet, everybody still frozen in their positions as if it was a grisly party game. Grant was the first to move, shouldering roughly past Phil and barging out of the door without saying a word. 'Grant!' Phil shouted, staring at the swinging door. The long, awkward silence continued.

'Look, I think everyone should leave,' Michelle said, taking charge. Slowly, the room came back to life, people putting down their glasses and filing out quietly. Sharon, in trepidation, approached Kathy.

'Look, Kathy,' she began, 'nothing happened ...'

'You slut!' Kathy, eyes blazing, slapped her hard across the face before collapsing on a chair in tears.

'Come on, everybody,' Phil herded the remainder towards the door. 'Time to go home. The party's over.'

While the repercussions between Sharon, Kathy and Phil continued inside the Vic, the crowd milling around outside were speculating about what Grant would do.

'Maybe he's gone to get a gun,' Bianca said, with ghoulish relish.

'Don't be silly,' Ricky snapped.

'Well he is a nutter, remember?'

Nigel, meanwhile, was arguing with Debbie. 'Look, he's my best mate, I can't leave him on his own.'

'You don't even know where he is,' Debbie pointed out.

'Then I'll have to find him,' he said, walking off.

A few minutes later, Phil appeared from the pub. 'Has anyone seen Grant?'

A lovelorn Natalie stepped forward eagerly. 'I have. Just now. He was going down towards George Street.'

'Right.' Phil set off, but Debbie scurried after him. 'Phil … look, why don't you let Nigel talk to him first, try and calm him down a bit?'

Phil ignored her and continued down Bridge Street. He passed under the viaduct and saw Nigel.

'Anything?' Phil asked anxiously.

'No, nothing.' Nigel ran a hand through his wild curls. 'I've checked the Arches and been through to Canal Street. I think we should leave it 'til tomorrow morning.'

'I can't,' Phil insisted. 'He's on his own.'

'Well, maybe he's better like that for now.'

'No! I've got to talk to him, explain what happened.'

Nigel put a hand on his arm. 'He ain't gonna listen to you. Not tonight.'

'Yeah, well, I've got to try.' Phil went on his way, leaving Nigel to return to Debbie.

They went back into the Vic, where Arthur, sent by a protective Pauline, had joined the small gathering left behind. Michelle was doling out brandies. Sharon was at the bar with her, while Kathy sat, head in hands, at a separate table. Nigel and Debbie chose the safest option and sat with Arthur.

'I don't understand why Phil's gone looking for him. He's only asking for trouble,' Arthur said.

Debbie turned to Nigel. 'It does seem a bit daft. Couldn't you have stopped him?'

'There's one thing I've learnt over the years,' Nigel said. 'Never get yourself in between the Mitchell brothers. You'll come out the other end like carrot juice.'

The street was deserted as Phil walked into Turpin Road from George Street, having found no trace of Grant either. Suddenly, he heard a tremendous crash and the sound of glass breaking. He cocked his head. It was coming from the Arches. Drawing a deep breath, Phil steeled himself and headed for the alleyway leading to the lock-up. It was pitch dark in the alley. Phil edged his way along it cautiously, coming out into the area in front where his Jag was parked. The windscreen had been completely smashed. The double doors to the lock-up were closed but he could make out a light inside. He walked over and tentatively pushed one of the doors open a foot or so. The garage was empty, his tools laid out neatly on the bench just as he'd left them earlier. Phil stepped inside and looked around, bemused, wondering whether he himself had left the light on by mistake. He was just about to give up and leave when the door slammed shut behind him. He turned round to see Grant barring his exit, back to the door, arms outstretched across it.

'Where've you been? I've been worried about you,' Phil said. He took a step towards him, stopping abruptly as Grant screamed, 'Stay away from me! If you come anywhere near me, I swear to God I'll kill you!' His face worked furiously, trying to fend off tears, but he lost the fight and broke down, sobbing uncontrollably. Phil, his heart torn to shreds, watched as Grant slid down the door and slumped on the floor, tears pouring unchecked down his cheeks.

Not heeding Grant's warning, Phil walked over to him. 'Come on, bruv,' he said, extending a hand to help him up.

'Get away from me!' Grant screamed again, lashing out wildly with a foot. 'I don't want you anywhere near me.'

Phil took a step back. Grant sat breathing heavily, attempting to compose himself. 'Worth it, was she?' he snarled eventually. Phil looked away. 'Come on ... on a scale of one to ten, what d'you reckon? A seven?'

'Grant, don't do this.'

'Come on, I'm interested. We're brothers. The least you could do is compare notes.' Grant paused, then he said bitterly, 'No? Maybe you want to explain ... only there's not a lot to explain, is there? You screwed my wife, not a lot more to say, is there, really?'

Phil did not reply.

'*Why*, Phil?' Grant's tone was beseeching. 'Why?'

'I don't know ...'

'You don't know? Did she come on to you?'

'No.'

'What then? You tried it on, just got lucky, was that it?'

'No.'

'It must have been one or the other.'

Phil looked at him wretchedly. 'It wasn't like that. It just happened.'

Grant thumped the concrete with his fist. 'She was my *wife*. You knew I loved her, you knew how much. Explain what was going through your mind? Did you think about me?'

Phil stared at the floor.

'I want to know!' Grant demanded, thumping the floor again.

'I can't change what's happened, alright.'

'Did you think about me?'

'Yes! I thought about you. I didn't think about anything else, alright?'

'When? While you were doing it? Before? After?'

'I don't know ... both of them.'

'But it didn't stop you?'

'No!' Phil suddenly retaliated, shouting. 'No, it didn't stop me. I thought about you, I saw your face and I just carried on.' He sank to his knees in front of Grant. 'And I've had to live with that ever since.'

'She was my wife,' Grant repeated, as if in a trance.

'Don't, bruv,' Phil said, welling up too.

Grant took Phil's head in both hands, cradling it to his chest. 'You're my brother,' he chanted. 'You're my brother.'

Back in the Vic, Arthur was taking down the decorations – including a large banner that read, 'Congratulations Kathy and Phil' – while Nigel and Debbie washed up. Kathy had left once the crowd outside had dispersed and Michelle had taken a shocked Sharon upstairs to comfort her.

Debbie took a soapy glass from Nigel, studying his pensive face. 'You're worried about Grant aren't you?'

He nodded. 'I'm frightened he'll do something stupid.'

'Phil will find him.'

'That worries me too.'

Debbie put her teatowel down and turned Nigel round to look at her. 'You think they might hurt each other?'

'Depends,' Nigel shrugged. 'Grant's only got three moods: happy, miserable and homicidal. It depends which one he's in when Phil finds him.'

'Well, he ain't exactly gonna be happy, is he?'

He bit his lip. 'Phil always used to say Grant would kill someone one day. Let's hope he was wrong, eh?'

'So what do you want to do?'

'I dunno.'

Debbie sighed. 'Okay, go and try to find him. Me and Arthur can manage here.'

'You don't mind?' Nigel was already pulling on his jacket.

''Course not. Just be careful.' Debbie stroked his cheek. 'Please.'

Grant got to his feet, walking away from Phil.

'Anyway, you can have her now, if that's what you want. I don't want anything to do with her,' he flung over his shoulder.

Phil stood up too. 'You can't do that.'

'Do what?' Grant swung round.

'Throw your whole life away, just because of this.'

Grant gave Phil a look of contempt. 'I'm not throwing my life away. You took it from me.'

'We can talk it out … we've always worked things out before, haven't we?' Phil said desperately.

'Phil, you slept with Sharon.' Grant paused, trying to control himself. 'I had two things in my life that meant anything. You. And her.'

'You've still got us both. She loves you and I love you.'

'I don't think you know what that word means,' Grant said menacingly, his anger starting to build. 'You want to know what love is? I'll tell you. Love is me not slamming your face through that wall. It's me not ripping down the Vic brick by brick while she's still in it. That's *my* love … brother!'

'Well, then, do that,' Phil said, surrendering himself. 'If that's what it takes for us to sort this out, just do it.'

Grant took a step towards him. 'Like that, would you? Want little brother to take the guilt away for you?'

'I don't want to lose you.' Phil stood his ground.

'You've already done that the minute you stood over *my* wife in *my* bedroom …' Grant was almost unable to say the words.

'That's not how it was,' Phil insisted again.

'No? Well you tell me how it was, I've asked you enough times.' Grant's voice rose. 'You want to make it better? Then take these pictures away.' He clamped his hands to his ears, as if he was being driven mad by demons.

'I wish I could,' Phil choked.

'Get out of my way!' Grant yelled, pushing past him to leave.

Phil caught hold of him. 'You can't go, not like this. Give it time,' Phil pleaded. 'You're hurting now …'

'Hurting? I can feel every stroke. You may as well have had a knife in your hand. Now get out of my way.'

'No.'

He faced up to Phil, head lowered, his chest rising and falling rapidly. 'I'm warning you. Don't do this.'

'Hit me, go on, that's what I want, I deserve it!' Phil begged, standing in his path. 'Come on, I want it over with!'

'Move!'

'No ... come on!' Phil shoved Grant backwards, trying to provoke him. 'Come on. Think about what I did. I want it out the way – come on, over with!' He pushed Grant again.

Suddenly, Grant let out a roar and charged at him, sending Phil sprawling backwards. He half-collapsed on the floor but made no attempt to get up. Screaming, Grant drove a boot into his side, and, when he continued to offer no resistance, he picked Phil up by his lapels and spun him round, hurling him across the lock-up as if he was a rag doll.

Nigel had combed the streets around the Square with no more success than the first time. He was on the point of calling it a night, when he decided to have another squint at the Arches. It was the only other place Grant could be, he thought. Funny there was no sign of Phil, though. The fact that neither of them had turned up made him feel distinctly uneasy. When he came across Phil's Jag with its smashed windscreen, he felt even more uneasy. There was a light on in the garage, but no noise. Slowly, he pushed open the door. Grant was sitting on the edge of the inspection pit with his legs dangling over the side. He could not see Phil anywhere. 'Grant?' he called hesitantly. Grant did not react. Nigel came in, his heart beating fast. Something was definitely wrong. Grant was staring down into the pit with a fixed expression on his face.

'Grant?' he said again. There wasn't a flicker; Grant was totally spaced out. Nigel walked towards him, ready to turn and run if necessary. As he drew nearer, he realized with a surge of horror what Grant was staring at. In the bottom of the inspection pit was a dark form. Nigel leaned over and looked in. Below him, lying twisted on the concrete in a pool of blood, lay Phil.

CHAPTER NINETEEN

It was Nigel who called for an ambulance. Had he not found him, Phil would probably have bled to death. Grant had gone into a zombie-like state and seemed barely to register what was going on. Nigel tried to make him leave before the police arrived, but Grant refused. As a crowd gathered outside the Arches, a hysterical Kathy pointed at Grant and screamed, 'He's the one who did it.'

Grant, passive, allowed himself to be led away for questioning.

At the hospital, Phil was found to have serious internal injuries requiring immediate surgery. The following day he was in a stable condition and allowed visitors. But Kathy, who had been waiting there all night, suddenly bottled out, declaring that she wasn't family and she hardly knew him, and Sharon was too terrified to leave the safety of the Vic. Two police officers arrived later, trying to get him to tell them what had happened, but Phil stonewalled them. His only other visitor was Ricky who'd been looking after the Arches since Phil got hurt.

With nothing to go on – Grant refused to speak to them and Phil would not press charges – the police were forced to release Grant. Nigel took him under his wing, putting him up on his sofa and trying to encourage him to talk about his feelings.

'What's there to talk about?' Grant replied listlessly. He had not bothered to dress and was still sitting around in his boxers and T-shirt, even though it was gone midday.

Nigel passed him a can of lager. 'I think maybe it would do you good – you know, get it out in the open.'

Grant was silent for so long that Nigel thought he'd gone

into some kind of trance. Then, at last, he said, 'Have you ever seen a bullfight?'

'No.' Nigel looked confused.

'I have. I remember this one – there was this bull – mad great thing it was, and this bullfighter, he just danced rings around it till, bit by bit, all the life was drained out of it.'

'Doesn't exactly sound like family entertainment.'

'You see,' Grant said, leaning forward, almost animated, 'this bull thought it was a fair fight, thought it could win, get away, but it couldn't. It didn't stand a chance.'

'But you're not like that,' Nigel exclaimed, realizing what he was getting at.

'Yes, I am.'

That night, Grant's nightmares returned. Nigel, startled out of sleep by the screams, padded through from his bedroom to see what had happened.

'Grant, wake up.' He shook him gently. 'You're having a nightmare.'

Grant rubbed his eyes. 'Oh, sorry, sorry mate.'

'What was it about?' Nigel assumed he was dreaming about the fight with Phil but Grant replied, 'Nothing. I used to get them all the time.' He looked at Nigel, as if trying to make up his mind about something, then said, 'I killed someone, when I was in the Falklands, up close.'

Nigel shifted uncomfortably. 'Yeah, well, that was what you were there for, wasn't it?'

'He was just a kid. Couldn't have been more than sixteen. I sat and watched him die in front of me.' He challenged Nigel with his blank-eyed stare. 'D'you know what? It was easy.'

There was another long pause.

Finally, Nigel said, 'He's gonna be alright, you know.'

'Who?' Grant's eyes were blank.

'Phil. Your brother.'

Grant showed no reaction. 'I haven't got a brother.'

★

It took Peggy's arrival in the Square to jolt Grant out of his morose mood. She had got wind of Phil's 'accident' from Kathy, who had relented and been to visit him. Peggy came straight over to Walford. Grant had been staying out of her way, but when he ran into her at the bus stop it was impossible for him to avoid her.

'Why didn't you call me, you useless great lump? Come on, give us a hug.' She embraced him and he clung to her for a second, desperate for comfort. 'Now that's what I call a hug. I couldn't get one from Phil so I just kissed his bald patch.' Grant smiled tightly but said nothing. 'He's going to be alright, isn't he?' Peggy asked anxiously. 'The doctor said he'd be home soon.'

'You know Phil, he always lands on his feet.'

'I wish he had. Do you know they had to give him a brain scan?'

'Did they?' Grant didn't know. He told himself he didn't care, either.

'Horrible, isn't it?' Peggy rattled on. They had seen little of her over the past few years, especially after Sam left to pursue supermodel stardom, so when Grant heard that she and Kevin had split up, he was surprised.

'I'm sorry,' he said, genuinely remorseful for having lost touch.

'So you should be,' Peggy remonstrated. 'It didn't used to be like this, did it? We were always together. When it mattered.' She eyed him beadily. 'Things can't go on like they are, Grant. I mean, what's more important than family? If it's good, you hang onto it. And if it's wrong, you've got to fix it.'

'I suppose you're right,' Grant said, an idea beginning to take shape in the back of his mind.

Phil had been in hospital for a fortnight and was making a good recovery when he suddenly developed a blood clot on the brain. Kathy took the call and telephoned Grant before rushing to the hospital. Grant, however, showed absolutely no interest in Phil's fate. In desperation, Nigel asked Sharon to go and talk to him, but the meeting only provoked Grant to hurl at her, 'I don't want to see you, I don't want to hear you, you don't exist! Get out!', repeating his shouts until she ran from the room in tears.

Nigel, who it took a lot to provoke, was incensed at Grant's selfishness.

'Can't stop thinking about yourself, can ya?' he demanded, momentarily unfazed by the prospect of Grant's savage temper.

'Oh yeah, and who else is going to think about me, Nige?'

'I'm Nige to my friends – and I don't think we're friends any more, Grant.'

'Alright, *Nigel*. Have a pop.' Grant stood in front of him and folded his arms. 'I mean, everyone else has. But you know something, I don't give a toss, 'cos if there's one thing I've learned lately, it's that if you don't care, you don't get hurt. From now on I'm looking after number one.'

'And what about Phil?' Nigel raged. 'Do you know what he said to me this morning when I went to visit him? He said, "Grant's my family". Despite everything that's happened to you, he still loves you. They both do, him and Sharon. Don't you think they've suffered enough? Do you have to keep twisting the knife?'

Grant sat down on the sofa and picked up a magazine. 'Believe me, I haven't started yet.'

Nigel, shaking with anger, leaned over him. 'You're a nasty piece of work, you know that, Grant? I don't blame Sharon for what she did. I don't blame either of them.' He took a breath, trying to control himself. 'After what you've put her through it's no wonder she jumped at the chance of a bit of love and warmth. Phil's worth ten of you. He's everything you're not.'

'Shut up, Nigel!' Grant's face darkened with fury.

'No I won't. Not this time.' Nigel was almost beside himself. 'I never thought I'd say it, but I'm ashamed of you, Grant. I used to think you were such a big man, but you're not, you're pathetic. You don't deserve a brother like Phil.'

'Too right I don't,' Grant sneered. Nigel, losing it, threw a punch, something he had never done in his entire life. It was Grant who defended him when they were at school; Nigel had always backed off a fight. Grant rode the punch easily but did not retaliate. He was too surprised.

Nigel's anger went down like a pricked balloon and he turned away, disgusted. 'Phil could be dead by tomorrow.' He caught Grant's sudden attentive look out of the corner of his eye and continued, 'Yeah, that's right, dead. But what do you care, eh? You're already dead.'

Kathy sat in the hospital waiting area, crying into her hanky. There were few people about, mainly nurses. She didn't care whether they saw her crying. She had a lot to cry about. Just as she had started to build some bridges with Phil, fate was threatening to take him away from her. She wasn't sure, yet, whether they still had a future but she did know that she loved him, despite everything, and she wanted him to recover. He was in theatre at that very moment. The wait was almost unbearable. She sniffled and blew her nose, trying to get a grip, then glanced up to check the time on the wall clock opposite. Instead, she found herself looking straight into the eyes of Grant. Saying nothing, he sat down on a chair a little way away from her. From his hunched posture and fixed stare, Kathy could tell he didn't want to be disturbed.

Peggy arrived in a tizz soon afterwards, but did not stay long. She hated hospitals and was agitated and ill-at-ease, preferring to go home and keep herself occupied there.

Kathy tried to persuade Grant to go as well, prompting him to snarl, 'I've spent most of the day having people tell me I should be here. Now you're telling me to go home.'

'You should be here because you want to be,' she said mildly.

'I'm the one that put him here, remember?'

'Yes, I know, but I don't think you wanted this.'

'Didn't I?' Grant's eyes glinted. He spun off into a rant

about Phil which made it clear he had not come to make amends.

'Then why are you here?' Kathy asked eventually.

'Maybe I'm waiting for him to come out of surgery so I can beat the crap out of him again.'

'You don't mean that, Grant.'

'Alright, so why am I here?'

'Because he's your brother. That must mean something.'

'It didn't mean anything to him. Why should it mean anything to me?'

'Because he's already paid for what he did. He's in there, now, fighting for his life.'

'So what, I'm supposed to feel guilty, am I?'

'No, but you should be talking about him getting better, about sorting this mess out. Not going over the same old ground. It's done, finished with. It's what happens now that matters.'

'Who are you trying to convince?' Grant said. 'Me ... or yourself?'

It was getting on for one o'clock in the morning before the surgeon appeared, apologising for the wait. He informed Kathy that the operation to relieve the pressure on the brain had been a success, but that they wouldn't know whether there was any brain damage until Phil woke up. Grant took no notice of the surgeon.

Bracing herself, Kathy followed the nurse into the high dependency unit, where Phil was the only patient. His head was swathed in bandages and he seemed to be attached to numerous tubes and drips and monitors. Kathy stared at him, willing him to be alright, begging the God that she wasn't sure she believed in to spare his life. Prayer was the only thing she had left.

'There's nothing more you can do now. Go home and get some rest,' the nurse advised.

'You will phone me, though, when he wakes up? Please?'

The nurse hesitated. 'We don't usually, but ... alright, I'll phone you.'

When Kathy returned to the waiting area, Grant had gone.

In the semi-darkened room, the machines were the only things that seemed to be alive: the ECG bleeping, the ventilator pumping rhythmically up and down. Phil lay in the bed immobile. For all Grant knew he was dead, but the instruments indicated otherwise. He sat down next to him, staring at his face. Kathy's voice echoed in his head, repeating, 'So why are you here?' Grant didn't know the answer to that one yet himself. He was so full of hate and hurt that he could hardly think straight. All he did know was that this night was the defining point of their lives. Whatever happened, he couldn't be anywhere else. Slowly, very slowly, he reached out and took Phil's hand.

A slight metallic clank of the drip stand being rocked jolted Grant awake instantly. He felt a rush of guilt at having dropped off, and glanced up at his watch: it was just gone six o'clock. He must have been asleep for a couple of hours.

'Bruv?' he whispered, his heart in his mouth. Phil's fingers pressed his palm. For a fleeting second, Grant thought that was all he was able to do. He heard again Kathy berating Sharon, who had turned up earlier at the hospital: 'They're operating on his brain at the moment. And if he survives that, which he may not, he might end up as a vegetable.'

'Bruv?' Grant whispered again, more urgently. Phil turned his head. He squinted, as if trying to focus on Grant, then smiled drowsily. 'They drugged me or something?'

'If they've got any sense,' Grant replied shakily, relief flooding through him. There was a beat between them.

'How have you been?' Phil said.

'Alright ... still kipping at Nige's.'

'Good old Nige, eh?'

'Yeah ... he was the one who got me to come here

tonight … I didn't want to.'

'I don't blame you for that,' Phil said quietly.

Grant's face hardened. 'Did you love her?'

'What?'

'Sharon.'

Phil looked away. 'I thought I did.'

'And now?'

Phil shook his head.

'Did you tell her? That you loved her?'

'Yeah.'

'And did she say it to you?'

'Yes. Look, what difference does it make?'

Grant, unheeding, continued his interrogation. 'Did she talk about leaving me?'

'No!'

'Liar,' he snarled.

'She never would have done it, it was all talk. You'd been a right bastard to her. She didn't know whether she was coming or going.'

'Both, by the sound of it,' Grant said nastily.

'She was mixed up, confused. She didn't know what she wanted.'

'Oh, and you were just helping her out?'

'No!'

'A shoulder to cry on, was that it?'

'Well, I listened to her, yes.'

'Slag me off, did she?'

'No!'

'Put your arm round her, told her everything would be alright?'

'You're not listening,' Phil sighed.

'Took her to bed?'

'That wasn't meant to happen.'

Grant leaned forward suddenly, resting his forearms on his knees. He glared at Phil. 'So you keep saying. So why do it?'

Phil paused, as if asking himself the same question for the

first time. He said, 'She never wanted me. All she wanted was you. I was just …'

'In the right place at the right time?'

'Wrong place, wrong time.'

Grant stood up and went over to the window, parting the blinds slightly. Outside, the sky was still quite dark, but streaked with strips of pink and yellow, a new day about to dawn. He did not know what to think or where to go. It was as if the two of them were lost in a desert. Any direction might bring them home or send them somewhere more remote. He turned round to look at Phil. He was fast asleep.

'Did we get anywhere?' Phil asked blearily, when he woke up again half an hour later.

'Not really.'

'I want us to.'

'Make a lot of people happy if we didn't.' Grant came and sat down next to him again. He had been prowling the room, unable to keep still. It was getting light now. They didn't have much longer.

'What?' Phil still wasn't with it.

'Ever since I can remember, people have wanted us to come a cropper. They always hated what we were, that we always had each other.'

'We still have,' Phil said.

Grant shot him a look, unconvinced. 'Sharon hated it. Me and you … she never liked the idea that all you had to do was shout, and I'd go running.'

'Same with Kathy.'

'They don't understand it, I suppose.'

'That's because they've never had it.'

'Maybe.' Grant paused. 'I don't know what to think any more. I've been thinking about moving out, getting out of London.'

'Why?'

'What is this — stupid question time?'

'Alright, you hate me now, and I don't blame you for that. So tell me what to do, how to make things better.'

'You can't.'

'Grant. I love you. You're my kid brother. Nothing can change that.'

'I've never betrayed you,' Grant said, wretched.

'I know,' Phil said, more softly, 'and I've never run away from you when you needed me.'

'We've always been there for each other. Until the day you screwed Sharon. "You thought about me". Your words. You thought about me, and it didn't make any difference. I needed you then, I needed you to walk away, but you didn't.' Grant leaned over Phil's prone body, until their noses were almost touching. 'So don't tell me what we had, I know. But you took it away.' He shoved his chair back and walked away from the bed. 'And if you take that away, what's left, eh? What makes us special?'

'So you're saying there's no way back?'

'How can there be?'

Phil went on the attack. 'Alright, so you move on, then what? You can't survive ten minutes on your own.'

'No?'

'No. A tenner says you're banged up within a year.'

'You finished?' Grant demanded.

'Yeah.'

'Then stop talking to me like we can chat about it for ten minutes and everything will be alright. You screwed my wife! Doing it was bad enough, but why wait for me to find out?'

'I wanted to tell you. I just didn't know how.'

'You told Kathy. Right at the start, when you got together in Paris. She told me while you were under the knife.'

'Grant ... I needed someone to talk to about it. She was there.'

'So was I.'

Phil sighed heavily. 'You think I didn't want to tell you? You think it didn't eat away inside me every time I looked at you?'

'But that's just it, though. Kathy knew something I didn't. So did Michelle. I sat in a room with you and Sharon and you both knew it and I didn't. So what does that make me? And what kind of a brother does that make you?'

Grant stared aimlessly out of the blinds, his face wet with tears. Day had come and from beyond the ward there were sounds of activity: doors banging, voices calling 'Good morning', the rattle of a trolley. He wiped his cheeks with the back of his hand. 'They'll be coming in soon. I'd better go.'

'No,' Phil begged, desperation in his voice.

'We've been round the houses, Phil. There's nowhere else to go. You can't take away what you did.'

'I can try, can't I? I can try by being the best friend you'll ever have, the best brother, by never letting you down again ...'

'But that's just it. I thought you were those things already.' Grant remained by the window, keeping his face turned away.

'I know. I always have been ... I just seemed to forget along the way somewhere. You married Sharon, moved out of the Arches, took over the pub – you were moving on but my life was stuck in limbo.' He paused. 'I suppose I envied you what you had. I thought, "That should be me, I should have that, I'm the eldest brother ..."'

'So you thought you'd take it away from me?' Grant said bitterly.

'No. That was just a moment of madness. Maybe I wanted to know that I could have what you'd got, if I wanted it.'

'I've never had anything that I wouldn't give you. Ever since we were kids, we've shared everything. I thought a wife may be different.' Grant tried to restrain a sob. 'I really loved her. She was the only decent thing I ever had. The only thing that was clean ... proper. Or at least, I thought she was.'

'I'm sorry, Grant,' Phil said, husky-voiced too.

'You and me both.'

'Don't go.'

Grant turned round at last, his eyes red. 'There's nothing left for me here.'

'Sharon still loves you, you know. Just talk to her, let her explain.'

'She can have reasons coming out of her arse. At the end of the day, she ended up on her back ... I don't know why I ever thought any different. The only thing she's ever cared about is that sodding pub, like it was some shrine to her old man. Well, I'm gonna rip it down around her ears.'

Phil was silent. 'And me?' he asked eventually.

'I don't know.'

'If you go, then we both go.'

'Kathy ain't gonna like that. But I appreciate the thought.' Grant smiled wanly.

'Tell me what you want and I'll make it happen.'

'Got a time machine in the Arches?' Phil shook his head. Grant walked back to the end of the bed. 'Looks like we're stuck with it.' He looked down on Phil, his anger blown out. 'You know I'll crush Sharon like a ping-pong ball.' It wasn't a question, it was a statement of fact.

'Yeah,' Phil said, resigned.

'You won't go stepping in? Sir Phillip on his white horse?'

'All I want is for us to be back where we were.'

'Maybe I should go away, give it time, a bit of space. I could always go and join the Foreign Legion. That's where you go to forget, innit?'

Phil saw Grant was only half-joking and tried once more to reach out to him. 'What about all those people waiting for us to come a cropper? Why give 'em the satisfaction, eh?'

Grant bowed his head. 'I don't know what to do,' he said, all his bravado gone. 'I still love her.'

'Then go back to her. Put it behind you.'

'I can't ... I've tried, but I can't.' Grant broke down and started to cry. Phil ached to get up and hold him, but he couldn't move from the bed.

'Don't, Grant ...'

Suddenly, Grant choked, 'Tell me it wasn't you.'

'What?'

'Tell me it wasn't you! That it was her!' he demanded ferociously.

'Okay.'

'Tell me!'

'It was her.'

'She led you on.'

'Yeah.'

'She threw herself at you. There was nothing you could do!'

'Grant!' Phil could see what he was doing. It wasn't the answer, piling lies upon lies. Then again, it was the only chance Grant was going to throw him.

'Say it!'

'Alright! There was nothing I could do.'

A load seemed to fall off Grant's shoulders. He came round to the side of the bed and embraced Phil as best he could with all the tubes and wires attached to him. 'You're my brother, right. Me and you again, eh? Sod 'em all.'

'Sod 'em all,' Phil chanted.

'You know the worst?' Grant said, his face relaxed now. He perched on the bed. 'The worst was I thought I'd lost you.'

Phil grabbed his hand, holding it tight. 'That ain't gonna happen.'

'After everything, the only thing I was worried about was not having a big brother any more.' Grant was laughing and crying at the same time, his face transformed with smiles.

'I'm sorry, Grant.'

'It wasn't you. I know that now.' He curled up next to Phil, laying his head on his chest. 'It was never you, only her ...'

'Grant.'

'No, say it. Say it. There's just you and me.'

Phil was silent.

Grant lifted his head and looked at him.

'There's just you and me,' Phil repeated, pulling Grant to him in a tender embrace.

CHAPTER TWENTY

Nigel rubbed his eyes blearily. The smell of bacon frying wafted in from the kitchen, accompanied by the sound of Grant singing along loudly to the radio. It didn't seem natural, not after the state Grant had been in for the past few weeks. Wondering what kind of a reception he would get – he had, after all, attempted to deck Grant the previous evening – Nigel went into the kitchen.

'One sausage or two?' Grant said, brandishing the pan. Nigel blinked. 'What's all this about?'

'All what?'

'This "new man" business.'

'I'm making a fresh start on everything.' He poured Nigel a mug of tea. 'Sit down mate, you look shattered.'

'Well, I ...' Nigel hadn't been able to sleep all night for worrying about Phil. Obviously he was better, he concluded.

'What is it they say?' Grant continued, almost bubbly. 'Today is the very first day of the rest of your life? Now eat your breakfast, it's getting cold.'

When Sharon learned about Phil and Grant's bedside reunion, she was surprised. Michelle broke the news as gently as she could. 'Nigel reckons they've made it up – sorted it – whatever that means.'

'It means the Mitchell brothers are back in business,' Sharon said grimly. 'Apparently, nothing can separate them.'

'Don't you believe it. Grant can't really forgive Phil for you.'

Sharon stirred her coffee slowly. 'I'm a woman, 'Chelle – a tart – hating me will help the two of them.'

'So where does that leave you?' Michelle asked, concerned.

'Look, it's good news, 'Chelle.' Sharon forced herself to smile. 'They need each other and I've got the Vic, and that's what I'm holding on to.' She said it with a show of confidence she did not feel. The prospect of confronting Grant again was petrifying enough; the idea of having both Grant and Phil ranged against her did not bear thinking about.

Sharon spent the rest of the day pondering Grant's next move and keeping a low profile in the Vic. She still didn't dare brave the Square: Kathy, who had reopened the café, was being venomous, and she didn't fancy a run-in with her or Pauline Fowler, or anyone else for that matter. It was hard enough just holding her head up in the pub. Having hidden herself away upstairs for a while, she was back behind the bar again and toughing it out. Some people had been sympathetic, like Pat Butcher, but Michelle was the only person sticking up for her publicly. Sharon had spent half the evening trying not to catch the whispered conversations and quick glances in her direction, but it was obvious what everyone was talking about.

Feeling very vulnerable and very alone, she was just about to lock up after closing when someone wedged a boot in the door. Recognising it as Grant's, she knew, with a terrible sinking feeling, that she wasn't going to be by herself any more.

Grant's campaign of hate against Sharon began immediately. By lunchtime the next day, his vicious remarks and sneering innuendoes had reduced her to a quivering wreck. Retreating to the living-room with Michelle and a large gin, she tried to explain things. One look at the drink slopping in her trembling hands was all Michelle needed to see.

'What is it, Sharon? What are you scared of? What's he been doing?'

'He's just so … cold. The way he looks at me, like I'm something he stepped in. Things he said …'

'Like what?'

Sharon shook her head. She couldn't bring herself to tell

even Michelle the vile names he had called her and the utter contempt with which he treated her. It was almost harder to deal with than his violent outbursts. At least she knew where she was with that Grant. This calculating, sadistic bully had unnerved her completely.

'Sharon, look at you!' Michelle put an arm around her. 'You can't let him terrify you in your own home.' She was itching to have a showdown with Grant, but Sharon insisted that she keep out of it. All the same, when Michelle pressed a spare set of house keys on her – 'just in case anything happens' – she pocketed them gratefully.

Michelle did not have long to wait before she and Grant clashed head to head. That evening, when she was working her shift, he came into the bar and helped himself to a beer.

'Where's Sharon?' Michelle asked protectively, concerned that she had not followed Grant down.

'Upstairs servicing the punters I expect. I mean, that is her job, isn't it?'

'I suppose you think that's funny.'

Grant slammed his beer bottle down. 'There's some tables over there need clearing. Do it.'

'Say please.'

'I said, do it!' he flared, taking a step towards her. Michelle stood her ground. The buzz of conversation suddenly fell quiet. Just at that moment, Sharon entered.

'What's going on?'

'Shut it. No one asked you.' Grant swung back to Michelle. 'I said, clear those tables.' Michelle did not budge. Sharon, noticing the back of Grant's neck turning red, cut in smoothly.

'Do what he says, 'Chelle.'

Michelle moved away. 'Of course, Sharon. You're the boss.'

'That's right,' Grant snarled. 'She's top dog around here. But I'm the one holding her lead. You'd do well to remember that.'

He took his revenge after closing by giving Michelle the

sack. 'Now, you can walk out of here, or you can go in an ambulance. Your choice,' he said, slapping her wages down on the bar.

'What you gonna do? Beat me up?' Michelle taunted.

'If you like.' He smiled menacingly.

'You touch me and I'll call the police.'

'And tell them what?'

'They'd be very interested in the robbery you were planning with Dougie. And that's just for starters.'

'You see, that's the very reason you should go, Michelle. Be a shame if anything like that happened again.'

'Going to shoot me, are you?'

Grant came up to her, putting his face close. 'You weren't shot. A couple of drunks were fighting and you got caught in the crossfire, remember? That's what you told the police. Happens all the time. It'll be a glass in your face, next, eh?'

'I ain't leaving,' Michelle said, pale but determined.

'You'll have to leave us alone sometime.' Grant went over to Sharon and put his arm around her.

'Tell her to go,' he said, making a play of affection. 'We're never going to patch up our marriage with her around, are we?' He kissed Sharon on the top of the head and left with an arch smile.

The two women looked at each other. ''Chelle …' Sharon began.

'You can't be serious.'

'He's right.'

'He's certifiable.'

Sharon fixed her eyes on the floor. 'Well, you working here won't make me any safer, will it? It'll probably make things a whole lot worse. You're going to send him off like that all the time.'

Michelle was dumbfounded. 'You want me to go, then?'

Sharon wanted nothing of the sort. But she did want to try again with Grant. And if he was offering an olive branch …

'Yes. I'm sorry.'

Michelle opened her mouth to speak, but Sharon interrupted her. 'Please, 'Chelle, don't make this any harder than it is. It's my mess and I'm the one that's got to clean it up.' She paused. 'Go on, before I change my mind.'

'I wish you would.'

'Well, I won't.'

'He does anything at all, you've got my keys.'

'Yeah.'

Michelle slipped out into the night, giving Sharon one, last, doubtful backward look. Sharon slid the bolts across and turned around to see that Grant had reappeared noiselessly in the bar. He had obviously been listening. Opening another bottle of beer, he took a swig, then emptied the rest of it all over the floor.

'I'll leave you to clear up, shall I? Like you said. It's your mess.'

A week later, Sharon received a divorce petition in the post. Michelle told her to sign it and send it straight back, but, despite Grant's regime of humiliation and insults, Sharon couldn't bring herself to do it. Somewhere in the back of her mind was the vague belief that if Grant could get all the poison out of his system by torturing her, they might be able to pick up again where they left off. If there was anything left of her by then. Another, equally masochistic voice, told her that this was all her own fault and it was only right that she should do penance by suffering. Phil was due out of hospital in a few days and the thought of what he'd been through, because of her, sliced into her conscience like a knife.

Grant, too, seemed rattled by the prospect of Phil's return, upping the ante and drinking heavily. 'Don't you think you've had enough?' Sharon said, as he sat slumped at the bar one lunchtime.

'There's only one thing I've had enough of, sweetheart, and that's you.' Grant stared at her with distaste.

'I'm not the only one, either. Poor Phil, better not run into you when he gets back, you'll set him back weeks. Now get me another drink.'

Michelle, who was hanging around in the Vic keeping an eye on Sharon, drew her to one side.

'How much longer is this going to go on? Just sign it, Sharon. Sign the damn thing. It doesn't matter who's right or wrong. Just sign it.'

To everyone's surprise, Phil did not return to Walford on his discharge from hospital, opting instead to convalesce at Peggy's for a while. Peggy had been insistent – it was part of her crusade to reunite the family – but Kathy was shocked. She still wasn't sure whether she wanted Phil back living with her, but at the same time she didn't like having the decision made for her. Especially by interfering Peggy Mitchell. She moaned to Grant about it, who was equally upset. He had been looking forward to spending Christmas with Phil, bonding under the tree with some good malt and putting the past few weeks behind them.

When he found Sharon putting decorations up in the Vic, he laid into her savagely. 'You must be really pleased. Not only did you nearly kill Phil, you've also succeeded in splitting him and Kathy up.' Sharon, who was standing on a chair, trying to position holly around the picture rail, looked down nervously. 'I'd call that a good day's work – I'm sorry, you only work nights, don't you? – even by your standards,' Grant hissed. 'Not that you've got any.'

Christmas Day dawned clear and cold. Sharon stood at the window with a hint of a smile on her face, looking out at children riding new bikes and skateboards in the Square. She heard Grant moving on the landing and her smile faded. The days when Christmas was a thrilling, magical time were over. Just to make the point, Grant slung the divorce papers down on the breakfast table.

'I got you something. Something you've had for weeks.'

'I've been busy.'

'You've got time now.'

'I want to be sure I'm doing the right thing. I need time to think.'

'What's there to think about? I don't want you as a wife.'

'I don't believe that. I can't.' She took a deep breath. 'I still love you, Grant.'

'Oh, grow up Sharon. I don't love you, we're not gonna get back together again, and there's no such thing as Father Christmas.' He hurled the petition in her face, catching her unawares. 'Now sign the sodding forms.'

Later on that morning Sharon found Grant back in the kitchen, nursing a glass of whisky and fingering the present she had left on the table for him.

'Aren't you gonna open it?' she asked, coming in and sitting down. He shoved it out of the way. Sharon sighed. 'Please talk to me, Grant.'

'Okay, darlin',' he said, with exaggerated warmth. 'What would you like to talk about?'

'Us.'

He laid his forearms on the table and leaned towards her. 'Well, let's talk about you, eh? Why did you sleep with my brother?'

'I ...' Sharon struggled to try and put her answer in a nutshell.

'You ...' Grant gave her an impatient 'I'm waiting' look.

'It's hard to explain ...'

'Yeah, of course, it must be. How about if I give you a list of possibilities and you pick one? Would that be easier?' He ticked them off on his fingers. 'One. It seemed like a good idea at the time. Two. You couldn't resist his aftershave. Three. It was dark, you couldn't see who it was.' He paused. 'Four. You're a slut.'

'That's not true, stop saying that.'

'Okay, and what would you call yourself?'

'I made a mistake.'

'No! A mistake is giving someone salt 'n' vinegar crisps when they ask for cheese and onion. Hardly the same, is it?'

'But you won't give me the chance to explain,' Sharon said, her bottom lip beginning to tremble.

'Why should I?'

'I don't know ... because you loved me once, because I'm still your wife ... because it's Christmas Day ... anything, just try,' she pleaded.

Grant stood up. 'Oh yeah, it's Christmas, the season of goodwill to all sluts. Well, let's get in the spirit of things, shall we?' He walked over to the sink, picked up a plate from the draining-board and smashed it on the floor. Very deliberately and very falsely, he began to sing. 'Jin-gle bells, Jin-gle bells, Jin-gle all the way', smashing more crockery in time to the beat. When he had cleared the washing-up in the rack, he started on the cupboards, hurling their contents – food, glass jars, mugs, dishes – around the kitchen in time with the macabre parody. 'Oh-what-fun-it-is-to-ride-on-a-one-horse-open-sleigh ...'

'Grant, stop it,' Sharon screamed, cowering in a corner and covering her ears. He came up to her weighing a saucepan in his hand.

'Sign the forms!' He held the pan aloft for a second, as if he might bring it down on her head, then dropped it on the floor with a clatter and walked out of the room.

As far as the Vic was concerned, Christmas was cancelled, Sharon decided, taking down the decorations in the bar. It was lunchtime and there were punters knocking on the door, but she merely yelled, 'We're closed' and carried on ripping down the paper chains and tinsel.

'What do you think this is going to prove?' Grant said, watching her.

'Nothing. I just don't see why I should stand behind that bar pretending to be happy when I'm not.'

'Feeling sorry for ourselves, are we?'

'Say what you like, I'm past arguing,' Sharon snapped, stuffing the decorations into a box.

Grant picked up the divorce papers from the bar. 'Then sign the forms.'

'I'm going to see a solicitor first, tell me what I'm entitled to, what my rights are.'

'You haven't got any rights.'

'We'll see.' She swung round to challenge him.

'Alright, you fight me. Take me to court. Everything they say you can have, I'll burn to the ground.' Grant's eyes blazed with a frightening intensity. 'I'll haunt you, everywhere you turn, I'll be looking at you. You won't have a life because I won't let you have one.'

'Grant, please!' Sharon stammered, increasingly distressed at his malevolence.

'You've got no idea what it feels like, have you? You ever had anybody ram their fist down your throat and pull out your insides?' His head was bowed, shoulders drooping in an attitude of utter despair.

Tentatively, Sharon walked up to him and put a hand on his arm. Turning him round towards her she said, 'I know you're hurting, darlin', but I can make it better if you let me, eh?' She kissed him gently on the cheek. 'I can always make it better ...'

He stood stock-still, letting her nuzzle and caress him. Then, just as Sharon thought she could feel him beginning to respond, he lashed out, sending her sprawling on her back.

'Is that how it was with Phil, eh? Is that how you came on to him?'

'No!' She tried to get up, but he was looming over her.

'Look at you – just like your mother, drunk and begging for it. He told me that's how it was. He told me everything. How you tried it on, how he tried to stop it, but you were all over him.'

'That's not true!'

Grant took her by the shoulders, shaking her. 'Don't lie to me. I know everything. He even said if it hadn't been him, it would have been someone else.'

'No!'

'You make me sick.' He shoved Sharon back on the floor and walked out of the room, leaving her crying bitter tears into the carpet.

After a while she picked herself up and went into the bedroom, dragging her suitcase down from the top of the wardrobe. Hastily, she began to pack.

It was too quiet in the bar. The silence and the emptiness was driving Grant crazy. He put down his whisky and got up. Even fighting with Sharon would be better than sitting by himself, his head clamouring with accusatory voices. Staggering slightly, he went upstairs. There was no sign of Sharon. He went into the living-room and, drawn by the sound of music, walked over to the window. Outside, in the middle of the Square, the Salvation Army band was playing in the gardens. All the local residents seemed to be there, under the tall Christmas tree, joining in with the carols: the Fowlers; Ian and Cindy and their brood; Michelle and Vicki; Kathy; Nigel, Debbie and Clare; the Jacksons; the Butchers, even Doctor Legg and Ethel. Everyone looked happy and together, the young couples – Ricky and Bianca, Mark and Ruth – with their arms around each other. For a second, Grant felt his eyes misting over and blinked furiously. Below him, a black cab threaded its way past the crowd and chugged out of the Square. Grant released the curtain and went into the kitchen, which was still a bombsite of broken crockery, burst flour bags and shattered ketchup bottles. The present and card Sharon had bought him were still on the table, untouched, with the divorce papers propped up against them. He picked them up and leafed through them. Sharon had signed them.

CHAPTER TWENTY-ONE

Grant didn't know that Sharon had left the country until Boxing Day, when he found Michelle opening up the Vic. She informed him tersely that Sharon had gone to Angie's in Florida, leaving her to run the pub. In spite of everything, Grant was stunned. Today was their wedding anniversary. Having got what he wanted at last – Sharon's signature on the divorce petition – he felt strangely hollow inside. He tried to swamp the emptiness with booze, but all it did was give him a bad head and a worse temper.

Grant took out his temper on Michelle. At least she was useful for something, he thought. He took a perverse pleasure in goading her until she couldn't stand it any more and handed over the reins to Pat Butcher. Pat knew the Vic of old – she and Frank had run it before Sharon and Wicksy took over – and she was not a woman to be messed with. Grant was forced to call a truce and they settled down to a guarded co-existence.

The arrangement worked well enough until Peggy started giving Grant stick about the Vic going to seed. Before he knew it, she had her feet under the bar and was organising a pub football team. Her intervention put Pat's nose thoroughly out of joint, but as far as Grant was concerned, that was tough. Prompted by Nigel's comment that the Vic had got some of its old family atmosphere back, Grant made Peggy's appointment permanent. The Mitchell family was back in business.

There was also a new addition to the clan – Kathy Beale. She and Phil had married secretly at a registry-office ceremony with Grant and Pat as witnesses. Peggy was initially disapproving. Kathy had been holding Phil at arm's length since his discharge from hospital and they had only recently been reunited as a couple. In Peggy's eyes, Kathy's offhand treatment of her son was deplorable, but she knew nothing of the cause, and Phil and Grant aimed to keep it that way.

Sharon returned to Walford in the middle of March, strolling up Bridge Street looking like a million dollars. She had a stunning tan, glossy hair, designer clothes and a manner that exuded confidence. Her reappearance in the Square sent ripples of excitement through the market traders, particularly Sanjay Kapoor, who had a clothes stall just down from Mark Fowler's fruit and veg.

'Sharon! You're looking great!' he drooled as she passed.

'Thanks,' she replied, 'You're not looking so bad yourself.'

Sanjay grinned. 'Good to see you back.'

'For God's sake, put your tongue away, Sanj,' Mark reprimanded him, as Sharon disappeared into the First 'Til Last, the food store next to the Vic. 'Lusting after Sharon only gets you one place – hospital.'

Phil was expecting fireworks from Grant when he told him he'd just spotted Sharon, but Grant was apparently unconcerned. 'I thought you should know first,' Phil said anxiously, watching as Grant humped empty barrels across the yard.

He stopped and looked at Phil. 'Why?'

'You know why.' Grant nodded, giving nothing away. 'It's not going to make any difference to any of us,' Phil continued, although it was more of a question than a statement.

'No.'

'We're going to carry on as we are, right?'

'Yeah.' Grant turned and started to walk inside.

'Where are you going?' Phil asked, concerned.

'Carrying on. I've got a pub to run.'

'What about Sharon?'

'What about her?'

Once Peggy heard the news, she did her utmost to persuade Grant to visit Sharon, assuming that she was the injured party and Grant was the one who had had an affair. When she told Phil her theory, he warned her not to get involved, but Peggy pursued the matter with a terrier-like persistence. A few days later, Grant gave in and went round to see Sharon at Michelle's, his curiosity piqued at having witnessed her roll up in the Square in a Porsche. Besides, he had something for her ...

Michelle was reluctant to let Grant put a foot inside the door, but Sharon, relaxed and smiling, called, 'It's okay, 'Chelle, I'm sure he only wants a friendly chat.' She made Grant a coffee – 'Two sugars, that's right, isn't it?' – and sat down at the kitchen table. 'Well?'

'We've got some business to sort out,' he said gruffly, unsure of how to interpret her chipper behaviour. 'The Vic. You've still got a stake in it.'

'So I have.'

'If you think I'm running away and leaving it all to you, you've got another think coming.'

'Fine,' Sharon said pleasantly. 'We'll work it out.'

'As easy as that.'

'Yeah, as easy as that. Only ...' she glanced at the clock, which said eleven-fifteen, '... not this time of night, eh?'

'Right.' Grant scowled.

'Don't look so worried, Grant. It'll work itself out, just wait and see.' Even Grant, with all his defences up, couldn't resist a slight smile and a shake of his head at her laid-back attitude. 'What?' she asked.

He decided to change the subject. 'So who was the geezer in the Porsche?'

'An acquaintance.'

'And you expect me to believe that?'

'Grant.' Sharon looked at him coolly. 'You can believe what you want. The truth is still the truth, however you decide to twist it.' She laced her manicured fingers together on the table. 'So is that it? We're separated and you're still worried about my love life? I can't believe you came over just for that.'

'I didn't.' He dug in his pocket and pulled out a letter,

dropping it in front of her. 'We're not separated, Sharon, we're divorced. This is your decree absolute.'

She picked it up and read it. 'At last, eh?'

'Yeah,' he said scornfully, 'and not a moment too soon for you, obviously. Ink's not dry on the divorce papers and you've got your claws into some other mug.' He sat back, regarding her. 'You don't fool me. Now I know why you haven't set foot in the Vic. Too busy on the streets. Back in the old routine.'

This time, though, his insults seemed to have no power to wound. Sharon merely smiled and pointed to the letter.

'You see this? It means we've got nothing more to do with each other. No more questions. No more accusations. No more lies, no more guilt. I'm not seeing anybody, but even if I was, I wouldn't have to justify it to anyone but myself, because as far as you and me are concerned, it's finished. End of story.'

What Grant did not know was that after she let him out, Sharon collapsed against the door, trembling like a leaf.

Even Michelle was having problems coming to terms with the new, super-confident Sharon. The impermeable shell Sharon had sprouted in America seemed to deflect not just Grant's barbed comments but Michelle's own intimacy with her. Sharon was not being straight about her motives for returning, and Michelle could not figure out why. It had the effect of making her hold back, too, although she desperately wanted to confide in her friend. Geoff had asked her to marry him and he was still waiting for an answer. It would mean a whole new life for her and Vicki – Geoff had been offered a university job in Scotland – but Michelle wasn't sure. She had a new job on the council as a housing officer, Vicki was settled at school, and, most important of all, she didn't love Geoff. Not enough.

Sharon found out for herself when she came across Geoff moping about with a hangover. He confessed that he thought he'd blown it with Michelle, and when Sharon interrogated her, Michelle finally came clean.

'I can't do it to him, Sharon. I mean, I like him and all that.

He makes me feel looked after and cared for. He's sweet and generous and kind and good with Vicki ...'

'... but it's like being with your favourite uncle, not a lover?' Sharon finished for her.

'That sounds terrible,' Michelle laughed.

'Well, you know what I mean. He doesn't ring your bell, light your fire, make your heart leap, all that stuff?'

Michelle shook her head. 'No.'

'But apart from that, he's Mr Wonderful?'

'Yeah.'

'So what are you waiting for? Marry him, Michelle.' For a moment, Sharon let her guard drop. 'Geoff's your ticket out of here. Do you want to be stuck in this dump for the rest of your life? Passion isn't necessary, not if you like and respect each other. That's what's important. Passion only gets you into trouble.'

When Peggy enquired about how Grant had got on with Sharon, he bit her head off. Phil continued to evade her questions too, and by bedtime she had come to a decision. Grant tripped over her suitcase when he came upstairs after closing. He found Peggy in the living-room. She was in her dressing-gown sipping cocoa and looked tired and fragile.

'What's this?' He plonked the suitcase on the floor. 'I fell over it on the landing.'

'I've outstayed my welcome. You need your space. I'm going home,' she replied, staring at her drink.

Grant was shocked. 'Mum. Don't go.' He came over and sat down. 'Please. I want to explain, but it isn't that simple.'

'I understand, love.'

'No you don't. If I hurt you – I'm sorry.'

'So am I, love,' Peggy said, blinking rapidly. 'So am I.' Her tears were more than Grant could bear. Most of all, he longed to have her comfort him, cuddle him, make things all better like she used to.

'Mum. It wasn't me who had the affair. It was Sharon,' he

blurted. Peggy was shocked, but not appalled.

'It doesn't have to be the end, you know. Affairs happen. You might still be able to work it out.'

'No.'

'Affairs are all sex,' Peggy said. 'Now marriage, that's different. You and Sharon have got so much going for each other. It stands out a mile how much you love her.'

'Mum. Don't. Please.' Grant was close to tears himself.

'Why didn't you tell me? We've always been there for one another. And where was Phil, eh?'

'Mum, leave it, please …' Grant began to weep silently, his shoulders shuddering as he held his face in his hands. Peggy put her arm around him, concerned.

'Why didn't Phil tell me? He knows Sharon better than I do. What did he have to say about it?'

'Not much,' Grant gasped, making an effort to control himself. 'He was too busy.'

'What do you mean?'

'He was too busy, in bed with my wife.'

Half an hour later, Phil received a telephone call from Peggy, summoning him to the Vic. Kathy was distinctly unimpressed: it was gone midnight and they were in bed. Phil shambled across, expecting a burst pipe or some such domestic emergency, and found himself on the receiving end of a hard slap across the face from Peggy. Once she had given him a piece of her mind – at length – he was excused. The next day, Kathy was also summoned, coming off rather better with an apology from Peggy over her earlier frostiness. Peggy reserved a special public humiliation for Sharon, dealing out another vicious slap in the middle of the crowded market.

'Right. Now I'll say this slowly so you understand it,' she warned. 'If I catch you anywhere near my two sons, I'll do time for you. I'll kill you with my bare hands. Now do we understand each other?' For once, even Sharon was too stunned to say anything at all.

★

Refusing to be cowed by Peggy, Sharon sauntered into the Vic two days later and, when Peggy told her to get out, threatened to repay the slap she had given her with interest. Grant looked on with mixed feelings. Despite the fact that his mother was standing up for him, it was Sharon he found himself feeling unexpected sympathy for. Her steeliness was one of the qualities that had attracted him right from the start. He had watched her slinging out drunks and thought, now there's a woman I could respect. Her grace under fire in the face of Peggy's onslaught rekindled the memory and, as she made a dignified exit from the bar, Grant looked after her with a prickle of desire.

Sharon's advice to Michelle was well-meant, but in the end, although she'd agreed to marry Geoff, Michelle could not go through with it. The Fowlers had all been up to Scotland for Ruth and Mark's wedding, accompanied by Geoff, who wanted Michelle to see the university-owned house they would soon be living in. Seeing Ruth's happiness and devotion to Mark in the face of their uncertain future made Michelle realize she could never love Geoff so completely. They parted full of sadness and a subdued Michelle returned to Walford single again.

Michelle's was not the only relationship in the Square to have come to grief. Bianca and Ricky had had an acrimonious split after Bianca walked in to the Arches to find him snogging her friend Natalie. A defeated Natalie eventually fled Walford, but Bianca would still have nothing to do with Ricky, preferring to flirt with David Wicks instead. After Bianca made a pass at him, he was forced to reveal that he was her father, a fact that her mother, Carol Jackson, had not had the nerve to tell her. Angry and confused, Bianca was exploiting David's guilt by doing serious damage to his wallet, aided and abetted by her streetwise friend Tiffany.

Meanwhile, at the Vic, things had reached crisis point, with both Pat and Binnie resigning. Binnie, the new barmaid, had left to travel the world with her girlfriend, Della (a relationship Grant had never been able to get a handle on) and Pat was going on a cruise with Roy Evans, a car dealer who had been courting her patiently for months. Peggy saw it as an opportunity to bring in new blood, but when Grant reminded her that Sharon, as licensee, was the only person who could appoint a temporary manager, the wind was taken out of her sails.

'The last person I'm gonna crawl to is Sharon Watts,' Peggy declared.

'You might have to,' Grant said grimly. 'If we don't have a manager, the Vic'll have to close.'

'Never!'

'Them's the rules, Mum.'

'She wouldn't do that.' Peggy was flabbergasted.

Grant hung a glass up above the bar, avoiding Peggy's eye. 'Who knows what Sharon's playing at?'

They did not have long to wait to find out. A few days later, Sharon walked into the bar and offered to make Peggy the new licensee. Grant was still reeling from the unexpectedness of this when Sharon added, almost as an afterthought, 'Oh, and perhaps you'd like to think about buying me out. I won't be around much longer so I'm selling my share in the Vic.'

That was when it hit home. For Sharon to abandon the place that meant everything to her, she must be leaving Walford permanently.

The thought of Sharon leaving sent Grant into a deep depression. The more he tried to imagine life without her, the less he relished it. It was the fiftieth anniversary of VE Day and Arthur Fowler had organised a street party in the Square. But Grant wanted no part of it. He wasn't in the mood to celebrate at home. Some of his old regiment were having a get-together at an ex-servicemen's club and Grant was planning on joining them. They had more recent dead to pay tribute to.

Dressed in his old uniform, he stared at his reflection in the mirror. He hardly recognized himself. The last time he had put on the uniform and the red beret was thirteen years ago. He remembered coming back from the Falklands on a ship, out of his nut and trying not to show it when his mum and dad and Phil and Sam greeted him rapturously on the quayside. They had feted him like he was some kind of hero, not a coward who had shot an unarmed soldier boy when he was trying to surrender.

The memory of that night on Mount Longdon churned his stomach and he sat down on the bed, his head in his hands. What had that boy's family got to greet them? A letter telling them their son was dead. Grant got up again and paced the room. He had developed a morbid curiosity about the Argentinian lad for a time after he was demobbed. Who was he? Where did he come from? Did he believe in what he was fighting for? He had even wondered about tracking down the boy's parents and writing them a letter. What he would have put in it, he had never decided. The urge, like the madness, had passed, and he had buried the memory, he thought, for good.

Grant stared out at the Square, at the bunting and flags and trestle tables. Thirteen years ago, I had everything to look forward to, he thought bitterly. What have I done with my life since then? With hindsight he had had only one real achievement – his relationship with Sharon. And I wasn't even clever enough to hold on to that, he thought. He watched Bianca and Tiffany cavorting in tight-fitting forties dresses and smiled faintly. Sharon had a better figure for those sort of clothes; a real, womanly shape. The thought of Sharon and everything they had together filled him with longing. There and then, he made a vow, he was going to win her back, no matter what he had to go through to get her.

CHAPTER TWENTY-TWO

Three weeks later, an opportunity presented itself to Grant. Peggy was having problems meeting the asking price for Sharon's share of the Vic and Grant suggested to Sharon that they meet somewhere away from the Square to talk about it. To avoid hassle, they agreed not to tell anyone about the rendezvous. Michelle, seeing Sharon dolled up, was told she was going out on business, while Peggy took one look at Grant's blazer and tie and assumed he had a new girlfriend.

The matter of the Vic was swiftly dealt with, Sharon agreeing to compromise on the price. 'Well, that was easy,' she said, brightly. 'What do we do now?'

Grant glanced around him. They were in a City pub, which was almost empty, even though it was eight o'clock. That was why he had chosen it, trade always dropped off early in City pubs after the dealers and the bankers had rushed off home.

'What happened to you? In America?'

'What do you mean?' she asked warily.

'Well, you're different, stronger.'

'Mum sorted me out, helped me put myself together again.'

Grant looked awkward. 'Anyway, I'm glad you're back,' he said, at last. He drew a deep breath. 'I miss you.'

'No, you don't.'

'Oh, I know I shouldn't. But I do.'

They sat in silence, both of them trying to absorb the implications of his remark.

Finally, Sharon asked hesitantly, 'Is that really true?'

'Yeah. Sometimes, when I think about what happened, I get so angry. No, not angry, I feel sick ... But then I think about what I did to you ... and that freaks me out, too.'

Sharon met his eyes. 'You *were* horrible.'

'I know. I didn't mean to …' He studied his glass. 'I hated you. And him. I nearly killed my own brother …'

'And when that didn't work …'

'I never laid a finger on you,' he insisted sharply.

Sharon's mouth tightened. 'There's more than one way of killing someone. You can frighten them and humiliate them until their insides curl up and die …' She stared at him, unsmiling. 'You think I've changed, Grant, but I haven't. I've just stopped being scared.'

Grant did not pick up on the note of warning. 'It's funny,' he said. 'All the things that have happened between us just seem to have drifted away. And all the things I loved about you are still there. Like it never happened.' He gazed at her, his expression soft. 'You know I want to see you again?'

'D'you think that's a good idea?'

'Probably not.' He smiled, not meaning it.

'Your mum and Phil won't be very happy.'

'Who says we have to tell them?'

Later, when they were standing outside looking for a black cab, Grant suddenly took her in his arms and kissed her. Sharon drew away, shocked. 'I don't think we should be doing this.'

'No,' he grinned, pulling her against him again, 'Good, innit?' This time, Sharon responded. Grant sighed, squeezing her tight. 'I've missed you so much.' Sharon, staring bleakly over his shoulder, did not reply.

Sharon and Grant's secret rendezvous continued over the next few weeks, although it was Grant who was making all the running. Sharon remained cautious, demanding more time to get used to being with him again and refusing to let Grant do anything more than kiss her. At first, he was frustrated and angry but, realizing it was not helping his cause, he promised to let Sharon take as long as she needed.

Peggy and Phil were agog to know who Grant's mystery woman was, but he merely tapped his nose and said, 'You'll find out when I'm ready.' Phil didn't like the sound of this, but kept his suspicions to himself.

Michelle was equally curious about Sharon's love-life. Sharon had spun her a story about dating a guy called Chris, which Michelle just about believed. Then, one night when she was returning from the chippy – Ian Beale's new venture – she spotted Grant and Sharon locked in an embrace in a dark corner near the viaduct.

When Sharon got home, Michelle was waiting up for her. 'Had a nice evening with "Chris"?' she asked sarcastically.

'Yeah. We went to that new theme pub out towards Bow.'

'Come home via the backstreets, did you?'

'What?'

'I saw you. In Turpin Road. Grant got a twin we don't know about, has he?'

'Oh.' Sharon looked flummoxed. 'I was going to tell you.'

'Sharon! What in God's name do you think you're doing? I can't believe it. Not even you …'

'… could be that stupid? That is what you were going to say, isn't it, Michelle?' Sharon flashed. She sat down at the table and said, more calmly, 'Look, 'Chelle, it isn't what you think.'

'So what is it? I know what I saw. And I know you, too. You always go running back to him. Only this time …'

'Only this time, 'Chelle, he's the one who's doing the running. And he's the one who's going to pay for hurting me. Big time.' Sharon's eyes were cold.

Michelle sat down opposite her. 'What do you mean?'

'I'm not falling for him again, not now, not ever. I'm stringing him along. It's like landing a fish: you gotta get him to swallow the bait.' She smiled. 'When he's hooked, you reel him in. Then you fillet him and have him for tea.'

Michelle gaped at her. 'You're playing with fire, Sharon. You know what Grant's capable of. If he finds out …'

'Don't worry. I ain't gonna get my fingers burned. I've got it all worked out. Grant's gonna wish he'd never been born.'

The death of Nigel's wife Debbie, who was killed in a road

accident, devastated everybody in the Square. Grant was at Nigel's side the moment he heard the news, sticking with him throughout the following day as Nigel fought desperately to hold himself together for Clare's sake. The experience made Grant reassess his own life, and in the evening, when he met up with Sharon in a hotel bar, he was edgy and tense.

'I needed that,' he said, knocking back a bottle of beer. 'It's been a long day.'

'At least you were there for him,' Sharon comforted.

'Yeah.' Grant was quiet for a moment, then he said, 'Nige and Debbie were good together, weren't they?'

'They were.'

'We were as good as that.' Sharon gave him a sceptical look. 'We were,' Grant insisted. 'Maybe even better … I just wish I'd tried to keep it going.' He fell quiet again. It wasn't easy to find a way to say what was on his mind. Shifting uneasily in his seat, he said, 'I want to ask you something.'

'Ask me what?' Sharon replied, her heart quickening.

'I'm not sure that I can now.'

'Try me.'

Grant reached into his jacket pocket and brought out a small box. Leaning forward, he took Sharon's hand. 'We can start again. Somewhere else. Somewhere new.' He opened the box, revealing a sparkling sapphire-and-diamond engagement ring. 'You and me. We can make it work this time.'

'Grant …'

'Marry me, Sharon,' he whispered, his eyes glowing.

The cremation service for Debbie was deeply moving, thanks not only to the sensitivity of the young Minister who took it, but also, unexpectedly, to Grant. Nigel had planned to address the congregation, but when the moment came he stared out at the assembled company as if he couldn't remember what he had so desperately wanted to say about his adored wife. Clare urged him on silently, but Nigel was lost for words. 'Er, Debbie was … she was …' He spread his hands helplessly.

On impulse, Grant went to the front and stood by his friend. Turning to the sea of faces, he spoke from the heart.

'I'm not surprised Nigel can't say anything. Sometimes, things hurt so bad ... when you lose the thing that's most important in the world to you – well, you can't even begin to talk about it.' He paused, thinking not just of Debbie, but of his own experience of loss. 'It's like you want something to take the pain away. Only nothing does.' He glanced at Nigel, who was still looking stunned. 'And I'm grateful to the Minister for what he said. It was good, only it just doesn't add up. Not to me. And not to Nigel, either, I don't think. Nigel's a decent bloke. He doesn't deserve this. He really doesn't.'

He put an arm around Nigel's shoulders and ushered him back to his seat, the total conviction and sincerity of his remarks bringing tears to many eyes.

Sharon did not attend Debbie's funeral, although she wanted to. With Peggy and Kathy giving her the cold shoulder, she did not want to run the risk of a confrontation spoiling the day. Being by herself while the rest of Albert Square mourned Debbie made Sharon feel even more isolated. The place she had grown up in no longer felt like home. The sooner she executed her plan, the better, she told herself.

Despite the blasé front she had presented to Michelle, her nerves were wearing thin. Wearing a mask for Grant, pretending she was falling in love with him again, was draining her. She was almost shocked at her own success. Six months after tormenting her into signing the divorce papers, Grant had proposed to her all over again. Michelle was astonished when she told her, but Sharon took no great pleasure in her achievement. As far as she was concerned, this was all part of her design. There was no turning back now. What happened next was critical.

'The decision is yes. I will marry you,' Sharon told Grant, when they met up again at the hotel that evening. 'But,' she continued, as relief flooded his face, 'there's a condition attached. I want you to propose to me again. Only this time, in the Vic. In front of all of them. Your mum, Phil, Kathy, all the regulars. Everyone who knows what's gone on.'

Grant opened his mouth to protest, but she carried on, 'I need you to put me first. And for everyone to see that. You owe it to me, Grant.'

To convince Grant, Sharon spent that night with him at the hotel. When she arrived back at Victoria Street the next day, Michelle took one look at her and said, 'You did, didn't you?'

'Did what?'

'You've slept with Grant. It's written all over your face.'

'So what else does my face tell you?' Sharon ran a hand through her hair distractedly.

'You ain't happy about it.'

'Michelle. I had to do it, to get him to trust me. There was no other reason, I assure you.'

Michelle shook her head, disbelieving. 'So what happens now in this great master scheme of yours? You jilt him at the altar? Cut off his goolies on your wedding night?'

'Better than that.' Sharon produced a one-way plane ticket to Miami from her handbag and showed it to her. 'Grant's going to ask me to marry him in front of everyone at the quiz night on Thursday. I'm going to humiliate him just like he humiliated me.'

'You're gonna turn him down? After leading him on like this?'

'He has to know what it feels like, to be reduced to nothing.' Sharon's fists were clenched tight. 'That's the reason I came back. Then I'm flying home. My new home. America.'

The morning of the quiz Grant awoke bubbling with excitement. He had a suitcase packed, which he was taking care to hide from Peggy. Not that she was in a state to notice anything; her licence had arrived that day and she had been crowing non-stop about being the new landlady of the Vic.

Grant was glad. Hopefully it would soften the blow when she found out that he and Sharon had gone off to start a new life together. The move meant cutting the ties with everybody dear to him, not least Phil, who he had told nothing. Once, not long ago, he'd had a straight choice between Phil and Sharon and chosen his brother. Now, things were different. Sharon was the only decent thing he'd ever had and he wasn't going to lose her again. If that meant being estranged from his family, then it was the price he would have to pay.

He caught up with Phil at the Arches later that morning. 'Just wanted to make sure you and Kathy'll be at the Vic tonight,' he said casually.

'What's this? Mum sent you to round us all up has she?'

'It's nothing to do with her. I've got a little announcement to make.'

'What sort of announcement?' Phil asked, distrustful.

'All in good time.'

'I thought we said no more secrets.'

'We said a lot of things. And one of them was you'd be there for me when I asked. Well, I'm asking now.'

Phil scratched his beard, regarding Grant quizzically.

'This has got nothing to do with Sharon, has it?'

Grant ignored the question. 'As my brother, you'll be there for me, no matter what, right?'

'Right,' Phil said, resigned.

By seven-fifteen, the pub was filling up and Peggy and Tiffany, who had recently been recruited as a barmaid, had their hands full. Grant surveyed the scene with a fast-beating heart, thinking about the end of the evening when he would be leaving with Sharon. He had arranged to let her in through the private door in the hall at nine o'clock, after the quiz had finished. His eyes swept the room, seeking Phil and Kathy. They came in at that moment, Phil looking strained. Grant continued to scan the room, taking it all in for the last time. He caught Michelle watching him and smiled the generous smile of a victor. She was one person he had no regrets about not seeing again. Unusually, she smiled back.

Michelle and Sharon had said their goodbyes earlier. 'Chelle was bereft at losing her best friend, but trying not to show it for Sharon's sake. She knew the seesaw of emotions over Grant would never go away if Sharon stayed in Walford, but still had doubts about the drastic measures she was taking. She told herself not to be selfish, Sharon had to do what she thought was right. It was her tape that had got Sharon into this mess; she couldn't interfere again. All the same, she had tried to talk Sharon out of it again, to no avail. Her mind was made up.

Sharon was waiting outside at the appointed time. Peggy was still calling out the quiz answers so Grant told Sharon to go upstairs for five minutes. She stood in the living-room, looking around her. With Peggy's furniture and knick-knacks in it, the room she had grown up in seemed totally alien. It was a room she now associated with raised voices – Den and Angie's, hers and Grant's – and suddenly she was relieved to be shaking it off for good. As far as she was concerned, the Vic was cursed.

Grant came and led her downstairs, encouraging her tenderly as she hesitated outside the bar.

'Don't worry, it'll be okay.'

He opened the door and hand-in-hand they stepped into the noisy, smoky, beery fug. As they made their way to the microphone Peggy had been using for the quiz, the room gradually fell silent.

Grant picked up the mike. 'Er, I've – we've – got a little announcement to make.' He fumbled in his pocket and produced the ring box. 'I've waited a long time for this. I never thought it would happen … I've not loved many things in my life … I didn't know how to, I suppose … ' He turned to Sharon, who was staring at him intently, digesting every word. 'I should be saying this to you …' He looked into her eyes, suddenly overwhelmed with emotion, blinking back tears, 'I'm just so …' Too choked to continue, he said, 'Well, help me out.'

Sharon turned to face the crowd, surveying the familiar faces, all watching expectantly. She turned back to him.

'Grant, I ...' She shook her head.

Grant put his arm around her, addressing the crowd. 'What we're trying to say is ...'

'Grant ... don't.' Sharon took his arm away gently. He stared at her, puzzled. 'I can't,' she said in a cracked voice. Her eyes were brimming with unshed tears. 'I'm so sorry.' She ran to the door, wrenching it open. The cab she had booked earlier was waiting for her outside, engine running.

'Sharon!' Grant ran out after her. People were beginning to spill out of the pub: Phil, Kathy, Peggy, Michelle, Pauline.

'It wasn't real, Grant. Any of it. I lied. I wanted to humiliate you in there, like you did to me.'

Grant looked as if he was in shock. 'But I love you,' he said.

'Have you any idea how much damage you did? You can't take that hurt away – ever. You treated me like a whore. You even offered me to your friends!' she screamed.

Grant was taken aback at her ferocity. 'Look, we can work it out.' He reached out to touch her, but she moved away.

'There's no way back, Grant. There never was.'

'But I was giving up everything. That's what tonight was all about.'

'No,' she said, softer now, 'tonight was to pay you back.'

He stood stock still. 'Revenge? That's what this is? You hated me that much?'

'I thought I did.' She paused. 'Maybe if I'd hated you enough, I could have gone through with it.'

He took a shaky breath. 'Okay, you've made your point. But it's still not too late ...'

'No.'

'I love you,' he pleaded.

'I love you too.' She pecked him on the cheek, then turned and got into the cab. The door slammed and the cab chugged away, taking Sharon from Walford for ever.

She did not look back.

CHAPTER TWENTY-THREE

In the days following Sharon's departure, Grant kept his head down and his mouth shut. He did not want to talk to anyone about what had happened, particularly Peggy, who was standing behind him wearing a concerned expression every time he turned round. Phil seemed to be avoiding the subject, which suited Grant fine. He had decided to draw a line under his past, starting from now. Sharon was history and all he wanted to do now was blot out her memory entirely. When he heard about Steve's plan to get up a group of lads for a week of sun, sangria and sex in Torremolinos, it sounded like exactly what he needed.

Peggy was keen for Phil to go too, 'to keep an eye on Grant'. Phil, who had spotted the pressure-cooker build-up of tension in his brother, was torn. It had taken so long to win back Kathy's trust after Sharon, and she was bound to object to him going away without her. On the other hand, Grant was all set to go off the rails and he needed Phil to look out for him. He had another, more personal motive: he owed Grant. His conscience had been nagging him non-stop since that night in the Vic. The sight of Grant's crushed face as Sharon left would stay with him forever. As far as Phil was concerned, the business with Sharon was his own fault and, if he could make it up to Grant in any way, he would.

After a couple of days of heavy boozing and all-night clubbing, during which Phil had to intervene several times to prevent Grant starting fights, he was relieved to get away from Torremolinos and head through the mountains to Seville, to look up Sam. Peggy had insisted that they visit their sister while they were in Spain. From the little news she sent home,

Sam was still, apparently, enjoying a successful modelling career, but her letters were scant on detail and Peggy was keen to know more about how her daughter was faring.

Phil and Grant took a hired car, leaving the rest of the group – Steve, David Wicks, Ricky and Bianca – behind. Grant spent the journey needling Phil about why he hadn't pulled and Kathy being his keeper, and demanded a night on the town – 'Just like we used to' – before they did anything about Sam. Phil's heart sank. This was Grant's screwed-up way of testing his loyalty to him. If he didn't want Grant going on a destructive bender, he was going to have play it his way. Or at least pretend to.

That night they hit the bars and discos of Seville. They soon picked up a couple of likely looking English girls, Angie and Bev, and went back to their apartment. After Grant had disappeared into the bedroom with Bev, Phil declined Angie's invitation to join her, explaining awkwardly that he was married. She flared at him for leading her on, but admitted to appreciating his honesty. They ended up playing an amicable game of cards instead and he spent the night on the sofa.

The next day, the Mitchells began their search for Sam. Strolling along Seville's narrow streets, listening to caged birds singing from the wrought-iron balconies above, Grant said, 'This is the life, eh, bruv? You and me, back in business, showing 'em all how it's done.' He turned his face up to the hot sun, breathing in the heady scent of flowers from numerous hanging baskets and floral displays.

'Yeah,' Phil said, noncommittal. He had asked Angie to act as if they'd spent the night together and fortunately, she had seen the funny side and agreed. Grant was none the wiser.

Sam was not at the address they had for her and, on making further enquiries, they discovered she was working in the seedy nightclub they had frequented two nights ago in Torremolinos, The Blue Parrot. Grant drove back as fast as the winding mountain roads would permit, but just as they arrived at the club they spotted Sam leaving in a taxi.

'When I find the bastard she's gone with, I'll kill him,' he swore. After getting hammered at the complex bar, they finally discovered their sister more easily than either of them had anticipated: back at their apartment, in bed with David Wicks.

Sam was dragged back to Walford with them in disgrace. Grant was raring to 'sort' David, but David had him over a barrel, threatening to tell Peggy that Sam had been dabbling in prostitution if Grant laid a finger on him. The holiday had repercussions for Ricky, too: having proposed to Bianca, the shock of seeing Sam – who was still his wife, on paper at least – had plunged his feelings into turmoil all over again.

Grant, meanwhile, was busy stirring things between Phil and Kathy, dropping hints about his brother 'misbehaving' while they were away. It became too much for Kathy, who eventually made Phil tell her the truth. When she flung it back in Grant's face he was furious and stormed off to take up an offer of temporary security work on a by-pass in Cumbria, venting his foul mood on anti-road protestors instead.

Grant returned three weeks later, still spoiling for a fight. He got his wish that evening, when Peggy's quiz night descended into a pub brawl after a row broke out about cheating. In the melee, Mark Fowler saved Grant from being glassed and was injured himself, falling and hitting his head on the bar. Grant spoke to him the next day to check that he was alright, and might not have thought any more about it, had not Michelle come steaming round to the Vic just as he was closing up.

'Who have you told?' she demanded.

Ruth was worried that Grant had overheard her telling the paramedics who attended Mark that he was HIV positive. Michelle, taking her brother's cause into her own hands, had come round to find out what Grant was going to do with the knowledge.

Before she realized it, she had given away more about Mark through her tirade than Grant might know himself. Grant quickly cottoned on. Staring hard at her he said, 'I love to see you squirm. You're really sweating, aren't you, wondering if you've blown it?'

'There's nothing to blow.'

'So why are you acting like a rabbit in a trap?'

'You wish,' Michelle said stoutly, turning to go.

'You never stop and think, do you?' Grant said. 'It's always feet first, jump in, never mind anything else. You were like that with Sharon.'

Michelle turned round. 'It's called caring for somebody, but you wouldn't know about that, would you?'

'It's called sticking your nose in where it's not wanted, and I know all about that because all the time I was married to Sharon, you were doing it.'

The row batted backwards and forwards, becoming increasingly personal, Michelle accusing Grant of being a coward and a bully; Grant accusing Michelle of driving Sharon away.

'Oh, and I suppose it was me that drove her into your brother's bed, that was my fault as well, was it?' she retaliated hotly. Her remark floored Grant and for a few seconds he was speechless. 'Why won't you admit it, Grant? Why won't you say it was as much Phil's fault as Sharon's?' she goaded him.

'Because it wasn't,' he said at last.

Michelle moved closer, her eyes flashing. 'Shall I tell you what happened, Grant?' He backed away, but Michelle kept coming at him, firing home truths at point-blank range. 'Sharon slept with Phil because you treated her like filth. And Phil, good old Phil, didn't give a monkey's about sleeping with his brother's wife. Then, you and your brother drove her out to save yourselves. To save your relationship. That's what happened, isn't it? For all your big talk, you were willing to let her go, so that you and Phil could carry on playing brothers . . . blood's thicker than water at any price. I'm right, aren't I?'

Grant sat down, his head in his hands. 'I trusted him,' he said in a quiet voice. 'I didn't want to believe he betrayed me.' He fell silent, as if facing up to the situation for the first time. Then he faltered, 'I didn't want not to have a brother. I couldn't let that happen. I knew I'd already lost Sharon ... so it was easy to blame her, easy to say it was all her fault. She'd gone already. Phil ... Phil was all I had left.'

Listening to Grant, Michelle felt almost sorry for him. She went over and sat down next to him. 'Sharon didn't leave because of what happened with Phil. She left because she'd just had enough ... of everything. She needed to start again. A clean break ... away from it all.'

Grant looked up at her, his eyes red. 'Does that include you?'

Michelle swallowed. 'Probably.'

Her admission signalled a brief truce and Grant poured them both a drink. It proved to be merely a lull in hostilities, with Grant going on the offensive again, accusing Michelle of wanting Sharon all to herself.

'You wanted to own her – her clothes, her looks, her life ... her dad ...'

'You bastard!' Michelle knocked back her drink and poured herself another from the bottle of scotch on the table between them. 'You enjoy hurting people, don't you?'

'Almost as much as you do,' he hit back. 'Do you know what hurt Sharon the most, the worst moment in her entire life? When you slept with Den.'

Michelle knew he was right and the truth made her flinch. 'Do you think I enjoyed telling Sharon? You know how you felt about Phil ... that's how Sharon must have felt about me ... and if you think that makes me happy, then you're wrong. It's just something I have to live with.'

'I just want you for once to admit you're like everybody else. You cock up. You make mistakes,' Grant insisted.

She paused. 'Alright ... I make mistakes.'

'And you hurt people.'

Michelle looked at him, her defences shot to pieces. 'Alright,' she whispered. 'I hurt people.' Grant topped up their glasses. They sat without speaking for a while, and then Michelle started to open up. 'The problem is ... what I did, getting pregnant – well, you're right, I messed up big time – but it gave me the one thing in my life I care about more than anything. Vicki. Without her, I'd have nothing.' She glanced at Grant, who was almost as drunk as she was. 'That's what you want, isn't it? You wanted Sharon to have your children. But you blew it.'

'Yeah,' he admitted. 'I blew it alright.' Staring into space, he continued reflectively, 'I always wanted things – cars, clothes, whatever, like most people do – but I just didn't *want* a kid ... It was like something else. It was like nothing I'd felt before. And I wanted it with Sharon.' He turned his face back to Michelle. 'It would have all been different, you know.'

'In what way?'

'I'd have been different.'

'Then it's a shame.'

'Thanks.' He caught Michelle smiling and asked, 'What's so funny?'

'That's the first time you've ever thanked me for anything.'

'It's the first time you've ever said anything nice to me.'

Michelle grinned. 'You're probably right.' She finished her drink and got up to go. 'I'd better get back.'

Grant followed her to the door. 'You missing Sharon?'

She nodded.

'Me too,' he said. He gazed at her keenly. 'It's a funny question, but do you snuggle up with Vicki, now Geoff isn't around?'

'Sometimes.'

'That must be nice.'

'It is.' She touched his shoulder lightly. 'One day, Grant, you'll have kids and I reckon you'll make a good dad.'

'If I'm half as good a dad as you are a mum, it'll do for me.'

For a few seconds, a question hung in the supercharged air between them, then Grant leaned forward and kissed Michelle on the lips. They drew apart, both trying to read the message in the other's eyes, then Michelle returned the kiss. Half-laughing, half-crying, they clung to each other, united by their sense of loss and a reconciliation that had taken more than five years to find.

Two things happened after that which turned Michelle's world around. The first was that she was offered a job as a research assistant on a housing project in the States, just a short drive from where Sharon lived. The second was that she fell pregnant with Grant's baby. After all that Grant had said about wanting a child, she felt honour-bound to tell him, but Mark, who was the only person who knew, talked her out of it.

'He'll make your life a misery, 'Chelle. Think about it. If you keep the baby, he'll want it – and if you abort it, he'll kill you.'

As far as Michelle was concerned, there was never really any question of doing the latter. She had always planned for Vicki to have a brother or sister. Just not like this. And certainly not by Sharon's ex. She really did have a penchant for wanting a piece of whatever her friend had, Michelle reflected. Grant had certainly made his point there. More potently than he would ever know ...

Thinking she'd blown her chances with the job by getting pregnant, Michelle contacted Dr Rose Markham, her prospective employer, and told her the situation. Dr Markham, a working-class woman who, like Michelle, had put herself through university, respected her honesty and told her that, as far as she was concerned, the pregnancy didn't change anything. Her resolve strengthened, Michelle made the decision to leave, and, after an emotional farewell with her family, disappeared with Vicki for a new life in America.

Grant didn't miss Michelle, but he did miss having a confidante. Marriage seemed to have made Phil more distant; there was a space between him and Grant that hadn't existed before and recently Phil had been behaving in an oddly secretive manner.

Nigel had also got other things on his mind. Liam, Clare's father, had reappeared at Debbie's funeral, wanting to take his daughter back. Nigel was embroiled in a bitter custody battle with him and Grant hadn't helped matters by giving his word to a distraught Clare that she would be able to stay with Nigel.

In a bid to honour his promise to Clare, Grant considered paying Liam off. His own capital was tied up in the Vic, but he knew Phil had the funds. But, when he approached him at the Arches, Phil was not keen.

'No can do, Grant. I'd like to help Nige, but me and Kath need the money.'

'You've got two businesses between you! Look, Nigel's just the manager of a poxy video shop. He can't raise the cash and I can't, not without remortgaging the Vic. But you can. If you really want to.'

Phil's face turned ruddy. 'It's not a question of whether I want to or not. I just can't. We've gotta lot of expenses coming up.'

'What — redecorating that rambling flea pit of Ian Beale's you've just moved into?'

'Yeah. But there's other stuff, too.'

'Like what? What's so important you'll refuse to put your hand in your pocket for an old mate when he needs a bit of support?'

Phil sighed. 'It was you that got him into this mess, Grant.'

'Okay, okay. But I'm asking you to help Nige, not me. If he loses Clare … it'll destroy him, Phil, you know it will.'

Phil turned his back, rummaging on his work desk. 'It ain't up to me.'

'Kathy wears the trousers now, does she?' Grant said scathingly. 'Shall I ask her instead? What does she do, give you your beer money for the week — if you've been a good boy?'

Phil spun round. 'Look, we need that money because — well, we weren't gonna tell you yet, but since you won't let it drop …' He took a deep breath. 'Kathy's pregnant, alright? And babies cost a fortune. There's cots and prams and all the gear.'

'Kathy's going to have a baby?' Grant's mouth fell open. 'You're going to be a dad?'

'Yeah.'

'You never mentioned having a family.'

'Well, it weren't exactly planned ... but the idea's growing on me.' He gave Grant an embarrassed grin.

'You didn't even want a kid and you've got one, just like that!'

'It ain't born yet, bruv,' Phil said. But Grant had already gone.

The months that followed were uneventful for Grant, although Phil had his fair share of traumas. Frank Butcher made a surprise return to the Square on Christmas Day, reawakening Phil's worries about the police investigation into the car-lot fire. Frank, who had spent the past eighteen months in psychiatric care, claimed to have the death of the young vagrant on his conscience and was threatening to confess. He milked the situation for three months, until Phil, who had torched the lot on Frank's behalf, arranged to meet him at the portacabin to negotiate a deal. An unknown arsonist set the place alight with Phil inside and he was only saved thanks to the heroic efforts of Ricky. The police suspected Frank, who disappeared, leaving a stricken Pat behind all over again.

Nigel, at least, had won custody of Clare after Liam was proved to be violent and abusive. But the Fowlers did not fare so well. Arthur was arrested for embezzling the funds of the Flowering Wilderness campaign, and was denied bail after he failed to make his court hearing. He spent Christmas in prison, becoming increasingly withdrawn and unstable, and refused to see any of his family.

Phil and Kathy's son was born on 21 March 1996, Peggy's birthday. Grant and Peggy were the first to visit, Peggy immediately taking the tiny bundle off Kathy and nursing him in her arms. 'He's just like his dad, strong and healthy,' she cooed admiringly.

'Poor kid,' chipped in Grant. He turned to Phil. 'So, have you sorted out some football boots yet? We'll have him kicking a ball around the park before he can say "Mummy and Daddy".'

'Give us a chance, will yer?' Phil spluttered.

'Listen,' Peggy intervened, 'the most important thing at the moment is finding a name for him. What do you think of Eric?' She beamed at Kathy and Phil. 'After his Granddad? He'd be so proud.'

Kathy cleared her throat. 'Actually, we've already decided on a name. He's called Ben.'

'Ben?' Grant smirked. 'It's a bit soft, innit? That's no name for a Mitchell.'

'Well, what would you prefer? Rocky? Sugar Ray? Grant?' Kathy snapped.

'The last one's not bad,' he teased. 'But whatever you call him, you're bringing him up into a tough old world, he's going to have to learn to stand up for himself.'

'Yeah, but we don't want him to grow up thinking that the only way to get on in life is to prove yourself with your fists,' Kathy said, looking meaningfully at Grant. 'We want him to have all the opportunities that we didn't. We want him to respect people, rely on brains, not brawn.' She sat back, arms folded, glaring defiantly at him.

'Good for you,' Grant said, taking them all by surprise. He bent down and stroked Ben's cheek with a finger. 'You're right. Look at him, he's perfect. If he was mine, I'd want something better for him as well.'

With Phil now a family man, Peggy turned her attention to Grant. Concerned about his bachelor status, she placed a lonely-hearts ad in a magazine, which a perky Tiffany spotted and read out to all and sundry. Grant, outraged, binned it, informing Peggy not to meddle, but Nigel rescued the ad and sifted through the replies, setting Grant up on a blind date.

'You'll thank me for it one day,' he gulped, when Grant

reacted with typical fury. 'Maybe not now, but when you realize I was just interested in your wellbeing, you'll think, I love that man.' Grant grimaced. 'Her name's Yvonne. In the letter it says she likes Bruce Willis films and does aerobics twice a week. Just your type, eh?' Nigel rattled on.

'Give it a rest, Nigel, eh?' Grant said warningly. Later, though, after he'd had time to think about it, he decided it might be a laugh, and when a willowy brunette with a mane of dark curls walked into the bar, he was pleasantly surprised.

'I couldn't help noticing ... are you looking for someone?' he asked.

She smiled. 'Yeah, I am, actually.'

'Oh, good, I was right.'

'I'm sorry?' She looked confused.

'You spoke to a friend of mine this morning. He said you'd be coming in. I'm Grant Mitchell, the landlord. Why don't you grab yourself a table and I'll bring you over a drink?'

'Well, that's very nice of you,' she said, smiling again. 'I'll have a dry white wine, please.'

He was surprised – and flattered – to discover she had travelled all the way from Bolton, and even more surprised when she said she had friends in the area. They were getting on well – although she seemed puzzled by his references to 'Die Hard' movies – and it wasn't until he asked her about her interest in aerobics that he began to realize they were talking at cross-purposes.

'I don't work out. Who told you that, David?'

'David who?'

'David Wicks. That's who I'm meeting. You said he was a friend of yours.'

'No,' Grant said, stonily. David Wicks had been his sworn enemy ever since Torremolinos.

The woman checked her watch and stood up to go. 'Oh, I'm sorry, Grant. I think there's been some sort of mix-up. Look, I can't wait any longer. Thanks for the drink.' She left, Grant's eyes following her as she walked gracefully to the door.

Nigel, who had been hovering nearby, came up to him. 'Is Yvonne coming back?' he asked excitedly.

'She was never here to begin with,' Grant retorted, going back behind the bar.

After Grant, the next item on Peggy's agenda was Ben's christening, which soon developed into an unholy war between herself and Pat, who Kathy had already asked to be godmother. To keep the peace, Peggy was eventually appointed godmother as well, with Ian as godfather. Phil had wanted Grant, but Kathy was not persuaded. However, when Grant revealed his gentle side, cradling Ben in his arms with tenderness, she saw him in a new light.

'It's funny … this time last year I thought it might be me and Sharon having a kid …' He paused, staring intently at Ben's little snub nose. Looking up at Kathy, he continued, 'When Phil talks about being a dad, all I can think of is, I wish it was me.'

'There's still plenty of time, Grant. You'll meet someone else,' she said consolingly.

He smiled at Ben again, then handed him back to her. 'No. Anyway, I'd probably make a terrible dad.'

'Would being Ben's godfather cheer you up at all?' Kathy heard herself saying. 'We've decided to have two. Match the number of godmothers.'

Grant was stunned. 'I didn't think you'd want me, of all people.'

'People change. You have.'

He smiled broadly. 'It would be an honour.'

Ben's christening went off well. Pat and Peggy made their peace and the party at Phil and Kathy's went with a swing. But later on news filtered through that Arthur Fowler had been rushed to hospital unconscious. Arthur had recently been released from prison, exonerated, after his friend Willy Roper confessed to embezzling the Flowering Wilderness money.

He had come out dazed and confused, all his spirit gone. Unable to face his friends at the christening, he had gone to dig his allotment instead, where he had suddenly collapsed. An ambulance was called but the doctors were unable to resuscitate him and he died of a brain haemorrhage at the hospital.

Michelle promised to fly back home as soon as Mark phoned her in America with the news. However, the day she was expected to arrive, Pauline received a call from Sharon saying that Michelle had gone into labour prematurely and had given birth to a baby boy. The baby – whom she had named Mark – was in an incubator, but doing fine. Pauline, her grief tempered with joy over her new grandson, insisted on making an announcement in the Vic, despite Mark's attempts to dissuade her.

Grant was serving at the bar when Pauline made her shock announcement. He listened, stunned. When did he and Michelle ...? It was the start of October, he recalled, thinking hard. They were at the end of May now, which meant ... He looked up and caught Mark Fowler watching him anxiously. Mark's pale face was a dead giveaway. It had to be his, Grant thought, his stomach flipping over. Michelle's baby had to be his. He had a little boy! The thought made him giddy with happiness. He was a father at last.

CHAPTER TWENTY-FOUR

'I thought I'd get a congratulations card for Michelle. Be nice if we both signed it.' Peggy bustled in from the back, bearing a box of crisps. Grant, who was already in the bar taking stools down off tables, did not reply. 'It's a funny old world, isn't it,' Peggy continued thoughtfully. 'There's Arthur not long dead and there's his daughter bringing a life into the world.'

'Who are we talking about?' Tiffany interrupted chirpily, coming in. She was living above the Vic in Steve's old room, Steve having left the Square to be with his girlfriend, Lydia. Sam had also vacated the Vic, returning to Spain with her new love, Guillermo – although not before making a play for Ricky and busting up him and Bianca.

'I was just saying, about Michelle ...' Peggy mused.

'Fast little worker, int she?' Tiffany laughed.

Grant looked up from what he was doing. 'And what's that supposed to mean?'

'Well, she's hardly been out of Walford five minutes. Must have met someone on the plane.'

'Tiffany ...' He growled warningly.

'What?'

'Shut it.' Grant threw down his cloth and went out, slamming the door behind him. He sat in the garden in the middle of the Square, his head whirling. Michelle would have to come back home, that was the first thing, he decided. He tried to imagine living with Michelle, raising a child with her, but his brain refused to co-operate. The idea of the two of them playing happy families was inconceivable. They had never got on, and they never would, despite their brief truce. If he'd learned one thing from his marriage to Sharon, it was that anything less than love wasn't worth having.

Mark Fowler came into the Vic later on that lunchtime, giving Grant the opportunity to quiz him more closely.

Pouring Mark's pint, he said, conversationally, 'Can't be easy for Michelle — what with Vicki, a new baby and being all alone in a foreign country.'

'What makes you think she's alone?' Mark replied.

'Well, she'll have made some friends, but it isn't the same.'

'There's the father.'

'The father?' Grant's hand shook slightly, slopping the beer he put down in front of Mark.

'Yeah, he's around. They're going to get married once the baby's out of hospital. They'd probably have done it earlier, but with the baby being three months premature ...' This was the story Michelle had instructed Mark to tell, making the baby sound more premature than it was, to throw Grant off the scent. It seemed to work.

'So who's the lucky fella?' Grant asked abruptly.

'Someone she met in the first week she was out there. They've fallen madly in love, and apparently he adores Vicki.'

'You must be pleased they've named the baby Mark.'

Mark beamed. 'She promised she would if it was a boy.'

Grant gave him a tigerish smile. 'Congratulations.'

Grant felt as if he'd been punched in the stomach. He carried on working, his expression grim, not bothering to talk to anyone else for the rest of the session. He didn't know whether to laugh or cry. Just as he was getting used to the idea of having a son, the carpet was yanked from under his feet again. He had spent the morning thinking about his kid, dreaming such dreams . . . Ruth's voice attracted his attention and he looked up. She kissed Mark fondly, and he whispered something in her ear, making her giggle. Grant's lips tightened. Mark Fowler might have built his hopes up for nothing, but there was another baby he, Grant, was responsible for. And there was no way Mark was going to endanger little Ben.

Grant did know about Mark being HIV positive. He had

strung Michelle along for the hell of it, and was concerned that Ruth could pass the infection on to his godson. So far, Grant had said nothing – it was Mark's business, and he had no intention of broadcasting the news. But, when Kathy mentioned she had asked Ruth to mind Ben, Grant became anxious. He tried to dissuade her, but his flimsy reasons – he did not reveal the truth – cut no ice and Kathy returned to work leaving Ruth in charge of Ben.

He caught up with Ruth that afternoon and gave her an ultimatum: quit or bear the consequences. Despite Ruth's protestations that Ben was in no danger, Grant persisted. He gave her until Arthur's funeral to make her mind up or he would go public.

But the situation with Ben wasn't the only thing worrying Grant. Phil had got himself into trouble after a car that he had done a service on had an accident caused by brakes failure. The owner had been injured and was threatening to sue for £10,000. The Mitchells' solicitor, Marcus Christie, had suggested Phil make an out-of-court settlement for 75 per cent of the amount. Phil, who had allowed his insurance to lapse, was working himself into a state and drinking heavily. A concerned Kathy, who knew nothing about it, had asked Grant to have a word with him.

Phil was well-oiled and in argumentative mood when Grant came down to the bar that night.

'I saw Kathy in the Square today.' He eyed his brother speculatively. 'You still haven't told her, have you?'

'Told her what?'

'About the lawsuit, what else?'

Phil flushed. 'Look, what is this? Can't I come in here for a quiet drink?'

'I just think she's got a right to know, that's all.'

'Yeah, well, let's face it, Grant. Marriage guidance was never your thing, was it? That's between me and Kathy, and I'll tell her when I'm ready.' He threw back his whisky, glaring at

Grant, and slammed the glass down on the bar. 'I'll have another of these and a pint if you've stopped playing agony aunt.'

'I was just trying to help, that's all.'

'Yeah, well, I don't need help.'

'That's not the way it looks from here.'

Phil was not so drunk that he didn't catch the intonation. 'And what's that supposed to mean?' he slurred.

'You've been spending a lot of time in here lately.'

'What? And I ain't welcome, is that it?' Phil got off his stool. 'I don't need this, Grant. Get off my back. Understand?'

It was going to be one of those nights, Grant thought wearily, after Phil had stormed out. Peggy had gone to Aunt Sal's, leaving him and Tiff behind the bar, but Tiffany was proving more of a hindrance than a help. She was already frosty with Grant because he had chucked her brother, Simon, out on his ear when he discovered him sleeping in her room. She had then served Ian Beale a mouthful of abuse along with his pint for trying to evict Simon from the squat he had moved into at number 29. Ian, who had big plans for his newly acquired property, was outraged, and Grant, mindful of losing custom, had ordered her to take the rest of the evening off.

When Grant went upstairs later, he found Tiffany on the sofa watching television. 'Oh good, you're still up,' he said, fancying a bit of company after the trials of the evening. Even Tiffany was better than sitting there by himself.

'Why? What have I done now?' she demanded suspiciously. Grant went over to the sideboard.

'Nothing. I just thought we could both do with a drink.' He poured two large brandies.

'No thanks, I'm going to bed.'

'Come on.' Grant sat down beside her. 'I didn't mean to upset you earlier. It's just that it's been a pretty tough day for me too.' He glanced at her mutinous face. 'So, what's wrong?'

'You wouldn't understand.'

'Try me.' He passed her a glass but she pushed it away.

'You're not interested in my problems. I mean, if it weren't for you ...'

'Well, what?'

She stared at him coldly. 'Kicking my brother out like that. You didn't have to do that, did you?'

'I thought he'd found somewhere.'

'Not for much longer.'

Grant sighed. 'You really care about him, don't you?'

'Yeah,' she said. 'He's the only person I do care about.'

'That's the way I feel about my brother.'

Grant's reflective voice seemed to take Tiffany by surprise. Seeing her soften a fraction, he offered her the glass again. This time, she took it. Finding Grant unusually prepared to listen, she told him about Simon, about how he had been in an abusive relationship and allowed himself to be knocked about.

'Sometimes I feel so angry with him,' she confessed.

'Why?'

'Oh, I don't know. For him not wanting something better.'

Grant shrugged. 'Still, if he thinks she's worth it ...'

'Yeah but that's not the point,' Tiffany snapped. She had not told Grant that Simon was gay and it didn't seem the best time to break the news to him. 'That's not what it's all about, is it? It's not love being in a relationship like that. Not when somebody hurts you.'

'What do I know about it? I've screwed up every relation-ship I've ever had. And there I am, trying to tell Phil how to run his marriage. It's a joke.' Grant paused, thinking about how, suddenly, their roles seemed to have been reversed and he was having to look out for Phil. Feeling sympathy for Tiffany, he said, 'Simon's two years older than you. Why do you feel so responsible for him? Shouldn't it be the other way round?'

She fiddled with her glass. 'Maybe it's what we've been through.'

'How do you mean?'

'Our dad wasn't a very nice man,' she said diffidently. 'Mum left him and he took it out on us – with his fists, with his belt, anything he could get his hands on. Drunk or sober, made no difference. Simon got the worst of it, though. I mean, I'm a girl, and you can't hit a girl, can you?' She stopped, obviously remembering something painful. 'He pushed me down the stairs once, though.'

'Mine too,' Grant said, his voice almost a whisper.

'What? Pushed you down the stairs?'

'No.' He gave her the ghost of a smile. 'We lived in a tower block. I wouldn't be here now if he had. But he did other things ...' Grant shut his eyes. The shadow of a giant fist raining down on him was as clear as if it were yesterday. 'He was a boxer. I was his punchbag, his everyday, knockabout tool.' He hunched his shoulders, as if anticipating a blow. 'Anything frustrated him, I got hit. Phil, too, sometimes. I don't think he took it out on Sam, though, or Mum. They didn't have a clue about what was going on. But he reckoned we were fair game, even though we were just kids.'

He glanced up and saw Tiffany blinking back tears. 'Do you hate him?' she asked tremulously.

'It's funny. I never think of him that way. I mean, we survived, we toughened up, we fought back and in the end – well, I think he respected us, for a bit ... He finished up this wizened, sad old geezer dying of cancer. I just felt sorry for him, I suppose.'

'I can't believe you don't hate him for what he did. I really, really hate my dad.' She started to sob and Grant, moved by her distress, put an arm around her. 'Hey, hey ...' he said, stroking her hair. She leaned her head on his chest, breathing in big, shuddering gulps. 'Sshh, it's alright.' He pulled her close, and the feeling of her body against his aroused him. He touched his lips to her forehead and she lifted her tear-streaked face to him. 'Tiffany,' he groaned, finding her mouth and kissing her. Her lips parted and he lost himself in her, devouring her body like a starving man.

Tiffany slipped out of Grant's bed in the early hours and went to her own room. The next morning, she and Grant faced each other over the breakfast table with some embarrassment. It wasn't the first time they had slept together – there had been a one-off occasion, ten months earlier, after Grant returned from Spain – but there had been no real spark, then or now. Both of them recognised that what had transpired the previous evening had been the result of mutual need, but neither wanted to admit to having been so vulnerable.

'Pass the marmalade' Grant said eventually. Tiffany slid it across the table. The kettle boiled and she leapt up.

'I'll make it. Coffee or tea?'

'Er, coffee, thanks.' He put down his knife with a clatter. 'Look, Tiff …'

'Sugar?'

'Two. Tiff, we've got to …'

'We're a bit low on milk.'

'*Tiffany!*'

She started. 'There's no need to shout. I ain't deaf.'

'Will you stop playing the little wifey or whatever it is you think you're doing and sit down for a minute.'

'Wifey? You gotta nerve, ain'tcha? Just 'cos we slept together, it don't mean I'm turnin' into your slave. In fact, it don't mean nothing, Grant.'

Relief flooded his face. 'Thank Christ for that.'

She snorted. 'Don't hold back, will yer? I was just tryin' to be nice, spare your feelings – *for once* – that's all.'

'Spare my feelings? That a joke or what?'

'Well, you know … after what you told me last night …'

'I was drunk,' he said shortly.

'Oh.' She studied him for a few seconds. 'Well, I weren't. Not to start wiv. And although, like I said, it don't mean I fancy you, I did – well, I did appreciate you listening.'

Grant was taken aback. 'No problem. Any time.'

'I don't think so, Grant.'

He started to smile. 'You're probably right. Let's forget about it, eh? Pretend it never happened.'

'Fine.' She left to get dressed, but Grant called her back.

'And Tiffany ... let's keep schtum about this, shall we?'

'Okay,' she said, adding under her breath, 'As if I'd tell *anyone* I slept with Guy the Gorilla ...'

Phil's drinking got heavier over the next weeks, making Kathy's life a misery. When she found out about the lawsuit – and that Phil was doing resprays on stolen cars to pay it off – she was even more angry and they ended up rowing bitterly. Kathy, distraught, took Ben and went to stay at Pat's, leaving Phil to console himself with a bottle.

The next day, at Arthur Fowler's funeral (which had been delayed because of a post-mortem), they were barely on speaking terms. When Grant intervened, in an attempt to get Phil to face up to his family responsibilities, Phil once again ripped into him.

'I'm fed up of you going on about Kathy and Ben every five minutes,' he exploded. 'You can cut the concerned god-father act, Grant. It don't suit you. Not with your track record. Just who do you think you are, anyway, telling me how to behave with me own wife and kid? You got no idea what it's like to have a kid – *or* how to keep a woman.' He paused, breathing hard. 'What is this? You trying to get your own back for Sharon?' Grant, shocked at the bile in his brother's voice, turned and walked away.

Arthur's funeral was also the deadline Grant had given Ruth, and he wouldn't let it go. But when, a week later, Ben was rushed to hospital with meningitis, Grant was suffused with guilt for not having stopped her earlier. Kathy and Phil were horrified when he told them about Mark, but even though the consultant reassured them there was no possibility of Ben having contracted HIV, their suspicions remained.

Fortunately, Ben made a good recovery, although his hearing was slightly affected by the illness. The repercussions for Mark and Ruth went on, with Peggy finding out and barring all the Fowlers from the Vic. Mark, appalled at the ignorance and prejudice he was met with, stood up in the pub and told everybody the facts: they were scared of something that one day only he would die of. Grant apologised and went out of his way to make amends, although it took Peggy much longer to come round.

Grant's 34th birthday was a low-key affair. He received a card from Sharon, which only served to remind him of how good his life used to be, and spent the rest of the day wandering miserably around the Square, dragging a reluctant Frieda, the Vic's new dog, along by her lead. Passing the entrance to a new nightclub that had opened recently, the Cobra Club, he stopped and studied a flyer advertising a Seventies Night. It was Nigel and Sanjay's idea. They were trying to persuade half of Walford to dress up for it and had asked Grant to distribute some handouts in the Vic. Grant had agreed, but he was anticipating an earbashing from Peggy. The club was another of her pet hates. Convinced that it was attracting drug dealers – and, more importantly, taking custom away from the Vic – she had got up a petition against it.

Grant had not been planning on going to the disco himself. However, he changed his mind when the woman he had mistaken for his blind date came into the pub again. Feeling stupid – it was now common knowledge that she was David Wicks' ex-wife, Lorraine – he went over to her and apologised for the mix-up. 'It's alright, you don't need to explain,' she said, laughing. 'Nigel's told me all about it.'

'Oh, has he?' Grant swivelled round and fixed Nigel with an interrogative stare. Nigel smiled and spread his hands helplessly. 'Yeah. He's been telling me all about the Seventies Night he's organising. Sounds a lot of fun. Are you going?'

Grant looked her up and down and said, 'Yes.'

'Then I'll give you the first dance,' she promised, with a toss of her curls. '*If* you wear flares.'

'Who do you think I am? John Travolta?'

Lorraine sucked in her cheeks as if the image amused her. 'You must have got a few old Seventies relics hidden away.'

'Yeah,' he grinned. 'My brother. But he's spoken for. I ain't.'

That night, for the first time since Sharon left, Grant had fun again. He had almost forgotten what it was like, dancing, joking, having a laugh. Lorraine — who consented to dance with him, despite his absence of flares — was different to any other woman he had fancied before. She was a mature, intelligent woman of Grant's own age and an astonishing beauty, although her generous smile seemed to hide a secret sadness. Watching her shake her slender hips on the dancefloor made Grant shiver with lust but, knowing she was planning to return to Bolton soon, he did not make a move. Lorraine was not the sort of woman to indulge in one-night stands and Grant sensed that his attraction to her was more than just passing. He could not afford to have his heart broken again.

Nigel, who spotted Grant talking to Lorraine in the Square the next day, saw straight through him. 'You're smitten,' he teased. Grant denied it, but when Lorraine announced she was going to settle in Walford permanently, he felt his spirits rising. Lorraine had a teenage son, Joe, from her marriage to David. Joe, who had run away from Bolton to find his dad, was refusing to go home to Lancashire. His behaviour was becoming increasingly bizarre and unpredictable and Lorraine felt she had no option but to move to London to look after him. When Grant offered her a job at the Vic, she accepted gratefully. Grant was less pleased to learn that Nigel had offered to put her up in his tiny flat. He had never seriously considered Nigel as a love rival, but still ...

He was distracted from thinking any more about Lorraine by Tiffany asking him to change a barrel. Tiffany had moved out into one of the scruffy flats adjacent to the Vic to be with her new boyfriend, Tony, and her brother, Simon. She had been looking a bit green about the gills recently and had been in late a few times. After overhearing Tony shooting his mouth off in the bar, Grant had guessed the reason why.

'So, is it true about you being in the club?' he asked, escorting her out of earshot of the punters.

'Might be,' she flounced crossly.

'Well, how do you know Tony's the father?' Grant said, enjoying winding her up. As far as he was concerned, Tiffany was a little tart. 'It might be me, mightn't it?'

'If it comes out with two horns and a forked tail, I'll let you know,' she replied, stalking off.

Her answer gave him food for thought, and he pressed her about it again later. 'Look, I was just joking, alright,' she insisted. 'Don't you think I'd have told you if it was your baby?'

'Well, I dunno. You have been known to be a devious little cow,' Grant said rudely. 'Anyway, I think you're making a big mistake, shacking up with a loser like Tony Hills. He's a drug dealer. You gonna bring the kid up in a flat full of syringes?' Phil had witnessed Tony dealing outside the Cobra Club and had broadcast the news in a row with his father, Ted, in the Vic.

'He ain't dealin' no more,' she snapped, sullen.

'Yeah? And what's he gonna do instead?'

'Look, he's got six months to get himself fixed up with something. That's plenty of time.'

'Six months?' Grant's mouth fell open. 'So, you're three months gone?'

'Good at maths, are you?' Tiffany retorted, realizing she had dropped herself right in it. The truth was, she wasn't sure who the baby's father was – she had first slept with Tony a couple of nights after Grant – but she wasn't going to tell Grant that. Tony had told her he would be there for her and the baby, and she believed him.

Grant grabbed her arm. 'This baby – it really could be mine, couldn't it?'

'No.' Tiffany struggled to free herself. 'Get your hands off me.' She pulled away from him and went back through to the bar, leaving a shocked Grant staring after her.

Grant was ready for her at closing time, and when she made an excuse to Peggy to be let off early, he caught her sneaking out of the back door of the Vic. 'Tiffany, wait ...' he shouted, pursuing her into the Square. 'Look, I've got a right to know if the kid's mine or not.'

'I told you it ain't.'

'But how do you know?'

'I just do.'

'Please. Tiff. I just wanna know the truth.'

'Why? Even if it was yours, you'd get me down the abortion clinic as soon as I could blink.'

'So – it might be mine?'

'What if it is?'

'I just wanna know if it's possible.' The pleading note in his voice made her stop and turn round. She looked at him and saw again the vulnerable Grant who had confessed his tortured childhood to her. 'Yes ... it's possible,' she admitted gently, adding more harshly, 'but you haven't got a look-in, so forget it.' Putting her key in the lock, she went into the flat and slammed the door. Grant, devastated, was walking slowly back to the Vic when he heard shouts behind him and saw Tiffany coming back out, pursued by Tony and Simon.

'Keep away from me! How could you?' she screamed.

'What's going on?' he asked, turning back and approaching. 'Tiffany, what's happened?'

'Look, this is none of your business,' Tony said. Simon hung back awkwardly.

'Well, I'm making it my business,' Grant growled, putting an arm around Tiffany.

She collapsed against him, sobbing hysterically. 'Grant, make him go away.' Surprised, he drew her close.

'What's he done to you?' A look passed between Simon and Tony. Tiffany clutched at Grant's clothes. Staring at Tony, she said, 'Grant, I lied to you earlier. The baby ain't Tony's ... it's yours.'

CHAPTER TWENTY-FIVE

'Look, why don't you stay here for the night? No strings attached,' Grant said, ushering Tiffany into the Vic. Realizing she had nowhere else to go, Tiffany agreed. There was no way she could face going back to the flat, not after what she'd just witnessed. She had walked in on Simon and Tony kissing. Humiliated and betrayed at the sight of her supposed boyfriend in a passionate clinch with her own brother, she had fled. When Grant materialized out of the dark like a rock in a storm she had said the first thing that came into her head. It was meant to hurt Tony and, by the shocked look on his face, it had. She took some pleasure in that, but Grant's unexpected reaction was making her feel uneasy about having lied.

Sitting with her in the deserted bar, Grant asked, 'You know what you said earlier ... that was the truth, wasn't it?'

'Yeah,' she said, feeling vulnerable and confused. Sticking to her story seemed the safest option, for now anyway. She didn't like to think about what Grant would do if he knew she was telling him porkies.

Grant regarded her still-flat stomach with awe. 'So that's my little baby in there?'

'Yeah.'

He looked up at her, eyes gleaming. 'Why didn't you tell me before?'

'I didn't think you'd be interested. I mean, you're hardly the fatherly type.'

'Ah, but I am.'

She glanced at him sceptically, but his face was serious.

'When Phil told me that he was gonna be a dad – well, I've never been so jealous in my life.'

Tiffany tried to collect herself. 'Look, at the end of the day it doesn't matter whether you want kids or not, we can't be parents. I mean, we've slept together twice and the rest of the time we're at each other's throats.'

'Doesn't mean I wouldn't stand by you.'

She sighed. 'Grant, this is the twentieth century. Men don't have to stand by women any more.'

Grant was silent, staring down at his hands. Finally he asked, 'You're not going to get rid of it, are you?'

'No,' she replied. 'Is that what you want?'

He took her hand, staring at her intently. 'No. I want you to keep it. I want us to keep it.'

When Peggy found Tiffany in Grant's bedroom the next morning — and discovered the reason why — she was furious. 'That girl's taking you for a right mug, you mark my words,' she lectured Grant. She did not spare Tiffany's feelings, either, accusing her of trapping Grant, but when Tiffany pointed out she was carrying her grandchild, Peggy was brought up short. Nor was she happy about Grant offering the spare room to Lorraine, who she also viewed with suspicion. Lorraine, who was feeling awkward about imposing on Nigel any longer, jumped at the chance, although she seemed surprised to find out about Grant and Tiffany.

Lorraine wasn't the only one. Bianca — who knew about Tiffany's history with Tony and Grant — was gobsmacked by the news. 'But Tiff, what are you going to do if he finds out?' she said. 'He'll go mental.'

'Well, he won't find out, will he? Not unless someone goes and opens their big mouth.'

'I won't say a word, you know me. But don't say I didn't warn you … Anyway, I've got some news too,' Bianca rushed on. 'Me and Ricky are gettin' married. I popped the question last night and he said yes! Innit marvellous? We're saving up for the best wedding Walford's ever seen.'

'That's great, B,' Tiffany said distractedly, noticing Tony approaching. 'Look, I gotta go. Catch you later, alright?'

★

Grant, basking in the glow of prospective parenthood, had never felt happier. Suddenly, his life seemed to have been given a meaning. He treated Tiffany as if she was made of china, bringing her breakfast in bed, insisting she had lie-ins and refusing to let her carry anything heavy. He was as excited as a kid at Christmas about Tiffany's first scan, surprising Lorraine with his confession that he longed for a daughter.

'I used to want a boy, a little mate to play with – you know, teach him footie and all that – but it's funny, just lately I keep imagining a little girl,' he said, looking faintly embarrassed. 'I can see exactly what she'd look like.'

As it turned out, the scan confirmed that Tiffany was carrying a girl, and the two of them returned to the Vic flushed and proud, laden with Mothercare bags. After sending Tiffany upstairs for a rest, Grant pulled out the scan photos and showed them to Lorraine.

'There's her little head, and that's her heart – you can just see it there. And in this one she's sucking her thumb, look.' His eyes met hers and he was touched by the warmth of her expression.

'She's beautiful,' Lorraine said softly.

'It was magical seeing her. Best feeling I've ever had. When I saw her little heart beating away …' Grant broke off, choked. Lorraine touched his arm.

'I know. I remember the feeling I had.' She smiled sadly. 'I knew the moment I saw Karen like that, that she was a girl.'

Grant wanted to say something, but could think of nothing that would comfort her. The thought of losing a life so precious, like Lorraine had – her daughter, Karen, had been killed in a car accident – had not occurred to him until then. Suddenly, he was seized with an icy fear.

The moment was broken by Nigel, who shambled over to the bar and squinted at the photograph.

'Tiffany giving birth to a rabbit, is she?' he enquired, jovial. He picked it up, holding the picture upside-down. 'Ah-ha. It all becomes clear. So, another Mitchell in the making. You must be proud, Grant.'

'I am,' Grant said, turning the photo the right way round. 'Meet my daughter.'

Had Grant not been so taken up with Tiffany and the baby, he might have given more thought to Kathy's concern over Phil's drinking.

'He's never out of the pub these days – and it's not just the Vic,' she complained when Grant came round to see Ben. 'He hardly bothers to turn up at the Arches and he disappeared virtually all last weekend. He ruined our holiday in Scotland. Why do you think I came back early? Since then, it's been one bender after another. You saw how he was the other night.'

'Are you telling me that wasn't an accident?' Grant asked warily. Kathy had appeared in the pub recently sporting a black eye, which she claimed to have got by walking into a door. When a sceptical Peggy put two and two together and accused Phil of hitting his wife, he had gone berserk.

'No. It wasn't,' Kathy admitted. 'But it was a one-off. Phil's not violent, not like that' she eyed Grant dubiously, 'But you try and have a conversation with him these days and before you know it you're in the middle of a full-scale argument.'

'What about?'

Kathy hesitated.

'Come on, Kath, spit it out,' Grant insisted.

'I – I think he's an alcoholic.'

Grant brushed off the suggestion without even stopping to think. 'You're kidding me, right? He's a boozer, Kathy. He always has been.'

'No, it's more than that.'

'No way,' Grant said firmly. 'Not Phil.'

Peggy, meanwhile, had been swept off her feet by her new man, George. He was a tall, silver-haired, distinguished-looking man whose air of discreet wealth suggested powerful connections. Phil and Grant were deeply suspicious, especially when they learned he was the owner of the Cobra Club, but by then George had whisked Peggy away on holiday to New Zealand. Peggy was unfazed by their concern on her return.

'Oh, I know all about that – and he's promised to clean up his act in future,' she said airily.

Unconvinced, Grant did some more digging and found out from Roy Evans that George used to deal in stolen cars. When he tried to discover what else Peggy knew of George's business interests, she was vague.

'He's got a gym, he told me that, but we've got better things to talk about than boxing rings and nightclubs, Grant.'

In the end, Grant took the matter into his own hands, spelling out to George exactly what he would do to him if he involved their mother in anything dodgy. George, apparently unruffled, promised it would never happen. Grant cracked his knuckles and gave George a menacing smile.

'I hope not, George, for your sake – 'cos she ain't gonna fancy you after I've finished with you'

The intimidation routine, which Grant and Phil had perfected over many years, came in useful a few days later. Ian Beale had been the victim of a drive-by shooting and when a stunned Kathy told them she suspected Cindy and David – who had been having an affair – Grant was only too happy to shop David Wicks to the police. Kathy asked Grant to put some feelers out about the shooting, but he insisted Phil be involved, too, hoping the gesture would put Phil back in Kathy's good books. The two of them were now estranged, with Kathy and Ben staying at Pat and Roy's, and even Grant could see Phil's drinking had spiralled out of control.

They decided to target Barry, Roy's son, who was thick with David. It didn't take much to make Barry squeal, and he gave Phil and Grant a lead on the gunman, John Valekue, who they tracked down to a bric-a-brac shop. While Grant pinned him down in the storeroom, Phil planted a mocked-up map of the Square under the till. They left, tipping off the old bill, who took Valekue in for questioning.

But it wasn't enough to prevent Cindy's next desperate move. With Barry and David's help, she snatched two of her three children – Steven, the eldest, and Peter, one of the twins – and fled to France. Phil and Grant, who discovered a Eurostar timetable at the car lot, gave chase, but when they arrived at Waterloo Station, the train was already pulling out.

Grant was champing at the bit to see to David Wicks, who was still strolling around the Square for all the world as if nothing had happened. Phil, arguing it wasn't the right thing to do, restrained him. But Grant couldn't resist following him to his flat that evening and delivering a warning.

'We're playing by my rules now,' he hissed. 'You put a foot wrong and something very nasty's going to happen to you.'

'Oh, yeah?' David said icily.

'Yeah.' Grant thrust his face at David, his eyes burning with hate. 'You might just go on a little journey. And I don't mean over to France to see lover girl.'

'You're mad,' David said, backing away. 'That's all over.'

'Too right it's over. And if those kids aren't back in the country soon, that ain't the only thing that's over.'

A return visit to John Valekue, who had been released by the police, gave Grant what he wanted to hear. After a couple of good whacks to the head, Valekue lost his cool and coughed up a name. David Wicks. Determined to get him this time, Grant lured David to the Arches, where he was just about to inflict serious damage when Carol Jackson arrived, saving David's skin.

It was time, Grant decided, to see Barry Evans again.

'I told you. I don't know where Cindy is,' Barry insisted, looking scared. Grant and Phil had collared him getting out of his car and had frogmarched him into his flat, dumping him unceremoniously on a chair. Grant was standing behind him, giving Barry the heebie-jeebies. Phil was sitting in front of him, conducting the interrogation.

'Wrong answer,' Grant said, curt.

Phil sighed and addressed Barry again. 'He's not a patient man, Grant. He's busy. And he don't like wasting time.'

'Maybe you should go and wait in the car. This won't take long,' Grant suggested to Phil, over the top of Barry's head. Barry's shoulders contracted slightly.

Phil returned to Barry again. 'If you think I was hard on you, you wanna spend a bit of time alone with my brother.' He stood up, making as if to leave.

'I can't tell you anything, honest,' Barry cried, panicking.

'Sorry, old mate.' Phil clapped him on the back. 'Well, I'll leave it to you, then,' he said to Grant. 'Want me to put some music on, drown out the noise?'

'Yeah, good idea.'

'Phil! Don't leave me with this psycho,' Barry protested, trying to get up. Grant pushed him back down.

Phil turned on his heel. 'Why shouldn't I?' He glanced back at Grant. 'Don't enjoy yourself too much.' Grant yanked Barry's head back and smiled at him. It was not a friendly smile. Barry went to pieces.

'No, please! She sent me a postcard. It's over there. But I don't know anything.'

Phil retrieved the postcard from a shelf. '"Barry",' he read out loud. '"Life is impossible. If D wants to talk, tell him to meet me outside the Concorde Metro at noon on 12 November. C."'

'Thank you,' Grant said, releasing Barry's head. Barry, relieved, deflated like a pricked balloon, until Grant walked round to face him and jerked him to his feet. 'David don't know about this, does he?'

'N – no.'

'You sure?'

'Yeah.'

'And you're not gonna tell him. Are you?'

Barry, too frightened to speak, shook his head.

Grant shoved him back in the chair. 'It's been a pleasure.'

★

Grant was all for going to Paris mob-handed and grabbing the children back, but Phil had a better suggestion.

'Why don't you take Tiffany on a little romantic break? That way, no one would suspect anything and you could suss out how the land lies, report back.'

Tiffany did not need asking twice. 'You're spoiling me, you know? Not that I'm complaining – I love surprises.' She gave Grant a hug. 'Just one thing. No sightseeing. I'm not walking up thousands of stairs in my condition.'

Grant ruffled her hair. They had become closer recently, the platonic relationship blooming into a sexual one, and he had hopes they might have a future as a couple.

'What about clothes shops?' he joked.

Tiffany laughed. 'That's different.'

Grant and Tiffany stayed away a week longer than planned and returned to the Vic with a shock announcement: they were married. Peggy received the news grim-faced and the next morning, hauled Grant into the living-room for a 'chat'.

'Before you say anything, it was my idea.' Grant held up his hands. 'Tiffany didn't push me into it. We talked about it and decided it was what we both wanted.'

'But what was the big hurry? Why couldn't you come back here and do it properly?'

Grant sighed. 'Look, mum, we didn't want a lot of fuss. And I'm sorry you missed your chance of buying a new hat.'

'Yet again!'

'But it was no big deal,' Grant continued. 'Just a formality.'

Peggy sat back and folded her arms. 'So you don't love her. Admit it!'

'It's not like it was with Sharon. How could it be? But I've got a lot of respect for Tiffany and we've come to an understanding about things …'

'You mean, she's having your kid and you wanted to make sure it had your name.'

Grant stood up. 'She's my wife, now, Mum. She's part of the family. And families stick together, right? That's what you always say.'

Trumped, Peggy could only purse her lips sourly. Grant, smiling to himself, went off to take Tiffany a cup of tea in bed.

While Tiffany was entertaining an avid Bianca with a blow-by-blow account of her wedding, Grant went round to report to Kathy and Phil, who had made an uneasy peace and were living together again. He had seen Cindy – she had been waiting by herself, no sign of the kids – but he had lost her in the crowd. His enquiries at local hotels had drawn a blank and in the end he had given up on the search. Kathy and Phil had some news for Grant, too: David Wicks had done a runner – without leaving a forwarding address.

'Just as well – otherwise I'd have gone and wiped that stupid grin off his face,' Grant snarled. 'I'm sorry, Kath,' he said, catching sight of her distress, 'I tried to find the kids ...'

'I know, I'm not blaming you.'

Ben started crying and she got up to see to him. When she had gone from the room, Phil said, 'So what about you and Tiff, eh? What brought that on?'

Grant shrugged. 'After seeing what happened to Ian, it made me think – if I wasn't married, I wouldn't have any say in what happened to my kid.'

'Sounds like a romantic proposal.'

'Well, there was a bit more to it than that. I could have done a lot worse, couldn't I? She's young, she's a looker and we've got on all right since she moved into the Vic. She likes the life there, she's happy to be a part of the business. And she doesn't want to bring a kid up on her own.'

'So you thought you wouldn't waste another moment.'

Grant laughed. 'The last thing I wanted was her and Mum getting in a state, planning a big wedding.'

Phil snorted and raised his beer can. 'Well, here's to your future happiness. Or whatever.'

CHAPTER TWENTY-SIX

Despite Grant's optimism about the future, his marriage to Tiffany ran into problems within days. Catching her at the bar taking a sip of Bianca's vodka and orange, he went ballistic, laying into her about the effect on the baby. Tiffany, upset at being so publicly berated, stormed off upstairs and when Grant went to find her she was curled up on the sofa in tears.

'I'm just a walking womb to you, aren't I? An incubator for your baby. Well, I've got feelings, you know. I'm still a person.'

'You know the damage alcohol can do to a baby,' Grant said, ignoring her.

'Not the odd sip. I'm not stupid, you know.'

'I never said you were.'

'Do you know what the worst thing is?' she continued, talking over him. 'I can't see any end to this. I can't see it getting any better once I've had the baby.'

Grant was silent at this, seeing her point. Eventually, he suggested they go out for dinner to talk things over, but Tiffany reminded him he had arranged to play snooker with Phil. Unwilling to pass up a session with his brother – it had been ages since they'd had a night out together – Grant invited Tiffany along too. To his chagrin, she said yes.

The evening turned out to be a disaster, with Tiffany being chatted up by some slimeball and Grant losing his rag and threatening to poke the bloke's eye out. His heavy-handedness enraged Tiffany, who insisted she was quite capable of looking after herself. When Grant begged to differ, telling her he expected her to act more responsibly from now on – including giving up work after Christmas – she was appalled.

★

Tiffany's moans about being oppressed by Grant led Bianca to suggest a girls' night out. Knowing how Grant would react to that, Tiffany declined, suggesting they had a quiet drink upstairs instead. Somehow, the quiet drink became a session, and when Grant came to investigate the noise and saw Tiffany with a beer can in her hand he broke up the gathering, slinging everyone out. Tiffany, embarrassed and humiliated once again, left with Ricky and Bianca and spent the night at their flat, refusing to come home until Grant apologised.

As his relationship with Tiffany grew increasingly volatile, Grant found himself confiding more and more in Lorraine. Her maturity and understanding made a refreshing change from Tiffany's schoolgirl petulance. The fourteen-year age gap between him and Tiffany was at times glaringly obvious. As far as Grant was concerned, he had nothing in common with her friends, although Tiffany had wrung a concession out of him that he would make an effort to get along with them before she agreed to return to the Vic.

Lorraine had been having a hard time with Joe, who was receiving treatment for psychotic depression caused by his sister Karen's death. David's departure had made him even worse, and he had refused to live in the Vic with Lorraine, telling her to keep away from him and saying that Grant was evil. Carol Jackson was the only person he seemed to trust and she had taken him in, but although Lorraine had given the arrangement her blessing, she was deeply hurt by Joe's rejection.

Grant listened to Lorraine with sympathy. She had been talking about returning to Bolton for Christmas, hoping that being back on familiar ground would benefit Joe. Grant was surprised at the intensity of the pang he felt when she told him; he had been trying to forget about his attraction to her, but it wouldn't go away. When she changed her mind and decided to stay, he felt a massive sense of relief. Trying to quash his feelings by telling himself he had more than enough on his plate with Tiffany and the baby, he encouraged Nigel, who was mooning around hopelessly after Lorraine, to ask her out. Nigel did, and was delighted when Lorraine agreed to go for a meal with him.

The build-up to Christmas was overshadowed by Peggy's announcement that she had breast cancer and needed a lumpectomy. One afternoon she gathered her immediate family around her and broke the news. It was clear that she was frightened about her prospects of survival. Having watched her husband die of cancer, she could not face putting George through such an ordeal and ended their developing relationship, telling him they were going nowhere. George, who worshipped the ground Peggy walked on, was mystified. He had, anyway, been given an ultimatum by Grant to finish things with Peggy after a gangland rival started causing trouble at the Vic, but he was deeply reluctant to do so. Instead, he made a full confession, telling her his businesses weren't entirely legitimate. Peggy, who had guessed as much, opened up to him about her cancer and they were reconciled. She returned from hospital on 23 December wearing a brave face and announced determinedly that the Mitchell family Christmas lunch would go ahead as planned.

By Christmas Eve, Grant was not feeling goodwill to anyone. He was as jealous as hell of Nigel, who was taking Lorraine out to a posh Italian restaurant in Stoke Newington, and furious with Tiffany, who had refused to work that night and was going to the Cobra Club with Bianca, Ricky, Simon and Tony. Peggy, who had noticed the two of them rowing, came over and issued a warning.

'Look, I don't know what's going on, but sort it out, fast. I want us to be one big happy family tomorrow, do you hear?'

'Fine,' Tiffany said with a tight smile.

Grant, glowering, stomped off into the back to fetch more crisps. He couldn't bear to look at Lorraine, who was the other side of the bar, waiting for Nigel. The sight of her made his stomach flip over, he wanted her so much. She was wearing a stunning black dress which showed off her slim figure perfectly. By comparison, Tiffany, who had squeezed herself into a too-tight mini-dress, looked like a tubby little tart. When Nigel arrived, spruced up and grinning like a big, happy puppy, Grant could not bring himself to wish his best mate a good evening out. Aching to be in Nigel's shoes, Grant watched enviously as Lorraine strolled out on his arm.

Grant was even more angry and fed-up by the end of the evening. The pervading atmosphere of seasonal jollity among the regulars only served to fuel his growing resentment and, without Tiffany to help, he had had a nightmare shift behind the bar. He retired to the living-room with a bottle of scotch and slumped on the sofa, brooding. When he heard footsteps on the stairs he thought at first it was Tiffany, and was just about to give her a mouthful when Lorraine came in.

'Hiya. You still up?'

'So, how did it go?' Grant asked.

'Fine. It was a lovely meal.'

'And?'

'And what?'

'He's a good bloke, Nige.'

'Yeah,' Lorraine agreed, smiling. 'He's a good listener, too. He didn't get a word in edgeways. He didn't seem to mind, though.'

'Do anything for you, Nige. Anything,' Grant said bitterly, pouring himself another scotch.

Lorraine, observing him closely, said, 'Are you sure that's a good idea?'

Grant chucked the drink back. 'I'm not sure about anything any more.'

She came and sat down next to him. 'Listen, would talking about it help?'

'Yeah, let's talk about it. Talk, talk, talk. We do a lot of that, don't we?'

'I think you've had enough,' Lorraine said, getting up. 'If I was you I'd get to bed. Goodnight.'

Grant put a hand on her arm. 'No, please, Lorraine. Don't go.'

She sat down again. 'So, are you going to tell me what's upset you? Is it something I've done?'

He shook his head. 'It's Tiffany. I've made the biggest mistake of my life, marrying her.' He poured himself more scotch. 'When she first told me the baby was mine, my instinct was to reach out, protect her, take care of her. She looked so sweet, all wide-eyed and innocent.' He thumped his leg. 'What a mug. What a prat.'

Lorraine looked at him, alarmed. 'What's she said?'

Tiffany had let slip to her that the baby might not be Grant's. Lorraine had been urging her to tell him, but Tiffany was dragging her feet.

'Does it matter? Whatever she says is pretty childish. Even by my standards,' Grant replied with self-loathing. 'I wanted the baby so much it blinded me to how stupid the whole situation was. We don't even get on, let alone love each other.' He dropped his head in despair. 'It's all my fault, I should have realized …'

'No,' Lorraine interrupted. 'You've really tried. I've seen you. Tiffany doesn't realize what she's got in you. You're a wonderful man, Grant, even if you don't see it yourself. If it was me, I …'

She broke off, aware that she had given too much away, but Grant had caught the wistfulness of her tone.

'If it was you?'

Lorraine stood up, agitated. 'It was just a figure of speech. I didn't mean it like that.'

Grant got up too. 'No?' he said, taking her into his arms. She resisted for a second but he pulled her to him and started to kiss her, a thorough, searching kiss. She stopped struggling and dissolved into the embrace, moulding her body against his as she returned the kiss with equal passion. Just then, a movement in the doorway made them both freeze. Lorraine turned round to see a shocked Joe standing there.

'I've come back to stay with you, Mum,' he said. 'If you still want me.'

Lorraine told Joe that Christmas away from Bolton had made her feel homesick and depressed and that Grant was just comforting her. He seemed to swallow the story. He was quiet the next day, causing Phil, who had turned up with Kathy and Ted Hills, her brother, to remark, 'Moody sod, ain't he?' Everyone was beginning to assemble in the bar, which was closed to accommodate Peggy's mammoth Christmas lunch. Two tables draped in snowy white linen had been set end-to-end, and were groaning with food and wine. Joe, who was sitting next to Tiffany at the opposite end to Grant, suddenly asked, 'You know Grant pretty well, don't you? Does he ever do things you can't explain?'

'Yeah, all the time,' Tiffany replied with feeling.

'What? Bad things?'

'Grant? Bad? You're kidding, aren't you?' She gave him a wry grin – Grant had been in a temper since they woke up – and continued tactlessly, 'There are days when sometimes I swear he's got that six-six-six mark.' Joe's eyes grew rounder and rounder.

The meal started with a thunderbolt from George, who announced that he had asked Peggy to marry him and that she had accepted. This earned the Mitchell brothers' displeasure, although they made an effort to hide it from Peggy. But the meal went downhill from there. Phil, who Kathy had warned off the drink, was knocking back red wine as if it was Ribena. George blotted his copybook by offering Tiffany a glass, who said yes to provoke Grant. Then, when Lorraine passed Grant the carving knife for the turkey, Joe went mad.

'No!' he screamed. 'Don't let him! He's got the mark of the devil, Mum!'

Phil snorted into his wine. 'Oi, Joe, what are you drinking

— 'cos I'll have some of it an' all.'

'Joe, it's alright, it's only Grant … remember?' Lorraine said, trying to pacify him.

'If you're looking for the black mass, the next one's at six o'clock on the allotments,' Phil continued, chortling.

Lorraine swung round. 'You think my son being ill is funny?'

Phil backed down. 'Alright, alright, it was a joke. Where's your sense of humour? Grant being the devil? That's funny, isn't it?'

The table erupted into a mass of accusations, Kathy reprimanding Phil, Phil snapping at Kathy, Ted defending his sister and Peggy furious with both of her boys. Into this, Joe dropped his second bombshell.

'If Tiffany is Grant's wife, right, why was he kissing my mum?'

For a moment, everyone was silent.

'It was a Christmas kiss. Under the mistletoe,' Grant explained in a strangled voice.

'She said you were comforting her.'

Peggy glared down the table. 'Grant?'

'He's mistaken, Mum.'

'Well, I wouldn't put it past you,' Tiffany joined in. 'You probably really fancy the idea of having two of us under one roof.' She leaned towards George. 'Give us another glass of wine, George. I need a top-up.' With that, the row broke out again, Grant launching into Tiffany, Tiffany shrilling at Grant and everyone else picking up their former arguments, until Peggy, mortified at having her Christmas lunch ruined, yelled, 'Shut up all of you!' at the top of her voice.

Tiffany was the first to leave. 'Well, that was good,' she said, getting up. 'We must do it again some time. In the next century, perhaps.' She turned to face Peggy. 'You're right, family is important. If anyone wants me, I'll be with mine.'

When the dust had settled and the disgruntled guests departed, Grant went upstairs to look for Lorraine. He found her sitting on her bed, sniffing into a tissue.

'Some day, eh?' he said, sitting down beside her. 'Where's Joe?'

'He needed to get out, clear his head.' Lorraine wiped her eyes.

'And what about you?' Grant asked gently.

'I'm alright.' She looked up at him. 'What about Tiffany? Aren't you going to go and get her?'

'No. She'll be at her brother's. Best place for her.'

'You can't leave it like this.'

'Yes, I can.' Grant stroked her cheek. 'I don't want to think about Tiffany, or Christmas, or anything else … Being with you is all that matters …'

He took her face between his hands as tenderly as if it was a flower, and kissed her. Lorraine responded with a sudden, desperate urgency.

'Close the door,' she whispered, her lips brushing his ear.

Grant looked at her, making sure he'd understood her right. Lorraine gazed at him steadily. He got up and closed the door, turning the key in the lock.

Boxing Day – Grant's wedding anniversary to Sharon – dawned with the realization that his second marriage was also well on the way to disaster. Grant didn't care for Tiffany, he knew that, but he did want the baby, more than anything. More than Lorraine?, a voice asked at the back of his mind That was the nub of it. Grant closed his eyes and sank into his bath, submerging himself completely. The warmth of the water comforted him. This must be what it's like for my baby, being suspended and protected in its sac of fluid, he thought, recalling the pictures in Tiffany's pregnancy book. The poignancy of the image affected him deeply. It wasn't a foetus now; at six months it was a recognisable baby. He had felt it moving in Tiff's tummy, seen her skin suddenly bulge when it kicked. Then and there, he decided, he couldn't let go of his little girl, whatever personal sacrifices it meant.

When he told Lorraine, later that day, she was angry and bitter, accusing Grant of using her. Grant was upset. He tried to reassure her that he would be with her if he could, but that he had to give his marriage another go first. Lorraine was initially scathing but then seemed to calm down and accept what he was saying.

Relieved, Grant went round to Simon and Tony's flat and made things up with Tiffany, who, after a night on the sofa, was secretly glad to be coaxed home.

'Listen, I know we didn't have a great time yesterday, but I do want to make things better between us,' she said, as they lay in bed that night. 'We just have to make more effort. Why don't we try really hard to make 1997 a good year for all three of us? Whaddya say?'

Grant, who had his hand on her belly, communing with the baby, leaned over and kissed her lightly on the cheek. 'Yes.'

After the fiasco of Christmas Day, Peggy was determined to make New Year's Eve in the Vic a night to remember. Nigel, who had been hired to DJ the party, was like a cat on hot bricks all day. After his meal out with Lorraine, he was even more smitten than before and was determined to tell her how he felt. Grant, who knew of Nigel's intentions, was very uncomfortable about the situation. He tried to dissuade him from getting his hopes up, but Nigel wouldn't listen. 'I've got a good feeling about this one, Grant. Sometimes, you just know.'

Nigel's words resounded in Grant's ears when Lorraine told him that evening that she was going back to Bolton. The party was well under way, the disco blaring out and the packed bar heaving with sweaty bodies. Lorraine signalled Grant out the back to talk.

'Please ... you can't,' he begged when she told him. 'We can sort something out.'

'Like what?' she said harshly. 'No, it's just impossible, Grant. I can't bear carrying on like this any more. You're making a fresh start with Tiffany, remember?'

'But I've waited so long to meet the right person – I don't want to lose you,' he cried. No matter how hard he had tried to put Lorraine out of his mind, she filled his thoughts constantly.

'It's too late,' she replied softly. 'You're married with a baby on the way. I should never have got involved.'

'I love you.' Grant reached out and touched her face. 'Really.'

For a moment, Lorraine looked as if she was going to respond and say the same, but then she pulled away.

'No, Grant. I can't do this. I just can't.'

She went back into the bar, shaking, and saw Tiffany sitting at a table, looking rather puffed. Tiffany, who was clad in another ultra-revealing mini-dress, had been dancing and was clearly regretting it. 'I just want to tell you I'm leaving Walford,' Lorraine said.

'Oh really? We'll miss you,' Tiffany replied, rolling her eyes. She was fed up with Lorraine banging on her about the baby's parentage and would be glad to see her go.

'Look, I know you don't want to hear this, but you have to tell Grant the truth about the baby,' Lorraine continued.

'Oh, change the record, will ya?' Tiffany shouted. 'He doesn't need to know. He never needs to know. I ain't gonna risk losing everything on the off-chance he ain't the father and if you can't see that, the sooner you go back to Bolton, the better.'

Grant, looking for Lorraine, caught sight of her rowing with Tiffany and came over. As soon as she saw him coming, Lorraine disappeared.

'What was that all about?' he asked Tiffany.

'Nothing,' she said sulkily. 'Lorraine just made some bitchy comment, that's all.'

It didn't sound like Lorraine to Grant, but with the bar like a madhouse and everyone drinking themselves under the table, he did not get a chance to quiz her until almost midnight.

Spotting her clearing glasses in the far corner of the room, he went over.

'What happened between you and Tiffany?' Lorraine hid her face behind her long hair. 'Lorraine, I want to know. Was it about us?'

'No.'

'Me?' She shook her head.

'Well, what then? Is it the baby?' Lorraine did not answer. 'It is, isn't it?' he said, with mounting horror. The pub was quietening, Peggy shouting for a little hush before the chimes of Big Ben. 'What's wrong with her? You've got to tell me!' He grabbed her arm, his eyes blazing.

'Nothing.'

'Then what is it?'

Lorraine, refusing to look Grant in the face, said hesitantly, 'She ... she might not be yours.'

The clock struck midnight, everyone counting to the chimes.

'But Tiffany told me ... she's my baby.'

'I'm sorry, Grant. She's been lying to you,' Lorraine said, tears in her eyes.

The final chime went and everybody cheered, popping champagne corks and kissing each other. Grant stared across the room at his wife, the traitor, and his face hardened.

CHAPTER TWENTY-SEVEN

'There you are!' Tiffany threw her arms around Grant's neck and gave him a smacker on the lips. 'Happy New Year.' Grant, his expression unchanging, detached himself. 'I want a word with you. In private.'

Tiffany waved a bottle of champagne at him. 'Come on Grant, lighten up. I'm celebrating.'

'Well you can stop celebrating right now and get upstairs.' He propelled her towards the door. Tony tried to intervene, but was shoved away by Grant, who told him to stay out of it.

'It's alright, I'm fine,' Tiffany insisted, sweeping out of the room. Grant followed her, granite-faced.

'So, let's hear it. What've I done?' she said rebelliously, walking into the living-room. Grant went to the sideboard and poured himself a drink, ignoring her. 'Oh, for God's sake, if you're gonna sulk ...'

'Sit down,' he barked.

'Oh, it talks.'

'I said, sit down.'

'I don't want to. Say your piece and then I'm getting back to the party.'

Grant rounded on her. 'You've been lying to me. I trusted you ... I believed everything you told me.'

'What do you mean?' Tiffany asked, unsettled.

'I know. About the baby. I want to know whose it is. Now.' Tiffany gulped. 'It's yours.'

'Don't mess me about, Tiffany. Lorraine told me about your little confession.'

'She's lying. She's got it in for me.'

'I had to drag it out of her. She ain't lying – you are. So is it mine, or Tony's?'

'Grant, we've been through all that. I wasn't sleeping with him then.' She touched his arm, trying to place his hand on her belly. 'This is your little girl in here.'

He looked at her in disgust. 'You'll say anything, won't you?' Tiffany stared at him, frightened at the fury in his eyes. He grabbed her by the shoulders. 'Tell me the truth ...'

'I am ...'

'Tell me ...' he screamed, trying to shake the truth out of her.

'I am! She's yours!'

'Tiffany ...' He shook her again, harder, losing control now. Tiffany's eyes were wide, her head rolling. She tried to speak, but was too breathless. Just as Grant felt the familiar red veil about to descend over his eyes, the door opened and Nigel came in.

'What's going on?'

'Go away, Nige,' Grant snarled, panting.

'No. I ain't standing by while you whack her. I've seen you beat one woman already, I ain't gonna let you do it again. Let her go, Grant.'

Grant relaxed his grip and Tiffany, tearful and shaking, made a bolt for the door.

'Get out of my way,' Grant said to Nigel, as she slipped past him. 'No. I've got something to tell you.'

'This ain't the time.'

'It is, Grant,' Nigel said harshly, 'It's perfect. I've just been having a chat to Lorraine. I told her how I felt about her and I told her that I really liked her – you know, just like you told me to.'

'What did she say?'

'Don't you know?'

'No.'

'You sure about that? Only I thought, since you're sleeping with her, you might have some idea,' Nigel said caustically. He brushed a hand across his face. 'Why didn't you stop me humiliating myself?'

Grant looked abashed. 'Nige, I'm sorry … I'd never do anything to hurt you.'

'Well, you have.'

'It wasn't intentional. I encouraged you because I saw how much you liked her. And it wasn't until Christmas Eve that anything happened between us.'

Nigel flinched. 'That's when we went out. What did you do, have a laugh about me in bed?'

'It wasn't like that.'

'You had a choice, Grant. You knew how much I liked her. You could have left well alone.'

'It was too strong for that.'

'I don't care how strong it was, I wouldn't do it to you.'

Grant sighed. 'You don't know how you'd feel if it happened to you.'

'No, I suppose not,' Nigel returned, shaking. 'I don't know anything about women, do I? I'm a total failure.'

'Nige – '

'Don't "Nige" me,' he shouted wretchedly. 'I'm sick of it, all your digs, your sarky comments – the same comments I've been hearing from you since I was six years old. Fat, stupid and a failure, that's how you've made me feel.'

He turned to go. Grant tried to stop him but he shrugged his hand off. 'Leave me alone. I don't want to be around you any more, Grant. You wreck people's lives.'

'Don't Nige, you're my best mate. You were there for me over Sharon. I was there for you when Debs died. We look out for each other.'

Nigel looked at him with red eyes. 'Not any more we don't. I don't ever want to see you again.'

When Grant got back downstairs, Tiffany had vanished. Lorraine fled to her room, refusing to talk to him and Peggy, most of whose bar staff had suddenly gone missing, was ready to kill him. Phil, who was virtually comatose with booze, slurred something about Tiffany having left with Tony, but when Grant burst into the flat – to the alarm of Tony and Simon – she was nowhere to be found. There was only one other place she could be at this time of night, he decided, Bianca and Ricky's.

He ran round there and pounded on their door, then began kicking it when they refused to let him in. Eventually, Bianca flung it open and told him to clear off, but Grant merely barged past her and went into the lounge, ignoring Ricky's protests.

Tiffany was sitting on the sofa, her hands on her tummy. She looked pale and drained and was a sorry sight with her streaked make-up and laddered tights. Grant told Bianca and Ricky to make themselves scarce, and, after reassurances from Tiffany that she would be alright, they reluctantly went outside.

'Well?' Grant demanded coldly, staring at Tiffany.

'I didn't want you to find out this way,' she said quietly.

'So it's true then?'

'Yes.' Tiffany hung her head.

'Whose is it?'

'I don't know.' She looked up at him. 'What do you want me to say? I lied to you and I'm sorry. It was stupid. I just panicked.'

'You should have been straight with me from the start.'

'Grant, I was scared. I didn't know what to do. I thought me and Tony would work out; next thing I find him snogging my brother. Then, that night at the Vic, you seemed so excited about it and it made me feel good, safe. The longer it went on, the more difficult it got.' She gazed at him appealingly. 'I mean, something started to happen between us. Didn't it? All of a sudden it wasn't just this kid, I really started to feel something for you. Then, of course, I wanted it to be true. I really wanted it to be our baby … I really wanted us to be together. I fell in love with you, Grant.'

'Love?' he scoffed. 'You lied to me. I really thought you had my baby inside of you. All these months, I've been thinking about the future, with my child, and you've just pulled the plug on it, just like that.' He snapped his fingers.

'But it still could be. We could sort things out.'

'No. It's too late. I don't want you, Tiffany. I never have,' Grant said witheringly. 'All I ever wanted was the baby. When it's born, get it tested. If it's mine, then I'm having it. If it ain't, for all I care you can drop it in the canal.'

The next day, when she called at the Vic to pick up some belongings, Tiffany walked in on Lorraine and Grant in a clinch. Grant, deliberately, made no effort to excuse himself or pull away, although Lorraine looked guilty. It was the final straw. Unable to bear living on their doorstep, Tiffany cleaned out hers and Grant's joint account and left Walford to stay with some friends in Spain. Peggy, who knew nothing of what had gone on, could not understand Grant's indifference to his pregnant wife's disappearance. He refused to enlighten her.

Conducting a clandestine relationship with Lorraine behind Peggy's back was hard enough, but when Aunt Sal descended on the Vic in the middle of January it became impossible. Lorraine, who was living in a constant state of tension, decided to move out and started making enquiries about flats, while Grant sought temporary sanctuary at Phil and Kathy's.

Kathy, who answered the door to Grant, made him welcome.

'Yeah, we can put you up, no problem,' she said, ushering him inside. 'Phil ain't here at the moment, but I'm sure he won't mind taking in his own brother.'

'So where is he?' Grant chucked Ben under the chin. Ben, who was sitting in his bouncing cradle, gave him a delighted smile.

'I dunno. Down the Arches, I suppose. That's where he says he goes,' Kathy added darkly. 'But since he only makes guest appearances here these days, who am I to say?'

Grant, who knew that the Arches was shut, was concerned. 'What do you mean?'

Kathy sat down wearily. 'Look, Grant, to tell you the truth, I don't know where Phil goes or what he's up to. He ain't here half the time and when he is, he's so pissed he don't make any sense. I'm getting absolutely sick of it.'

'I'm sorry.'

'There's no need for you to apologise.' She gave him a weak smile. 'Beside Phil, you look like Mr Sensitive. For once.'

'Makes a change, doesn't it?' Grant joked, feeling bad. So far, word had not got out about Tiffany and Lorraine.

'Yeah.' Kathy shot him a look. 'Stay as long as you like, Grant. You can help me with Ben, get in some practice with nappies and feeding. I'd appreciate the company.'

Phil returned that evening. He was not pleased to see Grant.

'What's he doing here?' he asked, swaying in the doorway to the living-room.

'Had to give up my room for Aunt Sal. She's having marital problems,' Grant answered before Kathy could say anything.

'Aren't we all,' Phil mumbled, lurching into the room.

Kathy's lips tightened. 'Where have you been all day?'

He glared at her. 'Drownin' my sorrows. Since I ain't got a business no more, it seemed the only thing left to do.'

'You what?'

'Got shut down. Bastard Health and Safety official said I ain't fit to trade.'

She got up, angry. 'I'm not surprised, if they saw you in that state. You ain't fit for anything.'

Phil regarded Grant sourly. 'I see you got a replacement in quick enough. Couldn't wait to start carrying on behind my back, could you?'

'Phil ...' Grant took a step towards him.

Phil squared up to him, holding up his fists. 'Wanna fight me for her? Even things up after Sharon?'

Grant took hold of his arms gently and lowered them. 'Nothing's going on between me and Kathy. I just need somewhere to stay for a while.'

'Well, you can get out of my house! I know your game, Grant.' Phil took a wild swing at him, missing by miles, and half-fell against a small table, knocking it over.

'For Christ's sake, Phil!' Kathy yelled. 'You'll wake Ben.' As if on cue, Ben's wail started up over the baby intercom.

Phil picked himself up and headed for the front door. 'Yeah, well, in that case I'll go somewhere I'm wanted,' he said, going out into the night.

Phil did not return that night, or the next. Kathy was beginning to go frantic and was even contemplating calling the police when a strange woman knocked on her door, demanding some money which she claimed she'd loaned Phil. She explained, awkwardly, that she'd met Phil the previous evening. They had had a drinking session and had ended up sleeping together. He had asked her for money and she'd lent him fifty pounds, which she needed back.

'He were driving me mad, banging on about how his wife didn't understand him. I gave him the money to get shot of him.' She glanced at Grant, who had appeared behind Kathy, holding Ben. 'I'm sorry,' she said, leaning towards Kathy and lowering her voice. 'It must be awful, hearing all this about your own brother-in-law.'

Kathy stiffened. 'This is my brother-in-law. You just slept with my husband.'

The woman took a step backwards. 'Oh no.' She put her hand to her mouth. 'You poor cow.'

After that, it was easy for Kathy to make her decision. She and Phil had no future. His drinking was wrecking her life and, more importantly, it was wrecking Ben's life. She told Grant, not knowing how he'd react, but he was understanding. He offered to look after Ben while she packed and Kathy was grateful.

She was even more grateful for his suppport when Phil eventually arrived home, drunk and abusive. After his forty-eight-hour bender, he had no idea what day it was and no recollection of having slept with another woman. When he saw Kathy's bags and Ben's baby stuff piled in the hall, he went mad.

'She ain't leaving me.' He stumbled into the house, Grant following. 'Let her go. Let her calm down and you can sober up and maybe …'

'Kathy!' Phil roared, standing at the foot of the stairs. Kathy descended with her coat on, Ben dressed and ready to go in her arms. 'Put him back. You ain't going anywhere.'

'Would you get out of my way, please?' Kathy said calmly. Phil made to start upstairs and she shrank back.

Grant grabbed his arm. 'Let her go!'

'Stay out of it, Grant!' Phil shook himself free and lunged again at Kathy. Thinking he was going to attack her, she gasped and clutched Ben tighter, appealing to Grant for help. He tackled Phil, dragging him away from the stairs. Phil lost his balance and stumbled against the wall, sliding down it until he subsided to the floor. He slumped, all the fight gone out of him. Kathy came down the stairs and picked her way carefully over his outstretched legs.

'Kath … don't go … Kath,' he called weakly.

She turned and looked at him in disgust. 'You know what you look like, Phil? One of them doorway winos.'

Kathy moved into Pat and Roy's, leaving Phil to fend for himself. After going on another binge, he was arrested for being drunk and disorderly and spent a night in police cells. Peggy, who took the call from the station, got him home the next day and was shocked to hear him making wild accusations about Grant and Kathy. Knowing them to be nonsense, she pressed him to tell her why Kathy had really left, and a pathetic Phil finally broke down and confessed his drink problem to her.

The dramas did not stop there: later that day Phil snatched Ben away from Clare and Sonia Jackson, who were pushing him round the Square in his pram. When Kathy found out, a search was mounted and Phil was discovered on the allotments, paralytic with booze, holding Ben perilously close to a billowing bonfire. Trembling with rage and fear, Kathy snatched him away, resolving then and there to divorce Phil. Her resolve faltered, however, when she went round later and saw how pitiable and incapable her husband had become. Unable to sink any lower, Phil agreed to go into a detox program, overseen by a community alcohol nurse. Kathy promised to help him but refused to move back until Phil proved he could stay dry.

Grant, who was still giving Phil a wide berth, turned his attention instead to trying to mend his friendship with Nigel, who had not spoken to him since New Year's Eve. He had spotted Nigel, purple in the face, running flat-footedly round the Square in a gaudy tracksuit. Concerned for his health – Nigel was clearly overdoing it – he gently intervened. Nigel, affronted, rejected his suggestions, but when he saw Grant was genuine he unbent a little and agreed to train with him.

Grant was relieved. He had been feeling like a leper – the news had got out about his affair with Lorraine and most of the Square was giving him the cold shoulder. Lorraine was miserable, too. She and Joe had moved out of the Vic into the flat above Tony and Simon's, but Joe's odd behaviour was increasingly giving her cause for concern. Not only that, but Peggy was livid with her for breaking up Grant's marriage and there was an atmosphere behind the bar you could cut with a knife.

To top it all, Tiffany had arrived home and was waddling around heavily pregnant. The baby was three days overdue and the wait seemed to be affecting Lorraine, who was tense and snappy, almost as much as Tiffany, who was heartily fed up with being so uncomfortable.

It was Nigel who pointed out the strain Lorraine was under, during his morning run with Grant. 'It must be hard for her, not knowing if it's your baby or not. I mean, if it is, it's gonna make things really difficult.'

'No it ain't.' Grant was adamant about that.

'But you'll be even more tied to Tiffany. You are married to her, after all.'

'Only in name.'

'Well,' Nigel panted, 'maybe Lorraine don't see it that way.'

His comment gave Grant food for thought and later on, when Peggy sent Lorraine out to the shops, he caught up with her half-way across the Square.

'Look, I just want you to know that whatever happens after the baby's born, nothing's gonna change between us.'

Lorraine looked away. 'It isn't that simple.'

'It is,' he insisted.

She turned back, flaring at him. 'Grant, if Tiffany has your baby, it's bound to affect things. How can you be so naive? Having a child completely changes your world view. You don't know how it's gonna make you feel. You might want to be with her again.'

'Listen, that's never gonna happen.' Grant put his hands on her shoulders, making her face him. 'I love you. You're the most important thing in the world to me.'

'Maybe that's true now, but in a few days, a week, who knows?'

'What have I got to say to convince you?' Grant cried desperately. Lorraine stroked his face, her eyes dark with concern. 'Let's just wait and see what happens, eh?'

Grant held her close, breathing in the scent of her hair. Whatever happened, he wasn't going to let Lorraine go. He wanted to be with her for the rest of his life. Suddenly, he knew what he had to do.

That evening, Grant proposed to her. They were on their way to a Seventies night at the Cobra Club when he pulled out a ring and asked her to marry him. Lorraine was touched at the gesture, but saw it for what it was.

'Grant … giving me a ring isn't going to guarantee anything …' she sighed, handing it back. 'When things have settled between you and Tiffany maybe we could think about it then.'

'It is settled.'

'No, Grant, it isn't. Ask me again when you're free.'

'What if I was free now, then what would you say?'

Lorraine was silent for a while, staring down the road into the distance. 'I'd say yes.'

Half an hour later, Grant slipped out of the club and went round to Tony's flat, where Tiffany was now staying.

'I'm glad you've come,' she said, letting him in. 'I know we live next door but I feel like I'm a million miles away.' She swallowed nervously. 'I've really missed you, Grant.'

'Look, the reason I came round was to get things straight, not to go over old ground,' he said brutally, sweeping aside her attempt at reconciliation. 'I want a divorce.'

'A divorce?' she echoed, shaken. 'But I thought you'd come to see how I was.'

'I don't care how you are. I don't love you. We've got no future together. I just want this sorted, before the baby comes.'

'Oh, and I suppose you've got a future with that slag Lorraine?'

Grant pushed his face at her. 'That's right. As soon as you and I get divorced. And she ain't a slag. You are.'

Tiffany refused to be intimidated. 'Well, if that's how you feel, you can whistle for your divorce.'

Grant, glared at her. 'All I want is to be rid of you.' He turned on his heel, heading back towards Bridge Street.

Tiffany stumbled after him. 'You get rid of me, you get rid of this kid an' all,' she screamed, hysterical. 'I won't let you see her. I'll claw your face off if you come anywhere near her.'

Grant continued to walk away, laughing. 'You really are out of control, aren't you?'

She attacked him from behind, hitting him and pulling at his jacket. 'I hate you, I hate you.' He pushed her away roughly and she slipped, falling to the ground. 'I hate you so much. I — oh — oh …'

Tiffany doubled up, wincing. She tried to stand, but a contraction seized her and she couldn't.

'You okay?' Grant tried to help her up but she yelled, 'Go away,' at him so ferociously that he backed off.

'Alright, alright,' he said, continuing down the road. He stopped and looked back. Tiffany was still in a heap on the ground and obviously suffering. She lifted her head, her face contorted.

'Grant,' she sobbed. 'It's the baby. Get me to the hospital. Now.'

Once at the hospital, Grant was going to leave, but Tiffany begged him to stay. She was so desperate, and in so much agony, that he couldn't bring himself to go and the midwife soon had him holding Tiffany's hand and doing the breathing techniques with her. Tiffany's labour was prolonged and exhausting and when, several hours later, the baby had still not emerged, the midwife began to look concerned. She checked the belt round Tiffany's belly which was monitoring the baby's heartbeat. The rate had slowed. Grant noticed the numbers dropping on the electronic display and caught her worried face. She rang the emergency bell and a doctor came in. They conferred briefly.

'Right. Straight to theatre.'

The doctor pulled a consent form out of his pocket. He turned to Grant.

'We'll need your wife to sign this. We've got to perform a Caesarean section. The baby's in distress and we need to get her out as soon as we can.'

Grant was allowed in to the operating theatre once he was gowned up. A screen had been placed over Tiffany's tummy, so they couldn't see what was going on. Tiffany, who had had an epidural, was awake but woozy.

'What's happening, Grant?' she asked, scared. 'I can't feel

a thing.' She started to weep. 'She's dead, ain't she? I've lost her.'

'No.' Grant squeezed her hand reassuringly, but he was as frightened as she was.

'Right, okay,' the surgeon said. Grant saw the midwife pull away from Tiffany and caught a glimpse of something red. She rushed over to a resuscitation table with a second doctor.

'Suction, now.' They huddled around the table, tense, not speaking, as the pump started to clear the baby's airways.

'What's going on?' Grant pushed his way over. 'Is she alive?'

'Please, Mr Mitchell!' The midwife held him back. 'You'll get in the way.'

'I just want to see her.'

'I'm sorry, you can't.'

Grant went back to Tiffany, who had lost consciousness and was lolling on the operating table being stitched up by the surgeon. The other group was still closed around the baby, the pump whining. Grant blinked back tears.

Suddenly, there was a cry, a newborn baby's mewling cry, and he held his breath.

'Mr Mitchell.' The midwife beckoned him over. 'You've got a lovely baby girl.' She placed a squalling, red-faced bundle in his arms wrapped in a hospital sheet. He looked into the little, screwed-up face with its shock of black hair and the sight of her made his heart lurch with love.

CHAPTER TWENTY-EIGHT

Grant held the baby in his arms most of that night while Tiffany slept. The midwives popped in every so often to check on her and give the baby a bottle, but for the rest of the time he was left undisturbed. Scared of waking the baby, he hardly dared move a muscle, but the discomfort of sitting still for so long was nothing compared to the joy he felt holding his little girl. You are mine, he told her silently, looking down at her sleeping face. I know you are. I can feel it.

After witnessing her traumatic birth, Grant was overwhelmed by the knowledge he had almost lost her. If the doctors hadn't operated when they had ... he couldn't bear to think about the consequences. Already, his life had taken on a new dimension. The baby stirred and opened her mouth once or twice, making sucking faces. He held her tiny fist, entranced, as her hand curled tightly around his little finger. Her grip was surprisingly strong. Reassured by the physical contact, she sighed and settled again. 'Don't worry, darling, I won't let you go,' he promised, his eyes welling with tears. 'We'll work it out. Somehow. I'll find a way ...'

When Tiffany came round, she was as overwhelmed as Grant. 'Look at her ... she's so beautiful,' she breathed.

'I know.' He smiled. 'She's perfect.' He placed the baby gently in her arms, cradling her head. 'Well, I'd better get going.'

There was an awkward pause. Tiffany looked up at him with shining eyes. 'Grant, I'm really glad you were here last night.'

'Yeah. So am I,' he said, meaning it.

She studied the baby's face, caressing her downy cheek. 'The baby's yours, Grant. Your daughter. Look at her eyes.'

'We don't know that.' Grant wasn't going to admit his feelings to Tiffany.

'Don't you want her to be yours?' He gazed at the baby, then looked away, unable to answer. 'Well, I do,' Tiffany continued. 'I want her to be yours more than anything in the world.'

'Why?'

'Because I love you.' She reached out to take Grant's hand. 'If we could just give it a second chance, start again from scratch, we could bring her up together.'

'No,' Grant said, snatching his hand away and getting up. 'It's too late. I'm in love with Lorraine.' He recited it almost like a mantra.

Tiffany named the baby Courtney. They came out of hospital a week later and moved back into Tony's cramped flat. Grant tried to keep a distance, but found it impossible. Sleeping with Lorraine in the flat above, he could hear Courtney crying downstairs and woke up almost as often as Tiffany did. He was frustrated by his lack of involvement with her, and envious of Tony, who had apparently taken to the duties of fatherhood like a duck to water. The thought of Tony Hills laying so much as a finger on Courtney riled Grant beyond measure. He did not allow himself to think that she might be Tony's child. He pushed Tiffany into having the paternity test done as soon as possible, while at the same time keeping up the pressure for a divorce.

Grant was disappointed to learn that he could do nothing to initiate divorce proceedings until they had been married a year. Not so Tiffany, who confided to Bianca that it gave her another six months in which to win Grant back. She resolved to go on a diet …

'Lorraine's pretty in a stick-insect way, but I ain't exactly giving her any competition,' she said, causing Bianca to groan. Bianca thought Grant was a pig and a bully and did not hold back from telling her so. Tiffany remained unmoved. 'Once he knows that she's his kid, he won't be able to stop himself from loving me.'

The results of the paternity test came through at the end of April. When Grant saw the official brown envelope, he could hardly bring himself to open it.

'Well, go on, Grant,' Peggy said eagerly. He stared at the envelope, turning it over in his hands.

'I can't ... I mean, what if, after all this time, I've just been kidding myself?'

'Shall I do it?' she asked gently, seeing the tension on his face. Grant shook his head. Ripping it open with his thumb, he extracted a single sheet of headed paper and read, disbelief spreading across his features.

'Well?' Peggy was almost hopping up and down. 'What's the matter, Grant? Is she yours?'

Grant put the letter down, looking a little stunned. 'Yeah.'

Peggy enveloped him in a hug. 'Oh Grant, I'm so pleased. Thank you for my beautiful granddaughter.'

'Thanks, Mum.' He turned to go but she called him back.

'Now you know for sure Courtney's yours, what about you and Tiffany?' Peggy had been waging a war of attrition against Lorraine ever since New Year and lost no opportunity to promote Tiffany.

Grant, aware of her tactics, replied defiantly, 'She's the mother of my child, Mum – end of story.'

When he went round to see Courtney, in his new, official capacity as dad, it was clear that Tiffany was harbouring the same hope.

'Now we know for definite she's yours, we owe it to her to both be there for her.'

'I'll be there for her, you can count on it,' Grant replied, gazing fondly at Courtney, who waved a rattle at him. He caught Tiffany's relieved smile and said, 'Look, Tiff, don't hold your breath. Nothing's changed between you and me. I mean that, okay?' Tiffany's smile faded.

★

Later that day, Grant hit upon a solution to his problem. It was so obvious, he wondered why he hadn't thought of it before. He called Lorraine, who was working behind the bar, out to the back.

'I'm going to fight Tiffany for custody,' he announced. 'What do you think?'

She looked surprised. 'Well, if that's what you feel you have to do.'

'The thing is,' Grant continued hurriedly, 'I don't know if I can do it on my own. I need to know you'll stand by me. Lorraine, I want us to be a family. So how do you feel about taking on Courtney?'

Lorraine was momentarily speechless. 'Are you serious? Have you any idea what you're asking? At a time like this? What about my child, for heaven's sake?' She stalked off, exasperated. Joe's behaviour had deteriorated again and it was worrying her greatly. He had taken to wearing tinfoil helmets to block out sinister messages and was filling scrapbooks with cuttings about catastrophes and disasters. After the previous evening, when he had invited in a load of drunken down-and-outs who he referred to as his 'disciples', Lorraine had been trying to talk to his psychiatrist, so far with no luck.

Joe's next trick was to vandalise some cars outside the Vic, saying they were from another planet. Lorraine was at her wits' end. But there was worse to come. Two days later she returned to the flat to find the place trashed and Joe in the grip of a psychotic attack. Telling her she was evil and 'one of them', he held her prisoner, threatening to hurt her if she moved. The siege ended with Joe being sectioned for 28 days for assessment and treatment. Lorraine, uninjured but badly shaken, was even more distraught when she subsequently learned that Joe had been diagnosed as suffering from schizophrenia.

Despite Lorraine's protests that she wanted nothing to do with it, Grant persisted in his plan to get custody of Courtney. His solicitor, Marcus Christie, advised him that his best recourse was to prove Tiffany was an unfit mother.

'You'll need evidence she's neglecting Courtney,' he said. 'It'll have to be utterly convincing.'

'I'll do whatever it takes.'

'It could turn nasty.'

'Like I said,' Grant showed him to the door, 'Whatever it takes.'

The first thing he did was offer to babysit Courtney so that Tiffany could go to a party. Tiffany was glad of the opportunity to put on her gladrags and dance, but Bianca was suspicious.

'I don't trust Grant. Why's he being so nice all of a sudden?'

'Maybe he's starting to realise what a mistake he's made,' Tiffany replied blithely, dragging her up for another dance. 'He wants Courtney and he knows there's only one way he's going to be able to be with her. With me.'

Back at the Vic, Grant was dropping heavy hints to anyone who would listen that he was worried about Tiffany returning drunk and being incapable of looking after Courtney. A few days later, he followed it up by swooping into the flat and forcibly taking Courtney off Simon, who was babysitting, after he saw a gas repair van parked outside.

'She's coming over to the Vic with me,' he said, picking up Courtney's carrycot and feeding bottle.

Simon tried to stop him. 'No, she's fine. I'm looking after her.'

'What if there's a gas leak? You thought of that? She could be poisoned.'

'Boiler's not dangerous, mate, it's just knackered,' the gas man said, putting his tools back in his bag.

'She's coming with me,' Grant repeated, giving Simon a stare that brooked no argument.

When Tiffany returned shortly afterwards from a night out with Bianca, she was furious to hear what Grant had done and stormed round to the Vic. Peggy took her side and made Grant hand Courtney back, which he did, pale with rage.

'Mum's got it all wrong, you know,' he said savagely. 'There's no way Courtney should be with you.'

'Don't say that,' Tiffany sobbed. 'I love her more than anything. She means the world to me. And you, Grant. If only you knew how much I …'

'I'm not waiting another minute, do you hear?' he shouted, interrupting her. 'I'm getting Courtney off you. And for good.'

Lorraine was exhausted by her daily trips to the hospital, which was miles away. Seeing Joe so sick was draining her. Sometimes he showed no flicker of recognition at all. At others, she found him rocking in a corner, or they would have bizarre, one-sided conversations which would leave her totally clueless. She felt guilt-stricken and inadequate. All she could do was bring him clean laundry and football magazines, none of which he appeared to read. On one occasion, Bianca, who was Joe's half-sister, had come to visit him too and had been shocked at his spaced-out appearance. Lorraine was doing her best to understand what having schizophrenia meant, but the idea that Joe might never fully recover haunted her.

Grant did his best to support Lorraine, but he was side-tracked by his preoccupation with Tiffany and Courtney. His single-mindedness was beginning to grind Lorraine down: she felt steamrollered by him and when, one evening, he produced the same ring he had offered her before, she reacted angrily.

'There,' she said, slipping it on her finger. 'Now all our troubles are over. It's a magic ring, isn't it? Just like Tiffany's.' She took it off again and laid it on the table. 'You have a wife and child. This doesn't mean anything.'

'But if we were married, things would be different,' Grant said, confused.

'Why do you still want me?' Lorraine asked, her voice tinged with bitterness, 'I don't want any more kids. I've already buried a daughter and I've got a sick son. I can't give you what you want.'

Grant retreated, wounded. Lorraine spent the night in

turmoil, unable to sleep. Too many people had been hurt already by what they'd done. However much she loved Grant, marrying him wouldn't make things any better. It would make them worse. Could she really do that? When she got up the next morning and saw the ringbox on the table, still surrounded by the remains of their meal, she knew there was only one answer.

With a small baby and no hot water – Tony and Simon's landlord was dragging his feet about replacing the boiler – Tiffany was having trouble coping. Eventually, she approached Peggy and asked if she could bath Courtney upstairs at the Vic. Peggy was only too delighted to cluck over her little granddaughter and, spotting an opportunity to do some matchmaking, suggested to Tiffany that she and Courtney move back in until the boiler was fixed. By the time Grant returned from the Cash and Carry they were installed in the spare room and Tiffany was back behind the bar looking as if she'd never been away.

Wrongfooted by Peggy and Tiffany's plotting, and unable to deny that it was the best thing for Courtney, Grant grudgingly allowed them to stay. Tiffany lost no time in letting him bond with his baby and, although he insisted he was going to pursue a residency order, his threats began to sound increasingly hollow. 'You're not really going to go through with it are you?' Peggy asked, as she and Grant watched over Courtney slumbering in her carrycot. 'You've seen what Tiffany's like with her. She's wonderful. If Tiffany was an unfit mother, I'd back you all the way. But face it, Grant, you can't split those two up.'

'I know,' he admitted, his expression unreadable.

Grant's life seemed to have reached an impasse. Lorraine was distant and frosty, flinching away from his touch and refusing to meet his eye.

'We need to talk,' she said, when he called round with a

bottle of wine in the hope of a reconciliatory chat.

'I agree.' Grant followed her up the stairs. He poured her a large glass and sat down on the sofa, patting the space beside him. Lorraine sat down gingerly, balancing on the arm. She put down her untouched glass, slopping the wine.

'I can't go on like this,' she gabbled. 'Look at us. This isn't a relationship. We're just a shoulder for each other to cry on.'

'It's not like that.'

'Be honest.'

'Not for me.'

Lorraine looked away. 'Then, I'm sorry. We don't feel the same way.'

Grant sprang to his feet. 'I don't believe this is happening.'

'It's not working. It's never worked,' Lorraine said tightly. 'We were kidding ourselves. The only thing that's kept us together is the fact that everything else is so messed up.'

'That's rubbish.' He pulled her to her feet roughly. 'I love you, you love me – what's so complicated?'

'Don't tell me how I feel!' Lorraine said, defensive.

She pushed him away but Grant came back at her, thrusting his face close. 'Then stop making excuses!'

Intimidated by his rigid neck and bulging eyes, she shrank from him. Grant, registering her reaction, backed off. 'Do I scare you that much?' He exhaled, blowing out his tension. 'Look, I would never lay a finger on you. I love you.'

Lorraine swallowed. 'I think you should go.'

The painful realization finally dawned. 'You don't love me, do you?' Grant said, reeling. 'Go on, say it. Say it!'

'I'm not in love with you,' Lorraine answered dully.

After that, Lorraine avoided Grant completely, refusing to return his calls or show up at the Vic. Instead, she poured her energies into caring for Joe, who had been discharged from the hospital and was still in a delicate emotional state. Joe, who had been primed by a manipulative Grant, seemed chuffed at the idea of the three of them being a family, and Lorraine, unwilling to risk disturbing Joe's mental balance, decided not to tell him that she and Grant had split up. It was a bad decision. When Joe discovered the truth he went spare, blaming Lorraine for ruining everything and accusing her of being the cause of all his problems. Lorraine crumpled, devastated.

Grant, who was standing by, could not contain his anger. 'Shut it,' he roared, slamming Joe against the living-room wall. 'She looks after you twenty-four hours a day. She sacrifices everything for you. She doesn't have a life because of you!'

'Get off him,' Lorraine screamed, pulling at Grant as he shouted in Joe's face.

'Someone's got to sort him out,' he ground, through clenched teeth.

'Yes, well it certainly isn't gonna be you.' Lorraine was vitriolic.

The quiet fury in her voice checked Grant's behaviour and, seeing Joe's petrified face, he let go. 'I'm sorry.'

Lorraine, shielding Joe, ushered him to his room. She returned and fixed Grant with a look so cold it froze his heart. 'Get out. Now.'

'Please,' he begged, 'look, I lost it for a minute, I couldn't help myself. It's just that I've had it up to here with Joe. It's him that ruins everything. If it wasn't for Joe, we could be together.'

'You live in a dream world,' Lorraine said, incredulous. 'It's not Joe, or Tiffany, or anyone else keeping us apart. It's just you and me. You're like a kid. You think the answer to everything is to smash things out of your way. You never stop and think about other people.'

'That's not true.'

'It is. You beat up Sharon. You hospitalised David. You put your own brother in a coma. It's a long list, Grant.'

'That's not fair.'

'And what you've been doing to Joe is, I suppose? Using him to get to me?'

'I haven't,' Grant protested weakly.

Lorraine came up close, the one with the power now. 'You

haven't any real feelings for him. You haven't the patience.' She paused, breathing hard. 'Don't you understand? Even if Joe didn't exist, if I was 21 and desperate to get married and start a family, I wouldn't choose you.'

Tiffany had hers and Courtney's stuff packed up and ready to go. The new boiler had been installed, but she had lied to Grant about it still not being fixed, hoping to buy more time. Peggy knew, and was protecting her, but Grant had found out anyway and had ordered her to leave. They were going the next morning.

It was late when she heard Grant come in. One look at his face told her something had happened. He swept past her and went into his room.

Curious, she followed him. 'Grant?'

He looked up as she entered. 'Look, I don't want to talk about it, right?'

'I just wanted to tell you that I'm sorry for lying to you earlier.'

'Forget it.' Grant slung his jacket on a chair and sat on the bed, his shoulders hunched. 'It doesn't matter now. Nothing matters any more.'

'Why, what's happened?' Grant did not answer. 'It's Lorraine, isn't it? What's she done?'

'It's over, finished.' He looked up at her. 'Happy now?'

Tiffany sat down next to him. 'Are you okay?'

'Do you really care?'

'You know I do.' She reached out and tentatively placed her hand on his.

'It's all my fault,' Grant said brokenly. 'I ruin everything. The closer I get to people, the more I hurt them. Two months ago, Lorraine loved me. Now she can't even bear for me to touch her.'

'That's just because she's the wrong one for you,' Tiffany said softly.

'No, it's me. Look what I've done to you.'

'It doesn't matter,' she whispered. 'I don't care about that any more. I love you, Grant.'

He stared at her. 'How can you say that?'

'I just do. I mean, I've seen all your sides before, all your bad ones, and I don't care.' She leaned forward to kiss him.

Grant pulled back. 'We can't do this.'

Tiffany stroked his jaw lovingly. 'Yes. We can.' She guided his face to hers and kissed him again. This time, Grant responded. They made love frenziedly, but afterwards he was separate and subdued. Tiffany, sensing what was wrong, said, 'Look, Grant, this is just the start for us. Your future is here, with me and Courtney, not Lorraine. No one else is gonna love you like I do.'

'Tiffany, I just don't feel the same way. If I was to get back together with you … we could end up hurting each other more than we've ever done before.' Tiffany was about to protest, when Courtney started crying in the room next door. Sighing, she got up to see to her. Grant was still lying in the darkened room when she returned carrying the baby.

'I thought I'd bring her in with us. Is that alright?'

Grant sat up, surprised and delighted. 'Yeah, of course.' Tiffany passed Courtney to him and he took her in his arms.

'Hello, my little princess.' Courtney gazed up at him with big eyes. Grant looked at her, then at Tiffany, who was watching father and daughter together.

'Grant, it's gonna be okay. I just know it,' she said.

He gave her a small smile, desperate to believe her.

CHAPTER TWENTY-NINE

After a shaky start, Grant and Tiffany settled back down into married life at the Vic. With Lorraine a constant presence in the Square, it was hard for Grant. His feelings about her had not gone away – every time he saw her crossing the Square his heart skipped a beat – but her shuttered expression forbade conversation and, after her wholesale rejection of him, Grant was too devastated to risk being knocked back again.

Being a full-time father to Courtney was more demanding than Grant had realized. The shock of being jolted out of sleep by her penetrating cry, night after night, made him begin to appreciate what Tiffany had been through. Working with her, sharing the changing, feeding and bedtime routine, the little anxieties over a cough or a raised temperature and the small triumphs when Courtney cut her first tooth or learned to sit up, brought them closer again. Tiffany bided her time. She knew Grant didn't love her, but he did respect her now, and that was a good start.

Peggy was ecstatic to have her family back together under her roof and was soon craftily manipulating things to consolidate Grant and Tiffany's marriage. 'I was thinking,' she said casually over breakfast, 'now that things are more settled between you two, have you thought about making it official?'

Grant raised his eyes to the heavens. 'What do you mean, Mum? Tiffany's my wife. How much more official do you wanna make it? Stick a plaque on the wall outside?'

'Well ... I was thinking more along the lines of renewing your vows. A church blessing. It's not as if any of us got to go to your wedding, is it?'

'What is this? Revenge for being done out of a new outfit?'

'No,' Peggy said calmly. 'I think you owe it to yourselves,

especially Tiffany. Look what she's had to put up with from you.' She stood up and began clearing the table. 'And I want everybody to know the Mitchells are united. One big happy family. That's worth celebrating, isn't it?'

Grant was distinctly underwhelmed but Tiffany was delighted with the idea and continued to push him until eventually Grant capitulated and they went to see Alex Healey, the vicar. When Alex told them they could push the boat out if they wanted, Tiffany got excited, but Grant was reluctant.

'Don't get carried away. We don't wanna invite the world and his wife.' She was downcast at this, but touched when he continued, 'The people that matter will be there – us and the family. That's what this was supposed to be about, wasn't it? Not how much money we spend.' He hadn't accounted for Peggy: that evening she stood up and announced a post-blessing party to the entire pub. Tiffany caught Grant's eye and shrugged helplessly. Grant set his jaw.

Later that day Phil came in to the Vic, looking troubled. 'Grant, I need to talk. It's important.'

'What's up?'

Phil glanced around. 'Not here, eh?' Grant raised his eyebrows and came round the bar, following Phil out into the Square. Now that Phil was off the booze and having counselling the two brothers had put their falling out behind them. Kathy and Ben had moved back in and the Arches was up and running again, thanks to Ricky, who had saved the day by doing all the alterations listed by the Health and Safety inspectors. As far as Grant was aware, things were running smoothly again, so he was concerned when Phil confessed that he and Kathy had had a row.

'It ain't just that,' Phil said awkwardly. 'I let things get on top of me and ... I wanted a drink. It was close, Grant. Really close.' He kicked the wall in frustration. 'I should have been able to handle it. I don't know how I'm gonna face Kath. I feel like I've really let her down.'

'So don't tell her. You didn't have it. And it ain't gonna happen again. Is it?'

'No,' Phil said, with a trace of uncertainty.

'What she doesn't know won't harm her. Now go home and make it up to her.'

Grant did not give Phil the same laid-back advice when, two weeks later, he confessed he was having an affair.

'Are you off your head? Who is she?'

'I met her through counselling.'

'I don't believe this. Is it serious or is she just a bit on the side?'

Phil, who had come upstairs to the kitchen for a cup of tea, was defiant. 'It's different, Grant. Lorna takes me for who I am. She don't look at me like she's waiting for me to make a mistake.'

'Oh, and Kathy does?'

'Yeah. She does. She's got no idea what it's like to be where I am. And neither have you.'

'You're right, I haven't. But I know what you've got,' Grant said shortly. 'You've got a wife who's been to hell and back because she loves you and you've got a fantastic kid, too.' He paused. 'Well, what do you want to hear, Phil? Do you want me to slap you on the back 'cos you've got something in common with a boozer, or congratulate you for getting your leg over a couple of nights a week?'

'It's not about that. Lorna understands me ...'

'Or do you want to hear the truth?' Grant continued harshly. 'I've been there, Phil. I know what it's like to betray someone's trust. And I know what it's like to be betrayed.'

Phil looked at him guiltily. 'I'll finish it with Lorna.'

Twenty-first of August, the day of the blessing, found Grant and Tiffany in a state of chaos. Peggy, who had gone to Spain to visit Sam, had been delayed by an air-traffic controller's strike, there was a problem with the cake, the caterers hadn't arrived and Courtney, who was picking up on the tension between her parents, wouldn't stop howling. Things did not improve. On the way to the church, Tiffany learned that, not only had Grant booked them into the same Parisian hotel for their post-blessing holiday that he and Sharon had once stayed at, but that Phil and Kathy were coming along, too. After a blazing row, which made them late, they travelled the rest of the way in silence. It was Tiffany's father, Terry, who turned up drunk and uninvited, who inadvertantly healed the rift. He accosted them outside the church. After he started shouting abuse at Tiffany, Grant waded in threateningly. Tiffany took Grant's arm.

'You stay out of my life,' she said coldly to Terry. 'You're no part of it any more, I've got my own family now.' Shaking, she led Grant into the porch. 'I'm not going to let him ruin this for me,' she said determinedly.

Grant took her hand and squeezed it. 'Ready?'

Tiffany nodded and they walked into the church; Bianca, who was waiting with a flower-bedecked Courtney, bringing up the rear. Just as they reached the front, where Alex was waiting for them, the doors at the back burst open and Peggy staggered in, laden with suitcases and wearing a straw hat.

'Phil!' she hissed in a stage whisper. 'I'm twenty quid short for the taxi! Could you …'

The ceremony was a moving one and, by its conclusion, Grant and Tiffany were smiling almost shyly at each other, their earlier row forgotten. Grant felt a rare sense of tranquillity as he stood, looking at his young wife holding their daughter. Perhaps things really would work out for them now. He wanted them to.

'You look great,' he murmured, as they posed for photographs afterwards. Tiffany smiled; not her usual coquettish smile but a smile of tremulous happiness.

'Thanks.'

'Any time.' Grant stared at her intently. Maybe now the love will come, he thought. It still hurt him to see Lorraine, but not as much. He was growing a skin over that wound. Tiffany was his future now. A real, believable future. At last. Tiffany caught Grant's look.

'Any regrets?' she asked, her smile fading momentarily. He shook his head and she clasped his hand, holding it to her. 'Oh, you've put your wedding ring back on.' Her grin broadened to full hundred-watt brilliance. 'Oh, Grant. You don't have to say anything else. This says it all.'

To get her own back on Grant for booking them into the Adelphi, Tiffany cancelled the reservation and booked the four of them into a hugely expensive chateau-style hotel on the outskirts of Paris. She did not tell Grant how much it cost. It was a party of six who eventually left Walford for a three-night break in Paris: newly-weds Bianca and Ricky were coming along too, but were staying with Ricky's sister, Diane, who lived in an apartment with a Cameroonian musician, Thomas, and her son, Jacques. Bianca, who had just discovered she was pregnant, was in turmoil; Ricky did not know about the baby and she wasn't sure how she was going to tell him. They had not planned on starting a family so soon and she was not even sure whether she wanted to keep it.

As soon as Grant saw the hotel, with its long drive through rolling acres of grounds, his face darkened. 'This is gonna bankrupt me.'

'Should have thought about that when you tried to palm me off with second best,' Tiffany replied with a toss of her head. 'Anyway, Kathy and I deserve the best, don't we?'

Kathy smiled in agreement. 'Yeah.'

'And Phil ain't bothered, are you Phil?'

'What?' Phil was looking distracted. 'No, 'course not.' Grant shot him a look but said nothing. The taxi drew up outside the front entrance, tyres scrunching on the gravel. A smartly attired porter appeared immediately and started unloading their luggage.

'I'll take them,' Grant said curtly, but the porter had already got the cases tucked under his arm and was carrying them inside. 'Yeah, well, you ain't getting a tip,' Grant muttered, and went to pay the cab. The others were waiting in reception for him when he went inside.

'Here are your keys,' said the receptionist, a glamorous young woman who spoke perfect English, 'And there's a letter for Mister Phillip Mitchell.' Kathy, who was standing nearest to the desk, took it and studied the London postmark. The letter was scented and written in a wobbly, rounded, feminine hand. Staring hard at Phil, she passed the letter to him. Phil swallowed and refused to meet her eye.

'What was that all about? The letter?' Tiffany quizzed Grant, as they sat at a pavement café in the village where the hotel was. Grant opened his mouth, but she carried on, 'And don't pretend to me. Married people shouldn't have secrets.'

'That's rich,' said Grant, referring to the hotel.

Tiffany gave him a warning look. 'Grant …'

'Alright!' He took a slurp of French beer and pulled a face. 'Phil's got another woman on the go. She must have got hold of the address of this place somehow. He was going to finish it but she's latched onto him. I told him to tell Kathy before she found out and made it ten times worse. He bottled out. End of story.'

Tiffany's eyes widened. 'Is it serious?'

'It is now,' Grant said grimly.

He was right. When they got back to the hotel, Phil had disappeared.

Grant tracked Phil down to a gloomy bar in the village, where he was playing a pinball machine as if on automatic pilot.

'How did you find me?' he asked, without looking up.

'I was just about to give up.'

'Don't let me stop you.'

Grant stood his ground. 'You've got to come back and face Kathy.'

'I thought you said if it all fell apart you'd have nothing more to do with me?'

'You're still my brother.'

'Did Kath send you?'

'No.' Grant sighed. 'Look, Kathy told me what you'd said about Lorna going off her rocker. You spun her a good yarn but she ain't stupid, she'll suss it out. What did the letter really say?'

'That I'm the worse lay she ever had – though I don't remember her saying that at the time. And that if she kills herself, it'll be all my fault.'

Grant put his hand over Phil's, stopping him playing for a moment. 'You gotta come clean to Kathy, bruv. Tell her everything. Then there's a chance she might forgive you.'

Phil removed Grant's hand deliberately. 'I'm not sure I wanna be forgiven. I don't deserve it.' He looked up at Grant for the first time. 'Leave us alone, Grant. I need time to think.'

Tiffany was working hard to make it a romantic getaway, but Grant's surly mood over their candlelit dinner stung her into picking on him. Watching Grant's belligerence with the wine waiter, she said, 'What were you thinking of when you booked us into the Adelphi?'

'We've been over all that.'

'What was it about her?' Tiffany had a deep-seated insecurity about Grant's feelings for Sharon. Compared with her, she would always come second, and the knowledge hurt.

'There was nothing about her,' Grant continued.

'I can't understand what you both saw in her.'

He laid down his knife and fork, glaring at her. 'I ain't gonna talk about it.'

'But you never do,' Tiffany complained. 'It's not like she was that good-looking or anything. What was she? Fantastic in bed or something?'

'Do you want a row?'

Tiffany went on, unheeding. 'And what is it about Phil? Does he only ever want the thing he can't have?'

'I said leave it!' Grant poured himself more wine, filling his glass to the brim.

'I always thought she was rather fat.'

If looks could kill, Tiffany would have died a sudden and very nasty death.

By the morning, Phil had still not returned. Tiffany was surprised at Grant's lack of concern for his brother.

'I ain't gonna go chasing round after him. It ain't worth it,' he said, as the two of them sat by the hotel pool, speculating about Phil's whereabouts. Kathy had still not appeared. Looking up at the closed shutters of her room, Grant said, 'I suppose I'd better go up and talk to her.'

Kathy was steaming with rage and all ready to go home. 'You knew, didn't you?' she yelled.

Grant looked at her guiltily. 'I told him to end it, Kath. Don't make me feel bad.'

She was not mollified and when Grant offered to take her sightseeing in Chantilly with him and Tiffany, she refused brusquely. 'I ain't up to it.' Softening slightly, she added, 'Go on. Go and have a good time. Some of us should.'

Grant paused in the doorway, looking at her as she sat tousle-haired on the bed. She had dark circles under her eyes and it was obvious she'd had a rough night. 'I did tell him to end it, Kath. Told him he didn't know how lucky he was. He's a fool. Always has been. And you're too good for him.'

When Grant and Tiffany returned from Chantilly, there was still no sign of Kathy or Phil. Grant went back up to Kathy's room to find her still in her dressing-gown, curled up on the bed in the semi-darkened room, surrounded by an assortment of empty miniature bottles from the mini-bar.

'What must I look like?' She sat up, raking a hand through her blonde hair. 'I'm not proud of meself. But I thought, if you can't beat 'em, join 'em. Phil said that nobody understands a drinker like another drinker. So I thought I'd give it a go. See what all the fuss is about.' She clutched her head. Grant sat down beside her. She smiled at him weakly. 'After two drinks I almost went to bed with the guy from room service. I could've done it. He was on for it. Get my revenge on Phil and all that.' A tear formed in her eye and she brushed it away angrily. 'But in the end, I caught a glimpse of meself. I thought: you sad old tart. I'm so useless. I'm even a useless drunk. I couldn't go through with it.'

'Listen.' Grant gripped her by the shoulders. 'You're not a sad old anything. And you're very far from useless. Nobody could have tried harder than you with Phil – look at what you've been through these past eighteen months. You stuck with it.' He looked away. 'I'm so ashamed of Phil. He don't deserve you.'

A moment of palpable electricity passed between them.

'Sharon didn't deserve you,' Kathy said softly. 'Her and Phil were made for each other.' She stared at him, drinking in his face in a way she had never done before. Grant felt the hairs on the back of his neck prickle, caught unawares by something that had been lurking in the background of his consciousness. 'Do you know what I sometimes think?' Kathy continued.

'What?' he breathed.

'I sometimes think maybe I married the wrong brother.'

She held the look and Grant stared back, mesmerised. It couldn't be. Not her. Not Kathy, his brother's wife. She couldn't be the one. Could she? Being with her was so natural that he had taken their familiarity, their ease together, as read. She was off-limits. He'd never even considered her that way before. But suddenly, it all made sense … Almost imperceptibly, he nodded. The sound of his heart hammering seemed to fill the room. Kathy's eyes were bright, her lips parted.

'I'd love to see their faces. That would be one for the scrap book.'

So she meant it. Grant swallowed. He wanted desperately to kiss her. But it was mad – he couldn't even begin to think about the consequences.

'Listen …' he began shakily.

Kathy detached herself. 'It's alright. I know what you're going to say. It's not on. Of course it's not. Only end up with more pain. And I've had enough pain. Besides, I like Tiff, she's a sweet girl.' She went to the bathroom and got herself some water. 'We won't mention this again, eh?'

'No,' said Grant, his head in a whirl.

Phil came back on the third day, coming up behind Tiffany in the hotel bar while she was ordering pre-lunch drinks for herself and Grant.

'I'll have a pastis, please,' he said, breathing alcohol fumes down her neck.

He was red-faced, as if he'd caught the sun, and he smelt unwashed. Tiffany, alarmed at his heavy hand on her shoulder, backed away. 'I don't think that's a good idea, Phil.'

'You know something?' Phil said, blinking at her. 'You're very pretty. Good company. But you're no Sharon. And you never will be. Grant ever talk to you about Sharon, does he? No, I don't suppose he does,' Phil continued, as Tiffany stared at him, open-mouthed. 'That's 'cos he's never got over her. And it don't matter what you do, he never will. No hard feelings,' he added.

'Well, well, well, look who it is,' Grant said sarcastically, coming up behind Phil. He got hold of his arm. 'I think you should go.'

'Don't order me around, you stinking hypocrite.' Phil pushed him off. He turned to Tiffany. 'It's alright for him to get his leg over with old what's her face – Lorraine. As soon as I do it, he's Cliff flamin' Richard.'

Tiffany ran out, suppressing a sob.

Grant glowered at Phil with hatred in his eyes. 'What's with the Mr Silent routine?' Phil drawled. 'I know it scares everyone else, but it don't scare me. I know you better than you know yourself. I know why you wanted me to tell Kathy. Come on, Grant, it's the truth! Let's just for once tell it like it is. You were out to get me.' Phil belched loudly. 'I forgive you because I understand. I know how lonely you are. 'Cos I'm just the same. But she's gone. She's in America and there's nothing you can do about it.'

'When I threw you down the pit ...' Grant began with quiet fury. He paused, staring at Phil with disgust. 'You're drunk. It's not worth it.'

'But don't you see, Grant – there'll never be another time. So tell me. What? You wish you'd killed me? Is that it? Well, let me tell you something. I wish you had too.'

Kathy, who had been alerted by Tiffany, appeared in the bar and was silently listening to the end of this.

Phil looked up and saw her. 'Look who it is! Come here darling and give me a great big cuddle. Isn't she amazing?' He waved his arm at Grant. 'Knocking on a bit but not bad for her age. What I used to refer to in my younger days as an OBG – Oldie But Goodie.' He leered at his brother. 'I can understand why you fancy her, Grant. But it's a bit of a disappointment, when she's got her kit off. That's where you see the tell-tale signs. Nothing personal, Kath, but it's as well he knows.'

Grant hauled him out of the room 'If you don't shut up right now, I'm gonna shut you up.'

After that, there was nothing to do but go home. Phil came begging for cash as they loaded up the taxi, but Grant steadfastly refused.

'I ain't gonna give you money to swill down your throat. Now go away. We're not talking to you.'

'What's this "we"? That's my wife!' Phil made a lunge for Kathy as she and Tiffany got in the cab and lost his balance. Almost in slow motion, he toppled to the floor, crashing onto the gravel. Grant stared at him in disgust, and got into the car.

'Let's go,' he said. The car moved off, leaving Phil lying on the ground. Neither Grant nor Kathy looked round.

CHAPTER THIRTY

Grant watched as Kathy swung little Ben into the air, hugging him as if her life depended on it. 'Oh, I've missed you so much.' She buried her face in her son's neck, unable to say any more for fear of breaking down. Grant's lips tightened. Kathy was totally wiped out. She had not spoken since they left the hotel and seemed to have retreated into a world of her own. He could still hardly believe what Phil had done, the terrible things he had said. He felt like disowning him completely. He had thrown Phil into the pit once and left him for dead. This time, Phil had thrown himself in and Grant had left him there just as surely. The difference was, he had made the decision in cold blood. It was a deliberate severing of their childhood bond, but Grant no longer cared. They were two grown men, he told himself, and Phil could watch out for himself.

Peggy was astounded when she found out the truth about Phil from an embittered Kathy. She summoned Grant and laid into him. 'You're his brother. You should have stopped him!'

'I tried,' Grant retorted, furious.

'Well, you didn't try hard enough, then, 'cos according to Kathy it's finished.'

Grant folded his arms and fixed her with a sullen look. 'Well, perhaps he doesn't want to come back. And who can blame him.'

'What do you mean?' she said, quivering.

'Maybe he's had enough of you interfering all the time. You've always been the same. Never satisfied, always demanding. Me and Phil have turned ourselves inside out trying to please you.'

'Don't you …'

'When we were kids, you played us off against each other.

Let us fight to see who loved you the most. And you loved every minute of it.' He put his face near to her. 'Is it any wonder we turned out the way we did with a mother like you?' Peggy's mouth fell open in surprise and dismay.

Massively hurt by Grant's words, Peggy took refuge at George's house. It was several days before she and Grant made it up, and although he said he hadn't meant it, she knew there was a core of truth in his harsh words. Grant, too, was shocked at what he'd said. It was almost unheard of for either of them to criticise Peggy like that. She was beyond reproach; he and Phil might moan about her behind her back but they had always walked on eggshells in her presence. Suddenly, Grant's life felt as if it was unravelling at the seams. He had left his brother, helpless, in a foreign country, and his mother, who he worshipped, would barely acknowledge him. Not only that, but he was wrestling with an attraction to his sister-in-law that had floored him with its unexpectedness and intensity. And all the while he was supposed to be starting over again with his wife.

Phil came back a week later. He had been sleeping rough, and drinking and looked like a derelict. Peggy was pleased and relieved to see him but Grant was cold and threw Phil's apologies back in his face. Kathy refused to give Phil the time of day and told him bluntly that their relationship was over. Vowing to make a fresh start, she took herself and Ben off to Florida to stay with Angie for a while. A rejected Phil spent the night in the Arches with a bottle of vodka and fled to Scotland the next day. Grant was secretly glad he did not have to front him. Apart from his disgust at his brother's behaviour, it made him uncomfortable to realize that, even drunk, Phil had been on the ball about his feelings for Kathy, sensing them more accurately than Grant had himself.

The Mitchell brothers were eventually reconciled when Phil returned from Scotland three weeks later, a sombre and now sober man. Kathy was back from America, too, but when Phil went to see her, buoyed up with renewed hope, she was un-impressed at his claims to have turned over a new leaf. Floored by her rebuff, Phil almost started drinking again, and would have done so had not Grant come into the living-room in the Vic and caught him red-handed.

'You know that ain't the answer, bruv.' Grant locked his arm around Phil's chest, clamping hold of Phil's wrist to prevent him lifting the bottle to his mouth. 'You wanna go back to hanging out with dossers and kipping in cardboard boxes?'

Phil shook his head mutely.

'Then put the bottle down,' Grant instructed. There was a beat. Slowly, Phil lowered his arm, placing the scotch on the sideboard. He was shaking visibly. He drew a deep breath, trying to compose himself.

'Does this mean you're talking to me again?'

'Depends.'

'On what?'

'On whether you plan on making a complete prat of yourself again.'

'I'm an alcoholic, Grant.'

'Yeah, I know. But you gotta stop blaming everyone else for it and deal with it.'

'I can't. Look at what I just did. If it hadn't been for you …'

'Yeah, well, I can't be there for you every minute of the day, can I?' Grant said gruffly. 'Better get back to that counselling group. Just don't go making any new little friends, that's all.'

Although Kathy allowed Phil limited access to Ben, that was the extent of her contact with him. So, when an opportunity came up to put himself in her good books by helping Ian track down Cindy and the kids, Phil let himself be talked into it by Grant. Grant had a different agenda. He thought Cindy would be hiding out with David Wicks and was still itching to sort him out. Ian had a lead. He heard that Cindy was staying around Lake Como in Italy and had put his private investigator, Ros, onto it. Unaware of the Mitchell brothers' intentions, he flew out to join her. He was in the middle of a pleasant cappuccino at a pavement café with Ros, when Phil and Grant drew up in a rented car.

'Here comes the cavalry,' Grant announced cheerfully. He plonked himself down at their table. 'We've come to help, mate. I'll have a beer.'

After they got into a brawl with a group of Italian youths over a game of pool, Ros decided the Mitchells were proving a liability and sent them off on a false trail. Phil, worried about the report Ian would give Kathy.

'It ain't gonna look good when he tells her we started a punch-up five minutes off the plane'

He was narked when Grant replied casually, 'Don't worry, I'll tell her the truth.'

'Oh, I forgot – you're mates, aren't you?'

Grant sighed. 'Look, I know you've been having a rough time, Phil, but it ain't been easy for me, stuck in the middle.'

'Alright, then how come you always took Kathy's side?'

'Because you were acting like a plonker.'

'So you gave her a shoulder to cry on?'

'Yeah,' Grant said. 'Same as you did for Sharon, remember? Only that's all Kathy got ... a shoulder.'

They sat in silence for several minutes, Grant drinking a beer, Phil, an orange juice. At last, Grant said, 'I was only looking out for you. It's what families do.'

Phil snorted. 'Great family we are. I'm an alcoholic like the old man, and you're a nagging old woman like Mum.'

'Kathy needed someone to talk to, that's all.'

'Pour out all her troubles, did she?' Phil's voice hardened. 'Did she tell you she'd married the wrong brother?' He caught Grant's astonished expression. 'She did, didn't she?' Phil started to chuckle, then burst into a full-bellied laugh. Grant, who had not expected this reaction, was wrong-footed.

'Come on, then, share the joke.'

'What's funny is, that's exactly what Sharon said to me.'

Grant did not find it amusing at all. 'If you were anyone else, I'd rip your head off,' he said.

Phil got up, defusing the situation. 'I'm gonna get back to the hotel, stop Ian doing a hatchet job on me with Kathy. I'll see you later.'

When Phil returned, Grant had moved to a table inside and was well into the beers. 'It ain't been easy for me, you know,' he slurred. 'Anything I did, you'd already done. I played football, you already had a shelf full of medals; I got a girlfriend, you had three ... That's why I joined the army. You hadn't done that.'

'I thought about it.'

'That don't surprise me ...' Grant finished the rest of his bottle and signalled the waiter to bring him a new one. 'I had a baby ... you already had one ...'

'So now you're gonna be an alcoholic?' Phil said tartly.

'Yeah, why not?'

'Believe me, it's no fun.'

Grant met his eyes. 'I know.'

Phil glanced over Grant's shoulder. 'Er, how drunk are you?'

'I've been worse.'

'Too drunk to run?'

'Definitely. Why?'

Phil pointed at a gang of youths guarding the doorway. They looked familiar. The ringleader started shouting something that was unambiguous in any language. Grant eyed them up. 'Which one do you want?'

'The little one.'

'One, two ...' And with that, the party really began. The Mitchell brothers had come out on top and were just finishing off the two remaining gang members – the rest had run away – when the police, who had been summoned by the bar owner, arrived in a van. Grant tried to shake them off, but when one of them put a hand to his holster, he got in the van willingly. They spent the night in the cells cooling their heels, but even the hardness of the bunks didn't quench Grant's high spirits. There was nothing like looking out for each other in a fight – especially against some foreigners – to bind the Mitchell brothers close again.

'This is just like old times,' he said happily. Phil grinned. 'Shame we couldn't fit a curry in as well, innit?'

They were released the next day with a caution. When they met up with Ian, Ros had tracked down Cindy and discovered where the children were. Grant was all for snatching them back and, although Ros was against it, Ian was eventually persuaded. While Ian detained Cindy by pretending to want a reconciliation, Phil and Grant took Steven and Peter when their childminder's back was turned. After a fraught journey to the airport, during which they scraped a car and almost got involved in a punch-up, they made the flight just in time.

Ian was genuinely grateful, but Phil's longed-for promotion in Kathy's eyes was not forthcoming. She thought it typical of the Mitchells to go lumbering in and was apprehensive about the legal consequences. Tiffany, too, although glad to see Grant – who greeted her with a warm, 'Ciao, Bellissima' – could not help putting herself in Cindy's place.

'I can't stop thinking how I'd feel if someone snatched Courtney from me.' Grant, remembering the time when he had tried to prove her an unfit mother, noticed Tiffany's vulnerable look and realized she was thinking about it too.

'You are a very different person from Cindy,' he said, kissing her gently, 'And besides, that was before I knew any better.'

That evening, Nigel was throwing a big party for Lorraine and Joe, who were returning to Bolton. Lorraine had been reunited with her ex-boyfriend, Peter, much to Joe's delight, and had taken up a job back in their home town. Most of the Square was going to the party, including Grant and Phil, although Tiffany was apprehensive.

'It's probably best if you say goodbye to Lorraine on your own,' she said quietly to Grant.

He put his arm around her. 'No way. I want to relax, have a few beers, and spend an hour or two with the mother of my kid.' He stroked her hair off her face and kissed her on the nose. 'Without the kid actually being there.'

Tiffany brightened. 'I'll go and get my coat.'

Despite Grant's reassurances, Tiffany found it hard to enjoy the party. When she caught sight of Lorraine talking to Grant and touching his cheek, it was the last straw. She disappeared off to the bedroom to get her things, agitated. Grant spotted her and followed.

'Lorraine was only teasing me,' he said, sitting down on the bed. He patted the space beside him. 'Come here.' Tiffany sat, reluctantly. 'You know it's all in the past, me and her, don't you?' Grant said.

She gave a little laugh. 'You've got an awful lot of past.'

'But it's me and you that's got a future.' He took both her hands in his. 'Look, I've got a wife, a daughter and a wedding anniversary coming up. That's worth one hell of a lot to me.'

'I thought you'd forgotten,' she said in a low voice. Grant, who had been saved by Nigel reminding him, smiled broadly. 'Oh right. Do I look like the sort of man who wants to be hit over the head with a shovel?'

She gave him friendly push. 'I would've, an' all.'

Peggy had arranged a surprise party for Grant and Tiffany's wedding anniversary, but Grant, who was wise to her plans, swept Tiffany off for a romantic meal instead. Tiffany was delighted, but Peggy was rather put out, especially when George told her she should have learned her lesson about not interfering with her children's relationships.

George had his own motives. It was almost a year since he had asked Peggy to marry him, but whenever he raised the issue, she dodged around it. Finally, he gave her an ultimatum, which did not have the desired effect. Peggy finished things, stating firmly that she didn't want to leave the Vic. After a few days apart being miserable, she agreed to give their relationship another go, and they went away together for the weekend.

Phil, meanwhile, was equally fed up with Peggy's constant nagging about him getting back with Kathy and had moved out of the Vic and into his old flat next to the Fowlers, which he had been renting to Bianca and Ricky. They, in turn, moved into the upstairs flat at number 47, adjacent to the pub, which had just been vacated by Lorraine and Joe.

With a baby on the way – Bianca had decided to keep it and Ricky was over the moon when he heard the news – Bianca was keen to decorate the smaller of the two bedrooms as a nursery. She soon had Ricky rushing around with tins of pastel paint and bunny borders. Carried away, he bought a cot and a small menagerie of soft toys as a surprise. Bianca was touched at his enthusiasm. When her twenty-week scan revealed that the baby had spina bifida and hydrocephaleus, both of which were severely disabling and incurable, they were totally crushed. Following the doctor's advice, Bianca made the heart-wrenching decision to terminate the pregnancy. It was a traumatic and emotionally devastating experience for both of them, especially Bianca, who had to go through an induced labour and give birth to the tiny baby.

The talk of the Square was Cindy's return. Ian, who had aspirations to become a councillor, was torn between the desire to prosecute his estranged wife on an abduction charge, and the bad publicity such an action would give his political career. When Cindy refused to budge over fighting him for custody of the kids, he went with the first option. Cindy was arrested. She was released on bail, and her passport was confiscated. However, Ian remained wary of her and decided to appoint a nanny to look after the children and be present at all Cindy's visits. Mary, a capable young Irish girl who was a relative of Pauline Fowler's, volunteered her services and Ian took her on.

The story of Cindy's arrest came out well in the local press for Ian, thanks to his agent, Annie. Annie was George Palmer's daughter, a shrewd, hard-nosed, independent young woman who was grooming Ian for political success. He missed winning a place on the council by a few hundred votes, but Annie, who foresaw profiting in the future, took a long-term view of things.

Currently, she had bigger fish to fry. Concerned that her father was intent on going legit to please Peggy, she was keen to take over George's business empire. Annie already ran the Market Cellar, a private club in Turpin Road set in one of the arches of the railway viaduct. Originally Strokes Nightclub, run by 'Dirty' Den Watts, it had provided a front for illegal gambling then and was continuing to do so now, with a secret back room to which only a select membership was invited. Phil, who had hit it off with Annie, was soon admitted to this inner sanctum. He also found himself excited by Annie's sense of danger.

As Christmas drew near, Tiffany found herself growing more and more frustrated with her domestic situation. Living under the same roof as Peggy was bad enough, but Aunt Sal was staying too and both of them were free with their advice about raising Courtney. But not only that, Peggy apparently had her future for the next twenty years already mapped out. Tiffany had overheard Peggy talking to Grant about having another baby; something they hadn't even discussed themselves. She had hoped that George might have persuaded Peggy to move out after their romantic holiday, but it was not to be.

'I told him I couldn't. I mean, how would you and Grant manage without me?' Peggy said chirpily when she enquired. Tiffany gnashed her teeth.

When Grant found her in their bedroom later, he immediately guessed the reason for Tiffany's bad mood.

'I know it's hard, sometimes, with her being here, but she is my mum,' he said, trying to placate her.

'And I'm your wife,' Tiffany countered, brushing her dark hair furiously, 'Only at times it doesn't feel like it. I feel like I'm someone's daughter-in-law, someone's mother.'

'What do you mean?'

'I married you because I love you. I wanted to be with you and I wanted to be a family. Just you, me and Courtney.' She looked at him in the mirror. 'I still want that.'

'So do I.'

'Do you?' she said, turning round. 'Or is it just that you want another baby?'

'I want that, too.' Grant came over and started to caress the back of her neck, kissing it softly. He pulled down the strap of her dress and kissed her shoulder, his breathing getting heavier. Tiffany pushed him away. 'What is it?' he asked, irritated. 'Are you playing some sort of game?'

'No,' she said, getting up and smoothing her dress.

'Then what?' Grant grabbed hold of her arm, his fingers pinching into her flesh.

'You really want to know? Well, alright,' she flung back. 'There's sex and there's love. I know the difference, even if you don't.' She exited from the bedroom leaving a thwarted Grant staring after her.

The needle between Tiffany and Grant notched up a gear on Christmas Eve, when she invited Bianca, Ricky and Frank (who had returned to the Square again, apparently in good health) for Christmas Day lunch at the Vic – without consulting Peggy.

When Grant had a go at her later for being impolite, Tiffany flew at him. 'I'm your wife. This is my home too. I can invite who I want.'

'You're my wife?' Grant sneered. 'In that case, start acting like it.' Enraged, Tiffany booted him out of the bedroom.

Grant took his revenge by flirting with two girls who had been eyeing him up in the bar earlier, inviting them in to the by-now closed Vic for a nightcap. Tiffany, who witnessed the scene from the window – as Grant intended – was mortified. When she came down to the bar the girls had gone and Grant was waiting for her, playing schmaltzy Christmas music.

'Nothing happened,' he said, in response to her interrogation. 'I was just proving a point. Now, can we go to bed?'

He walked out of the bar, switching off the lights; Tiffany, feeling humiliated and put upon, trailing behind.

Christmas Day saw no improvement. Grant, uptight about Tiffany's refusal to kowtow, eventually stormed out when he saw her give Conor, Mary's father, a flirtatious smile. Phil, who found Grant sitting in the garden in the Square, drunk, advised him to give Tiffany some space, but Grant was enveloped in a maelstrom of resentment and refused to go back inside. He stayed the night at Phil's, drinking himself into oblivion, and returned to the Vic the next day in a foul mood. Discovering Tiffany trying on skimpy dresses with Bianca for the party in the Vic that night, he laid down the law, but Tiffany wasn't having any of it. 'Why don't you like me enjoying myself, Grant?' she demanded. 'You're only happy when I'm stuck behind that bar thinking of babies. I want to have some fun for a change.'

'I don't want my wife behaving like a slut,' Grant snapped, stalking out.

Tiffany stared at his retreating back, her lips compressed.

'I think he's just declared war.'

Peggy's wheeze for getting the party going was working well. A game of forfeits was underway, producing some notable performances by some of the Vic's regulars (Pauline Fowler's can-can) and some equally dire ones by others (Dot Cotton's joke-telling). When Bianca was called up to do an Irish jig, Conor, infected by the music, grabbed Tiffany and pulled her out to the front too, whooping and dancing with her. Shrieking with laughter, Tiffany pulled Phil up, who shambled around quite energetically, but when she tried to get Grant to join in as well, he refused and walked off.

She found him out the back in the hallway, his face livid. 'Are you trying to make a fool out of me?'

'No. Of course not.' Tiffany, hearing Courtney crying, started to go upstairs.

'Where are you going? I'm talking to you.'

She turned to look at him. 'Yeah, but I've heard it all before, Grant. And it's boring me.' She paused. 'Come to think of it, maybe that's why I don't sleep with you, because you're boring in bed as well.'

Grant made a lunge for her foot through the banisters. 'Don't you touch me,' she cried, shrinking back.

'Touch you? I'm gonna kill you,' he snarled, racing up the stairs after her. Tiffany ran to the bedroom and locked the door. Grant pounded on it, rousing Courtney, who was in Peggy's room, to cry even harder.

'I should have sorted you out a long time ago,' Grant bellowed, shaking the door handle. 'You're a little slag. That's what you are – a slag.' He pulled back his fist and smashed it through the door panel, sending splinters of wood flying. Tiffany screamed.

Downstairs, Frank was leading the regulars in a roaring hokey-cokey. Nobody heard anything unusual.

CHAPTER THIRTY-ONE

Grant didn't bother undoing the lock. He wrenched his fist free and with one almighty kick, bust the door open. Tiffany shrieked and backed away, her eyes wide with fear. Grant slammed the door behind him, advancing on her with a manic face. 'Keep away from me,' she cried. 'I'm warning you, if you touch me ...'

'You'll what?'

'I'll scream the place down.'

'Go ahead,' he said. 'I don't care. No one's gonna hear you.' His tone sent a chill down Tiffany's spine. She scrambled around the bed, knocking over a chair in her haste. Grant kept coming at her. 'You got no right to do this,' she quavered.

'And you got no right to humiliate me. Carrying on like that. Flirting. Making a fool of me.'

'I was just having a good time dancing, that's all.'

'Well, I'm sick of it. You don't think about me or Courtney. All you care about is yourself. You ain't got the faintest idea about being a mum, having a relationship ...'

'Oh, and you do?' Tiffany scoffed.

'Yeah. It means treating each other with respect.'

Tiffany gave a hollow laugh. 'What like Lorraine did, when she threw you out? Oh, and then there was Sharon. She really respected you.'

Grant's lip curled. He took another step towards her, backing Tiffany into a corner. 'Shut it.'

'Why? Afraid of the truth? Fact is, you ain't ever had a decent relationship with anyone.'

'Me and Sharon had things good for a long time. She knew how to make me happy.'

'Not only you, eh?' Tiffany said, hitting Grant where she

knew it would hurt, then rapidly wishing she hadn't. Grant stood right in front of her, his bulk blocking her escape.

'What's that supposed to mean?'

Tiffany glowered at him defiantly. Her only recourse now was to face him out. 'She knew how to make Phil happy, too. You weren't the only one keeping her bed warm.'

Grant looked momentarily shaken. 'You don't know the first thing about Sharon and me. You're just jealous.'

'Of her?'

'Yeah, 'cos you know whatever she did, I still loved her.'

'Grant.' Tiffany's voice softened a fraction. 'You love me, only you're too proud to admit it.'

He gave her a twisted smile. 'No I don't. I don't love you, I never have. You're just a second-rate scrubber who happened to have my baby. If it weren't for Courtney I'd have dumped you ages ago.'

Tiffany began to tremble. 'I don't believe you.'

'It's true. You disgust me. Sometimes I can hardly bear to even look at you.' He grabbed her arms and thrust his face close, so that all she could see was his mad, blazing eyes and flaring nostrils. 'Sometimes, just watching Sharon cross the room used to make my skin prickle. I was crazy about her. I've never felt anything like that for you.'

'Get off. You're hurting me.' Tears sprang to Tiffany's eyes.

'Oh, I'm getting to you now, am I? Well, I'll tell you something else.' She pressed her hands to her ears, unable to bear listening to Grant's outpouring of hate. He yanked her hands away, pinning them by her sides. 'When we make love, I ain't thinking of you. In my head I'm always with Sharon.'

'No.' Tiffany tried to pull away but Grant held her firmly.

'Yes. She's the one, Tiffany, and she always will be.'

'No,' Tiffany screamed again, struggling free. Grant smiled at her distress. Provoked beyond measure, she lashed out at him, slapping him across the face. He caught her wrists and held them as Tiffany continued to scream and claw at him, then something inside him snapped and he pushed her away forcefully, sending her flying backwards. She flailed, trying to regain her balance, and fell against the corner of the bedside cabinet, knocking her head and sending a lamp crashing to the floor. For several seconds she lay motionless. Grant stood stock still, holding his breath. He took a step towards her and she flinched, drawing up her knees and curling into a ball, clutching at her head. He regarded her sobbing, heaving form. 'You had enough now? Well, have you?'

Tiffany sobs grew louder. She tried to move away from him but she was pinned between the bed and the wall. He stared at her with revulsion, then turned and left the room.

Downstairs, the pub was packed, punters queuing three-deep at the bar and baying for refills. Grant, ignoring Peggy's pleas for help, wrenched a whisky bottle from the optics and stomped out to the back. Alerted to trouble, Peggy insisted that Phil go after him. Phil, who had been nursing an orange juice and keeping himself to himself, followed him out of the Vic reluctantly. Grant brushed off his entreaties to stop, yelling at Phil to leave him alone. Shaking his head, Phil returned to the Vic's private entrance. He was about to go into the bar when he heard the sound of crying coming from upstairs. Going up, he found Tiffany in the kitchen, standing by the sink with a bloody tea-towel in her hand. She spun round when he entered, a look of fear on her face.

'What happened?' he asked, catching sight of a big gash on her forehead. Tiffany said witheringly, 'What do you think?'

'Grant? I don't believe it.'

'I didn't think you would. You've probably been encouraging him to hit me, sort me out. The two of you are just the same.'

Phil looked at her intently. 'That's not true.'

'Oh no? You both despise me ... well, I ain't gonna take it. I don't deserve to be pushed around.' She started to cry again, great big tears rolling down her cheeks. Phil put his arms around her. 'Come here,' he said gently, holding her close. He felt her body stiffen then relax as the sobs broke loose and she cried uncontrollably, her tears soaking his shirt right through.

When she was all cried out, she let Phil attend to the cut, sitting obedient as a child while he bathed it. Phil tried to persuade her that Grant hadn't meant the cruel things he'd said, but it was more to try and alleviate her pain than because he really believed it. Tiffany saw straight through him. 'Grant's given up on me, Phil. He's crossed the line and you know it.' She bundled Courtney into a blanket, hoisting a changing bag on her shoulder. 'Where are you going?' Phil asked.

'Bianca's. And tell Grant not to bother coming over. After tonight, I've got nothing to say to him.'

Grant had not gone far. He sat down on the memorial bench in Turpin Road and slugged back the whisky. It seared his throat and made his eyes water, but he was glad. So long as it numbed him, took away all the anger and bitterness and hate, he didn't care. He felt raw, as if he'd been turned inside out. Tiffany did that to him, he thought. She had an instinct for sussing out his weak points and homed in on them unswervingly. But this time, she'd overstepped the mark. She'd pushed him too far. And she deserved all she'd got.

He took another burning gulp of whisky and looked up at the sound of voices. Three teenage girls were emerging from the fish and chip shop, giggling, followed by Tiffany's father, Terry. 'You don't know what you're missing! Scrubbers!' he shouted, as they tottered off on high heels, ignoring him. Terry swaggered into the street, bag of chips in hand, and began stuffing them down greedily.

Terry Raymond had become something of a fixture in Albert Square since the Blessing. He had palled up with Ted Hills' ex-wife, Irene, although they were currently at loggerheads and she had chucked him out. He was sleeping on the sofa at the Vic – against Grant's wishes – after Peggy had taken pity on him and given him a job clearing tables.

Tiffany and her brother, Simon, had not been happy to see

their father again, but were treating him with slightly more tolerance after he'd been hospitalised a second time with pancreatitis. Terry was a drunkard and a letch with a history of violence towards women. He had beaten his ex-wife, Louise, so brutally that she ran out on the family, abandoning her children. After that, Tiffany and Simon had borne the brunt of their father's foul temper, culminating in an incident that had caused Tiffany to miscarry a teenage pregnancy.

Grant had no time for the man, who he regarded as a loser and a waste of space, so he was annoyed to see Terry making a beeline for him. 'Drowning your sorrows, eh?' Terry said, champing on a mouthful of chips.

'Nah, just trying to forget who I'm married to,' Grant replied unpleasantly. To his surprise, Terry was sympathetic. 'I don't blame you. If I was shacked up with that daughter of mine, I'd never be off the bottle. You're too good for her, you know.' He slumped down next to Grant, who glared at him. Terry got the message and edged away a little. 'Listen, I know we ain't exactly seen eye-to-eye in the past, but you're alright.'

'Thanks,' Grant said, heavily sarcastic.

'No, really.' Terry was immune to sarcasm. 'You're a man after me own heart. Don't take stick from anyone.'

Grant tried making his dislike of Terry plainer. 'Go away.'

'Ah, don't be like that. This is a chance for us to talk, man to man, father-in-law to son-in-law. Whaddya say?'

'Beat it.'

Terry did not move. 'Daughters, eh? They don't half give you some grief. You wait 'til Courtney grows up. Come fourteen, she'll be out of control. Boyfriends, drugs, all the scum off the street knocking on your door. Tiffany weren't always a cheap little scrubber, you know. Naughty, maybe; a bit lippy. But she was alright. A sweet kid.'

'So, what happened?' Grant asked carelessly.

'Hormones. Once she got a taste for it, there was no stopping her. If they had trousers and their own teeth, she'd have 'em. Flash a tenner at her and she'd be flat on her back.'

'Maybe if she'd had a proper father, a bit of discipline ...' Grant began, revolted at Terry.

'Oh, I gave her discipline, alright. She put a foot wrong, I sorted her. When she got up the duff with that teacher, I made her pay.'

'I heard. You pushed her down the stairs. She lost her kid 'cos of you.'

Terry looked uneasy. 'That's not true.'

'She was a whore,' Grant said, exasperated. 'A good slapping's what she needed and that's what she got. You ought to try it sometime.' The words escaped from him with a vehemence that shocked him. He was talking about Tiffany then but thinking about Tiffany now. Terry nodded sagely. 'You don't let 'em know who's boss, they walk all over you.' He smiled. 'We ain't so different, you and me ...'

Grant stared at him with a sensation of growing horror. What had he turned into, swapping notes on beating women with Terry? Had he sunk that low? Was he the same? 'You make me sick,' he said in a low growl. 'If you ain't out of my face in five seconds, I'm gonna rip your throat out.' Terry looked up from his chips and saw that Grant was deadly serious. He scarpered.

The bedroom was still in the same state of disarray that Grant had left it in. There was no sign of Tiffany. Grant knocked on Peggy's bedroom door and, when there was no answer, stuck his head inside. Courtney had gone, too. His half-hearted notion of apologising vanished in an instant. Hearing a noise in the kitchen, he went to investigate and found Phil, who was putting on his jacket. When Phil informed him, curtly, about Tiffany's cut head, Grant was taken aback. 'I didn't see any blood.'

'Oh, well, that's alright, then,' Phil said bitterly. The fact that he was sticking up for Tiffany provoked Grant even further, and when Phil tried to stop him going after her by physically blocking Grant's way, the two brothers faced each other in a standoff. 'Let her be, Grant. Talk to her in the morning.'

'Get out of my way.'

Phil refused to budge. 'No. I ain't gonna stand by and see you muck things up again.'

'I wouldn't be in this mess if it weren't for you.'

'How d'you work that out?'

'I'd still be with Sharon.'

Phil sighed. 'Every time we get in a ruck, you get that stupid look on your face and drag out Sharon. It's all in the past. The important thing is, you've got a new life now. And you're blowing it.'

Grant clenched his fists. 'You don't understand. You don't know what Tiffany does to my head.'

'Listen to yourself. For once, Grant, try and see what's really going on, instead of getting all worked up. You gotta put the brakes on this now or you'll end up like Dad.'

'I'm nothing like Dad,' Grant said with a shudder.

'Nah? Blocked that out, too? Don't you remember what he used to do? We only had to give him a bit of lip, he'd start punching.'

'I ain't like that.' Even as he denied it, Grant caught the shadow of a giant fist looming over him, as if it had been projected onto the back of his skull by a creaky home cinefilm. The image made him feel physically sick.

Phil just gave him a look. 'And that's all Tiff did, ain't it? Talked back a bit. You can't punish her for that. She loves you, Grant. You got something better than you realize. And if you ain't careful, you're gonna lose it.'

Grant got his retaliation in with Phil with a few home truths of his own. Phil was adamant it was not too late for him and Kathy to make another go of things, so Grant challenged him to prove it, then and there. 'What about Tiffany? I don't see you heading for the door,' Phil replied, defensive. They glowered at each other in silence. The gauntlet had been thrown down. Suddenly, the mood had changed. This was no longer about protecting each other, or facing facts, or mending relationships. It was a straightforward, head-to-head contest, a battle for dominance between the two brothers. 'Watch me,' Grant said, going out.

Bianca had just talked Tiffany into leaving Grant and moving in with them when he appeared on their doorstep. She tried to shut him out but Grant stuck his foot in the door and marched inside. While Bianca and Grant had a screaming match, Tiffany stood by in silence, until the volley of abuse became too much and she yelled at both of them to stop. Grant pleaded with her to give him a few minutes alone and, despite Bianca's attempts to dissuade her, Tiffany eventually gave in. Bianca, issuing Grant dire warnings if he laid so much as a finger on her friend, went over to the Vic, looking back over her shoulder as she went.

Tiffany and Grant stood apart in awkward silence. 'Does it hurt?' he asked tentatively, indicating her cut.

'I'm alright. Just say what you gotta say and then go.'

Grant swallowed. 'I'm sorry. I didn't mean to hurt you. Things just got out of control. I – I feel lousy about the whole thing.'

'Yeah, now you do. But what about in a couple of weeks?'

'It'll never happen again, I promise you. From now on, I'm gonna treat you like a princess.'

Tiffany looked at him, irritated. 'Half an hour ago I was a second-rate scrubber. Now I'm a "princess" …'

'I didn't mean it. I just wanted to hurt you. You'd been driving me crazy,' he said weakly.

'And all that stuff about Sharon? Was that lies too?'

'Yes.'

She narrowed her eyes. 'You make me sick, Grant. I don't believe a word of it. As far as I'm concerned, it's over. I'm leaving you.'

'What?' Grant reeled visibly. He hadn't expected this.

'I mean it. Tonight I saw you for what you really are. You knew you were hurting me, knew you were scaring me, but you kept on going. I can't live with you no more. I want you to go. Now.'

'No,' Grant said, panicking. 'I wanna see Courtney.' As if on cue, Courtney, who was in Bianca's spare room, began crying. Tiffany, yelling at Grant to get out, went to tend to her. Grant remained in the middle of the room, refusing to leave.

Tiffany emerged fifteen minutes later, angry at seeing Grant still there. This time, however, he was more willing to listen to her grievances. 'I don't wanna be changing nappies all me life, Grant. I wanna be able to see me mates, get a different job, go back to college maybe.

'I just don't think the sun sets and rises over the Queen Vic. I can't breathe in that place, what with Peggy watching me every move and you – you got me pinned to the spot like some kind of insect. I ain't gonna end up like me mum, being pushed around and taking a beating on a Saturday night.'

'I ain't Terry.' Grant shuddered at his recent encounter with him.

Tiffany raised an eyebrow. 'No? When you pushed me across the room, I saw all that hate in you. You looked just like him.'

Terry, his dad – how many more comparisons did he need, Grant thought dully. He had hit Sharon, nearly murdered Phil, half-killed Eddie. He'd even been about to beat up a kid, Joe. The memory sickened him. 'I'll try harder. I'll sort it. won't let things get that far again,' he said, meaning it. 'I'll change. I just don't want what happened with Sharon to happen again. I – I couldn't hack that.'

Tiffany regarded him almost sympathetically. 'They really did a job on you, didn't they?' Her understanding of the fear that undermined Grant's confidence was like a lifeline. 'Sometimes, I – I get scared, sort of panicky. Like tonight, I saw you enjoying yourself, not needing me ...' he admitted falteringly.

'I did need you. You've been the one freezing me out, remember?'

He drew a shaky breath. 'Okay, fine. From now on, things

are gonna be different. You wanna go off, do different things, do 'em. Whatever it takes to keep you loving me, I'll do it. Just give me a chance, let me prove to you I can change.'

She stared at him for a moment, tempted, then sighed. 'How can I? After all those things you said?'

He moved towards her. 'I lied. I promise you, I just want you now. I love you.'

'As much as Sharon?'

Grant looked at his feet. He knew he had to be honest with Tiffany. But would it burn his boats? He was so nearly home and dry ... He looked up and saw her eyes boring into him and knew she had to hear the truth. 'No ... not yet.' He saw her face fall and reached out to hold her arms. 'But I do love you. And it's getting there. You've just gotta give me a little more time.' He tried to stroke her hair but she jerked her head away. 'Please, Tiff. I ain't hiding anything. I want to be with you now. If Sharon came back, I wouldn't have her, I'd choose you.' Tiffany raised her eyes to his, a single tear shimmering on her dark lashes. Grant brushed it away delicately with his finger. This time, she did not flinch.

Phil stood on the steps outside Kathy's house, alone. He was glad of the dark. Kathy had told him she didn't love him any more and that she wanted a divorce. Phil was gutted. He heard a door slam and saw Tiffany coming out of Bianca's flat, carrying Courtney. Grant followed. As if she was aware of his gaze, Tiffany glanced over. She caught sight of Phil and looked faintly embarrassed. Grant noticed his brother, too. Holding his gaze, he deliberately put his arm around Tiffany's shoulders as he steered her into the Vic.

CHAPTER THIRTY-TWO

New Year's Day saw several of Albert Square's residents resolving that 1998 would be a fresh start for them. Grant, who was handling Tiffany with kid gloves, had vowed to put a lid on his temper once and for all, while Tiffany was planning to make it the year she got herself a career. Grant had encouraged her to sign up for a part-time aromatherapy massage course at the local tech (and even, with a gleam in his eye, offered himself for practise). Best of all, he had sealed their new beginning by presenting Tiffany with an eternity ring, a gesture that had touched her deeply. She welcomed him back into their bed with open arms and they settled down to a period of comparatively harmonious – or at least uneventful – married life.

Ian Beale was also hoping to make a new beginning for himself and his children, despite the machinations of scheming Cindy. Cindy, who had the benefit of the best brief her rich boyfriend could buy, won a surprising victory by changing her plea to guilty. That, however, was only round one. The next hearing, for possession of the three children, was equally fraught, but the tables were turned when Ros and Annie visited the gunman who had shot Ian and 'persuaded' him to grass. Cindy was charged with attempted murder, leaving a delighted Ian with responsibility for Steven, Peter and Lucy.

Nigel, too, was facing a new future. After the wrench of Lorraine's departure – the two of them had become very close friends – he had found himself drawn to Clare's teacher, Julie Hayes. When, at last, they consummated their relationship, Nigel felt disloyal to Debbie's memory and ended it shortly afterwards. With Julie and her teenage son, Josh, due to move away to Scotland, the prospects seemed hopeless, but just as the two of them were leaving the Square in a cab Nigel changed his mind. Flagging it down, he told Julie that he and Clare would be going with them. 'Do you really mean it?' Julie asked, throwing her arms around his neck. Nigel hesitated for a split-second. 'As long as kilts aren't compulsory.'

Phil was also considering branching out, and in more ways than one. Annie Palmer had been offered the chance to buy into a lucrative protection racket and Phil, unknown to Grant or Peggy, had put himself forward as her business partner. Conor was roped in to help with the strong-arm stuff and in no time they were raking it in. It was easy money until a turf war broke out with a rival gang. Annie and Phil fronted them out and when she produced their trump card – her father's name – they were given the respect accorded to the daughter of a notorious underworld figure. The territory was carved up amicably between them – or so they thought – and Annie and Phil left well satisfied with their night's work.

Phil felt he and Annie were two of a kind and was hoping to turn their association into a more intimate arrangement. She was a tough cookie and appealed to his thrill-seeking side. Annie, turned on by the danger of their work, had rewarded him with a hot-blooded kiss, but that was as far as it had gone. Telling him she did not mix business with pleasure, she had kept him at arm's length, although Phil was encouraged enough to accept his divorce from Kathy with something like equanimity.

Kathy was astonished – and not a little hurt – at Phil's ready co-operation over the divorce. She had been confused about her feelings ever since Christmas, when her relationship with Alex Healey, the vicar, had moved beyond that of confidante after they had shared a passionate kiss. They both agreed nothing could come of it, but the sizzling sexual chemistry between them was impossible to resist and a few days later she and Alex ended up in bed. The next morning, guilt-ridden, they made a pact to forget about it, but it was proving harder to do than either of them had imagined.

The situation was further complicated by Kathy's secret yearning for a reconciliation with Phil. Phil's distant and uncommunicative behaviour did not make this easy, and when Lorna reappeared, drunk and destitute, Kathy decided the two of them deserved each other. Essentially kind-hearted, she eventually found she had more sympathy for Lorna than her erstwhile husband and took her in, promising to help her dry out and get back on track. Phil was furious, but by this time Kathy was past caring. The divorce papers had been signed and he had no further hold on her. Or so she told herself.

At the end of March, Kathy received a letter from her brother, Ted, who had made a new life for himself in South Africa. In many ways, it contained the answer to all her problems. She had written to Ted, pouring her heart out about the divorce, and in his reply he had suggested that she and Ben move to South Africa. Pat was sceptical. 'You don't want to live in South Africa. This is your home, Walford.'

'Yeah, happy, sunny, fun-filled Walford. I must be mad to want to leave.'

Pat sighed. 'You gotta do what you feel is right, Kathy love. I just hope you hate the place and can't wait to get back, but that's me. Selfish. I don't want to lose my best mate.'

'All I know, Pat, is that I'm forty-seven and I've lived here all my life and what have I got to show for it? Two failed marriages and a greasy old café. There's nothing left for me and Ben here any more.'

'Well ...' Pat put an arm around Kathy's shoulders and gave her a squeeze. 'What are you waiting for?'

It was Ian who gave Kathy the push that she needed, presenting her with a one-way ticket to Cape Town, leaving Good Friday. Apart from Pat, Kathy told only one other person: Grant. He was still a good friend and she felt she owed him an explanation. They arranged to drive out to a quiet country pub where they could talk without being overheard.

Grant felt his stomach lurch when Kathy told him. He swallowed hard. 'I'm going to miss you.' He gazed at her, trying to imagine life without seeing Kathy every day, and found it impossible. 'We've been part of each other's lives for so long now, I just can't believe you're not going to be there.'

'Grant. Please. This isn't the time ...' Kathy said, looking awkward.

He continued to stare at her intently. 'It might be the only time we have. I've watched you ... I've watched you with Ben, when he was ill and I've watched you holding it all together even when Phil was ...' Grant broke off, his voice catching. He took a deep breath and continued. 'You're the best thing that ever happened to my brother and he just threw you away. You're kind and you're strong and you're decent and you deserve every break you get. So go and be happy. Just don't try to forget me, eh? Looking at you now, I really think I ...'

Kathy held up her hand. 'Don't, Grant, please. Don't ruin it. Be my friend. I haven't the room for anything else.'

There was a long silence. 'Okay', Grant said at last, feeling anything but okay inside. Suddenly, he was in the throes of an emotional earthquake and, for the first time in a very long while, Grant was really, truly scared.

Later, when Tiffany quizzed Grant about his whereabouts – she had seen him leave in the car with Kathy – he gave her short shrift. His head was still in a turmoil, all sorts of mad ideas racing through his brain. He couldn't stop thinking about that moment in Paris; the moment when everything had suddenly become clear and out of the murk of compromises and recriminations and failures that had dogged his adult life, the answer had become shiningly obvious. Kathy was the one. He had shut that message down. It wasn't possible then, and it wasn't possible now. Or was it?

For all his oft-repeated promises to Tiffany, Sharon had

always been the best he'd ever had. Grant had given up expecting to find a relationship to equal that. In retrospect, Lorraine was a life-raft he had clung to when he discovered the gulf between himself and Tiffany. Despite their attempt at starting over again, Grant knew his marriage to Tiffany was nothing more than muddling through, making the best of the situation. Back in January, he had convinced himself that muddling through was enough, but when he thought about Kathy, the truth was undeniable. He was going to muddle his life away, while the one woman who could match – and possibly even exceed – what he had with Sharon was about to fly off to another continent.

When Phil found out from Lorna that Kathy was leaving, he was furious. They had a short, terse exchange, which had failed to persuade Kathy to change her mind, and since then he had not spoken to her. He had tried, once, to go back and talk to her, but the prospect of another brutal rejection was too much to bear and, after skulking in the shadows outside the house, he had left without ringing the bell.

Peggy was frantic. Ben was her only grandson and she was determined to make Kathy see sense. Good Friday morning had hardly dawned before she was giving Grant an ear-bashing about seeing Phil in the hope that he would have some influence on Kathy. Grant, who was in a stinker of a mood, merely snarled, 'Phil can make up his own mind' and stalked out. He had to talk to Kathy, for reasons of his own.

Grant had just dialled Kathy's number when he heard Tiffany descending the stairs and replaced the receiver hastily. 'Who were you phoning?' she asked, coming into the hall. He refused to tell her, but instead of shutting her up, his surly responses merely provoked her to ask more questions. 'What's the big deal? Why won't you tell me?' she persisted.

''Cos of the way you're asking.'

'What do you mean?'

'Just listen to yourself,' Grant said nastily. 'Your voice. Do you know how sick and tired I am of listening to your voice?'

But Tiffany would not be intimidated. 'I'm sorry, there's not much I can do about that. Do you mind telling me who you were phoning, O Lord, O Master?'

'Jeez!' Grant exploded, smashing his fist into the banisters. One of the balusters snapped like a matchstick. Tiffany stood her ground. 'What were you doing, phoning her anyway?' she said, guessing correctly. Grant ignored her. Pulling out the broken baluster he headed for the door. 'I'm going to the High Street, to get another one of these.'

It was a blatant excuse. Baluster in hand, Grant beat a path straight round to Kathy's. 'I need to talk to you,' he demanded, when she opened the door.

'Should I ask what about?' she asked, vaguely amused at his odd appearance.

'Don't go.'

'What?' The smile left Kathy's face.

'I'm saying don't go. Stay here.'

She frowned. 'Has your mother sent you round here?'

'No,' Grant said. 'This has nothing to do with her. I'm saying stay here. Or, rather, don't stay here. Come away with me.' Kathy's mouth fell open. 'You'd better come in.' He followed her through to the living-room. 'Grant, the flight leaves at four-thirty this afternoon. I've got tickets,' Kathy said, turning to him. He looked at her with glowing eyes. 'Well, let me come with you.'

'What?' She could hardly believe she was hearing this.

'Well, it doesn't have to be South Africa. It could be anywhere,' he continued, inspired. 'And we'd never tell anyone where we were. We both know how we feel about each other. We've been given a chance here. Let's not throw it away.'

'And how do we feel about each other?' she said, trembling.

'Have you forgotten what you said to me in Paris? There hasn't been a day since then when those words of yours haven't gone through my mind.'

'I was drunk,' Kathy said starkly.

'Are you saying you didn't mean it?' Grant took her by the shoulders, searching her face. 'Alright, look me in the eye and say that. Go on.' Kathy lowered her eyes, brushing away a tear. Grant raised her chin with a finger, forcing her to make eye contact with him. 'D'you know what I think?' he whispered. 'I think we could love each other in a way we've never loved anyone else before.'

Kathy shook her head. 'It's not on, Grant.'

'What? You telling me you don't care for me?'

'No. I can't say that because it's not true.'

Grant breathed a sigh of relief. 'Well then.'

'How many reasons do you want? Tiffany. Phil. Your mother.'

'All I get from them is aggravation.'

'And Courtney? You're just gonna wash your hands of her an' all?' A look of surprise passed across Grant's face, as if he had, in the heat of the moment, forgotten about his beloved daughter. 'And what about me and Ian? And Peter, Lucy, Steven?' Kathy persisted. 'It's not such a clean break, is it?'

'We can sort all those things out once things have settled down,' he said stubbornly.

Kathy looked upset. 'Grant, part of me would love to run off and be with you ...'

'Well, listen to that part then!' he urged. He pulled her towards him and she lifted her mouth to his without hesitation. Their kiss was long and thirsty. Kathy broke it, pushing Grant away from her in frustration. 'Oh Grant, you gotta stop this. You gotta go. Now.'

He remained where he was. 'That was the real you just then. You weren't pretending anything.' He grabbed her hand. 'Kathy. I've never kissed anyone and meant it like I meant it just then. And I know you feel the same.'

'I – I can't make a decision just like that,' Kathy said, knowing he was right.

'Alright. I'll give you some time to think about it, then ring you. In a couple of hours, we could be on our way. It's the right thing, Kathy.' She nodded numbly. 'It is,' he repeated, smiling confidently.

When Grant rang, later that morning, Kathy was even more confused than before. 'I'll be in my car outside the Tube station at two o'clock.'

Kathy winced. 'I haven't made up my mind yet.'

'Just remember what it felt like when we kissed,' he said. 'I'll be waiting for you.'

Kathy put the receiver down, her head spinning. Since Grant's unexpected offer, she had had two more encounters. One with Alex, who wanted to resign the priesthood and marry her, and one with Phil, who didn't really say anything at all. It was clear that Peggy had sent him, but when Kathy gave him the opportunity to ask her to stay, he copped out. His resignation angered her. More than anything, she wanted Phil to show he cared. Apparently, he did not. Grant's proposal was looking increasingly attractive. A car horn tooted and she hurried outside to meet Pat, who was waiting to take her for a short drive to the cemetery. There was one other person she needed to say goodbye to. Her first husband. Pete.

Grant was saying his goodbyes, too. He was upstairs, gazing at Courtney asleep in her cot, when Tiffany came in. 'What are you doing up here? We could do with a hand in the bar.'

'Well, you're gonna have to manage without me. I'm off out ... get some paint for the banisters,' Grant improvised. He turned to her. 'Listen, I'm sorry,' he said suddenly.

'What, about this morning? Forget it.'

'No, not just this morning. For everything.'

Tiffany put her head on one side and gave him a bright-eyed look. 'Come here.' She kissed him gently. 'What are we gonna do about you and your temper, eh? I'd be lost without you. You know that, don't you?' She enveloped him in a big hug, then stood back and stared at him. 'What are you looking at me like that for?' Grant did not answer.

CHAPTER THIRTY-THREE

Grant was just about to get into his car when Phil came running across the road. 'Grant! Quick as you can! It's an emergency!' Reluctantly, he followed Phil to his flat, where, it transpired, a suicidal Lorna had locked herself in the bathroom with a bottle of pills after Phil had rejected her. By the time Grant had bust the door down, Lorna was unconscious. When the ambulance arrived, the paramedics insisted they come to casualty to provide information about her. It wasn't until Lorna had been wheeled away on a trolley to have her stomach pumped that the two of them were able to talk. Too late, Phil, who had been primed by Pat that Kathy was thinking of marrying Alex, had been jolted into taking action. When Grant saw the earnestness on his brother's face, something gave way inside him. Pulling out his car keys, he said, 'Here, take my motor. They don't need both of us here now. See if you can catch Kathy before her flight leaves.'

'What about you?'

'I'll be fine,' Grant said abruptly. 'Go on. You'd better hurry.'

By the time he got back from the hospital, Tiffany was on the warpath. 'I've been really cross with you. The pump on the lager's not working and me and Peggy have been trying to do it but it's hopeless,' she said, hands on hips. The normality of the situation was, suddenly, an enormous relief to Grant, so much so that he felt quite light-headed. 'I'll see to it,' he said gruffly. 'Is Courtney okay?'

'She's fine. Why?'

'No reason.' He went upstairs to see his daughter, who was playing in the living-room with a distracted Peggy. 'How's my princess?' he said, sweeping her off the floor and cuddling her close. He breathed in the scent of her soft baby skin and was overwhelmed by the thought that he had considered abandoning her. It was a moment of madness, he told himself. A fantasy. A rush of blood to the head. He wouldn't have gone through with it ... But what if you had? a little voice said at the back of his mind. Think how different your life could have been. You could have been with Kathy. You could have escaped ... Courtney patted his cheek with a chubby hand and he pulled a face at her. 'Who's my little love?' he crooned. 'Who's Daddy's best love in the whole wide world?'

Phil made it to the airport in time to see Kathy ascending the escalator for the departure lounge. Ian, who had come to see her off, persuaded him not to follow. 'Just let her go, Phil,' he said, putting a hand on his sleeve. 'For the first time in her life, she's doing what she wants. What are you going to do — drag her back and make her miserable again? If you really love her, you'll do the decent thing.' Phil, who knew that Ian was right, fought back the tears as he watched his wife and son disappear out of his life for good.

He returned home to yet more trouble. George's house had been razed to the ground by a fire, which had been confirmed as arson. Annie, who had done some investigations of her own, discovered it had been started by the gang they were having the turf war with. It was clearly a warning. She collared Phil the next day and told him to stop the extra collections they'd been making. Unlike Annie, who appeared to be laid back about the whole thing, the news made Phil as jumpy as a kitten. The fact that they had given the gang George Palmer's name meant that anyone linked with him was also in danger. And that meant Peggy. When Phil confessed it all to Grant, he went ballistic. 'You've got to warn Mum,' he said furiously. 'If you don't, I will.'

Phil put it off as long as he dared, but with Grant breathing down his neck, he had no choice but to come clean. Peggy was shocked when she learned the scale of George's criminal activities. George had lead her to believe it was petty stuff, about which she had been broad-minded, but when she discovered her boyfriend was a major-league villain, her face grew grim. George got his marching orders that night and Peggy refused to take him back on any terms. He left for New Zealand a few days later, leaving Peggy, who loved him dearly, broken-hearted.

Grant, meanwhile, was missing Kathy terribly, while at the same time having to prop up Phil, who had gone to pieces over losing her. Keeping his misery bottled up had put him in a grumpy, uncommunicative mood, which was exacerbated by Tiffany's attempts to cheer him up. Everything she said and did grated on his nerves and he was rude and snappy with her.

Frustrated at his surliness, Tiffany accepted an invitation on their behalf to the opening of the new Italian restaurant, Guiseppe's, in Turpin Road. It was managed by the De Marco family, who were friends of George's. Grant, who had already had a couple of run-ins with the two De Marco brothers, attended with bad grace. He spent the evening standing in a corner, drinking and brooding and watching Tiffany, who was enjoying herself talking to Beppe and Gianni. Finally, he could take it no longer and went over to her. 'Why don't you go and do a bit of washing up,' he snarled at Gianni. Tiffany gave Gianni an apologetic nod and he went away. 'So what's going on with you and the bolognaise brothers?' Grant demanded. 'First you're flirting with one, then the other. What's the matter – can't make up your mind?'

'We were just talking,' Tiffany replied calmly.

'Right. Get your coat, we're going,' he ordered.

'I ain't going anywhere.'

'Do you wanna make a scene in here?' Grant threatened.

'You wouldn't dare.'

'Watch me.' He got hold of her arm and dragged her to her feet, physically hauling her across the restaurant. Tiffany yelled in protest. 'Grant, you're hurting me.' Frog-marching her out of the door, he dumped her on the pavement. Gianni, who had observed all this, followed them outside. 'Everything alright?' he asked Tiffany, ignoring Grant.

'Yeah, I'm fine. Honestly.' He studied her intently, weighing the situation up, then disappeared back inside. Tiffany exploded at Grant. 'How dare you show me up like that!'

'What, I was supposed to stand there and watch you flirting with those two greaseballs, was I?'

'I wasn't flirting.'

'You were all over them!' he shouted, enraged.

'Grant, I'm warning you. You touch me again and I'll …'

'You'll what?'

'Just try it,' Tiffany said, sure of her ground. She held Grant's eye for a few seconds, then turned and marched off, head held high. Grant, realizing that Tiffany had his measure, let her go.

Tiffany continued to be glacial with Grant the next morning. When he attempted to make it up to her by giving her a quick cuddle, she squirmed free.

'Look, either we pretend we're getting on, or have Mum on our case,' Grant huffed.

'Oh and that's your suggestion for putting things right, is it? "Let's pretend for Peggy's sake."'

'That's it,' he said fiercely. 'I give up. I'm fed up with apologising for existing. Now, you going to tell me what's going on?'

'It's not me that's been acting strange, Grant, it's you.'

'Of course I'm acting strange, you're doing my head in. And what was it with all that business last night?'

'Grant. Do you really think, if I was going to flirt, I'd be stupid enough to do it in front of you?' Tiffany said, blowing her top.

'Well, at least Boxing Day taught you something,' he returned.

Tiffany gasped. 'What did you say?' They were interrupted by Terry, banging on the door, eager to get a drink. 'It's one minute past! Open up!' Grant strode across the bar to unbolt the doors, leaving Tiffany open-mouthed at his viciousness.

The needle between them lasted all day, culminating in a row that evening after Grant got in another dig about the De Marco brothers. Tiffany retaliated, and within seconds they were slagging each other off until a well-placed shot about Sharon prompted Grant to pull Tiffany through to the back. 'I've told you before, Sharon has nothing to do with you,' he growled.

'No? How many Boxing Day presents did you give her?'

Grant saw red. 'Do you want to talk about it upstairs?' he threatened. Peggy, who had witnessed the tussle in the bar and, unknown to Grant and Tiffany, caught the conversation, intervened. 'What do you think you're doing?'

'We're talking,' Grant thundered. Tiffany tried to make good her escape, but he grabbed her arm. 'I ain't finished with you yet.' She struggled, making him hold on to her tighter. 'Ow, Grant, let go!'

Peggy stepped forward. 'Let her go, Grant.' He gave Tiffany a menacing stare. 'Grant!' Peggy barked again. There was a long pause, then he loosened his grip. Tiffany shrugged him off and he turned and stormed upstairs. Peggy followed him up, white with anger.

She found him in the living-room, pacing the floor, and immediately began interrogating him about what Tiffany had meant about Boxing Day. Grant, wound up to breaking point, held her off for as long as possible, but she prised the truth out of him in the end. 'I don't believe you! Where will this all end?' Peggy said, appalled.

'Don't start, Mum. Just because you've fallen out with your fancy man.'

'You leave George out of it.'

'Well, it ain't our fault the bloke's a con, is it?'

Peggy squared up to him, a diminutive sparrow to his hulking bull of a figure. 'A con he may be, but when it comes to women, at least the man has principles. George has never so much as raised his voice to me. And there you are, a grown man, hitting your own wife in front of your own child.'

'I didn't hit her!' Grant shouted. 'You picked the wrong man, you can't handle it and you're looking for someone to take it out on.'

'Yes, well, I wish you was half the man,' Peggy shouted back. 'It's not surprising Sharon left you. I wouldn't blame Tiffany if she went as well. I'm surprised she's stuck it so long with you as that child's father…'

Grant felt his pulse hammering in this temples. 'I don't want to hear this,' he screamed, starting to lose control.

'No, course you don't. Because it's the truth.'

'Just leave it, alright! Leave it.'

But Peggy didn't heed the warning. 'Apart from your fists, you've got nothing going for you. Do you hear? Nothing! And if I wasn't Courtney's gran, I'd have that child taken away from you. You're unfit to be a father.'

Her voice seemed to be filling his head. Grant's breathing was ragged, his heart pounding. He knew what was coming if he didn't do something and had just enough presence of mind to move away from her. 'Don't you dare turn your back on me!' Peggy ranted, trying to pull him back towards her. Grant swung round to get her off and before he knew what he was doing, struck her across the face. The loud smack seemed to reverberate in the silence that followed. Peggy was frozen to the spot, her hand to her cheek. 'You alright?' Grant said, feeling the anger draining out of him.

'Get out,' she whispered, almost inaudibly.

'I'm sorry,' he said, shocked. 'I didn't mean to …'

'Just get out, Grant.' She looked at him with an expression he had never seen on her before. It was total and utter loathing.

Grant spent the weekend hiding out at Phil's. He told Phil he and Peggy had had a fight, but left it at that. He was too ashamed to tell him the truth. He tried to psyche himself up to return to the Vic, but every time he thought of Peggy he remembered the look on her face and could not go through with it. He had committed the ultimate sin. Even his dad, who had beaten the hell out of them, had never – to Grant's knowledge – hit Peggy. What had he himself told Sharon, all those years ago? 'I have never laid a finger on a woman in my life?' He was proud of that. He could knock seven bells out of another bloke with his bare fists, but he never struck a woman. He recalled Sharon's prophetic rely. 'You'll get round to it. But it's damn well not going to be me.' Only, of course, it had been. He had hurt both his wives and now he had hit his own mother. He was out of control. His rage was a like some sort of monster that reared up within him and took over his personality. Its power terrified him. What if he lost it and hurt Courtney? It was too awful to contemplate. He had to get away before he did any more damage.

He remembered the letter he'd received a week before from a mate of his, 'Tiny' Johnson. They'd been in the same regiment and had seen action together in the Falklands. Tiny had seen Grant at his very worst. If anyone would understand, he would. Tiny had opened a bar in Cyprus and had invited Grant out for a holiday. Now seemed like a good time to go. Whether it would be just for a holiday, or whether he would stay there for good, Grant did not know.

He co-opted Nigel, who was packing up for the move to Scotland, to get his passport and some clothes from the Vic. Nigel was deeply unhappy about Grant running away, and told him so bluntly. Grant would not be dissuaded. 'I wouldn't expect you to understand. Everyone who knows you is going to be sad to see you go. Who's going to miss me, eh?'

'I am.'

'No. You'll be well shot of me.'

'Why do you think I've hung around with you all these years? You're my best mate. Who else can get away with calling you pathetic?' He paused. 'This is where we're meant to hug.'

'Don't push it.'

Nigel almost smiled. 'I hope it works out for you. You've got a great wife, a beautiful baby. Don't blow it, Grant.'

'Thanks for everything,' Grant said, suddenly desolate. Nigel had stuck with him more loyally than his own brother had and he knew he was letting him down now. But it couldn't be helped. Staying in Albert Square was not an option. He gave him an awkward hug. 'Right.' Nigel stared at his feet, embarrassed. There was so much left unsaid, but they could both fill in the gaps. 'Yeah. Good luck.' Grant was equally diffident. Nigel left, leaving Grant staring at the door and wondering if he would ever see his best friend again.

Grant was half out of the house when Tiffany ran up the steps. She assumed he was returning to the Vic and said, breezily, 'Come on, then, you've got a lot to sort out with your mum.'

'I'm not coming home.'

'Oh. So d'you mind letting me know where you're going?'

He glanced at his watch. 'Cyprus. Flying tonight. You'd better come in.'

Tiffany was outraged. 'You can't just up and leave. You need to sort things out here, with your family.'

'It's my family I want to get away from.'

'What are you talking about? What about Courtney?'

'I'm not much of a dad, am I?'

'Don't be stupid. I know how you love her,' Tiffany said, her voice softening. 'I've seen you playing with her at three o'clock in the morning when she's woken up crying.'

'I just want to get from this place. Nigel's doing it. Kathy's done it.' Grant sighed heavily. 'I feel stifled. There's no one I can talk to.'

'You can talk to me,' Tiffany said, looking hurt. 'I want you to. We talked after what happened at Christmas, didn't we?'

'Yeah. And now look where we are.' He got up, hefting his kit bag over his shoulder. Tiffany barred his way. 'You're not leaving, Grant. Come on, talk to me. Ever since Easter it's been like you weren't really here.'

'I don't want to have this conversation.'

'Why not?'

'I'm telling you, it's better if we leave it.' He knew if he tried to explain, he would have to tell her about Kathy, which would open up a whole new can of worms. If he was honest, it wasn't just what he'd done to Peggy that he was running away from – he needed to lick his wounds in secret, get over what could have been the greatest love of his life. Even Tiffany wouldn't want to hear that. They stood in silence, the shouts of the market traders just heard from outside. Gently, Grant moved Tiffany away from the door. 'Whatever I touch, I end up wrecking. Just let me go.'

'I don't want you to,' she said, catching her breath in a sob.

'I'm doing this for you and Mum and Courtney.' Grant opened the door. 'I'm sorry Tiff.'

He went down the steps and into the Square. Walking past the Vic, he glanced up at an open window. He thought he heard Courtney's faint cry, but he wasn't sure. He stopped for a second, listening, and heard it again, stronger this time. It was her frightened cry, a yelping noise she made when something startled her, different from her hungry cry or bored cry or frustrated cry. Every atom of his being wanted to drop everything and go inside and race up the stairs to comfort her. But it wouldn't just be Courtney up there. Peggy would be there, too. She'll make sure Courtney's alright, he told himself, moving on past the café towards the bridge. Someone – Sanjay possibly, or Mark – shouted a greeting to him, but he dared not stop. If he had done, they would have seen him crying.

EPILOGUE

A girl in a yellow bikini slid onto the bar stool next to Grant and flashed him a smile. He smiled back. 'I've seen you round here a lot,' she said, running a hand through her thick blonde bob. 'Are you on holiday?'

'Something like that.' He eyed her up. She was tanned and bouncy with cat-like eyes. The resemblance to Sharon was striking. 'Can I buy you a drink?'

'Thanks. I'll have a Bicardi and Coke.' Grant nodded to Tiny, who was serving behind the bar. Tiny shot him a knowing grin and began filling a tall glass with ice. 'I'm Linda, by the way.' She held out her hand.

'Grant.' They shook.

'So … are you here by yourself, then?' she asked casually.

'Yeah.'

'Where's home?'

'London, East End.'

Tiny put the drink down in front of her. 'For Gawd's sake give her a bit of encouragement, mate,' he hissed at Grant. 'You're in there.'

Grant blanked him. 'Cheers.' He raised his glass and they both drank. Linda regarded him over the top of the paper umbrella Tiny had stuck in her drink. 'You look fit. Do you work out?'

'Nah. This is down to lugging barrels of ale, mainly. I'm a publican.'

'Really? My dad used to run a pub.' This was getting too close for comfort. Grant listened to the waves crashing on the beach. He did not know what to say. 'Yeah,' Linda carried on, trying to keep the conversation going. 'I know all about life behind bars.' She giggled. 'Oops. I didn't mean it like that.'

Grant winced. 'Me an' all.'

Linda didn't catch on. 'Sounds like we've got something in common then.' She hesitated, giving him an opening, but Grant did not take it. She gave it one last shot. 'Fancy meeting up later for a drink? I know some cool bars. You could call it research.'

Grant couldn't do it. It just didn't feel right. He downed the rest of his beer and got up. 'I can't,' he said, not looking at her. 'I'm sorry, I should have told you. I'm married.'

'You never told me about a wife,' Tiny said later, when they were relaxing back at his apartment.

'Must have slipped my mind.'

'Why ain't she here, then? You're turning down busty blondes left, right and centre, so she must mean something to you.'

'She does.'

'So …?'

'I couldn't hack it, alright? Relationships and me are a total disaster.'

Tiny grimaced. 'You're not the only one. Do you know how many from our regiment are happily married family men? Practically none that I've heard of. That's why I came out here. Me and the wife bust up. I thought I'd start over again in Cyprus, but I dunno …'

Grant shrugged. 'Same here. Couple of losers, ain't we?'

'Are we? Maybe we're just the same as everyone else. I mean, who does have an easy time of it, eh?' he sighed. 'You just think all the rest can handle it.'

'Yeah, well, all the rest don't go mad and hurt people.'

Tiny cocked an eyebrow. 'Something you want to get off your chest?'

Grant stood up and went to the window, looking out over the sparkling blue ocean. 'You remember … how I was … in the Falklands?'

'That night on Mount Longdon?'

'Yeah.' Grant took a shaky breath. 'Something happened to me in that trench. And it's been happening ever since.' He turned back to face Tiny. 'I lose control. Black out. Go crazy. Lash out. Next thing I know someone's calling an ambulance.'

'Killing people can do that to you. Look at Dougie Briggs.'

Grant shuddered. 'I met him,' he said grimly.

Tiny shook his head. 'Dougie was always a nutter. But you – you're not like that. You're damaged, Grant, but you can recover. You gotta put it behind you. It wasn't your fault about the Argentinian kid. I thought he was going for a gun, too. You did what you had to do. What you were trained to do.'

'But he was a boy ...'

'And so were you.' Tiny moved over to Grant and put a hand on his shoulder, towering over him. 'He's dead, Grant, long dead. Lay him to rest.' He gazed at him with burnt-out blue eyes, his face kindly. 'Lay the boy you were to rest, too. I know who you was killing. You were shouting all kinda stuff afterwards when we carted you off, screaming about you and your dad.'

'He's dead now, too.'

'So, let 'em all go. Look to the future. You got kids?'

'One. A girl, Courtney.'

'And your wife?'

'Tiffany.' Grant smiled. 'Wicked little brunette with a heart of gold.'

'You miss 'em?'

'Every day.'

'Well, then, go home to 'em. You've been here two months.' Tiny grinned. 'It's not that I don't like the company, Grant. But what you gonna solve, drinking my beer all day?'

Grant looked down at the kids playing on the beach in the distance. He knew Tiny was right. His sojourn in Cyprus had been like living in limbo. Every day he woke up to cloudless skies and hot sun, but it was all the same. There was nothing in his life; it was all on hold. He had to go back.

★

Walford East Tube station looked pretty much how Grant had left it: grimy, litter-strewn and covered in grafitti. He descended the stairs into the ticket hall, following a trickle of early-morning market traders, and stopped outside. It was seven o'clock but there were signs of activity already, people setting up stalls, collecting milk from their doorsteps, opening shops, walking dogs. Robbie Jackson jogged up to him and said a friendly 'Hello', stopping long enough to spray him with sweat before sprinting off again, lank hair flopping. Grant took a deep breath and picked up his bag. He walked up George Street and into Turpin Road, where he caught sight of Rosa, the De Marco boys' mother, sweeping the pavement outside the restaurant. She looked up as Grant approached. 'Hello. You look well.' Grant glanced down self-consciously at his tanned arms. 'Thanks.' He sat down at one of the tables outside — Walford had gone continental with the arrival of the De Marcos — and asked, 'Any chance of a cup of coffee?'

'We don't open 'til lunchtime,' Rosa said. 'Don't you want to go home?'

'Yeah, of course. It's just been a bit of a long journey, that's all.' The truth was, he was putting off seeing Peggy and Tiffany for as long as he could. Now that he'd got this close, he would do anything to delay the moment of reckoning.

'Go on, then, sit down. Think we can manage a cup of coffee for you,' Rosa smiled, taking pity on him. She bustled off and returned with a steaming cappuccino. Grant took his time drinking it. Unable to stretch it out any longer, he was about to go when a woman he hadn't seen before sat down at an adjacent table. 'It's closed,' he explained politely. She glanced at his cup. 'Oh, sorry. You work here?'

'No, I, er … know the owner, sort of.'

She flopped back in her chair. 'I don't think I've got the energy to get up. Long journey,' she explained.

'Me too.'

'Been anywhere nice?'

'Isn't everywhere, compared to this place?'

'Oh, don't be like that,' she scolded him, with a laughing intimacy that made him examine her more closely. She was an attractive redhead of about Kathy's age, slim, self-assured and sexy in a way he couldn't quite put his finger on. Grant felt a tell-tale prickle on the back of his neck. 'Well, it's home, I suppose,' he returned, managing a grin.

'At least you've got a home.' She looked sad, lost. He noticed her suitcase. 'You visiting?'

'Yeah. I'm here to see my kids.'

'See much of them?'

'Not enough,' she said regretfully. She did not tell him their names – Tiffany and Simon – so Grant remained none the wiser that he was talking to his mother-in-law, Louise.

Grant stood up. 'Yeah, well, you can't always be there for them.' He considered, fleetingly, shaking her hand, then rejected the thought. There was no point in getting friendly with a stranger. He had a life of his own to sort out. 'Right, I'd better go.' She looked up at him with a hint of a twinkle. 'See ya.'

'See ya,' Grant replied. Squaring his shoulders, he walked off down the road towards the Vic.